Gunmen and Gangsters

To my father, who introduced me to these men as if they were old friends

Gunmen and Gangsters

*Profiles of Nine Actors
Who Portrayed Memorable
Screen Tough Guys*

MICHAEL SCHLOSSHEIMER

McFarland & Company, Inc., Publishers
Jefferson, North Carolina, and London

Acknowledgments: I would like to express my gratitude to the following people: Keith Andes, Harry Carey, Jr., Karen Steele, Tom D'Andrea, Frances Drake, Samuel Peeples, and the late Walter Abel, Mary Astor, Marguerite Chapman, Frank Faylen, Paul Fix, Viveca Lindfors, Joshua Logan, Nedda Logan, Una Merkel, Ray Milland, Marjorie Reynolds and Mary Wickes. I am grateful to Wendy Roine for typing this work for me.

Library of Congress Cataloguing-in-Publication Data

Schlossheimer, Michael.
    Gunmen and gangsters : profiles of nine actors who portrayed memorable screen tough guys / Michael Schlossheimer.
        p.   cm.
    Includes bibliographical references and index.
    ISBN 0-7864-0989-4 (softcover : 50# alkaline paper) ∞
    1. Gangster films—United States—History and criticism.
2. Motion picture actors and actresses—United States—Biography. I. Title.
PN1995.9.G3 S34   2002
791.43'028'092273—dc21
[B]   2001030551

British Library cataloguing data are available

©2002 Michael Schlossheimer. All rights reserved

No part of this book may be reproduced or transmitted in any form or by any means, electronic or mechanical, including photocopying or recording, or by any information storage and retrieval system, without permission in writing from the publisher.

Front cover: Brian Donlevy in a 1930s western.

Manufactured in the United States of America

McFarland & Company, Inc., Publishers
  Box 611, Jefferson, North Carolina 28640
    www.mcfarlandpub.com

Table of Contents

Acknowledgments iv
List of Abbreviations vi
Introduction 1

William Bendix 5
Charles Bickford 31
Ward Bond 69
Broderick Crawford 121
Brian Donlevy 159
Paul Douglas 189
William Gargan 217
Barton MacLane 256
Lloyd Nolan 295

Bibliography 337
Index 339

List of Abbreviations

The following abbreviations are used in the filmographies to indicate releasing companies.

AA	Allied Artists
ABC	American Broadcasting Company
AIP	American International
BV	Buena Vista
Col	Columbia
CBS	Columbia Broadcasting System
DCA	Distributing Corporation of America
EL	Eagle Lion Classics
Fox	Fox Film Corporation
GN	Grand National
Lip	Lippert
Med	Medallion
MGM	Metro-Goldwyn-Mayer
Mon	Monogram
NBC	National Broadcasting Company
Nat Gen	National General (Cinema Center)
Par	Paramount
PRC	Producers Releasing Corporation
Rep	Republic
RKO	Radio Keith-Orpheum Pictures and Radio Pictures
20th	Twentieth Century–Fox
UA	United Artists
Univ	Universal and Universal-International
WB	Warner Bros.

Introduction

The motion picture audiences of the 1930s might very well have appreciated the *Godfather* films (and their imitators) of the 1970s. But they did not require that type of entertainment, for they had the real thing. The elite of the underworld, whether it was Al Capone in Chicago or Lucky Luciano in New York, did not maintain the low profiles of their modern-day counterparts. Those who survived the Roaring '20s and lasted into the Depression era remained constant subjects of press coverage. These were larger-than-life characters who enjoyed public attention. And to portray their kind on the movie screens required actors of a special kind.

Screen legends Humphrey Bogart, James Cagney and Edward G. Robinson received great acclaim for their portrayals of racket bosses. Or did they? Cagney was the only one of the three to be Oscar-nominated for portraying an underworld denizen. Academy voters liked Bogart more as a drunken boat captain (*The African Queen*) or a mentally deteriorated naval commander (*The Caine Mutiny*), and they appeared to like Robinson not at all, though he gave great performances from his first film in 1923 to his last some 50 years later. (He *was* awarded a special Oscar, presented posthumously.)

Evidently, enacting the role of a snarling gangster was not likely to win the plaudits of the professional community. So it was that when these three leading portrayers of underworld types reached top stardom, they stopped playing socially repellent characters. Thereafter, the gangsters they played were mostly reformed or comic. For the most part, these stars were out of the crime business, and replacements were needed. This was where a group of second-stringers came in to play the tough guys, the gunmen and gangsters.

These men rarely starred in films, and when they did, it was usually a small budget production. Several of them had the talent to go from playing a villain or a character role in an expensive feature to doing a breezy Cagney-type hero in a cheapie. Some were more adept at playing thugs, both serious and comedic. Some were better suited to being on the right side of the law, playing those tough cops or private eyes. Two of them did star in films that today are regarded as semi-classics, but they retained their second-string status nevertheless.

Not all of these men were admirable human beings. One of them was known to have made anti–Semitic remarks about his studio bosses. Another had a penchant for making controversial and sometimes slanderous remarks for publication. A third is still despised by many, years after his death, for contributing greatly to the blacklisting of some of his colleagues. On the other side of the coin, several dealt courageously with tragic illness, either their own or that of a loved one.

But their personal traits or experiences were not the reason they were selected for their roles. They were chosen because they had the ability to project images unlike their real-life personalities.

Because they were part of an era when good looks were worshipped, none of these men attained the type of stardom enjoyed by latter-day counterparts like Charles Bronson, Peter Falk and Lee Marvin (who each made an early screen appearance with at least one of the actors in this text). In almost all cases, the older actor easily took the honors in any sequence shared by the two.

These actors were often in competition for parts, and they sometimes appeared in the same film. Broderick Crawford and Brian Donlevy appeared in several films together. Crawford also worked with Charles Bickford and Lloyd Nolan on several occasions and appeared in *The Time of Your Life* with both William Bendix and Ward Bond. Donlevy worked with Bendix and Bickford, as well as Barton MacLane. The only "loner" is Paul Douglas, who never acted with the others. He did, however, play some stage roles which at other times had been played by Bendix, Crawford and Nolan, and William Gargan recreated one of his best film roles on television.

Today's tough guys are the stars of their films, and the vehicles of an actor like Bronson are main features, not the kind of programmers the older actors starred in. With sheer professionalism, men like Bickford, Gargan and MacLane brought some quality to the cheapest junk that Hollywood's "Poverty Row" could turn out in the '30s.

Introduction

Stardom eluded these men, whether due to personal tragedy or mere chance, but they have left their marks. Anyone who has favorite films from the Golden Era must remember some of them. Rarely does a day go by when no television station runs a film featuring one of them. Perhaps it's because all were still active in films through the '50s, with six of them still filming in the '60s. Crawford and Nolan were still acting on television as the '80s began. (Of course, they had long since become character actors, leaving all those crime lords and general heavies to younger men.) Over the years, the tough guys learned that you can make points without resorting to violence in film after film. In *Earthquake*, Nolan, playing a doctor, shares the last scene with George Kennedy. As they survey the devastation caused by the natural disaster, the quiet eloquence in the older actor's stare says it all. When someone has been stealing scenes for 50-odd years, it gets easier.

The actors chosen for this text are personal favorites and they all meet the criterion of having played tough guys on both sides of the law. These men had a Depression era resilience that enabled them to survive in spite of years of inferior material, with only a rare cinematic bone tossed to them. Having lasted without benefit of a great deal of publicity, they may be closer in kinship to the modern lords of the underworld. But, as the movie gangsters of old, they have provided some of film's most enduring images.

William Bendix

The great Depression of the '30s is often cited as the primary reason many unlikely types became actors. In those days, the handsome "matinee idols" still outnumbered the Wallace Beerys and Louis Wolheims. So, as in the case of William Bendix, a scarcity of other types of employment led many into the theatrical arena. And not even the world's greatest optimist could have predicted the future in motion pictures awaiting someone as unphotogenic as Bendix. If anyone had told him in the years he was struggling to provide for his family that in a decade or so, he would be stealing scenes from Tallulah Bankhead, singing with Bing Crosby and cast as a man he had idolized in his youth (Babe Ruth), he probably would have laughed in that person's face.

In the category of lovable tough guys, Bendix reigned supreme through the '40s. He portrayed his share of sidekicks to handsome heroes, but sometimes he was the hero. Bendix was also called upon to play a number of straight character parts. Unfortunately, dramatic roles were often his undoing; without the guidance of a director like Alfred Hitchcock or William Wyler, a meaty part would turn rancid in his heavy hands. His tendency to mug, an asset in comedy, was not appropriate in drama. He was enjoyed for what he could do best, and those are the parts that have withstood the test of time.

He was born on January 4, 1906, to Oscar and Hilda Bendix, a musically inclined couple. They lived on New York's Third Avenue and 45th Street. When young Bill was five, his father worked in Vitagraph Studios and started getting him bit parts in films. But he did not adapt to performing the way other future movie tough guys did. William Gargan and Paul Kelly, starting about the same age, quickly graduated from the extra ranks to featured player status.

If Bill Bendix had one passion as a boy, it was baseball. He went

William Bendix's standard *film noir* look.

to the Polo Grounds so often that he became a bat boy for the Giants and later for the Yankees. Working in silent films could not compare with that. He attended Townsend Harris High School, where his desire to graduate had little to do with scholastic ambition. At age 17 he was playing both semi-pro baseball and football. Had he been able to make a living through such endeavors, he might have continued in that direction. But in 1928, he married Theresa Stefanotti and no longer could a young sports enthusiast indulge himself. He just was not good enough to step into the major leagues; he could not afford to make the attempt. A full year before the stock market crash, Bendix was feeling burdened by financial need.

During this period, his only brush with performing was as a member of the Henry Street Players, a neighborhood drama group on Manhattan's Lower East Side. Gruff-voiced Bendix even worked for a time as a singing waiter. The arrival of a daughter, Lorraine, supplied additional impetus for obtaining steadier work. For almost five years, he managed a grocery store. But economic conditions forced it to close, sending him one step closer to his life's vocation.

The early days of the New Deal saw the formation of a number of federally subsidized acting groups. Bendix worked for a time with the Theater Project in New Jersey. His work there brought him to the attention of the Theater Guild's Cheryl Crawford. Through the late '30s, Bendix was seen in a number of plays, generally undistinguished. The big breakthrough was his being cast by the Guild in its production of William Saroyan's *The Time of Your Life*. The play gave a career boost to a number of young performers—including a dancer named Gene Kelly, who went from chorus boy to star by way of this show. Opening on October 25, 1939, the play went on to win both the Pulitzer and New York Drama Critics Awards for the year. And as the argumentative patrolman Krupp, Bendix did not go unnoticed by Hollywood.

Film producer Hal Roach was looking for able comedy actors who would work economically in features barely an hour-long. James Gleason starred in a few military comedies and Roach, wanting to start a simultaneous series about cab drivers, thought Bendix would be ideal. The Saroyan play had a short initial run of 185 performances, so it was easy to lure an actor who feared unemployment into the motion picture business. Bendix and veteran screen tough guy Joseph Sawyer were teamed as brawling Brooklyn cabbies and for the remainder of his career, Bendix and Brooklyn were inseparable, despite his Manhattan origins.

Actors rarely stayed with Roach when the major studios came calling, and bald, 55-year-old Jimmy Gleason was no exception. That fine character comedian had been consigned to Poverty Row a few years earlier, but a 1941 Oscar nomination had renewed interest in him. Joseph Sawyer was called upon to replace Gleason as a harried army sergeant and was probably expected to continue in the series with Bendix. However, when the first Roach film, *Brooklyn Orchid*

(1942), was released, it did not make much of a splash. Almost simultaneously released was MGM's *Woman of the Year*, the first of the great Spencer Tracy–Katharine Hepburn films, in which Bendix had the relatively minor role of Pinkie, Tracy's bartender pal. The George Stevens–directed comedy got so much attention that Bendix got more notice than such a part would usually receive. This notice led to a Paramount contract. Before Bendix's first year in films ended, he was seen in three major Paramount productions. They appeared before his last film with Roach, *Taxi, Mister?* (1943), made its debut.*

His first for Paramount was *Wake Island*, which was rushed through production so that it would be Hollywood's first topical war film. (This rush job required some reshuffling of the facts.) The most enjoyable sequences featured the bantering dialogue of a pair of heroic non-coms (Bendix and Robert Preston). Although everyone guessed the film would be popular, probably no one (least of all Bendix) expected him to receive an Oscar nomination for Best Supporting Actor for his role as Smacksie Randall. This nomination was proof of his almost immediate popularity with American audiences. Like others who made it big during the War years, he was not the ideal movie actor; yet, typecast for a while as the homely, baseball-loving serviceman, he became a perfect symbol of the times. (Asthma kept him out of the real war.)

Bendix and Brian Donlevy rushed from *Wake Island* to *The Glass Key*. In this instance, Paramount's rationale was to get another release out of their hot new property, Alan Ladd, after the smash success of *This Gun for Hire*. Based on a Dashiell Hammett story, *The Glass Key* supplied Bendix with a small but memorable role: a brutish thug named Jeff (a part played by Guinn "Big Boy" Williams in the 1935 version of the Hammett tale). Bendix's main contribution was his sadistic beating of Ladd. In real life, a strong friendship developed between the two actors and they would work together on eight other pictures. Despite their dissimilar background, both men were rather nonchalant about their newfound success (in both cases, it followed years of struggle). They were also fated to die within a year of each other. Despite the success of his heavy role in *The Glass Key*, Bendix was not to play another real villain until the end of the '40s.

The Bendix family settled on the West Coast; he had too many film offers to even consider stage work at this point. The success of

---

Since Roach kept his comedies at minimum length, there was enough footage remaining for a third film, The McGuerins of Brooklyn.

William Bendix and Mary Anderson in *Lifeboat* (1944). (Director Alfred Hitchcock fulfilled his own requirement for a cameo appearance in this limited-cast movie via the newspaper advertisement.)

Wake Island and the war itself shaped his film career. Most of his '40s tough guys were devoted to good and even approached sainthood in their acts of self-sacrifice. Even when playing a hard-as-nails character, beneath it all he was a softie. He became content with the typical role as the guy who looked like a brute, but usually behaved with gentleness and a touch of heroism. That year, the Bendixes adopted an infant girl named Stephanie.

After appearing in a sketch with Bob Hope in the all-star *Star Spangled Rhythm* (1942) and in another comedy bit in *The Crystal Ball* (1943), Bendix embarked on a series of heroic roles. He was a courageous resistance fighter in *Hostages* (1943), Luise Rainer's last film. He and Ladd fought the Japanese in *China* the same year. He began appearing, on a non-exclusive basis, in 20th Century–Fox films, beginning with *Guadalcanal Diary* (1943), almost reprising his *Wake Island* characterization.

Bendix then landed his finest screen role. His second picture for

Fox was Alfred Hitchcock's *Lifeboat* (1944), in which he received second billing to Tallulah Bankhead (*Lifeboat* was the only film where her own enigmatic personality transferred well on the screen). Bendix played Gus, a badly injured seaman aboard a crowded lifeboat, and he perfectly embodied the type of character John Steinbeck described in the original story. Gus is the only character who has not accepted the grim reality of the war and is living in the past, in a world that to him was wonderful. Could just any actor, no matter how gifted, make growing up in Brooklyn and winning a dance contest at Roseland sound as wonderful as Bendix does? It is this quality that makes Gus the personification of those true victims of twentieth century inhumanity. He trusts the others on the lifeboat, yet it is they who must amputate his leg. Their action to save his life is in his own mind an act of destruction. He trusts a Nazi (Walter Slezak) who has been hauled aboard the lifeboat, but the others are rightfully wary of him. When Slezak throws Gus overboard, this provides the others with the motivation to kill him. Alfred Hitchcock's direction of this claustrophobic one-set picture is superb. Yet, if there is one thing audiences would not forget, it was most likely Bendix's Gus. Everyone else was too battle-hardened; he was the only one in the film who was meant to be liked.

Regrettably, Bendix was unable to follow up this acting plum with similar parts. His very next role, on the surface a choice role, turned out to be a step in the wrong direction. Eugene O'Neill's plays have rarely worked on film and no O'Neill play was more lacking in substance than *The Hairy Ape*.* There was little that director Alfred Santell, or any other director, could do with what was supplied. The play could be called a monologue of hate, since the leading character, a "repulsive" seaman, complains bitterly throughout the length of the play. He turns into a raving maniac when a society girl takes one look at him and is appalled. Eventually is done in by a circus ape. Not exactly the stuff that makes great movies. Filmmakers ignored the most important characteristic in the actor's makeup, his humanity. There was no humanity, not even a bit of warmth, in the character of Yank. The picture, never expected to be a popular success, didn't even make it with the critics. Bendix's limitations as an actor were made all too evident and only Susan

---

O'Neill's tribute to Charles Darwin's theories was a big Broadway success for Louis Wolheim in the twenties. Wolheim was so naturally "ugly" that he did not require any special makeup for the part. The play helped make his reputation and led to such worthwhile parts as Flagg in the original stage version of What Price Glory?

Hayward, in the beefed-up girl's part, attracted any positive reviews.

Bendix, next cast in a slew of poor comedies, was definitely in a slump. Fox cast him in a supporting role in *A Bell for Adano* (1945); star John Hodiak had been billed below Bendix in *Lifeboat* the previous year. The studio starred him in *Don Juan Quilligan* (1945), in which he played a tugboat skipper who was an unwitting bigamist. Bendix couldn't seem to get away from the sea. Paramount gave him a meatier role in *Two Years Before the Mast* (1946): Mr. Amazeen, a mate loyal to his vicious captain (Howard da Silva) until he finally revolts against this sea tyrant. Alan Ladd, Brian Donlevy, Barry Fitzgerald, Albert Dekker and Ray Collins were also in the cast. Another Ladd picture, Raymond Chandler's original *The Blue Dahlia* (1946) showed both actors to better advantage, with Bendix playing Ladd's disturbed returning war buddy.

Bendix completed his commitment to Fox* with his first really villainous role since *The Glass Key*. In Henry Hathaway's *The Dark Corner* (1946), one of the better *films noire* of the '40s, Bendix played a mysterious character known only by the white suit he wears as he shadows private eye Mark Stevens. Their performances, as well as those of Lucille Ball as Stevens' secretary and Clifton Webb as an urbane chief villain, keep the film entertaining. Since Bendix's home studio, Paramount, did not keep him busy enough, the actor obtained a three-picture deal with Universal. He played a shady night club owner in *White Tie and Tails* (1946) and the protector of Deanna Durbin in *I'll Be Yours* (1947), a poor updating of Ferenc Molnar's *The Good Fairy* (which Universal had done very well by in 1935. (After viewing the results of this, one of Durbin's last, the studio gave up their literary rights to the property so that a Broadway musical version could be produced.) His third role for the studio was a bland police detective in *The Web* (1947).

While films were offering Bendix little prestige, he won new popularity in a totally different medium. Gravelly voiced Lionel Stander had been cast in the radio show *The Life of Riley*, a comedy series about a welder at an aircraft factory and his misadventures at work and at home with his family. Even before the House Un-American Activities Committee began investigating the entertainment

---

*In their review of his next-to-last Fox film, Sentimental Journey *(1946), The New York Times said Bendix gave "a droll and refreshing representation of a person who might possibly exist"—an obvious putdown of the picture.*

media, Stander was known as a left-winger. His conservative co-workers, when asked to name an actor they considered subversive, always cited Stander. His outspokenness had made him *persona non grata* at all the major studios, except when someone like director Preston Sturges insisted on having him in one of his pictures. At the height of "The Red Scare," radio and television advertisers were demanding the dismissal of scores of actors. Stander was one of the first radio actors replaced for being too controversial; this occurring soon after the end of World War II.*

Bendix, offered the role of Riley, was hesitant about taking on a radio series. Actors with any stature in the motion picture industry usually confined themselves to appearances on programs like *Lux Radio Theater* or as guests on comedy shows. It was felt that only those who were finished in films went into radio, since no one would want to go out to see a performer they could hear week after week in their own homes. But Bendix's decision to play Chester A. Riley was a sound one, for he and the program would go on to become one of the most popular in the history of broadcasting. Here was a perfect blend of actor and part: Riley was a lovable dope, the kind who would get into the most idiotic situations and try to cajole or lie his way out of them, with little success. Only the understanding of his long-suffering wife Peg would bail him out. He played the part for all it was worth, running the gamut of emotions. In the ten years-plus that he played the role, Bendix never let it become one-dimensional, even with the most idiotic scripts.

Bendix did not curtail his film work, even though his radio work had won him more fans than his largely undistinguished movies of this period. There was hardly a good scene in any of his four Paramount releases of 1947, *Blaze of Noon*, *Calcutta*, *Where There's Life* and *Variety Girl*; the only good thing one could say about the latter was that it was the last of that studio's all-star musicals. (Bendix had been shoved into all of them.) His amended Paramount contract allowed him to accept parts at other studios, and he found what must have appeared to be ideal projects: a screen biography of Babe Ruth and an independent James Cagney production based on the play that did so much for Bendix, *The Time of Your Life*. Although he managed to do both films, the results were not as beneficial as he might have hoped.

Stander brazenly rode out his blacklist, returning to film work in the sixties and eventually a regular TV role on Hart to Hart *in the 1980s.*

Bendix's casting as Ruth, considered by many to be the greatest baseball player of all time, seemed natural but was all wrong. Bendix came close to the physical appearance of the chunky "Bambino" at the height of his career, but it all fell apart on the screen. The idea of playing one of his own idols may have blinded Bendix to the ridiculous things he was asked to do. He was first seen as the oldest-looking kid in Charles Bickford's Catholic orphanage and then proceeded through any number of embarrassing scenes. The writers were obviously trying to wring every bit of pathos out of the script and they even had Bendix crying over the death of manager Miller Huggins, a man who in actuality had made Ruth's life miserable. *The Babe Ruth Story*, ironically released the year of Ruth's death, was unfortunately a typical, cheaply budgeted product of a small studio (Allied Artists).

The Time of Your Life (1948) was also not made by a major studio, but did not suffer from penny-pinching. The film's producers, Cagney brothers James and William, recognized the need to fill all the colorful Saroyan roles with the best actors available. Cagney, submerging his usual dynamic personality, was fine as the play's centerpiece, a barroom philosopher who manipulates the people around him. His sister Jeanne played a prostitute. Two other Warners alumni, Wayne Morris and Gale Page, were well cast as Cagney's chief stooge and a lady to whom Cagney is briefly attracted. James Barton played a gabby old cowboy who wasn't as crazy as he seemed. Bendix played a bigger part than he had in the original play: Nick, the bar owner, who's on stage almost as much as the play's leading character. (Broderick Crawford played Bendix's stage role.) None of the performances could be faulted, but the film was seen as no more than a photographed play.

That same year, RKO (newly acquired by principal stockholder Howard Hughes) signed Bendix. Hughes was hiring a number of performers he personally liked and—unfortunately—Bendix was one of them. The films Bendix made for RKO did his career no good. His first, *Race Street* (1948), found him in a standard cop role in a George Raft crime vehicle. His subsequent films were in the same vein; he played good or bad cops or gangsters in forgettable films with such stars as Victor Mature and Robert Mitchum. Back at Paramount, he was cast in two mediocre remakes. He was an unlikely English knight in *A Connecticut Yankee in King Arthur's Court* (1949), in which he sang "Busy Doing Nothing" with a most unlikely pair, Bing Crosby and Sir Cedric Hardwicke. In the same year's

Streets of Laredo, a remake of 1936's *The Texas Rangers*, he was a reformed outlaw pal of William Holden. During that period, the only work Bendix did that was at all popular was his radio show.

When Universal decided to make a film of *The Life of Riley*, Bendix was signed for the lead. He was, however, given a different supporting cast: Rosemary DeCamp replaced Paula Winslow as Peg and James Gleason played Riley's best friend, Gillis. (Years later, when Bendix was doing *Riley* on television, Gleason guested as his very *Irish* father.) The radio show's writer-producer Irving Brecher began thinking of bringing *Riley* to television, but when Bendix was approached about the idea, he immediately refused to consider it. He said he would stay with the radio show as long as it lasted and play Riley in other movies, but he drew the line at television.* So a little-known comic in his early thirties, Jackie Gleason, was given the TV Riley part. Outside of a few small parts in films, Gleason was then primarily known for his work in Broadway revues. The TV producers gave him the same scripts and they put gray die in his hair to make him look old enough to have a teenage daughter. It was the best thing for Gleason's career when LOR disappeared the following year and he began working in the variety format that would make him a star.

On April 1, 1949, actor Wallace Beery's sixtieth birthday, the MGM star died. He had been scheduled to appear in an independent production called *Johnny Holiday*, to be directed by former Metro director Willis Goldbeck. Needing a quick replacement, Goldbeck thought of Bendix. The part had been a natural for the late star; an old soldier-type trying to reform a juvenile delinquent. Bendix wisely decided to underplay the role and this, coupled with the film's unpretentious quality, made it a moderate success when released in early 1950.

Bendix followed that film with another freelance role, in Columbia's *Kill the Umpire* (1950). He played a Riley-type family man whose love of baseball does not prepare him for the rigors of the job of umpire. Considering his real-life feeling for the sport, he was perfect in the role, as his feelings about his new job change from revulsion to understanding. The great comedy director Lloyd Bacon made this mild B picture seem much better than it was. In several

---

*In 1949, practically all Hollywood actors did, feeling sure that television would end their careers. And TV producers could not afford to offer the salaries that might have made some of them more willing to gamble. Some prominent actors from films, such as Stuart Erwin, Paul Hartman and Charlie Ruggles, gave up making movies when they became stars of early TV situation comedies. Bendix, with film commitments at RKO and Paramount, wasn't ready for that.

scenes, Bendix was paired with comic actor Tom D'Andrea, whose option had recently been dropped by economy-minded Warners. They worked so well together than D'Andrea was tapped to play Gillis to Bendix's *Riley* on TV a few years later. *Kill the Umpire* turned out to be the last time Bendix was the sole star of a film.

In 1951, Bendix played in two Paramount pictures and then ended his decade-long association with the studio. *Submarine Command* was a rather ordinary naval drama in which, for the third and last time, he merely stood around and watched William Holden perform acts of heroism. William Wyler's film of Sidney Kingsley's play *Detective Story* was one of the year's popular successes and it appeared on a number of ten best lists. Bendix played Detective Lou Brody, a sympathetic man powerless to curb the self-destructive nature of co-worker and friend Kirk Douglas, who gave a dynamic performance which blended well with Bendix's underplaying. Wyler used some actors who had appeared in the play and they also fitted in well with the Hollywood name actors he cast. The drama was so realistic and powerful that few minded that the film took place almost completely within the walls of a police precinct. (The single-set drama was more noticeable in the dream-like *The Time of Your Life* than it was here.)

During his relatively brief tenure at RKO, Bendix was usually cast in dramatic roles, often of a sinister variety. Director Josef von Sternberg's last film, *Macao* (1952), with Bendix portraying a tourist who is not what he appears, was an unfortunately typical role for him. The studio planned this film as the initial starring vehicle of their "sizzling" duo Robert Mitchum and Jane Russell, but it was decided that their second film *His Kind of Woman* was better box office and the release of *Macao* was held up for over a year, a fairly standard strategy for Howard Hughes.

Hughes did not give Bendix comedy roles, simply because the studio rarely made comedies. However, Groucho Marx had a commitment to do a picture for RKO, so he and Bendix were teamed in *A Girl in Every Port* (1952). No chemistry was created by Marx and Bendix as a pair of sailors who become involved with a racehorse. Marie Wilson was thrown into the female lead, since she had a three-picture deal with RKO, but no one could save this bomb. Bendix returned to the sea in his next film, playing the villainous mate "Evil Eye" in *Blackbeard, the Pirate* (1952). RKO rounded up a prestigious director, Raoul Walsh, to take charge and he gave the film some badly needed humor to go with the color. Bendix remained in the background while Robert Newton hammed it up in the title role; Bendix would have done better to slip off the set altogether. He completed his contract with *Dangerous Mission* (1954), a quickie in which Bendix tried to figure out whether Victor Mature or Vincent Price was a syndicate killer.

Just prior to making *Dangerous Mission*, Bendix finally acceded to a request to do *The Life of Riley* on television. By this time, radio was in a bad slump and many successful shows were making the transition to TV. (Besides, NBC was willing to meet his price and give him a Friday night 8:30 time slot.) Most of the radio characters were retained with the exception of Digger O'Dell, the friendly undertaker.* Besides Tom D'Andrea, the new cast included former Paramount leading lady Marjorie Reynolds as a rather youthful Peg; Lugene Sanders and Wesley Morgan as the children, Babs and Junior; Gloria Blondell as Honeybee Gillis; Sterling Holloway as Waldo Binney; and Emory Parnell as Hawkins, Riley's Cunningham Aircraft plant foreman. Henry Kulky was later brought in as co-worker Otto Schmidlapp, the only man who could qualify as being even dumber than Riley, and Bendix's own daughter Lorraine made several appearances as Riley's visiting niece. When the script called for her to have a father, Bendix donned a mustache and an Irish brogue and played his own brother.

The program premiered in 1953 and ran for five seasons; it was even more popular than it was on radio. Producer Tom McKnight allowed the show to develop (the children grew normally with Babs marrying and have a baby). Later, the Rileys moved and for one season were given a new set of neighbors (George O'Hanlon and Florence Sundstrom), but that didn't work out and D'Andrea and Blondell were brought back as the Gillises. One of the highlights of any episode was Bendix's talent for facial expressions, reflecting the disgust, humiliation and fear that the poor sap who is in most of us feels when his best-laid plans are stomped upon. Some of the radio gimmicks worked well, even the use of a narrator at the beginning to introduce Riley as one of the "little people." The plots were simple, based primarily on the blue collar worker's desire to get something for his family—more often than not something they neither needed nor wanted. Every time a situation threatened to become

---

John Brown, the actor who played the part on radio and in the earlier TV series, had become a victim of the blacklist, so the character, usually extraneous to the plot anyway, was dropped.

maudlin or a character turned suddenly serious, something humorous would be injected. For moralizing, audiences could tune to Riley's contemporary *Father Knows Best* with its more intelligent but much duller father.

One of the staple comedy situations of all time is the leading character's mistaken belief that he is dying. In one such segment of Bendix's show, Riley has a long talk with Junior. He tells him he will soon be going away on a long trip and promises his son a number of things before he goes. Just as Bendix is reaching an emotional peak, the boy, excited about all he is to receive, shatters the drama by exuberantly saying, "Gee, Dad, I hope you go real soon." When Babs is about to make him a grandfather for the first time, Riley paces the floor of the maternity ward. A nurse comes in and tells another man that he has just become a father and an indignant Riley says to her, "Wait a minute, I was here first." Most memorable of all are Riley's famous catchphrases, spoken at the very end, usually after his latest venture has ended in disaster. If he wasn't too unhappy and was just letting Peg have her way, he would look at the camera and say, "It's a losing fight." But his most famous comment was reserved for those situations where an old problem had been compounded by a new one. Everything would stop as Bendix would turn to the camera, a look of utter frustration on his face, and say, "What a revolting development *this* is!"

It has become fashionable for some to deride the old situation comedies and the image of the doltish, ineffectual father. But Chester Riley is rightfully the proper ancestor of Archie Bunker. This is especially noticeable during *All in the Family*'s later years, when the bigotry was played down and Archie became just a blunderer. These men, as well as Jackie Gleason's bus driver Ralph Kramden (*The Honeymooners*), are better remembered than the upper-middle-class TV fathers in their business suits who came home, ready to hear their offsprings' latest problems. Although the situations were outlandish, Riley's basic inability to fight back made him the most human of them all. Like *The Honeymooners*, *The Life of Riley* proved durable and was still being rerun more than 20 years after its cancellation. It is the second oldest comedy TV series (the first being *I Love Lucy*) still regularly scheduled as of this writing.

The burden of starring in a weekly half-hour series put a dent in Bendix's already floundering movie career. During the series' run, he found time for just three theatrical films. He should have avoided playing the unredeemably evil leader of a group of escaped convicts in *Crashout* (1955). The other two pictures were traditional naval war dramas: Columbia's *Battle Stations* (1956) and Warner Bros.' *The Deep Six* (1958) cast him in stereotypical fashion. The latter provided a reunion with old pal Alan Ladd, whose production company Jaguar produced most of his latter-day starring vehicles. Except for a temporary rift between the two men (caused by a careless remark made by Sue Carol Ladd, Alan's wife, about Bendix's non-military status during World War II), they had remained friends over the years. In *The Deep Six*, their last film together, Ladd played a pacifist Quaker officer and Bendix a career sailor named "Frenchy" Shapiro, who teaches Ladd the true meaning of camaraderie under fire.

Much better than all his '50s film work was a half-hour drama he did for TV's *Ford Theatre* in October 1954. He played the henpecked husband of Rosemary DeCamp (a former Peg Riley, seen here in a change-of-pace as a domineering shrew). While staying at a hotel, the husband begins to crack under the constant nagging and turns on his wife. Their daughter, played by young and almost-unknown New York actress Joanne Woodward, notifies the police when she can't reach her parents on the phone. Detective Ward Bond sizes up the situation and has sharpshooters stationed across from the hotel room. Bendix has refused to let his wife go and is brandishing a broken bottle, but he is beginning to weaken when the marksman, misinterpreting a sudden move, shoots him in the arm. In the final scene, we see the husband once again docile and the wife once again making demands, as they depart for home. We know just from the look Bendix gives her that the explosion that happened before might very well happen again. This forgotten little drama is notable mainly due to the wide range of emotions Bendix got a rare chance to display. The usual awkwardness he brought to brutish parts was still there, but this time it worked because he was supposed to be a mild-mannered man coping with a spell of temporary insanity. Bendix got more critical notice for a performance in an hour-long Sunday night *Alcoa-Goodyear Playhouse* drama (February 1956). "Kyria Katina" was a rare opportunity for him to participate in a love affair; he played a driving inspector who finds love with Greek widow Viveca Lindfors. Bendix performed this role without any of his usual cloddish gestures. Two months later, he followed that episode up with a lesser drama, "Footlight Frenzy," on the same program.

Bendix's activities during his 1956 "*Riley* hiatus" were curtailed when he went into the hospital for an operation on his ulcers. This was the actor's only long-standing medical problem during his years in Hollywood (he'd always claim to have had a bad attack after seeing himself in *The Babe Ruth Story*). His ulcers could perhaps be attributed to his worry about the series; he believed its respectable ratings would climb if the show was moved to another night, but the network declined. Nevertheless, its ratings were good enough to knock off such popular CBS fare as *Topper*, which gave up the ghost after two seasons of Friday night opposition from *Riley*, and *Our Miss Brooks*. *Riley*'s fans were so loyal that the other stations were practically conceding the time slot to that show in its later years. Due to Bendix's operation, he had no new films released in 1957, but did manage to star as a police captain in a segment of the series *The 20th Century–Fox Hour*.

In 1958, *The Life of Riley* and several other famous comedy shows were given the ax; Westerns and detective shows were in, and comedies weren't. Bendix went into one segment of the anthology series *Desilu Playhouse* (Rod Serling's "Time Element"). Bendix plays a man who, because of a time warp, is explaining to a psychiatrist (Martin Balsam) how he predicted the Japanese attack on Pearl Harbor before it happened. The doctor later learns that Bendix was in Hawaii on that fatal morning 17 years earlier; in fact, he died on December the 7th. Once again, Bendix proved himself in quality drama, here portraying a man we must believe completely though what he says is incredible. The actor was actively pursuing the most un–Riley like roles he could find. In his interviews of that period, he usually complained about his image as the lovable lunkhead and talked about gaining acceptance as a serious performer.

In March 1958, Bendix's work in another area was recognized. His contribution to the sale of U.S. Savings Bonds won him an honorary title as "roving ambassador of good will" at ceremonies in Washington. When Alan Ladd's production company took a plunge into television, Bendix did a pilot film for his old friend but nothing came of it. It would be their last professional connection. Bendix also worked on many of the anthology series. He began 1959 with a role on the prestigious CBS show *Playhouse 90*. The drama, "A Quiet Game of Cards," co-starred Franchot Tone, Barry Sullivan and E. G. Marshall and the plot involved several middle-class men who play cards together once a week. Their idle talk about "the perfect murder" leads them to form the hypothesis that a killer cannot be caught if he has no motive. They become so stirred up that they plot the murder of an elderly professor they do not know personally.

The implausibility of this drama was overshadowed by the fine ensemble playing of the cast.

Like many American actors who had not made a Hollywood film in some time, Bendix went to England, only to find that British films featuring American actors were invariably potboilers. *Idol on Parade* (1959), conceived as a spoof of Elvis Presley's Army induction, pitted rock singer Anthony Newley against Bendix's stereotypical top sergeant. Despite Bendix's participation, the film did not have many U.S. bookings. His second, Robert Siodmak's *The Rough and the Smooth* (1959) should have been better. Its U.S. title *Portrait of a Sinner* tells the story, the well-worn tale of a lovely femme fatale (Nadja Tiller) who ruins the lives of all her men. Bendix appeared out of his element, since he usually played a guy too realistic about his looks to ever let a woman use him.

After these experiences, it was a relief to get back to American television. In the second half of 1959, he did an adaptation of O. Henry's "Ransom of Red Chief" as a Sunday night special; it reunited him with Hans Conried, who had appeared on the *Riley* radio show. He then played another villain, mobster Wally Leganza, on the new hit ABC series *The Untouchables*.

While doing a stint on TV's *Wagon Train*, Bendix was asked to appear in a new NBC Western called *Overland Trail*, a mid-season (1959-60) entry. The actor played Kelly, the flamboyant manager of a western stage line. The similarities to *Wagon Train* were noticeable; one early episode used the same plot as a *Wagon Train* (singer Monica Lewis played a part enacted on the earlier show by Agnes Moorehead). It also resembled another new NBC series, *The Deputy*, in which week after week Marshall Henry Fonda would trick Allen Case into doing a dangerous job for him. On *Overland Trail*, Bendix would do just about the same to his young assistant Flip (Doug McClure). Bendix got a better percentage deal from NBC on *Overland Trail* than he had had on his previous series; NBC even moved the "waterlogged *Wagon Train*" *Riverboat* out of its Sunday night spot to make room for it.

Experienced Western writer Samuel Peeples, who became a personal friend of the star, worked on the scripts, but the time element was against him. Meanwhile, Bendix argued with the criticism that the show was highly imitative and in doing so he pointed out that all Westerns were alike. A running feud seemed to develop between them and *Wagon Train*, caused by the latter's co-star Robert Horton, always one to make flamboyant remarks. However, this time he was on target; *Overland Trail* was a carbon copy of Horton's show. By this time it was apparent that *Overland Trail* was a loser; it was the only new NBC Western that was not renewed. Two other hour-long Western series that premiered that season, *Bonanza* and *Laramie*, were unqualified hits even though their stars were relatively unknown compared to Bendix; he was unprepared for this, his first TV failure.

This early cancellation, however, enabled him to return to Broadway for the first time in two decades. He also did a limited tour with *Born Yesterday*, playing the character of Harry Brock (a role mostly associated with Broderick Crawford and Paul Douglas). He was signed to replace TV's first Chester A. Riley, Jackie Gleason, when Gleason left the hit musical *Take Me Along*. (Gleason had a personal success as the alcoholic practical joker Uncle Sid in this version of Eugene O'Neill's lightest work, *Ah, Wilderness*, but he had a contract with CBS to start a new program in January 1961.) Bendix had to step in just before Christmas, with several of the original cast (Walter Pidgeon, Eileen Herlie and Robert Morse) still co-starring.*
Since Bendix had to "sing" all or part of six songs, he was fortunate that his predecessor in the role had the same sort of croaking voice. By doing a sensitive duet with Herlie, "But Yours," he won the critics' plaudits.

For Bendix, the worst thing about settling into an extended stage run was the separation from his family, so firmly ensconced in California. He found that only a few show business pals were in town, but he had never been much of a socializer anyway. Eventually, Theresa Bendix and daughter Stephanie joined him, staying in a hotel. So close to his roots, Bendix felt like a stranger: He found the New York winter uncomfortable after two decades in sunny California. But the warm reception he got on stage wiped away many negative feelings and he considered further theatrical projects. After completing the Broadway run, he took the show on a tour of Eastern dinner theaters in the summer of 1961. He later worked with other touring companies, often cast in roles he was not exactly ideal for. Though he had played Jews before, the character of Mr. Baker in Neil Simon's *Come Blow Your Horn* was a bit too ethnic for him.†
But he easily captured the bombast displayed by Lou Jacobi in the Broadway play and Lee J. Cobb in the subsequent film. Fans flocked to see him.

**The role had been originated by Gene Lockhart in the straight play. Both Wallace Beery and Frank Morgan had played Sid on the screen.*

†*The character became somewhat more "gentile" thanks to the casting of future talk show host Merv Griffin as Bendix's playboy son.*

That fall, he was approached about starring in a new Ira Levin play, playing the title role of *General Seeger*. The idea of originating a role, a dramatic one at that, in a brand new play was too tempting to resist. Veteran actress Ann Harding was his co-star. The director, who also had an interest in the play, was George C. Scott, who at the time was somewhat preoccupied with telling everyone that he did not want the Oscar for his performance in *The Hustler*. There were early indications of trouble, so it was not surprising when Bendix left the show before it got to New York. It was February 1962 and the show was in Detroit, still being worked on, when he made the usual excuse: He was leaving due to a "difference of opinion" and said no more about it. Director Scott stepped into the role and went to Broadway, where the critics tore the play apart. Bendix's departure, for whatever reason, was the right move.

Prior to this abortive stage venture, he returned to MGM for the first time since *Woman of the Year* for a guest spot in *Boys Night Out* (1961). It appeared as if nothing had changed in the intervening 20 years: Bendix was again playing a bartender. He also squeezed in another overseas foray, first to Germany to play another non-com in an oddity called *The Phony American*. Then came *Johnny Nobody*, filmed in late 1961, but not released in the U.S. for three years. This British-made feature was directed by actor Nigel Patrick, who also played the priest-hero. Bendix appeared only in the opening scenes, playing a famous and blasphemous author who is shot to death by a mysterious stranger (Aldo Ray). The film was intended as a religious allegory, but was so muddled it didn't come off. All this did not faze Bendix, who was glad to take these short-term jobs where he got an expense-paid trip, did a few days work and could fly home to his family before the finished product was even in the can.

Bendix realized that the greatest security was a TV series, especially for a man who wanted to stay home with his family. He had once considered *The Life of Riley* to be an anchor around his neck, but the business was different now. He began in earnest to try and find just the right pilot for himself. In the meantime, he contented himself with whatever film work was available. He became one of the members of producer A. C. Lyles' stock company of veteran performers, cast in his low-budget productions. Dana Andrews, Richard Arlen, Bruce Cabot, James Craig, Linda Darnell, Brian Donlevy and Barton MacLane were among the players who worked for Lyles, usually in some rehash of a standard Western plot. Although most of his films would be made at Bendix's old stomping grounds, Paramount, his first for Lyles was an MGM release. In *The Young and the Brave* (1963), he and Rory Calhoun played American soldiers in Korea who, separated from their company, became closely attached to an orphan boy (Manuel Padilla). Some of the plot paralleled an earlier Bendix success, *China*, and he played his scenes with the boy with his customary warmth. His next role reunited him with director Michael Gordon, with whom he had worked in *The Web* and *Boys Night Out*. Although Bendix's part was bigger in the latter film, his name was farther down in the cast listing of Universal's *For Love or Money* (1963). This weak comedy had wealthy Thelma Ritter hire attorney Kirk Douglas to marry off her three daughters. Bendix was a private detective in Ritter's employ, assigned to watch Douglas perform his duties. Although Bendix and Ritter suggested an interesting team, the script left them hanging without any amusing situations.

In August 1963, Bendix was back on the summer theater circuit, teamed with Nancy Carroll in *Never Too Late*. They played an older couple shocked to learn she is expecting a baby after many years of marriage. The stars were well received, which was particularly gratifying to Carroll, a major film star of the early '30s who had recently started on the comeback trail. Bendix was playing the role which was enacted on Broadway (and later on film) by Paul Ford. Back in Hollywood, he was cast as a lawman in the first Lyles' production under the Paramount banner, *Law of the Lawless* (1964). This was the best film of the whole Paramount group, stressing character over action. But the violence lovers won out: In all the producer's subsequent Westerns, a traditional climactic gunfight settled matters. And Bendix, who had not enjoyed learning to ride a horse for *Overland Trail*, did not relish the idea of continuing in a string of B Westerns.

Things looked up somewhat when a CBS comedy pilot, *Bill and Martha*, was picked up. This show teamed him with Martha Raye, who had not had a regular series of her own since she was under contract to NBC in the mid-'50s. Everyone seemed to like the idea of these two TV veterans working together and the usual comparisons with Wallace Beery and Marie Dressler were starting. The series was set to begin in the fall of 1964, at the start of CBS' Tuesday night lineup. But in May of that year, the network dropped the show, giving its time slot to a Joey Bishop comedy series. They gave as their reason the failing health of co-star Bendix. Bendix, somewhat surprised that anyone would think that he would allow any health problem to keep him from fulfilling a commitment, promptly brought suit against the network. However, despite his surgery in 1956, he did continue to suffer from intense stomach discomfort, aggravated in times of stress. (With the cost of film escalating, various production people were asking certain performers to undergo physical examinations so that they could be insured for the length of time they were needed on the set.) CBS settled with Bendix out of court.

Before the lawsuit was settled, he signed for another theatrical tour only to prove his stamina. This time, the show was *Take Her, She's Mine*, in which he played another upper-middle-class father. The part was not exactly right for him. On the West Coast, he guested on ABC's *Burke's Law*, which used name performers in cameos as murder suspects. Then A. C. Lyles paged him for another Paramount Western, *Young Fury*. Unfortunately, it was all too evident that Bendix's health was indeed failing. Due to his painful stomach problems, he had all but stopped eating and undergone a tremendous weight loss. His role in *Young Fury*, that of a blacksmith roughed up by a gang of juvenile delinquents, was drastically cut. The film, which starred Rory Calhoun and Virginia Mayo, was released as a second feature in the spring of 1965.

He would never have been able to finish a larger role. In December 1964, he was admitted to Good Samaritan Hospital suffering from malnutrition. His condition was further complicated when lobar pneumonia set in. On Monday, December 14, William Bendix passed away. Fittingly, he was eulogized as a superb comic actor, with Riley prominently mentioned. The newspapers had no trouble finding people willing to say kind words about him. Some writers put him in the same league with three comedy greats who had passed on earlier that year: Gracie Allen, Eddie Cantor and Harpo Marx. While Bendix rightly considered himself an all-around actor and his film work was largely dramatic, the compliments sent his way were richly deserved.

The best description of William Bendix was his own, taken from his interview with Whitney Bolton in the *Morning Telegraph* during his Broadway comeback run in December 1960: "A tenement kid with a pushed-in nose and I turned into a movie star and TV star. Anybody knocks a country that did that for me and I'll bust 'em one." Who says Bill Bendix couldn't play the tough guy when he wanted to?

The Films of William Bendix

The film title is followed by studio, release year, director and cast members.

1. ***Woman of the Year.*** MGM 1942. George Stevens. Spencer Tracy, Katharine Hepburn, Fay Bainter, Reginald Owen, Minor Watson, Roscoe Karns, Gladys Blake, Dan Tobin, Sara Haden, William Tannen, Ludwig Stossel. WB debuts as saloonkeeper Pinkie.

2. ***Brooklyn Orchid.*** UA 1942. Clarence Marks. Grace Bradley, Joseph Sawyer, Marjorie Woodworth, Skeets Gallagher, Florine McKinney, Leonid Kinskey, Rex Evans. Cab driver WB starts his own business.

3. ***Wake Island.*** Par 1942. John Farrow. Brian Donlevy, Macdonald Carey, Robert Preston, Albert Dekker, Walter Abel, Mikhail Rasumny, Don Castle, Rod Cameron, Bill Goodwin, Barbara Britton. WB's only Oscar nomination as courageous Smacksie Randall.

4. ***The Glass Key.*** Par 1942. Stuart Heisler. Brian Donlevy, Veronica Lake, Alan Ladd, Joseph Calleia, Bonita Granville, Richard Denning, Frances Gifford, Donald MacBride, Moroni Olsen, Margaret Hayes, Pat O'Malley. WB is the thug Jeff, who brutalizes Ladd.

5. ***Two Mugs from Brooklyn.*** UA 1942. Kurt Neumann. Grace Bradley, Joseph Sawyer, Max Baer, Marjorie Woodworth, Joe Devlin. Sequel to *Brooklyn Orchid* has cab driver Tim (WB) become concerned with fitness.

6. ***Who Done It?*** Univ 1942. Erle C. Kenton. Bud Abbott, Lou Costello, William Gargan, Patric Knowles, Louise Allbritton, Don Porter, Thomas Gomez, Jerome Cowan, Mary Wickes. WB out-dumbs Costello as Gargan's police aide.

7. ***Taxi, Mister?*** UA 1943. Kurt Neumann. Grace Bradley, Joseph Sawyer, Iris Adrian, Sheldon Leonard, Frank Faylen. WB's final film as the cabbie.

8. ***The Crystal Ball.*** UA 1943. Elliott Nugent. Ray Milland, Paulette Goddard, Virginia Field, Gladys George, Cecil Kellaway, Ernest Truex, Iris Adrian, Donald Douglas. WB as another cab driver.

9. ***China.*** Par 1943. John Farrow, Loretta Young, Alan Ladd, Phillip Ahn, Iris Wong, Sen Yung, Richard Loo, Irene Tso, Tala Birell. WB is Johnny, the sidekick of the more mercenary Ladd, aiding Chinese during the Japanese invasion.

10. ***Hostages.*** Par 1943. Frank Tuttle. Luise Rainer, Paul Lukas, Arturo De Cordova, Katina Paxinou, Oscar Homolka, Roland Varno, Hans Conried, Reinhold Schunzel. Typical Nazi vs. partisans drama, with WB as a courageous freedom fighter.

11. ***Guadalcanal Diary.*** 20th 1943. Lewis Seiler. Preston Foster, Lloyd Nolan, Richard Conte, Anthony Quinn, Richard Jaeckel, Roy Roberts, Lionel Stander, Minor Watson, Ralph Byrd, John Archer. WB's "Taxi" is a retread of his *Wake Island* role, serving another Pacific tour of duty.

12. *Lifeboat.* 20th 1944. Alfred Hitchcock. Tallulah Bankhead, Walter Slezak, John Hodiak, Mary Anderson, Hume Cronyn, Henry Hull, Canada Lee, Heather Angel. WB at his best as the injured but optimistic Gus.

13. *The Hairy Ape.* UA 1944. Alfred Santell. Susan Hayward, John Loder, Dorothy Comingore, Roman Bohnen, Alan Napier, Tom Fadden, Eddie Kane. Eugene O'Neill's embittered seaman (WB) shares the same profession, but not the same outlook, with his previous film character.

14. *Abroad with Two Yanks.* UA 1944. Allan Dwan. Dennis O'Keefe, Helen Walker, John Loder, John Abbott, George Cleveland, James Flavin, Arthur Hunnicutt, William Forrest, Janet Lambert. WB and O'Keefe are American Marines who get in trouble in Australia.

15. *Greenwich Village.* 20th 1944. Walter Lang. Don Ameche, Carmen Miranda, Vivian Blaine, Felix Bressart, The Four Step Brothers, Tony & Sally DeMarco, B. S. Pully, The Revuers (Betty Comden, Adolph Green, Alvin Hammer, Judy Holliday). WB is a club owner during the Roaring Twenties.

16. *It's in the Bag.* UA 1945. Richard Wallace. Fred Allen, Don Ameche, Binnie Barnes, Jack Benny, Robert Benchley, Victor Moore, Rudy Vallee, John Carradine, Sidney Toler, John Miljan, Steve Brodie, Dave Willock. WB is a gangster sought out by Allen, who is determined to retrieve a fortune in cash hidden in a chair.

17. *Don Juan Quilligan.* 20th 1945. Frank Tuttle. Joan Blondell, Phil Silvers, Anne Revere, George Macready, Mary Treen, B. S. Pully, Veda Ann Borg, Richard Gaines, John Russell, Thurston Hall. Sea captain WB innocently becomes a bigamist.

18. *A Bell for Adano.* 20th 1945. Henry King. John Hodiak, Gene Tierney, Richard Conte, Glenn Langan, Henry (Harry) Morgan, Stanley Prager, Eduardo Ciannelli, Hugo Haas, Luis Alberni, Monty Banks. WB is sergeant to the American major (Hodiak) in charge of forces occupying an Italian village.

19. *Sentimental Journey.* 20th 1946. Walter Lang. John Payne, Maureen O'Hara, Sir Cedric Hardwicke, Glenn Langan, Connie Marshall, Mischa Auer, Trudy Marshall. WB is a loyal family friend of a theatrical couple; the wife (O'Hara) has a terminal illness.

20. *The Blue Dahlia.* Par 1946. George Marshall. Alan Ladd, Veronica Lake, Howard Da Silva, Doris Dowling, Tom Powers, Will Wright, Hugh Beaumont, Howard Freeman, Frank Faylen, Walter Sande, Vera Marshe. WB is Ladd's buddy, a war vet with a plate in his head.

21. *The Dark Corner.* 20th 1946. Henry Hathaway. Lucille Ball, Clifton Webb, Mark Stevens, Cathy Downs, Kurt Kreuger, Constance Collier, Reed Hadley, Donald MacBride, Ellen Corby. WB is the nameless white-suited killer.

22. *Two Years Before the Mast.* Par 1946. John Farrow. Alan Ladd, Brian Donlevy, Barry Fitzgerald, Howard Da Silva, Esther Fernandez, Albert Dekker, Darryl Hickman, Roman Bohnen, Ray Collins, Frank Faylen, Tom

Powers, Duncan Renaldo, Luis Van Rooten. WB is the loyal first mate of a cruel sea captain.

23. *White Tie and Tails.* Univ 1946. Charles Barton. Dan Duryea, Ella Raines, Clarence Kolb, Frank Jenks, Scotty Beckett, John Miljan, Richard Gaines. WB is a night club operator.

24. *I'll Be Yours.* Univ 1947. William Seiter. Deanna Durbin, Tom Drake, Adolphe Menjou, Walter Catlett, Franklin Pangborn, Bess Flowers. WB becomes Durbin's unofficial protector.

25. *Blaze of Noon.* Par 1947. John Farrow. Anne Baxter, William Holden, Sonny Tufts, Sterling Hayden, Howard Da Silva, Johnny Sands, Jean Wallace, Edith King, Lloyd Corrigan, James Burke, Will Wright. WB is a friend and co-worker of four barnstorming brothers.

26. *Calcutta.* Par 1947. John Farrow. Alan Ladd, Gail Russell, June Duprez, Lowell Gilmore, Edith King, Gavin Muir, John Whitney, Benson Fong, Don Beddoe. Once again, WB and Ladd are two-thirds of a trio of veterans, this time flying cargo in the far east.

27. *Where There's Life.* Par 1947. Sidney Lanfield. Bob Hope, Signe Hasso, George Coulouris, Vera Marshe, George Zucco, John Alexander, Harry Von Zell, Joseph Vitale. WB is one of a family of cops trying to make sure radio entertainer Hope does right by his fiancée, WB's sister.

28. *The Web.* Univ 1947. Michael Gordon. Ella Raines, Edmond O'Brien, Vincent Price, Maria Palmer, Howland Chamberlain, Fritz Leiber, William Haade, Tito Vuolo. WB in the first of his "sympathetic cop" roles.

29. *The Time of Your Life.* UA 1948. H. C. Potter. James Cagney, Wayne Morris, James Barton, Ward Bond, Jeanne Cagney, Broderick Crawford, Paul Draper, Jimmy Lydon, Gale Page, Tom Powers, Natalie Schafer. William Saroyan's play gave WB his first big break. In this film adaptation, he is elevated to the larger role of bar owner Nick.

30. *The Babe Ruth Story.* AA 1948. Roy Del Ruth. Claire Trevor, Charles Bickford, Sam Levene, William Frawley, Gertrude Niesen, Lloyd Gough, Paul Cavanagh, Fred Lightner, Richard Lane, Bobby Ellis, Ann Doran. Corny script defeats WB's effort as the Bambino.

31. *Race Street.* RKO 1948. Edwin L. Marin. George Raft, Marilyn Maxwell, Frank Faylen, Henry (Harry) Morgan, Gale Robbins, George Chandler, Mack Grey, Jason Robards, Sr. Detective WB maintains a friendship with bookmaker Raft.

32. *The Life of Riley.* Univ 1949. Irving Brecher. Rosemary DeCamp, James Gleason, Beulah Bondi, Richard Long, Bill Goodwin, Meg Randall, John Brown, Lanny Rees, Ted De Corsia, Mark Daniels. WB recreates his radio role as the aircraft worker planning a proper marriage for his daughter.

33. *A Connecticut Yankee in King Arthur's Court.* Par 1949. Tay Garnett. Bing Crosby, Rhonda Fleming, Sir Cedric Hardwicke, Virginia Field, Henry Wilcoxen, Murvyn Vye, Alan Napier, Richard Webb, Joseph Vitale. WB is an Arthurian knight who befriends a transplanted Crosby.

34. *Streets of Laredo.* Par 1949. Leslie Fenton. William Holden, Macdonald Carey, Mona Freeman, Stanley Ridges, Alfonso Bedoya, James Bell, Ray Teal, Clem Bevans, Grandon Rhodes. WB is a Western outlaw who goes straight, joining the Texas Rangers with pal Holden.

35. *Cover Up.* UA 1949. Alfred E. Green. Dennis O'Keefe, Barbara Britton, Art Baker, Ann E. Todd, Doro Merande, Virginia Christine, Russell Arms, Helen Spring. Small town cop WB helps protect a "do-gooder" killer.

36. *The Big Steal.* RKO 1949. Don Siegel. Robert Mitchum, Jane Greer, Patric Knowles, Ramon Novarro, John Qualen, Don Alvarado, Pat O'Malley, Pascual Garcia Pena. WB is a detective tailing Mitchum into Mexico.

37. *Johnny Holiday.* UA 1950. Willis Goldbeck. Allen Martin, Jr., Stanley Clements, Jack Hagen, Hoagy Carmichael, Herbert Newcomb, Donald Gallagher, Greta Granstedt. Do-gooder WB runs a ranch for wayward boys.

38. *Kill the Umpire.* Col 1950. Lloyd Bacon. Una Merkel, Ray Collins, Tom D'Andrea, Gloria Henry, William Frawley, Robert Wilke, Connie Marshall, Jeff York, Richard Taylor, Alan Hale, Jr., Luther Crockett. WB is an umpire-hating baseball fan forced to take that detested position.

39. *Gambling House.* RKO 1950. Ted Tetzlaff. Victor Mature, Terry Moore, Zachery A. Charles, Basil Ruysdael, Donald Randolph, Cleo Moore, Damian O'Flynn, Ann Doran, Eleanor Audley, Gloria Winters, Don Haggerty. WB is an underworld character.

40. *Submarine Command.* Par 1951. John Farrow. William Holden, Nancy Olson, Don Taylor, Arthur Franz, Darryl Hickman, Peggy Webber, Moroni Olsen, Jack Kelly, Charles Meredith. For the third time, WB plays the buddy of Holden, here the skipper of a submarine.

41. *Detective Story.* Par 1951. William Wyler. Kirk Douglas, Eleanor Parker, Warner Anderson, Frank Faylen, Bert Freed, Gladys George, Lee Grant, Craig Hill, George Macready, Horace MacMahon, Gerald Mohr, Cathy O'Donnell, Michael Strong, Joseph Wiseman. One of WB's best, as compassionate cop Brody.

42. *Macao.* RKO 1952. Josef von Sternberg. Robert Mitchum, Jane Russell, Thomas Gomez, Gloria Grahame, Brad Dexter, Vladimir Skokoloff, Phillip Ahn, Edward Ashley, Emory Parnell, Philip Van Zandt, Don Zelayo. WB is a tourist in the title city. There's more to him than meets the eye.

43. *A Girl in Every Port.* RKO 1952. Chester Erskine. Groucho Marx, Marie Wilson, Don DeFore, Gene Lockhart, Dave Willock, Dee Hartford, Hanley Stafford, Teddy Hart, Percy Helton, George E. Stone. Oddly coupled sailors WB and Marx become involved with a racehorse.

44. *Blackbeard, the Pirate.* RKO 1952. Raoul Walsh. Robert Newton, Linda Darnell, Keith Andes, Torin Thatcher, Alan Mowbray, Richard Egan, Irene Ryan, Anthony Caruso, Skelton Knaggs, Jack Lambert, Dick Wessel. WB, a pirate nicknamed Evil Eye, backs his captain (Newton, in the title role).

45. ***Dangerous Mission.*** RKO 1954. Louis King. Victor Mature, Piper Laurie, Vincent Price, Betta St. John, Walter Reed, Steve Darrell, Dennis Weaver, Harry Cheshire. WB is a policeman in Glacier National Park.

46. ***Crashout.*** Filmakers 1955. Lewis R. Foster. Arthur Kennedy, Luther Adler, Gene Evans, William Talman, Marshall Thompson, Gloria Talbott, Beverly Michaels, Percy Helton, Chris Olsen, Morris Ankrum. WB, at his meanest, is one of six convicts on the lam.

47. ***Battle Stations.*** Col 1956. Lewis Seiler. John Lund, Keefe Brasselle, Richard Boone, William Leslie, James Lydon, George O'Hanlon, Claude Akins, John Craven, Eddie Foy III. WB is another World War II Navy man.

48. ***The Deep Six.*** Warners 1958. Rudolph Mate. Alan Ladd, Dianne Foster, Keenan Wynn, James Whitmore, Efrem Zimbalist, Jr., Joey Bishop, Barbara Eiler, Ross Bagdasarian, Jeanette Nolan, Perry Lopez, Walter Reed, Ann Doran. In this reunion with Ladd, WB is the improbably named sailor Frenchy Shapiro, whose sacrifice teaches pacifist officer Ladd an important lesson.

49. ***Idol on Parade.*** Col 1959. John Gilling. Anthony Newley, Anne Aubrey, Lionel Jeffries, Susan Hampshire, Harry Fowler, Sidney James, David Lodge, Dilys Laye, John Wood. Sergeant WB deals with rock 'n' roll star Newley.

50. ***Portrait of a Sinner.*** AIP 1959. Robert Siodmak. Nadja Tiller, Tony Britton, Donald Wolfit, Adrienne Corri, Joyce Carey, Geoffrey Bayldon, Ed Chapman, John Welsh, Martin Miller. A lovely temptress (Tiller) affects the lives of many men, WB included.

51. ***Boys Night Out.*** MGM 1961. Michael Gordon. Kim Novak, James Garner, Tony Randall, Howard Duff, Janet Blair, Oscar Homolka, Anne Jeffreys, Jessie Royce Landis, Howard Morris, Patti Page, Jim Backus, Fred Clark, Frank Devol, Zsa Zsa Gabor, Larry Keating, Ruth McDevitt. As understanding barkeep Slattery, WB's career returns to its roots.

52. ***The Phony American.*** Signal International 1962. Akos Rathony. Michael Hinz, Christine Kauffman, Ron Randell, Karl-Otto Albert, Inge Benz, Fred Durr. WB is an American non-com fooled by a German youth.

53. ***The Young and the Brave.*** MGM 1963. Harry F. Hogan. Rory Calhoun, Richard Jaeckel, Richard Arlen, John Agar, Manuel Padilla, Robert Ivers, Weaver Levy. WB is an American soldier behind enemy lines.

54. ***For Love or Money.*** Univ 1963. Michael Gordon. Kirk Douglas, Mitzi Gaynor, Gig Young, Thelma Ritter, Julie Newmar, Leslie Parrish, Dick Sargent, William Windom, Elizabeth MacRae, Willard Sage, Alvy Moore, Don Megowan. WB is a private detective who works for a rich lady.

55. ***Johnny Nobody.*** Medallion 1963. Nigel Patrick. Nigel Patrick, Yvonne Mitchell, Aldo Ray, Cyril Cusack, Niall MacGinnis, Noel Purcell, Jimmy O'Dea. WB is seen briefly as a drunken and blasphemous author who is murdered by Ray.

56. ***Law of the Lawless.*** Par 1964. William Claxton. Dale Robertson, Yvonne De Carlo, John Agar, Richard Arlen, Bruce Cabot, Lon Chaney, Jr., Barton MacLane, Kent Taylor, Bill Williams. WB is a sheriff.

57. ***Young Fury.*** Par 1965. Christian Nyby. Rory Calhoun, Virginia Mayo, Lon Chaney, Jr., Richard Arlen, John Agar, Linda Foster, Dal Jenkins, Preston Pierce, Merry Anders, Jody McCrea. Frail WB is a small-town blacksmith victimized by a gang of Old West juvenile delinquents. The actor has little more than a bit in this, his last film.

WB also appeared as himself in three all-star Paramount films: *Star Spangled Rhythm* (1942), *Duffy's Tavern* (1945) and *Variety Girl* (1947).

Charles Bickford

In these days of great independence for actors in films, the term "rebel" has become a cliché. Since the end of World War II, it has been applied at one time or another to almost every new young actor. Many of these so-called rebellions, however, were meaningless because they were against a system of movie making that was already near death. Things were different in the thirties and probably the two men best characterized as true rebels were Spencer Tracy and Charles Bickford. Others would have specific complaints, but these two never stopped fighting the producers who employed them but could not boss them.

There were several similarities between the two. Both were of Irish stock and both gained prominence playing criminals in socially conscious plays. They helped prove that on-screen lovers did not have to be handsome glamour boys. But there was one difference. If Bickford had not told MGM production chief Louis B. Mayer just what he thought of him, he might have become a major star at that studio, the way Tracy did five years later. Tracy had enough patience to wade through the inferior pictures until the right role came along, but Bickford did not.

The resulting careers practically speak for themselves. Tracy was a star for 30 years. But the 1930s, the movies' "golden age," were not golden for Bickford. A respected stage actor when brought to films in 1929, he was just a villain in second features at the end of the '30s. His only crime was being brutally honest in a town that had only recently learned how to talk, let alone talk honestly.

Charles Ambrose Bickford was born at exactly one minute after midnight on January 1, 1889, into the already large Bickford family of Cambridge, Massachusetts. The majority of future tough guys generally did not come from such affluent stock. Young Charles was

Charles Bickford's early '30s demeanor.

the type of boy who could never quite adapt to attending the best schools. At a time when children were seen but supposedly never heard, he gained the reputation of a bad boy. Before he was even in his teens, he went to court for shooting a trolley car motorman with an air rifle. The trolley car had run down his beloved dog and had not even stopped, so the boy felt justified. But young Bickford proved to be so incorrigible that even his mother did not have a softening influence; Mary Ellen Bickford had all but given up on him. After all, he was a redhead and redheaded boys were usually considered hopelessly brattish, particularly around 1900.

If there was ever a time when the boy was well-behaved, it was when he listened to the stories of his sea captain grandfather. A great wanderlust developed within Charles and he impatiently waited for the chance to satisfy it. When he found he could wait no longer, he ran away from home before completing his senior year of high school. He never continued his education, although in later years he claimed to have garnered more knowledge from the books he read. He drifted across the country, from east to west, taking whatever jobs were available when necessity dictated. A chance meeting with a burlesque comic got him a job with the show. He found performing to his liking. He had great expectations of playing in New York, not knowing that there would be ten thankless years of touring before he realized this goal. However, he built a solid reputation as a stock company actor. As he gained experience and maturity, he became an actor-manager of his own stock company, which toured some of the worst towns in America. He was only in his twenties, but he was wise enough to know that before he tackled Broadway, he had better have a good vehicle.

Bickford joined the Army at the time of the American entry into World War I and served in the Engineering Corps. After the war's end, April 22, 1919, he opened with Thomas Mitchell in a play called *Dark Rosaleen*; it ran for 87 performances. It may not have been an electrifying debut, but he made some of the biggest producers aware of his commanding stage presence. That same year, he married Beatrice Loring. Although she was his only wife and mother to his two children, Doris and Rex, Bickford hardly discusses her in his autobiography.

Many felt that the reason Bickford failed to fully capitalize upon his first Broadway role was his physical stature. Many of the stars of the day were rather small and may have felt intimidated by the tall, rugged-looking Bickford's very appearance. (Also, a crippling actors' strike of 1919 limited the number of serious dramas that opened the following season.) Whatever the reason, Bickford had to continue touring for three more years. Like many other legitimate actors, he discovered that vaudeville offered opportunities to the out-of-work stock actor; at least it allowed him to continue to work in show business. His next notable role was as the replacement for

George Abbott (soon to become one of the stage's most respected directors) in *Zander the Great*. Then he joined the touring company of celebrated actress Alice Brady. When she learned that Bickford kept in shape by sparring with former boxing champ Jim Corbett, she demanded that it stop. Although it had been a quarter of a century since Corbett lost his heavyweight title and he was approaching 60, Brady feared for her leading man's physical appearance. Bickford acceded to the lady's wishes, no doubt grudgingly, and finished out the tour.

The time finally come for his physical power to be properly used and appreciated. The noted playwright Maxwell Anderson, who would be responsible for Bickford's best parts on Broadway, had seen him in a supporting role. Anderson was adapting a story by hobo-turned-author Jim Tully to the stage and decided the actor would be ideal for the lead, a tramp known as Big Red. The play was called *Outside Looking In* and the character seemed almost made to measure for him. Bickford understood the man he was playing very well, partly because of his own period of bumming around. A younger actor, also a redhead—James Cagney—was cast in the show, and together these two little-known performers garnered the kind of reviews actors dream of.* Cagney developed the inner warmth which, together with his wonderful cockiness, made him one of the most loved stars of all time. As far as films were concerned, Bickford never developed this kind of audience empathy. The success of *Outside Looking In* not only established him, but the prototype for the character he would return to time and again: that of the sullen, unfriendly loner. Today, such heroes are popular in films, but over a half century ago, a character like that could only be the bad guy.

Cagney and Bickford never worked together again, despite their many years in films. Both would pen an autobiography, a none-too-common endeavor for actors of their generation. While Cagney's was a reasonably straightforward analysis of his career and interaction with others, Bickford's was anything but. Titled *Bulls, Balls, Bicycles and Actors*, it glossed over his personal life while taking an irreverent look at the acting profession. One who had never seen him perform might come away from this book with the idea that he

---

**The respected drama critic of the* Daily News, *Burns Mantle, compared the two little-known actors to the most celebrated performer of the time: "I believe Mr. Barrymore's celebrated performance as Hamlet would be a mere feat of elocution if compared to the characterizations of either Mr. Bickford or Mr. Cagney."*

wasn't much of an actor and didn't care enough to try and become a better one. Bickford even claimed to be so uninterested in the critic's reception of him in that first hit that he went to sleep before the glowing reviews came out. His book is more a tribute to his stubbornness rather than his talent: he painted himself as a man more interested in being a star than an actor and alienating many along the way. The reader never once sees the sensitivity that went into his best performances, since Bickford has buried it under mounds of conceit. The book may be more readable than the more serious tomes of other actors, but it's still an elaborate joke. It is only satisfying for those who want to know how Bickford made his enemies or for lovers of name-dropping, but serious students of acting will get nothing from it.

The popularity of *Outside Looking In* helped Bickford get his first picture offer, a role in the silent version of *Beau Geste* which he rejected out of "love for Broadway." When the play's run ended, he appeared in some less spectacular works. He had supporting roles in *Houses of Sand* (1925) and *Chicago* (1926); he wrote the unsuccessful *Cyclone Lover* in 1928. Even *Gods of Lightning*, now considered one of the decade's notable plays, was poorly received when it opened. Maxwell Anderson collaborated on the play, one of several based upon the headline-making Sacco and Venzetti case. Bickford played a Sacco-like anarchist called Macready; Sylvia Sidney and Barton MacLane were also in the cast. The public was tired of the subject matter, resulting in the play's failure. After this, Bickford no longer discouraged Hollywood. It was 1928, talkies had arrived, and Metro-Goldwyn-Mayer was making him offers.

MGM was already a top studio. Studio boss Louis B. Mayer kept an eye on the "taste of the nation"; production head Irving Thalberg was determined to elevate the artistic quality of the motion picture. Thalberg signed more theatrical players than any of the other studios: His tireless efforts netted Metro the temporary services of Ethel Barrymore, Helen Hayes, Alfred Lunt and Lynn Fontanne. Cecil B. DeMille, fresh from making one of his greatest films, *King of Kings*, was also set up on the lot. With all this activity, it would have been very easy for Bickford to have gotten lost among the other "New York talent." But when he arrived in California in late 1928, he already had his first film set: He was to play the male lead in DeMille's first talkie, *Dynamite*.

After DeMille made his silent Biblical epics, he wanted to do some modern-day stories, beginning with *Dynamite*. Bickford soon learned that even though he had been hired because of his stage credentials, he was now expected to behave like a film star. Hollywood stars were expected to meet publicity requirements, and he didn't. Bickford was 40 (hardly the right age for a screen newcomer) and, because he was married, he frowned on studio-arranged dates. He did not take his wife to the parties and premieres that stars often attended. He had no desire to amass the entourage of followers that some stars had. So he was given the label of "prestige star," which may have gone along with Thalberg's plans but was hardly designed to ring up ticket sales.

Those who had seen the actor on the stage predicted that once he was seen, he would pull the audiences in with his magnetism. Magnetism or not, it didn't take MGM executives long to become disenchanted with him. When DeMille first read the script of *Dynamite* to cast and crew, Bickford noticeably dozed off. Yet, for some perverse reason, the director took a liking to the arrogant actor and would use him in four other films. While his first film was being made, MGM was planning to cast him as seaman Mat Burke in the film of Eugene O'Neill's *Anna Christie*, which was to be Greta Garbo's sound debut. Most actors would have jumped at the chance, but when Garbo visited the set of *Dynamite*, Bickford told her he didn't want the role because it was too subordinate to hers. The studio heads were furious and decided that a few loanouts would make this actor see the error of his ways.

In the DeMille film, Bickford played a convict sentenced to death. He marries Kay Johnson so that she may claim an inheritance and then is exonerated at the last minute. The rest of the film has him trying to win his wife away from Conrad Nagel (an actor who seemingly never got the girl once talkies arrived). A big mine cave-in was DeMille's one concession to spectacle. For Bickford, it was the first of many screen roles as a gruff character who romances a genteel lady.

He was immediately loaned to Fix to co-star with stage star Lenore Ulric in *South Sea Rose* (1929). He was cast as a mercenary sea captain who wants to marry Ulric, mainly because of her supposed claim to a fantastic treasure. The film was directed by Allan Dwan. Bickford did not gripe as much about this quickie as he did about his next movie (and its director). *Hell's Heroes* (1929) was the first really important film in the career of William Wyler, who was then considered just another house director (and a relative of executive Carl Laemmle) at Universal. Bickford, like most of Hollywood, considered Universal a step down from MGM and Fox. To add to his annoyance, *Hell's Heroes* was to be shot on location in the desert, to capture some of the realism which had been achieved by Raoul Walsh in *In Old Arizona* earlier that year. The story was based on the oft-filmed *Three Godfathers*, about a trio of outlaws who sacrifice themselves for an infant they found in the desert. Raymond Hatton and Fred Kohler co-starred; all three had to work under less than pleasant conditions. Bickford developed an intense dislike for the director; his feelings would still be strong more than 35 years later. In his autobiography, Bickford takes Wyler to task for his "lack of talent"; after working with Wyler again three decades later in *The Big Country*, he claims that the director hadn't changed. Bickford's book never mentions Wyler by name, calling him "The Golem" because of what Bickford considered Wyler's rather lifeless direction.

By the time Bickford returned to MGM, *Anna Christie* was ready to be filmed. The studio refused to consider Bickford's objections to his role. Bickford was right about his role being far subordinate to Garbo's; with Marie Dressler in the film, it was practically unnoticed. But with all the publicity about Garbo talking, the film was a success. (Garbo was practically the only foreign-born performer to retain the stardom she had won in the silent days.) Bickford was one of those rare leading men who was able to get through to the elusive actress when out of character. Though he may have derided the Burke role, it appears that Bickford enjoyed working with the actress.

There was little doubt about how he felt on his Metro follow-up assignment, *The Sea Bat* (1930). Although he was not yet a proven money-maker, the studio knew how much they were paying him and it was enough for him to be carrying a picture by himself. The picture that was to establish him as a rugged action star was a contrived sea story about an escape from Devil's Island over choppy seas. Raquel Torres was Bickford's leading lady and silent screen favorites Nils Asther and John Miljan backed them up. The director was Lionel Barrymore, who had decided to leave acting to his celebrated siblings now that talkies were in. But Barrymore did not have a flair for direction and within a year, his Metro contract would be amended to a straight actor's agreement. Barrymore was replaced in mid-production by Wesley Ruggles, who was given sole directorial credit when the film came out. Ruggles would soon be going over to RKO to direct Edna Ferber's *Cimarron*. Everyone seemed to sense that this was one film that would be an unqualified success and the leading character, Yancey Cravat, was a part Bickford really wanted. But his constant griping had made Mayer and the other executives particularly vindictive and they refused to loan him out to RKO.

Anna Christie was rushed into release early in 1930, and soon other studios were interested in Bickford. While MGM hesitated sending him into some other company's hit (like *Cimarron*), they did not mind his being cast in an unproven property somewhere else. Bickford was loaned to Warner Bros. for *The River's End* (1930), a programmer which offered Bickford a challenge: He played a dual role, a Canadian Mountie and his fugitive quarry. Michael Curtiz, Warners' most prolific director, was at the helm, and the volatile Hungarian invested it with pace.

Back at MGM, Bickford found that *The Big House*, an important prison picture which had been cast, was being made with Chester Morris and Wallace Beery. In its place, the studio provided him with a film called *Passion Flower* (1930), directed by William DeMille, Cecil's brother. A remake of a 1921 Norma Talmadge film, it found Bickford cast as a chauffeur who romances two wealthy women (Kay Johnson and Kay Francis). He seemed somewhat out of place—too modern to be convincing in this outdated soap opera. He looked more at home in his next film, Cecil B. DeMille's third version of *The Squaw Man* (1931), playing a rough westerner. However, there was little comfort in this assignment: He was not playing the title role (Warner Baxter has been borrowed from Fox for that purpose), he was there to provide villainy and support. He was being told in no uncertain terms that MGM did not think of him as a star, at least as far as big-budgeted films were concerned.

Seeing no future for himself at the studio, Bickford asked Thalberg for his release. Had he left it at that and not had one final encounter with Mayer, his film career might have taken a different turn. But the famous Bickford temper flared. Among other things, he called the production boss of Hollywood's greatest studio a "posturing little ignoramus." Mayer would continue to dominate the studio for two decades, during which the actor would occasionally return for individual roles. Those parts could best be characterized as Louis B. Mayer's revenge.

It seemed as if all of Hollywood was united in a plot to teach Charles Bickford humility. He had been led to believe that there was a great deal of interest in him at all the major studios, but the lucrative offers soon vanished. In his book, he claims to have travelled abroad in order to wait out this shadowy "blacklist," but that wasn't quite true. He and his family moved into what would become their permanent home in Playa Del Ray; whatever roles were available to Bickford in Hollywood had to be taken. Fortunately for him, there were some people in town who would hire someone *because* he was on MGM's enemies list. Columbia's Harry Cohn was constantly making deals with people Mayer didn't want and he gave Bickford the leads in four programmers in the year and a half after his departure from MGM. Universal summoned him for two films, *East of Borneo* (1931) and *Scandal for Sale* (1932), in which he was, respectively, a doctor and a publisher being redeemed by an understanding wife; Rose Hobart in both instances was the lady fending off the advances of another man. In fact, most of Bickford's roles in this period found him at one end or another of a romantic triangle. Like many actors who clung to the lower rungs of the Hollywood ladder in the '30s, he accepted the fact that B-pictures were better than breadlines.

RKO used him as a weak lead for Helen Twelvetrees in *Panama Flo* (1932) and for Irene Dunne in *No Other Woman* (1933). The pictures were designed to prop up the heroine and the best that could be said about them as far as Bickford was concerned was that he was cast in sympathetic roles. He was also summoned to Paramount, a studio that had wanted to sign him as early as 1926. For his first Paramount assignment, he was cast as Tallulah Bankhead's husband, whose imminent blindness aids him in keeping his wife out of Paul Lukas' arms, in a very typical '30s drama, *Thunder Below* (1932). But, unlike the other studios that employed Bickford, Paramount did not see him as a leading man type. They didn't even see him as a rugged loner. They saw him as a villainous tough guy. In Bickford's next Paramount picture, *Song of the Eagle* (1933), he was a murderous bootlegger outwitted by clean-cut hero Richard Arlen. But it was Cecil B. DeMille, the man who gave Bickford his first film role, who delivered the *coup de grâce* to his career as a romantic lead. DeMille starred him in *This Day and Age* (1933) as a racketeer so vile that he inspires a group of youths in his community to kidnap him and torture him into a confession. The kids were the open-faced, all–American types who populated '30s films, so the contrast was all the more notable. Nobody seemed to mind the film's not-so-subtle fascism as long as the fascism was directed against someone as mean as Bickford. Not that too many people saw it; it remains one of DeMille's few complete failures.

But the die had been cast and more parts of an unsavory nature came his way. He was not as mean as was Charles Laughton in *White Woman* (1933); Bickford played the overseer of a jungle outpost who somewhat nobly allows Laughton's wife (Carole Lombard) to leave with her handsome lover (Kent Taylor) while he and Laughton remain to face some murderous natives. His acting in the last scene is particularly effective, quite restrained in contrast to Laughton's hamming as they play games, awaiting imminent death. Laughton was probably the finest actor detested by Bickford. He was also allowed some last minute nobility in his next film, *Little Miss Marker* (1934). In one of the better screen versions of a Damon Runyon story, Bickford played Big Steve, a hard-hearted gang boss, the last character to be softened by little Shirley Temple, whose life he saves by giving her a blood transfusion. Being up against the most amazing child star of all time and a fine and sensitive performance by Adolphe Menjou as Sorrowful Jones, few actors could have come off as well as he did. (When Paramount did a poor remake, *Sorrowful Jones*, Bruce Cabot played the Big Steve role and was left unredeemed.)

Bickford returned to MGM for the first time since his contract ended for *Wicked Woman* (1934), in which he supported Mady Christians and several newcomers, including Betty Furness and Robert Taylor. The best thing that could be said about the role was that it was so small, it couldn't do much damage to his career. He was then signed to be directed by Paul Stein, an Austrian who had made American pictures, in *Red Wagon*, a British production about a Latin American rebellion. At least it got Bickford a trip to England and an opportunity to work with a lot of British actors and leading lady Raquel Torres. The picture, based on an adventure novel by Lady Elinor Smith, was shot in 1934, but it took a few years for a company called Alliance to get it across the Atlantic, where it went largely unnoticed.

His career in this country followed the familiar pattern: leads in low-budgeters and supporting roles in big studio products. In the latter category came roles in two Fox films, *Under Pressure* and *The Farmer Takes a Wife*, both 1935 releases. The first was the last of Raoul Walsh's offshoots of his old success *What Price Glory?*; for almost a decade, he had been directing Edmund Lowe and Victor McLaglen in various reincarnations of their original Quirt-Flagg roles. This was to be the last, with both Walsh and Lowe at the end of their contracts. Centering around the construction of a tunnel under New York, *Under Pressure* found the two brawling stars united against a common antagonist—Bickford, of course. In *The Farmer Takes a Wife*, Bickford was cast to contrast with Henry Fonda, who in his screen debut recreated the role he had played on Broadway. Bickford had replaced Spencer Tracy in the film (Tracy was glad to break his Fox contract).

Bickford made a good impression in these films and had no call for his services from Paramount, so he considered signing with Fox. The studio was in the midst of its merger with Twentieth Century, which made Darryl F. Zanuck chief of production. Zanuck, whose only previous connection with Bickford was at Warners when *The River's End* was made, liked the actor well enough to offer a contract. It was announced that his next film, *The Littlest Rebel*, would reunite him with Shirley Temple. But Bickford did not appear in this film or, for that matter, any film under Zanuck's aegis for another eight years.

Bickford had also been picking up leading parts in several Universal programmers. In *A Notorious Gentleman* (1934), he was an unscrupulous criminal lawyer who plots revenge after he is jilted by Helen Vinson for a more successful man. (In the '40s remake *Smooth as Silk*, the Bickford role was played by Kent Taylor.) The following year, Universal reunited the star and the director (George Melford) of the 1931 film *East of Borneo* for a cheap (and similarly titled) adventure film, *East of Java*. To give its audience something extra, Universal decided to capitalize on the success of its earlier film *The Big Cage* (1933), starring famed animal trainer Clyde Beatty. They stocked the film with loads of "trained" animals, forgetting that the only thing their present star had in common with Beatty was the same initials. Bickford, playing the captain of a ship transporting these animals to the States for use in circuses, jumped into the project with typical enthusiasm. The actor who had once squared off against Jim Corbett now took on a 400-pound tiger. And this time his foolhardiness almost cost him his life. The tiger pounced upon the actor and ripped away at his neck and shoulders. Fortunately for Bickford, the animal was more frightened by his strange surroundings than intent upon the kill, and it was relatively easy for others to pull it off Bickford. Bickford was rushed to the hospital; he had lost a tremendous amount of blood, and there was a chance he might not survive. Universal, already in despair over mounting financial reversals, feared a lawsuit. They were comforted by the knowledge that he had completed enough footage that they could finish the film. But they had learned their lesson; in the future, they would either use Clyde Beatty or some actor small enough to have Beatty double for him in any jungle epic they made. It would be many years before Hollywood let any of its actors near a wild jungle beast.

During his long recuperation, Bickford had no idea whether his film career would continue. Even though his appearance was not terribly altered by the accident, the motion picture industry seemed unaware that he still existed. *The Littlest Rebel*, which had been delayed until Shirley Temple had completed another film, was not delayed for his benefit. There was no longer any mention of a contract. But his greatest annoyance was remaining inactive during the convalescent period. Fortunately, he had taken an interest in painting and developed that talent during this time. (He would become one of the best of the actor-artists.) In the meantime, his family's financial status was improved by his wise investments, such as the one he made in a tungsten mine. *East of Java* was released towards the end of the year and quickly forgotten amid all the other second features.

As soon as Bickford was able, he got back into film work and did seven films in less than two years, all but one for Paramount. That exception was a Harry Cohn potboiler called *Pride of the Marines*. After playing a claim jumper whose primary function seemed to be to keep Gladys Swarthout (as a proud señorita) and John Boles (a government man) from singing too much in the outdated *Rose of the Rancho* (1936), he landed in one of the decade's best adventure films and one of Cecil B. DeMille's finest of all time. This was *The Plainsman* (1936), which starred Gary Cooper as Wild Bill Hickok and Jean Arthur as Calamity Jane. One of the best things about it was that this time DeMille did not rely exclusively on spectacle to carry the movie. Rather than recreate the Custer massacre at Little Big Horn, DeMille has Hickok learn about it from a Cheyenne brave (played by a very young Anthony Quinn), and the audience sees only a brief visual montage as the Indian communicates with sign language and a few guttural sounds.

Throughout DeMille's career, he was frequently attacked for discarding facts and making up his own history. However, in this film, he came out in favor of truth, despite some studio pressure. Even though one of the screen's greatest heroes (Cooper) was playing Hickok, DeMille chose to end his film with a scene of Hickok being shot in the back during a card game, just about the way it actually happened. But Paramount was aghast at the notion of killing off two great American heroes (Cooper and Hickok) in one fell swoop. Seedy little coward Jack McCall was the real-life backshooter. The studio sought a compromise by having Bickford, as evil gun trader John Lattimer, be the culprit instead of actor Porter Hall's weasely McCall; the studio perhaps felt that it would be a lesser disgrace to have Cooper gunned down by a bigger man. But since Lattimer had already been dispatched by Hickok in a previous scene, DeMille stuck to his guns. After more than 60 years, the film's last scene is still telling, almost duplicated by the last scene in *The Shootist* (1976), in which John Wayne is shot in the back by the bartender. It emphasizes a great paradox: larger-than-life men are almost never gunned down by a physical or social equal, but rather by some cringing little nobody. *The Plainsman* was one of the year's top grossers.

After this interlude of quality, Bickford's career fell into another slump. He did one other A-product for Paramount, a standard villain in an original Jerome Kern–Oscar Hammerstein musical, *High, Wide and Handsome* (1937), directed by Rouben Mamoulian. It was obvious that his career was not in an upswing since he was billed far below star Irene Dunne (he was her leading man in a movie just four years earlier). The best thing to come out of the film was the beautiful song "The Folks Who Live on the Hill." Bickford's other 1937 films were all B's; *Thunder Trail*, a Zane Grey Western, *Daughter of Shanghai*, a melodrama about the smuggling of Chinese aliens into the U.S., and *Night Club Scandal*, in which he played a homicide detective. The latter film gave him the opportunity to work with the bad boy of the Barrymore clan, John, here playing the hardly taxing role of a doctor whose wife has been murdered. (Bickford, who would work with Ethel Barrymore in the '40s, performed with all three of the famous siblings.)

Nineteen thirty seven was a poor year, and the following one was a disaster. Bickford reached the lowest rung of Poverty Row, making the first of three appearances in Republic films. He once again played a dual role in *Gangs of New York*, which at least gave him the opportunity to be a hero and a villain in the same film. However, he felt he needed more of a challenge than films like these offered and he was spurred to try his first Broadway role in a decade: He starred in a play about the legendary railroad engineer, *Casey Jones*. Critics allowed it to roll along for a scant 25 performances.

Back in Hollywood, Bickford performed with another actor with directorial experience, Donald Crisp in Warners' *Valley of the Giants* (1938). There was a similarity in their careers: Crisp had also played brutish villains in earlier years, and both actors would later specialize in kindly doctors or other fatherly types. In *Valley*, Bickford clashes with local boy Wayne Morris, who blocks Bickford's attempt to cut down giant redwood trees. The film displayed a great deal of the color red; it was Bickford's first in color, so shocks of his red hair were seen on screen for the first time.

Evidently, some producers still saw some softness in Bickford's countenance, for when he and Barton MacLane landed in the same film, MacLane would invariably be the meaner of the two. This was true in Universal's *The Storm* (1938), a seagoing adventure, and in Monogram's *Mutiny in the Big House* (1939), in which Bickford was the prison chaplain to MacLane's vicious convict leader. Bickford and MacLane next appeared opposite that champion of gruffness Wallace Beery in *Stand Up and Fight* (1939). It was an MGM picture and Bickford's standing at that studio had not improved a bit: He received very little footage in this film, which concentrated on a feud between Beery's stage-line workers and Robert Taylor's railroad employers. MacLane was given equally shoddy treatment.

The period between 1939–1942 was a low point in Bickford's career, though these were the years of Hollywood at its best. During this time, he made many potboilers for Monogram, Republic, Columbia and Universal. The *Times* critic reviewing Universal's *One Hour to Live* (1939) thought Bickford so bad that he appeared to be merely rehearsing his role. Fortunately, there was a cinematic oasis in Bickford's desert of mediocrity: He was cast in one of that year's finest, portraying the foreman Slim in Hal Roach's independently produced version of John Steinbecks' *Of Mice and Men.**
With Academy Award winner Lewis Milestone directing, Aaron Copland composed the music and Bickford accepted the fourth-billed spot under three leading performers whose names had even less marquee value than his. Slim is not the sort of rough and unfeeling character Bickford was usually called on to play; he was a three-dimensional character of warmth and compassion who takes an interest in his ranch hands. Some cast members, particularly Burgess Meredith and Roman Bohnen, had better roles, but Bickford's

---

*While the play Of Mice and Men *was racking up 207 performances on Broadway, Bickford was only occupied for 25 performances in* Casey Jones.

competent and likable foreman also made a strong impression. He had not made the wrong move in allowing his name to come after Meredith, Betty Field and Lon Chaney, Jr. (in the role of Lennie the simpleton created on stage by Broderick Crawford). The film was one of the first United Artists film to be nominated for an Oscar.

Bickford returned to Poverty Row. At least Republic attempted to vary the types of parts they offered him: In *Thou Shalt Not Kill* (1940), he was a Protestant minister who hears the confession of a murderer who mistook him for a Catholic priest. In the same year's *Girl from God's Country*, he was a lawman who traces fugitive Chester Morris to the frozen north, where both become involved with doctor Jane Wyatt.

Programmers at Universal had not progressed from the *East of Java* days, the locales changed but the stories remained identical. Bickford was reteamed with his Java co-star (eternal kid brother Frank Albertson) in 1941's *Burma Convoy*. The script offered a passing nod to the worsening situation with the Japanese in Burma, as war clouds thickened around the world, film writers began using the international situation as a hook for many adventure films. That same year, Universal also cast Bickford in his first and only serial. *Riders of Death Valley* was given better production values than the average serial, with Lon Chaney, Jr., rejoining his *Of Mice and Men* co-star in supplying the villainy while Dick Foran and Buck Jones wore the white hats. Since the casts of serials were usually made up of has beens or nobodies, it appeared that Bickford's career had reached a dead end.

Even Cecil B. DeMille failed Bickford at this point. The part the director gave him in *Reap the Wild Wind* (1942) set a few records: He was dropped down to eighth billing and had the least amount of screen footage ever accorded him. To add insult to injury, his character was not even given a name, identified only as the "Mate of the Tyfib," who shanghais crewmen for his vessel. This was to be the last heavy he would play without any psychological shading at all.

Bickford resolved to make one more attempt at obtaining quality parts: He began turning down the majority of "dog" parts he was always being offered (something he hadn't done in a decade). Reasoning that with a war on, the bigger studios might have a need for older leading men, he figured this was his last good opportunity. At first, there were no appreciable results. After the DeMille film, he only had one other 1942 release, playing a dastardly character in MGM's *Tarzan's New York Adventure*. A lighter-than-usual entry in the Tarzan series, it had Bickford again working for a circus, this time capturing Boy (Johnny Sheffield) instead of the more dangerous jungle denizens he had tried to bring back alive in *East of Java*. Ironically, this programmer was better than what Metro usually offered him; the Tarzan films were always given good production values and fine supporting casts.*

Mr. Lucky (1943) is a prime example of what was wrong with wartime films; a routine comedy at best, it was made almost unbearable by an overdose of sloppy patriotism. Since no film starring Cary Grant could be *all* bad, he may be the only reason for its box office success. Third-billed Bickford played Swede, the skipper of Grant's gambling ship, a sympathetic character who was little more than a prop with no real personality of his own.

Bickford's next assignment would be as rich in quality as its predecessors were shallow. It was the film's writer, George Seaton, who recommended Bickford for the major role of Peyremaie, Bishop of Lourdes, in Fox's major production *The Song of Bernadette* (1943). Of Bickford's performance, film historian Frank Magill wrote that he showed the man's "depth of sincerity without the benefit of one obviously dramatic personal scene." Bickford later said about his contribution to this film that "a great character actor was born" when it was released at Christmas of 1943. Bickford's work was noticed by the critics for the first time in years, singled out in a uniformly excellent cast. The warmth and kindness that was suggested in *Of Mice and Men* and few other films was much in evidence here. The Bishop is a man who, through years of service to his church, is understandably skeptical that a peasant girl (Jennifer Jones) actually saw the Blessed Virgin, but he nevertheless defends her from those who would do her harm. The picture is a rarity, a lengthy religious film (two and a half hours) which is never slow-moving or dull—a credit to Henry King's direction. Jones as Bernadette, Gladys Cooper as a disapproving nun and Bickford were all nominated for Oscars, but only Jones received the award (Bernadette was her first major assignment). Her win, and Bickford's loss to Charles Coburn for *The More the Merrier*, started something of a trend: He would be nominated two more times for films where the leading actress captured an Oscar and he lost all three times to older actors. A

More than a decade earlier, in his waning days as an MGM contractee, Bickford had been briefly considered for the role of the Jungle Man, before Johnny Weissmuller was chosen.

happier trend also began here: He had found his niche in the movie business, the type of character he would most often play through the remainder of his career—the supporter of the underdog.

The most immediate result of this success was that Fox signed him for three more pictures. The first two parts were nice, and rather dull. In *Wing and a Prayer* (1944), he played the captain of a U.S. Navy aircraft carrier. Most of the action involved the conflicts between executive officer Don Ameche and pilots Dana Andrews and William Eythe. Bickford was one of several name actors playing small roles in *Captain Eddie* (1945), a highly fictionalized bio of World War I flying ace Eddie Rickenbacker that was being used as another flag-waver for the current war. Fred MacMurray played the title role and Bickford was seen in a flashback as his decent, hard-working father. Bickford had barely enough time to impart some typically meaningful advice to young Eddie (Darryl Hickman) before being killed off in an accident at work. His fourth Fox film in two years was somewhat better, even though it put him back in an unsympathetic role. In Otto Preminger's *Fallen Angel* (1945), he was cast as an ex-city cop seeking the murderer of Linda Darnell, a small town tramp he was romantically involved with. The film was Preminger's middle-class version of his prior year's success *Laura*, though it doesn't stand up as well today. Bickford and Darnell (who played the Blessed Virgin in *The Song of Bernadette*) were the ones audiences remembered, rather than the film's nominal leads, Alice Faye and Dana Andrews.

While shooting *The Song of Bernadette*, Bickford had helped the fledgling actress who played the role. Consequently, Jennifer Jones was eager to have Bickford in another one of her films and persuaded her fiancée David Selznick to add him to the all-star cast of his deluxe production *Duel in the Sun* (1946). (Jones and Bickford remained friends until his death.) The making of this epic, with several directors and years of filming, has become part of Hollywood legend, and the stories do not flatter Selznick. In his determination to make this the *Gone with the Wind* of Westerns, he created an almost ludicrous effect; many scenes recall his former triumph, but the characters here do not measure up to those in *GWTW*. However, the picture does have several things to recommend it, particularly the photography. And any time the camera focuses on either Lillian Gish or Lionel Barrymore, some fine acting is captured. King Vidor received sole directorial credit, but *Duel in the Sun* was truly a collaborative effort.

Jones is seen as a sultry half–Spanish girl who is taken in by a wealthy family after her father is killed. She causes a conflict between the family's two sons, upright Joseph Cotten and black sheep Gregory Peck. Bickford has the small role of a rancher who wants to marry Jones and is goaded into a gunfight by Peck. The final desert shootout between Jones and Peck is the most famous scene in the film—possibly the most flagrant use of violence as a "sexual symbol" in a movie made by the Hollywood establishment. It was not a typical movie contrivance to have the leading man and woman mortally wound one another and die in each other's arms. But it was scenes like that that helped *Duel in the Sun* become one of the top-grossing films of all time (despite a critical lambasting). After cleaning up in 1946–47, it was given a major re-release in 1954 before being sold to television. In spite of the fact that the story appealed to its audience's baser interests, *Duel*'s size and cast established it as a film of quality. And any time an actor like Bickford appeared in such a film, it boosted his stock. His newfound prestige would help him land important roles in at least eight films which became top moneymakers. His second 15 years in films would be far more remunerative than the first 15.

Bickford followed *Duel* with the very popular *The Farmer's Daughter* (1947), working again with Joseph Cotten and another Barrymore, Ethel; they played a Congressman and his mother. Bickford was cast as Clancy, their loyal Man Friday, and he received his second Academy Award nomination.*

Most of the attention was focused on the film's star—Loretta Young—as the Swedish farm girl who changes all their lives. She received the Best Actress award that year, while Bickford lost out in the supporting category to Edmund Gwenn in *Miracle on 34th Street*.

Jules Dassin's *Brute Force* (1947) was a violent prison drama distinguished by its fine acting. Bickford's role as a convict who plans an ill-fated breakout is sympathetic; in this film, it is the prison administrators who are the real villains. This was the first of three films in which Bickford supported Burt Lancaster, who was then new to the movies. *Woman on the Beach* (1947) was one of Jean Renoir's few American films, somewhat below his usual standards. However, the film offered Bickford an unusual (and unusually nasty) role: a blind painter whose wife (Joan Bennett) becomes romantically

---

*In the early 1960s, Bickford reprised his Clancy role in a television version with Lee Remick, which helped spawn the successful Inger Stevens TV series.

involved with Coast Guardsman Robert Ryan. The film did manage to generate some amount of suspense and was helped considerably by the acting of the three principals.

Bickford's first 1948 release was *Four Faces West*, released by United Artists. He played a relentless Western lawman tracking "good badman" Joel McCrea. When Bickford discovers how his quarry has risked capture to help a Mexican family, he allows him to escape. Once again, the acting elevated a relatively simple, though warm, story. The film represented a reunion with McCrea, who had played a small part in *Dynamite* two decades earlier. His next film *The Babe Ruth Story* offered no saving graces; he just did his bit as he again donned a cassock to play the head of the orphanage where the baseball star (William Bendix) grew up. (The old tough guys were often called upon to play mentors of great athletes: Lloyd Nolan in *Crazy-legs*, Ward Bond in *The Bob Mathias Story* and Bickford again in *Jim Thorpe—All American* are good examples.) In this film, his role is confined to a few brief words of wisdom.

Johnny Belinda (1948) is an example of how fine craftsmanship in all departments can turn a simple, sensitive story into a film of beauty. Directed by Jean Negulesco, this Warner Bros. release had the benefit of superb acting by Jane Wyman, Lew Ayres, Jan Sterling, Agnes Moorehead, Stephen McNally and Bickford. Wyman won the Academy Award for her role as a deaf mute. Ayres, Moorehead and Bickford were all Oscar-nominated, the latter for skillfully playing the mute's gruff but ultimately decent father. Although Bickford's character is killed well before the film's end, his characterization has left a strong impression. In the three televised versions of this film, time limitations curtailed the effectiveness of the performances of Victor Jory, Barry Sullivan and Roberts Blossom, who inherited the role of the father.

His last feature film at MGM was *Command Decision* (1948), which was also big box office thanks to its Broadway reputation and all-male all-star cast. As Brockhurst, a nosy war correspondent at an American air base in England, Bickford received fifth billing under studio regulars Clark Gable, Walter Pidgeon, Van Johnson and Brian Donlevy and *above* such important contractees as John Hodiak and Edward Arnold. This seemed to indicate that his newfound status as a freelancing character actor had destroyed the old blacklist. It was something of a vindication for Bickford to be in a Metro prestige picture after all these years, even if acting honors rightfully went to Gable and Pidgeon, playing generals of differing temperaments and priorities. Under Sam Wood's straightforward direction, the entire cast performed in true ensemble style. The greatest irony may be that Bickford never made another MGM picture. The vagaries of Hollywood saw to it that he did not again return to the studio that once wanted to make him a star, even after his bitter enemy Mayer was no longer the big man on the lot.

Producer Samuel Goldwyn considered every one of his films prestigious, but *Roseanna McCoy* (1949) did not live up to expectations. *Roseanna McCoy* was *Romeo and Juliet* transplanted to the hill country, with the Montagues and Capulets changed to the Hatfields and the McCoys, those famous feuding families of the mountains. A vehicle for the producer's new young stars Farley Granger and Joan Evans, the film offered little to the veterans in the cast, Bickford and Raymond Massey as the clan leaders. This was Bickford's only Goldwyn feature. He returned to Fox to work for Otto Preminger in *Whirlpool* (1949), playing a somewhat colorless role. Once again he was a stalwart upholder of the law, this time trying to nab phony hypnotist Jose Ferrer, who is using Gene Tierney in his diabolical plotting. Bickford finished out the year with his first top-billed role in eight years—but still in the cheapie division, unfortunately. He once again donned religious garments to portray the real-life Cardinal Mindszenty of Hungary, who was imprisoned by the Communists, in *Guilty of Treason* (1949). Because of its timely subject matter, the subject would not be touched by a major company and therefore the film had to be made by a shoestring outfit, Eagle Lion. As was the norm in those days of vehement anti–Communism, the script was damaged by an overabundance of propaganda, as well as the limited budget, most of which was used to pay the salaries of stars Bickford and Paul Kelly.

In 1950, the actor returned to Paramount for two films which were designed primarily as vehicles for the studio's top male stars, Bing Crosby and Alan Ladd, respectively. *Riding High* was Bickford's only Frank Capra film, a somewhat disappointing remake of the director's 1934 film *Broadway Bill*. He played the wealthy prospective father-in-law of incurable horse lover Crosby, a role played originally by the late Walter Connolly.*

**In 1956, when Dick Powell directed a musical version of Capra's* It Happened One Night *(1934), he cast Bickford in another millionaire role originated by Connolly. If one was to choose the films in which Bickford was most miscast, it would have to be* Riding High *and the Powell film (*You Can't Run Away from It*), in which he had to be a very straight man in the midst of some rather weak musical comedy doings.*

Many of the character actors who worked in the original film repeated their roles enabling Capra to incorporate whole scenes from the earlier work. The Alan Ladd film, *Branded*, turned out to be one of that star's biggest moneymakers though it had a fairly predictable plot. Back in the saddle again, Bickford played a wealthy rancher who develops a liking for Ladd, an impostor pretending to be his long-lost son.

Bickford got to do his mentoring bit again, this time playing a famous sports figure in *Jim Thorpe—All American* (1951). He played the real-life coach Pop Warner, who is remembered for the "Pop Warner kids football leagues." Once again he championed an underdog, the great American Indian athlete Thorpe, played by Burt Lancaster. Unlike *The Babe Ruth Story*, this was a slickly professional job, sparked by Lancaster's own athletic prowess as well as his acting ability. The film returned Bickford to Warner Bros. under the direction of the man who helmed his first Warners film two decades earlier, Michael Curtiz. He then returned to Universal for *The Raging Tide* (1951), a routine programmer in which he played a kindly Swedish ship captain who takes in fugitive Richard Conte and develops fatherly feelings for this hunted man—feelings he never displayed around his own son (Alex Nicol).

Elopement (1951), directed by Henry Koster for Fox, was a rarity for Bickford, a comedy that allowed him to be part of the proceedings rather than just a sourpuss observer. The key to the film's success was Bickford's teaming with the brilliant Clifton Webb; the plot is quite meager and it is the interplay between their two diverse types that creates interest. The two actors play strangers who are thrown together on a cross-country chase when Bickford's professor-son (William Lundigan) elopes with his pupil, Webb's daughter (Anne Francis). Practically the only humor in the film is derived from scenes in which Webb's acid tongue is used against Bickford's hardheaded gruffness. The actors were cast as types, but their playing of these types transcended the material.

Past 60 now, Bickford chose to ease up on his number of film commitments, usually averaging three a year. He also opted not to jump into the television waters, as their minuscule shooting schedules made some of his old quickie products seem luxurious by comparison. He still had his love of painting and his home in Playa Del Rey and enough money put away to enjoy both without having to worry about his next paycheck. Bickford made no screen appearances in 1952, the first year he hadn't made a movie since his 1929 arrival in Hollywood.

The following year, he returned to films, and to villainy, in a neat little Western called *The Last Posse*. He played a well-to-do rancher who relentlessly hunts down and murders the poor men who were forced to rob him. Directed by Alfred Werker, this example of the new form of "adult Western" benefits from a strong cast, particularly Bickford and Broderick Crawford as a basically decent lawman who sacrifices his life to ensure that the evil rancher gets what he deserves. Once again, it was interesting to see which of the two tough guy leads would play hero and villain. By virtue of being a contractee of the studio, Columbia, as well as a recent Oscar winner, Crawford won hands down.

Bickford then embarked upon a series of big budgeted films, starting with George Cukor's *A Star Is Born* (1954) at Warner Bros. In this Judy Garland film, he was called on to do his usual "father confessor" bit as a movie studio bigwig. He was so stereotyped that Bosley Crowther of *The New York Times* remarked, "Charles Bickford's calm and generous producer is a bit on the idealized side." In truth, Bickford was a more sedate Oliver Niles than was Adolphe Menjou in the 1937 version of the story (Menjou was a lot closer to the studio heads Bickford had dealt with).

Judy Garland's comeback, bolstered by James Mason's excellent performance and a fine Harold Arlen–Ira Gershwin score, are the only reasons for viewing this overlong film today. But its cult status is deserved when one compares it to the later Barbra Streisand version, which is simply wretched.*

Bickford remained in "show business" for his next, *Prince of Players* (1955) at Fox. Giving moral support to yet another famous person, the nineteenth century actor Edwin Booth (Richard Burton), Bickford played his manager and loyal friend. Much of the film dealt with Booth's torments, not the least of which were caused by his brother John Wilkes Booth (John Derek). The film allowed Burton a rare opportunity to do excerpts from Shakespeare, but has little other value. It was such a major disappointment that it ended up playing three-day engagements, the exhibitors not deeming it worthy of a week's run in the neighborhoods.

In the mid–'50s, Bickford began sandwiching TV work in between his theatrical films. He remained selective, choosing roles

---

*In the 1976 rock version of the story, actor-director Paul Mazursky played the record entrepreneur in much the same way as the Bickford counterpart. Probably both roles were diminished so as not to detract from the film's female stars.

on prestigious anthology series, like *Ford Theater*. On the short-lived *Screen Director's Playhouse*, he played personal physician to Robert Ryan's Abraham Lincoln in a half-hour drama called "Lincoln's Doctor's Dog." He also played a doctor who administers to the nuns at a convent in the fine *Hallmark Hall of Fame* production "The Cradle Song," co-starring with Helen Hayes and Judith Anderson. A few seasons later, he did the *Hallmark* show again, playing a disillusioned judge in an adaptation of Maxwell Anderson's *Winterset*, also starring Don Murray, Piper Laurie and George C. Scott. And he starred as a newspaper tycoon who refused to hold back on the story of a kidnapping, thereby endangering the victim's life, in "The Man Who Couldn't Wait" on *The Twentieth Century–Fox Hour*.

During this period of increased activity, Bickford had one of his finest screen roles: Dr. Runkelman in *Not as a Stranger* (1955). In a superb cast which included Robert Mitchum, Olivia de Havilland, Frank Sinatra, Broderick Crawford, Gloria Grahame, Myron McCormick, Lee Marvin and Lon Chaney, Jr., Bickford's performance as a small town general practitioner was the standout. Producer Stanley Kramer, here making a successful directorial debut, avoided many of the soap opera pitfalls usually inherent in those "doctors are human, too" films. The script followed ambitious Lucas Marsh (Mitchum) from medical school to assisting Bickford in his private practice. The elderly Dr. Runkelman teaches him the true meaning of being a member of the medical profession. Runkelman has all the characteristics of the actor's other top roles: shrewdness in his field, gruffness when dealing with inept, younger men and gentleness with his patients. So deeply does Bickford's Runkelman impress us that, when Dr. Marsh is unable to save him on the operating table, *we* feel the intense grief *he* feels. Perhaps Kramer intended to blunt the tearjerker aspects of the story by casting rugged tough guys in the major roles, but it is doubtful that any "softer" actor could have aroused more audience sympathy than Bickford does here. He had recognized a great part and seized it. Neither he nor any other member of the distinguished cast received an Oscar nomination, which was surprising since the picture did well at the box office. But this brilliant performance did not go unnoticed: Bickford was named Best Supporting Actor of 1955 by the National Board of Review.

Before the year was out, Bickford was back on the screen in *The Court-Martial of Billy Mitchell*, teaming with Gary Cooper for a second time and director Otto Preminger for a third time. Some critics, seemingly forgetting the old Bickford, thought him miscast as a general who was so antagonistic towards the hero, Billy Mitchell, he had convened the court-martial. Still, the talky debates about the future of American air power (the film is set in the 1920s) consign the two actors to relatively passive roles. Second-billed to Cooper, Bickford sits among the other officers while acting honors go to prosecutors Rod Steiger and Fred Clark and defense lawyers Ralph Bellamy and James Daly. Though not a typical Cooper vehicle, it made money like one, giving Bickford his third box office hit in a year's time.

After *You Can't Run Away from It* (1956), a mediocre *It Happened One Night* retread, Bickford went over to Universal to co-star with Tony Curtis in *Mister Cory* (1957). This time, he was the mentor of a fledgling gambler who wants to break into society. The picture was rather trivial and he plunged back into television work. These were the days of *Playhouse 90* and he obtained several roles on that show. Unfortunately, all series were not the gems memory would have us believe. Particularly poor were the series made by Columbia's TV outlet Screen Gems, whose production values were practically nil. Bickford starred with Jan Sterling in Screen Gems' *Clipper Ship* as a rugged sea captain who loved his vessel.

Bickford was back on horseback for William Wyler's spectacular Western *The Big Country* (1958). Whenever cast as a ranch owner, Bickford was called upon to enact the ruthless tough guy. Here he played Major Henry Terrill, engaged in a brutal range war with Burl Ives, who feels entitled to the land the Major supposedly owns. Caught in the middle is Gregory Peck, a former sea captain engaged to Bickford's daughter Carroll Baker. The problem is solved when the two violent old men gun each other down. The film, which also starred Jean Simmons and Charlton Heston and ran close to three hours, was filmed on location near Stockton, California. The amazing thing was that Bickford would have ever gone on any location with William Wyler, who had been responsible for one of his most unpleasant filming experiences. According to Bickford's book, he did not see any change in "The Golem" of nearly 30 years earlier.

Bickford's next film was also a big Western in the *Duel in the Sun* tradition, John Huston's *The Unforgiven* (1960). The stars were Burt Lancaster and Audrey Hepburn, but another alumnus from the Selznick spectacular, Lillian Gish, neatly stole this film. Huston was a director more to Bickford's liking than Wyler. He was once again cast unsympathetically, playing a rancher who turns against his neighbors when he learns that the daughter of the family (Hepburn) is really a full-blooded Indian adopted as a baby. He turns them out, leaving them to defend themselves against the attacking Indians alone. Far more melodramatic than *The Big Country*, *The Unforgiven* is also more compact and has better character development than the somewhat pretentious Wyler film. But it has dated badly, along with two films that swiftly followed on its heels, *Flaming Star* (1960) and *The Outsider* (1961)—well-meaning films that preached against bigotry towards Native Americans.

The difficult location shooting of his last two films convinced the now 70-year-old Bickford to further curtail his movie schedule and concentrate on Hollywood-based television shows. It would be close to three years before he would be seen on the big screen and when he did, it was to recreate a role he had originated on television. Back in October 1958, he acted in an excellent *Playhouse 90* that remains one of the series' most illustrious productions. The drama was J. P. Miller's "Days of Wine and Roses" with Piper Laurie and Cliff Robertson as a young couple whose lives are smashed by a growing dependency upon alcohol. Bickford was cast as Ellis Arnesen, the girl's father, a hardworking farmer stunned by his daughter's drinking. The play was deeply effective. Four years later, its producer Martin Manulis made the film version and Bickford was the only one of the principals reprising a role. Much as he did in *Johnny Belinda*, Bickford lent a quiet dignity to the role of a compassionate man with a child he loves but is unable to deal with. Jack Lemmon was brilliant as his son-in-law, while Lee Remick as the daughter who eventually sinks deeper than her husband is somewhat weaker than Laurie was. Both were Oscar-nominated in the 1962 race, but the film's only winner was the haunting title song. *Days* was recognized as a deeply moving study of the alcoholic and one of the best directorial efforts of Blake Edwards.

Bickford continued to pick up some quality television work. Dick Powell had become a major force in television drama via his work at Four Star productions. From a rotating anthology series to the very popular Zane Grey Western shows to his own weekly hour-long drama series, Powell led the field in production values and taste. Powell gave Bickford some solid dramatic roles on *Dick Powell Theatre*. He played the senior member of a unique trio of robbers (his partners being Cliff Robertson and Dean Stockwell) in "The Geetas

Sleeping Charles Bickford about to have a rude awakening courtesy of drunken daughter Lee Remick in *Days of Wine and Roses* (1962).

Box." Another starring role, "The Old Man and the City," was telecast after Powell's untimely death in 1963.

Working in television gave Bickford an opportunity to appear with several more great ladies of the screen. He guested on Barbara Stanwyck's dramatic series as a typically gruff rancher who gives a home to Stanwyck, who is trying to live down being an outlaw's wife. They proved that the combined talents of two veterans could enhance the value of an ordinary half-hour drama. Bickford worked with Joan Crawford in a pilot for a new series called *Royal Bay*. Both performers had long resisted being tied up in a regular show. Four Star Productions did as much as they possibly could to prove to them that this would not be an ordinary series so they made the pilot feature-length and added two promising younger performers, the excellent actress Diane Baker (who had already worked with Crawford in a pair of theatrical films) and Paul Burke (fresh from the successful series *Naked City*). Crawford played a small town woman whose house concealed the standard "terrible secret" while Bickford got into his father confessor role again as chief advisor to Burke. Much of this smacked of soap opera. Despite the *Royal Bay* cast, it apparently did not have the presold marketability of another "small town soap opera" pilot, *Peyton Place*, which did become a series (*Royal Bay* did not). Later in the decade, this lengthy pilot was sold to local stations and shown as *Della*. (*Della* may have been the first series pilot to make the TV rounds as a "movie," since actual TV movies did not appear until a couple of years later.)

Bickford, like most of the pros who worked frequently on TV, had become resigned to appearing in a series. Some of the dramatic series of the '60s featured veteran actors like Sam Jaffe, Dean Jagger and Raymond Massey in support of younger actors (in these cases, Vince Edwards, James Franciscus and Richard Chamberlain). Bickford reasoned that at 75, he was entitled to the shorter hours these men enjoyed while the newcomers carried the heavier schedule. He also wanted to avoid the far-flung locations current moviemaking demanded. So it was not surprising when he chose a series co-starring not one, but several youthful performers.

The program was *The Virginian*, an already established series which had enjoyed four successful seasons before Bickford joined its cast. This 90-minute western produced by Universal through its TV outlet (Revue) had benefitted from the participation of one of the best actors in the business, Lee J. Cobb, as the judge who owned the Shiloh ranch. Cobb was the perfect authority figure to be surrounded by a number of young actors (James Drury, Doug McClure and Clu Gulager, among others). But the distinguished actor had not expected to be tied up for so many years, finding his ability to accept outside work severely limited. So, in the fourth season, he gradually eased himself out, somewhat buoyed by the renewed interest sparked by his televised appearance in his classic stage role in *Death of a Salesman*. The studio felt the need to have some father-figure hold together a show that was too lengthy to be carried by one or two stars. Once it was decided that a new character would be introduced as the ranch owner, the selection of Bickford was a natural; he had certainly played a number of grizzled old ranchers in his time. The character of John Grainger was created along with a new storyline. And in his late seventies, Bickford finally found himself acting in a regular series.*

Before beginning work on *The Virginian*, he made another

**Bickford served as host-narrator of the nearly-forgotten* Man Behind the Badge *in 1954, but did not act in this syndicated documentary series.*

feature film which wound up being his last. *A Big Hand for a Little Lady* (1966), directed by Fielder Cook and written by Sidney Carroll, had its origins on television, where it was presented on *The Dupont Show* as "Big Deal at Laredo." It is a delightful comedy about a yearly poker game played by a bunch of wealthy Texans and how it is disrupted by a strange turn of events. The cast couldn't have been much better: Henry Fonda, Joanne Woodward, Burgess Meredith, Paul Ford and, as the rich poker players, Jason Robards, Jr., Kevin McCarthy, Robert Middleton, John Qualen and Bickford, as wealthy undertaker Benson Tropp. As the most dour of the group, he has the least lines of dialogue, but his facial reactions to the others say everything, and indicate that this is one character that is not easily outsmarted. When Tropp does succumb to sentiment, it creates the most ironic moment in the film; few other actors could have succeeded at this. Seldom does a screen veteran appear in a farewell film quite so touching as *A Big Hand for the Little Lady*.

Bickford was also represented in another area in 1966, when his autobiography appeared in book stores. Despite its somewhat negative look at Hollywood, *Bulls, Balls, Bicycles and Actors* is entertaining because its author was an unknown quantity to the general public, not having any regular cronies who talked about him behind his back, and having rarely given interviews.

In the fall of 1966, his episodes of *The Virginian* began appearing on Wednesday nights on NBC. Bickford's character, Grainger, had two grown grandchildren, a boy and girl, who had to warm to the ways of the West as well as to the grandfather they were estranged from. Don Quine and Sara Lane played Stacey and Elizabeth. Each of the regulars starred in a certain number of episodes, while appearing only briefly in others. Bickford adapted well to the schedule, which constituted his full professional activity during what would turn out to be the last year of his life.

Bickford began suffering from recurring bouts with emphysema and, after completing work on episodes for the fall 1967 season, he was hospitalized. One of the last episodes guest-starred Charles Bronson, still a character actor, but soon to become the film world's highest-paid tough guy star. Also in that show was former western star Dick Foran, who had worked with Bickford on the very same lot in the serial *Riders of Death Valley* more than a quarter of a century earlier. Universal, of course, had been one of the few studios that gave Bickford work when he was considered poison in Hollywood (he had practically sacrificed life and limb for them), so it was fitting that his last work would be for them. On November 9, 1967, Bickford died in his sleep at the age of 78; the official cause of death listed as emphysema. The studio quickly filled the void left on *The Virginian* by bringing in John McIntire as John Grainger's brother Clay. (McIntire had been the actor called upon to fill the wagonmaster's shoes when Ward Bond died during the run of *Wagon Train*.)

Perhaps a career as a major character actor can be considered a failed career for someone who could have been a star. But it is doubtful that any star parts could have made Bickford's record any more distinguished than it stands. By letting his temper get the best of him and sounding off early in his film career, Bickford may have set in motion the wheels that deposited him in his rightful niche. More amenable actors, all talented, had fallen by the wayside because they did not have the charisma and looks of a Gable or the gruff lovable quality of a Beery. Some who tasted stardom could not resign themselves to the small parts they were later offered. And none of Bickford's starring parts can hold a candle to his role in *Not as a Stranger*. So, while he may have been a failure as a tough guy hero, Charles Bickford was, in the final analysis, a true success.

The Films of Charles Bickford

1. ***Dynamite.*** Pathé 1929. Cecil B. DeMille. Kay Johnson, Conrad Nagel, Julia Faye, Joel McCrea, Muriel McCormick, Robert Edeson, Leslie Fenton, Rita Leroy, Carole Lombard. A convicted killer, CB enters into a marriage of convenience on the eve of his scheduled execution.

2. ***South Sea Rose.*** Fox 1929. Allan Dwan. Lenore Ulric, Kenneth MacKenna, Ilka Chase, J. Farrell MacDonald, Elizabeth Patterson, Roscoe Ates, Daphne Pollard. Sea captain CB wants to marry a woman because of her supposed claim to a treasure, but she loves a schoolteacher.

3. ***Hell's Heroes.*** Univ 1929. William Wyler. Fred Kohler, Raymond Hatton, Fritzi Ridgeway, Maria Alba. CB is one of three outlaws and gives up his life to save an infant found in the desert.

4. ***Anna Christie.*** MGM 1930. Clarence Brown. Greta Garbo, Marie Dressler, George Marion, Lee Phelps, James T. Mack. CB, as Eugene O'Neill's Irish seaman Mat Burke, almost gives up Anna (Garbo) when he learns of her sordid past.

5. ***The Sea Bat.*** MGM 1930. Wesley Ruggles (replaced Lionel Barrymore). Raquel Torres, Nils Asther, John Miljan, George Marion, Boris Karloff. CB is a phony minister on a stormy boat trip in the area of Devil's Island.

6. ***The River's End.*** WB 1930. Michael Curtiz. Evelyn Knapp,

J. Farrell MacDonald, Zasu Pitts, Tom Santschi, Junior Coghlan, Walter McGrail, David Torrance. CB has a dual role as a Canadian mountie and a fugitive he is pursuing.

7. *Passion Flower.* MGM 1930. William DeMille. Kay Francis, Kay Johnson, Lewis Stone, Zasu Pitts, Bobby Dukes, Dickie Moore, Winter Hall. CB is a chauffeur who married a wealthy girl and then strays with her cousin.

8. *The Squaw Man.* MGM 1931. Cecil B. DeMille. Warner Baxter, Lupe Velez, Eleanor Boardman, Roland Young, Paul Cavanagh, DeWitt Jennings, Julia Faye, Lawrence Grant, Lillian Bond, Mitchell Lewis. CB is a villainous westerner clashing with a disgraced Britisher (Baxter) who has become a rancher.

9. *East of Borneo.* Univ 1931. George Melford. Rose Hobart, Georges Renavent, Lupita Tovar, Noble Johnson. A woman finds her missing doctor husband (CB) in the employ of an evil rajah.

10. *Pagan Lady.* Col 1931. John Francis Dillon. Conrad Nagel, Evelyn Brent, Roland Young, William Farnum, Leslie Fenton, Lucille Gleason, Gwen Lee. CB's mistress has an affair with the son of an evangelist.

11. *Men in Her Life.* Col 1931. William Beaudine. Lois Moran, Victor Varconi, Donald Dillaway, Luis Alberni, Adrienne D'Ambricourt, Oscar Apfel. Rough-hewn CB and a suave foreigner become romantic rivals.

12. *Panama Flo.* RKO 1932. Ralph Murphy. Helen Twelvetrees, Robert Armstrong, Maude Eburne, Paul Hurst, Marjorie Peterson, Ernie Adams. CB is the man who does right by a fallen woman.

13. *Scandal for Sale.* Univ 1932. Russell Mack. Rose Hobart, Pat O'Brien, Glenda Farrell, Berton Churchill, Tully Marshall, Claudia Dell, Harry Beresford, Lew Kelly. CB builds up a scandal sheet on the misfortune of others.

14. *Thunder Below.* Par 1932. Richard Wallace. Tallulah Bankhead, Paul Lukas, Ralph Forbes, Eugene Pallette, Leslie Fenton, James Finlayson, Edward Van Sloan. CB is the blind husband Bankhead wants to leave.

15. *The Last Man.* Col 1932. Howard Higgins. Constance Cummings, Robert Ellis, Alec B. Francis, Kit Guard, John Eberts, Jack Richardson. CB faces the snobbishness of his girl's well-to-do family.

16. *Vanity Street.* Col 1932. Nick Grinde. Helen Chandler, Raymond Hatton, George Meeker, Mayo Methot, Arthur Hoyt, Claudia Morgan. CB is again softened by the love of a sweet young girl.

17. *No Other Woman.* RKO 1933. J. Walter Ruben. Irene Dunne, Eric Linden, Gwili Andre, Buster Miles, Leila Bennett, Christian Rub, J. Carrol Naish. Sudden wealth has a damaging effect on the marriage of CB and Dunne.

18. *Song of the Eagle.* Par 1933. Ralph Murphy. Richard Arlen, Mary Brian, Louise Dresser, Jean Hersholt, Julie Haydon, Andy Devine, George E. Stone, Gene Morgan. Bootlegger CB causes the death of a brewery owner, making him the target for revenge by the man's son.

19. ***This Day and Age.*** Par 1933. Cecil B. DeMille. Richard Cromwell, Judith Allen, Eddie Nugent, Ben Alexander, Harry Green, George Barbier, Bradley Page, Sterling Holloway, Fuzzy Knight, Nella Walker, Oscar Rudolph. CB is a vicious racketeer who is destroyed when a group of young students torture a confession out of him.

20. ***White Woman.*** Par 1933. Stuart Walker. Charles Laughton, Carole Lombard, Kent Taylor, Charles Middleton, Ethel Griffies, Percy Kilbride, James Bell, Marc Lawrence. CB is a tough overseer at a jungle outpost threatened by murderous natives.

21. ***Little Miss Marker.*** Par 1934. Alexander Hall. Shirley Temple, Adolphe Menjou, Dorothy Dell, Lynne Overman, Frank McGlynn, Sr., Jack Sheehan, Warren Hymer, Tammany Young, Gary Owen, Willie Best, Frank Conroy. CB is hard-hearted gambling boss Big Steve, a Runyonesque character to be softened by little Temple.

22. ***A Wicked Woman.*** MGM 1934. Charles Brabin. Mady Christians, Jean Parker, William Henry, Betty Furness, Robert Taylor, Jackie Searle, Bonita Granville, Paul Harvey, DeWitt Jennings, Sterling Holloway. Newspaper editor CB falls in love with the self-sacrificing mother of four children who has a terrible secret in her past.

23. ***A Notorious Gentleman.*** Univ 1934. Edward Laemmle. Helen Vinson, Onslow Stevens, Sidney Blackmer, Dudley Digges, John Darrow, John Larkin, Alice Ardell. Unscrupulous lawyer CB plots revenge when the woman he loves spurns him for a more successful man.

24. ***Under Pressure.*** Fox 1935. Raoul Walsh. Victor McLaglen, Edmund Lowe, Florence Rice, Marjorie Rambeau, Sig Rumann, George Walsh, Roger Imhof, Warner Richmond. Another Walsh-directed offshoot of *What Price Glory?* finds the two protagonists digging a tunnel under New York while battling each other and common enemy CB.

25. ***Red Wagon.*** Alliance 1935. Paul Stein. Greta Nissen, Raquel Torres, Anthony Bushell, Don Alvarado, Frances L. Sullivan, Paul Graetz, Frank Pettingell. CB is a circus manager, facing problems while on a tour of Europe.

26. ***The Farmer Takes a Wife.*** Fox 1935. Victor Fleming. Janet Gaynor, Henry Fonda, Andy Devine, Jane Withers, Slim Summerville, Margaret Hamilton, John Qualen, Kitty Kelly, Robert Gleckler. Fonda makes his debut in a role he played on the stage. The story concerns boatmen on the Erie Canal, with captain CB a rival for the affections of Gaynor.

27. ***East of Java.*** Univ 1935. George Melford. Frank Albertson, Elizabeth Young, Leslie Fenton, Ivan Simpson, Sig Rumann, Clarence Muse, Charles McNaughton, Fraser Acosta. Sea captain CB battles the villains and man-eating tigers.

28. ***Pride of the Marines.*** Col 1936. D. Ross Lederman. Florence Rice, Ward Bond, Robert Allen, Billy Burrud, Thurston Hall, Joseph Sawyer, George McKay. CB and his Marine pals raise the son of a dead buddy.

29. ***Rose of the Rancho.*** Par 1936. Marion Gering. John Boles, Gladys Swarthout, H. B. Warner, Benny Baker, Grace Bradley, Willie Howard, Don

Alvarado, Minor Watson, Herb Williams. Claim jumper CB causes trouble that temporarily interrupts the singing of señorita Swarthout and government man Boles.

 30. ***The Plainsman.*** Par 1936. Cecil B. DeMille. Gary Cooper, Jean Arthur, James Ellison, Helen Burgess, Porter Hall, Victor Varconi, Paul Harvey, Frank Albertson, John Miljan, Francis McDonald, Fred Kohler, Sr., George "Gabby" Hayes, Anthony Quinn. In one of DeMille's simplest and finest films, CB is an illicit gun trader and the bitterest enemy of Wild Bill Hickok (Cooper).

 31. ***Night Club Scandal.*** Par 1937. Ralph Murphy. John Barrymore, Lynne Overman, Louise Campbell, Harvey Stephens, Evelyn Brent, Elizabeth Patterson, J. Carrol Naish. CB is a police detective, investigating the murder of doctor Barrymore's wife.

 32. ***High, Wide and Handsome.*** Par 1937. Rouben Mamoulian. Irene Dunne, Randolph Scott, Dorothy Lamour, Elizabeth Patterson, Akim Tamiroff, Alan Hale, Raymond Walburn, Ben Blue, William Frawley, Irving Pichel, James Burke, Edward Gargan. A Jerome Kern–Oscar Hammerstein original musical for the screen about the battle for oil rights in nineteenth century Pennsylvania. CB is a roughneck working for the greedy villain.

 33. ***Thunder Trail.*** Par 1937. Charles Barton. Gilbert Roland, Marsha Hunt, J. Carrol Naish, Monte Blue, Barlowe Borland, James Craig, William Duncan, Billy Lee. CB makes it difficult for Roland to find his brother.

 34. ***Daughter of Shanghai.*** Par 1937. Robert Flory. Anna May Wong, Larry "Buster" Crabbe, Phillip Ahn, Cecil Cunningham, J. Carrol Naish, Evelyn Brent, Anthony Quinn, Fred Kohler, Sr., Frank Sully, Mae Busch, Paul Fix. Wong goes to Shanghai to find the alien smugglers who killed her father. CB is an alcoholic bad guy who employs her.

 35. ***Gangs of New York.*** Rep 1938. James Cruze. Ann Dvorak, Alan Baxter, Maxie Rosenbloom, Harold Huber, Fred Kohler, Sr., Jonathan Hale, Charles Trowbridge, John Wray. A good-and-evil twin role: CB as a clergyman and his convict brother.

 36. ***Valley of the Giants.*** WB 1938. William Keighley. Claire Trevor, Wayne Morris, Frank McHugh, Alan Hale, Donald Crisp, John Litel, Jack LaRue, Dick Purcell, El Brendel, Russell Simpson, Cy Kendall, Helen MacKellar. CB is an unscrupulous businessman with his eye on the giant redwood trees of northern California.

 37. ***The Storm.*** Univ 1938. Harold Young. Preston Foster, Barton MacLane, Tom Brown, Nan Grey, Andy Devine, Dorothy Arnold, Samuel S. Hinds, Frank Jenks. Brothers CB and MacLane feud until Mother Nature causes problems that reconcile them.

 38. ***Stand Up and Fight.*** MGM 1939. W. S. Van Dyke. Wallace Beery, Robert Taylor, Florence Rice, Helen Broderick, Barton MacLane, Charley Grapewin, John Qualen, Jonathan Hale, Selmer Jackson. A rivalry flares up between Beery's stagecoach line and the railroad represented by Taylor, with CB running interference for his own self-serving reasons.

39. ***Romance of the Redwoods.*** Col 1939. Charles Vidor. Jean Parker, Gordon Oliver, Marc Lawrence, Lloyd Hughes, Don Beddoe, Ann Doran. Lumberjack CB feels threatened in his relationship with a woman by a young newcomer to his logging crew.

40. ***Street of Missing Men.*** Rep 1939. Sidney Salkow, Harry Carey, Tommy Ryan, Mabel Todd, Guinn "Big Boy" Williams, Regis Toomey, Nana Bryant, Ralph Graves. CB and a young boy bond as they help each other survive.

41. ***Our Leading Citizen.*** Par 1939. Alfred Santell. Bob Burns, Susan Hayward, Elizabeth Patterson, Gene Lockhart, Joseph Allen, Jr., Clarence Kolb. An industrial strike threatens a small town but folksy Burns resolves all problems despite CB's typical opposition.

42. ***One Hour to Live.*** Univ 1939. Harold Schuster. Doris Nolan, John Litel, Olin Howlin, Paul Guilfoyle, Robert Emmett Keane, Jack Carr. CB is a police detective out to nab a shrewd criminal.

43. ***Mutiny in the Big House.*** Monogram 1939. William Nigh. Barton MacLane, Dennis Moore, George Cleveland, Nigel DeBrulier, Dave O'Brien, Charley Foy, Jack Daley. Prison chaplain CB redeems a young convict who was falling in with bad elements like MacLane's con boss.

44. ***Of Mice and Men.*** UA 1939. Lewis Milestone. Burgess Meredith, Lon Chaney, Jr., Betty Field, Roman Bohnen, Bob Steele, Noah Beery, Jr., Oscar O'Shea, Granville Bates, Leigh Whipper, Leona Roberts. Excellent adaptation of John Steinbeck's book and play with CB as a compassionate ranch foreman.

45. ***Thou Shalt Not Kill.*** Rep 1940. John H. Auer. Owen Davis, Jr., Doris Day, Sheila Bromley, Paul Guilfoyle, George Chandler, Granville Bates, Charles Waldron. Criminal CB reforms to save an innocent young man from execution. Leading lady Doris Day is not the singing star of later films.

46. ***Girl from God's Country.*** Rep 1940. Sidney Salkow. Chester Morris, Jane Wyatt, Mala, Kate Lawson, Spencer Charters, Ferike Boros, John Bleifer. CB and Morris are rivals for the love of nurse Wyatt.

47. ***South to Karanga.*** Univ 1940. Harold Schuster. Luli Deste, James Craig, John Sutton, Maurice Moscovitch, Abner Biberman, Paul Hurst, Addison Richards, Frank Reicher. CB is an African plantation overseer.

48. ***Queen of the Yukon.*** Monogram 1940. Phil Rosen. Irene Rich, June Carlson, Dave O'Brien, George Cleveland, Melvin Lang, Guy Usher. A Jack London tale, but very similar to Damon Runyon's oft-filmed *Madame La Gimp*: CB helps his shady lady friend put on a front for her visiting daughter.

49. ***Burma Convoy.*** Univ 1941. Noel Smith. Evelyn Ankers, Frank Albertson, Cecil Kellaway, Keye Luke, Turhan Bey, Truman Bradley, Willie Fung. CB avenges his brother's death while fighting the Japanese in Burma.

50. ***Reap the Wild Wind.*** Par 1942. Cecil B. DeMille. Ray Milland, John Wayne, Paulette Goddard, Raymond Massey, Robert Preston, Susan Hayward, Lynne Overman, Walter Hampden, Martha O'Driscoll, Janet

Beecher, Hedda Hopper, Louise Beavers, Victor Varconi, Oscar Polk. CB's role as a villainous seaman who shanghais sailors is one of his smallest.

51. *Tarzan's New York Adventure*. MGM 1942. Richard Thorpe. Johnny Weissmuller, Maureen O'Sullivan, Johnny Sheffield, Paul Kelly, Virginia Grey, Chill Wills, Cy Kendall, Russell Hicks, Charles Lane, Howard Hickman. When CB kidnaps Boy to use in his circus, Tarzan and Jane pursue him to New York.

52. *Mr. Lucky*. RKO 1943. H. C. Potter. Cary Grant, Laraine Day, Gladys Cooper, Henry Stephenson, Alan Carney, Paul Stewart, Kay Johnson, J. M. Kerrigan, Vladimir Sokoloff, Florence Bates, Walter Kingsford. Routine comedy with timely patriotism thrown in. CB is the skipper of a gambling ship run by Grant.

53. *The Song of Bernadette*. 20th 1943. Henry King. Jennifer Jones, Vincent Price, Lee J. Cobb, Gladys Cooper, Anne Revere, Roman Bohnen, William Eythe, Mary Anderson, Edith Barrett, Charles Dingle, Aubrey Mather, Patricia Morison, Sig Ruman, Blanche Yurka, Tala Birell, Jerome Cowan, Marcel Dalio. A beautifully crafted film for which CB got his first Academy Award nomination. He plays the Bishop of Lourdes, who has his doubts about Bernadette (Jones), but defends her against those who would harm her.

54. *Wing and a Prayer*. 20th 1944. Henry Hathaway. Don Ameche, Dana Andrews, William Eythe, Sir Cedric Hardwicke, Henry (Harry) Morgan, Richard Jaeckel, Glenn Langan, B. S. Pully, Roy Roberts. CB is the captain of a World War II aircraft carrier.

55. *Captain Eddie*. 20th 1945. Lloyd Bacon. Fred MacMurray, Thomas Mitchell, Lynn Bari, Lloyd Nolan, James Gleason, Spring Byington, Richard Conte, Darryl Hickman, Mary Phillips, Stanley Ridges. Highly fictionalized biography of World War I flying ace Eddie Rickenbacker (MacMurray). CB is seen briefly as his hard-working father, who dies in an accident when Eddie is only a boy.

56. *Fallen Angel*. 20th 1945. Otto Preminger. Dana Andrews, Alice Faye, Linda Darnell, Anne Revere, Percy Kilbride, Bruce Cabot, John Carradine, Jimmy Conlin. CB is a small town detective investigating the murder of a waitress he himself was involved with.

57. *Duel in the Sun*. Selznick-International 1946. King Vidor. Jennifer Jones, Gregory Peck, Joseph Cotten, Lionel Barrymore, Lillian Gish, Walter Huston, Herbert Marshall, Harry Carey, Joan Tetzel, Otto Kruger, Sidney Blackmer, Tilly Losch, Butterfly McQueen, Scott McKay, Charles Dingle, Victor Kilian. Epic Western with several strong performances. CB, a ranch foreman enamored of half-breed Jones, is drawn into a fatal encounter with the black sheep son (Peck) of a wealthy family.

58. *The Farmer's Daughter*. RKO 1947. H. C. Potter. Loretta Young, Joseph Cotten, Ethel Barrymore, Rose Hobart, Rhys Williams, Harry Davenport, William Harrigan, Harry Shannon, Anna Q. Nilsson, Keith Andes, James Arness, Lex Barker, Art Baker, Charles McGraw. CB is the secretary-confidante of a Congressman (Cotten) and his mother (Barrymore). He was again Oscar-nominated.

59. ***Brute Force.*** Univ 1947. Jules Dassin. Burt Lancaster, Hume Cronyn, Ann Blyth, Yvonne De Carlo, Howard Duff, Sam Levene, Ella Raines, Whit Bissell, Roman Bohnen, Anita Colby, Jeff Corey, Richard Gaines, John Hoyt, Frank Puglia. A violent, excellently acted prison drama, with CB as a con engineering a big breakout.

60. ***Woman on the Beach.*** RKO 1947. Jean Renoir. Joan Bennett, Robert Ryan, Nan Leslie, Irene Ryan, Walter Sande, Martha Hyer. CB is a blind artist whose wife (Bennett) has an affair with Coast Guardsman Ryan.

61. ***Four Faces West.*** UA 1948. Alfred Green. Joel McCrea, Frances Dee, Joseph Calleia, William Conrad, Argentina Brunetti, Houseley Stevenson, Eva Novak. CB is a relentless lawman of the Old West, tracking bank robber McCrea.

62. ***The Babe Ruth Story.*** Allied Artists 1948. Roy Del Ruth. William Bendix, Claire Trevor, Sam Levene, William Frawley, Gertrude Niesen, Lloyd Gough, Paul Cavanagh, Richard Lane, Bobby Ellis, Fred Lightner, Ralph Dunn, James Flavin. In this poorly conceived biography, CB again dons a cassock as the head of the home for boys where Babe was raised.

63. ***Johnny Belinda.*** WB 1948. Jean Negulesco. Jane Wyman, Lew Ayres, Agnes Moorehead, Jan Sterling, Stephen McNally, Rosalind Ivan, Dan Seymour, Mabel Paige, Ida Moore, Alan Napier, Douglas Kennedy, Monte Blue. CB received his third Oscar nomination for his performance as the farmer-father of deaf-mute Wyman.

64. ***Command Decision.*** MGM 1948. Sam Wood. Clark Gable, Walter Pidgeon, Van Johnson, Brian Donlevy, Edward Arnold, John Hodiak, Warner Anderson, Ray Collins, John McIntire, Cameron Mitchell, Moroni Olsen, Richard Quine, John Ridgely, Michael Steele, Clinton Sundberg, Marshall Thompson. A worthy adaptation of the outstanding Broadway play. CB is a nosy war correspondent at an Allied air base in World War II England.

65. ***Roseanna McCoy.*** Goldwyn-RKO 1949. Irving Reis. Raymond Massey, Farley Granger, Joan Evans, Richard Basehart, Aline MacMahon, Marshall Thompson, Gigi Perreau, Lloyd Gough, Arthur Franz, Richard Miles, Frank Ferguson. Romeo and Juliet transplanted to hillbilly country with the Hatfields and McCoys subbing for the Montagues and the Capulets. Massey and CB are the clan leaders.

66. ***Whirlpool.*** 20th 1949. Otto Preminger. Gene Tierney, Jose Ferrer, Richard Conte, Barbara O'Neill, Constance Collier, Eduard Franz, Ruth Lee, Fortunio Bonanova, Alex Gerry, Randy Stuart, Helen Westcott, Larry Keating. CB is a police detective trying to nab a phony hypnotist.

67. ***Guilty of Treason.*** Eagle Lion 1949. Felix Feist. Paul Kelly, Bonita Granville, Richard Derr, Roland Winters, Berry Kroeger, Elisabeth Risdon, John Banner. CB is Hungarian Cardinal Mindszenty, who was imprisoned by the Communists.

68. ***Riding High.*** Par 1950. Frank Capra. Bing Crosby, Coleen Gray, William Demarest, Raymond Walburn, Ward Bond, Douglass Dumbrille, Frances Gifford, James Gleason, Margaret Hamilton, Paul Harvey, Charles

Lane, Glenn Langa, Gene Lockhart, Marjorie Lord, Clarence Muse, Harry Davenport, Joe Frisco, Oliver Hardy, Percy Kilbride. This remake of Capra's own 1934 film *Broadway Bill* incorporates whole scenes from the original. CB is the wealthy prospective father-in-law of horse-loving Crosby.

69. ***Branded.*** Par 1950. Rudolph Mate. Alan Ladd, Mona Freeman, Robert Keith, Joseph Calleia, Selena Royle, Tom Tully, Peter Hanson, Martin Garralaga, Milburn Stone, George Lewis, Robert Kortman, Natividad Vacio. Drifter Ladd is persuaded to pose as the long-lost son of wealthy westerner CB.

70. ***Jim Thorpe—All American.*** WB 1951. Michael Curtiz. Burt Lancaster, Phyllis Thaxter, Steve Cochran, Dick Wesson, Jack Bighead, Al Mejia, Nestor Paiva, Suni Warcloud, Jimmy Moss. CB plays the real-life Pop Warner, mentor to the famed Native American athlete (Lancaster).

71. ***The Raging Tide.*** Univ 1951. George Sherman. Shelley Winters, Richard Conte, Stephen McNally, Alex Nicol, John McIntire, Tito Vuolo, Chubby Johnson. CB is a kindly Swede who hires hunted criminal Conte to work on his boat and unwittingly reforms him.

72. ***Elopement.*** 20th 1951. Henry Koster. Clifton Webb, William Lundigan, Anne Francis, Reginald Gardiner, Margalo Gillmore, Evelyn Varden, J. Farrell MacDonald, Tommy Rettig, Willis Bouchey, Julia Dean. Webb's daughter elopes with CB's son and the two enraged fathers give chase.

73. ***The Last Posse.*** Col 1953. Alfred Werker. Broderick Crawford, John Derek, Wanda Hendrix, Warner Anderson, Henry Hull, Skip Homeier, Will Wright, Tom Powers, Raymond Greenleaf, James Bell, Jim Kirkwood. An off-beat Western marking CB's return to villainy after years of kindliness. He plays a bitter rancher who hunts down and murders the poor men who were forced to rob him.

74. ***A Star Is Born.*** WB 1954. George Cukor. Judy Garland, James Mason, Jack Carson, Tommy Noonan, Amanda Blake, Lucy Marlow, James Brown, Louis Jean Heydt, Irving Bacon, Joan Shawlee, Hazel Shermet, Dub Taylor, Chick Chandler, Mae Marsh. The new Harold Arlen–Ira Gershwin score and Garland's comeback performance were sufficient reasons for this remake. CB is a more sedate studio head than was Adolphe Menjou in the 1937 version.

75. ***Prince of Players.*** 20th 1955. Philip Dunne. Richard Burton, Maggie McNamara, John Derek, Raymond Massey, Elizabeth Sellars, Eva Le Galliene, Dayton Lummis, Ian Keith, Sarah Padden, Mae Marsh. A biography of eighteenth century actor Edwin Booth (Burton), with CB as his loyal manager.

76. ***Not as a Stranger.*** UA 1955. Stanley Kramer. Olivia de Havilland, Robert Mitchum, Frank Sinatra, Gloria Grahame, Broderick Crawford, Myron McCormick, Lon Chaney, Jr., Lee Marvin, Jesse White, Henry (Harry) Morgan, Virginia Christine, Whit Bissell, Mae Clarke, Jack Raine. CB's finest screen performance as an aging small town doctor who takes ambitious Mitchum into his practice and teaches him the true meaning of

being a part of the medical profession. For this performance, Bickford was honored by the National Board of Review as 1955's Best Supporting Actor.

77. *The Court-Martial of Billy Mitchell.* WB 1955. Otto Preminger. Gary Cooper, Ralph Bellamy, Rod Steiger, Elizabeth Montgomery, James Daly, Fred Clark, Darren McGavin, Jack Lord, Peter Graves, Charles Dingle, Robert Simon, Will Wright, Dayton Lummis, Tom McKee, Phil Arnold. CB is the general who opposes Billy Mitchell (Cooper) and his campaign for greater American air power in the years following World War I.

78. *You Can't Run Away from It.* Col 1956. Dick Powell. June Allyson, Jack Lemmon, Allyn Joslyn, Stubby Kaye, Jim Backus, Paul Gilbert, Henny Youngman, Jacques Scott, Walter Baldwin, Louise Beavers, Byron Foulger, Howard McNear, Jack Albertson. A mediocre musical version of *It Happened One Night*. CB is the millionaire father of Allyson.

79. *Mister Cory.* Univ 1957. Blake Edwards. Tony Curtis, Martha Hyer, Kathryn Grant, William Reynolds, Russ Morgan, Henry Daniell, Willis Bouchey, Louise Lorimer, Joan Banks, Harry Landers, Dick Crockett. CB helps Curtis rise in the world of gambling in order to crash society.

80. *The Big Country.* UA 1958. William Wyler. Gregory Peck, Jean Simmons, Charlton Heston, Carroll Baker, Burl Ives, Alfonso Bedoya, Chuck Connors, Chuck Hayward, Dorothy Adams, Buff Brady. CB is a cattle baron embroiled in a feud with homesteaders. His prospective son-in-law (Peck) finds himself in the middle.

81. *The Unforgiven.* UA 1960. John Huston. Burt Lancaster, Audrey Hepburn, Lillian Gish, Audie Murphy, John Saxon, Joseph Wiseman, Albert Salmi, June Walker, Doug McClure, Kipp Hamilton, Arnold Merritt, Carlos Rivas. CB, again a rancher, turns against his neighbors when he learns the daughter of that family (Hepburn) was born an Indian.

82. *Days of Wine and Roses.* WB 1962. Blake Edwards. Jack Lemmon, Lee Remick, Jack Klugman, Alan Hewitt, Jack Albertson, Debbie Megowen, Katherine Squire, Maxine Stuart, Tom Palmer, Ken Lynch. J. P. Miller's powerful *Playhouse 90* TV episode about an alcoholic young couple comes to the big screen, with CB repeating his "small screen" role as the girl's father.

83. *A Big Hand for the Little Lady.* WB 1966. Fielder Cook. Henry Fonda, Joanne Woodward, Jason Robards, Burgess Meredith, Kevin McCarthy, Robert Middleton, John Qualen, Paul Ford, Gerald Michenaud, James Kenny, Virginia Gregg, Mae Clarke, Chester Conklin, Milton Selzer, Ned Glass. Another adaptation of a teleplay, Sidney Carroll's "Big Deal in Laredo." CB is a wealthy and dour undertaker who participates in a big poker game and says very little until the end.

Director David Butler's *The Littlest Rebel* (1935) is sometimes listed as one of CB's credits. This was the film he was supposed to make immediately following the disastrous *East of Java*, but due to his long recuperation, the role of the Union colonel was played by Jack Holt.

CB played the chief villain in Ford Beebe's Universal serial *Riders of*

Death Valley (1941), which also starred Dick Foran, Buck Jones, Lon Chaney, Jr., Leo Carrillo and Noah Beery, Jr.

CB once again played a sea captain in the Screen Gems TV film *Clipper Ship* (1957). Oscar Rudolph directed and his co-stars were Jan Sterling, Steve Forrest, Helmut Dantine and Paul Fix. It was made for *Playhouse 90* and has also been shown as a TV movie.

Ward Bond

A good majority of actors have long been seen as politically liberal and everyone thinks that's good; it means they are concerned about those who have lower incomes than they. Any enemies they have will usually keep any negative talk about them confined to private conversations. But when an actor openly declares himself to have conservative beliefs, especially in recent times, he becomes a subject of public humor, if not out and out ridicule. In the post–McCarthy era, John Wayne's politics were treated in this manner, especially by his fellow performers who could not understand how anyone at this point in time could still be so reactionary. Some equated his stance with bigotry.

Wayne, however, seemed a moderate in comparison to his friend Ward Bond, whose vehement anti–Communist pro–American outlook pre-dated the "Red baiting" period of the late '40s. He was successful in his campaign to cut off revenue to many colleagues he considered enemies, but this did not win him any friends among the more secretive of movieland's conservatives. Perhaps Ward Bond had no friends, though he was never at a loss for cronies.

His screen image was that of the American patriot and this led to his being put down as a stereotype, particularly in the years since his death. In an April 18, 1976, *New York Times* article, Wallace Markfield, appraising several actors of the past, had this to say of Bond: "With his Merrie Melodies bulldog face and brain, he was ideally suited to serve all those 25 year hitches in John Ford's cavalry." This one sentence is unfair to the actor and the more varied parts he played (and also suggests a dislike for the films of Ford). Most purists respect Bond's position as a figure of authority in the later Ford films. And Bond had spent many years in the depths of show business, as a movie bit player. Since he had no professional

Ward Bond publicity shot from the '40s.

training, it was years before even a friend like Ford gave him a worthy part. Bond worked at his craft for three decades, rising to the position of respectable (if not respected) screen actor and finally television star. Thanks to his latter-day popularity, newspaper and magazine writers became genuinely interested in what he had to say. And after that very slow climb, death snatched it all at the very peak of his career.

He was born Wardell Bond in Denver, Colorado,* on April 9, 1905. He was the son of John and Mabel Bond and he had one sister. He grew up in a time when a staunch love of country was not an awkward stance for a young American and he was imbued with such ideas early in life. Riding a horse and hunting with a shotgun were talents that came easily to young Wardell. All of this would, of course, comes in handy in an occupation this rugged boy would never have imagined.

He began playing football in high school and his prowess won him a scholarship to the University of Southern California in 1923. He was no great shakes as a student: USC represented his first break from the country life and he did not do well off the gridiron field. The husky Bond looked older than other boys his own age. If he was to get by in the world, it appeared that he would have to rely on his skill with a football. Football grew in popularity during the Roaring Twenties, and moviemakers were aware of this phenomenon. They responded in the mid- and late '20s with many pictures on the order of *Brown of Harvard* and *The Drop Kick*, as well as some comic takeoffs on the sport.

For authenticity's sake, producers imported college and semi-pro footballers to show the actors the ropes and often double as extras. Some well-known actors had their first film experience in this manner, including Wesleyan star running back Barton MacLane. But generally the movie people were inclined to look closer to home. Aside from a few name players brought from other parts of the country, most of their gridiron experts came from nearby USC. One of these was Iowa-born Duke Morrison, who took a liking to film work and began doing odd jobs at Fox Studios. The director who most often used Morrison as an extra was John Ford, already a movie veteran although he was only in his early thirties. Ford decided that the first talking picture of George O'Brien (whom he had made a star in *The Iron Horse*), should be about football. He reasoned that sports pictures combined sound and action as well as any other genre, and he asked Morrison to recruit some average football players.

Morrison returned with more than enough, and in that group was Bond. While the two men did not know each other personally, Morrison was aware that Bond, who was two years older than he, was no longer a USC student. Morrison was, in essence, just letting

---

*Some sources give his birthplace as Bendleman, Nebraska, but they are unsubstantiated.

the burly Bond come along for the ride. Having done extra work himself, he knew that the director always sent for more people than were actually needed and then chose from the group. When Ford picked Bond out of the group because he was "big and ugly," his assistant allegedly objected, claiming he had a friend who was bigger and uglier. But Ford's will prevailed and Bond won a noticeable bit in his first film, *Salute* (1929).

Ford made arrangements to shoot much of the film at the U.S. Naval Academy and the Fox people agreed, feeling it would lend more authenticity (not to mention publicity value) to this tale of the traditional Army-Navy football rivalry. This meant footing the bill for transportation of the cast and crew to Annapolis, Maryland. Duke Morrison found himself sharing his facilities on the cross-country train ride with the big bruiser Bond. Morrison, also a big guy, found it difficult to keep out of Bond's way. Bond was anxious to take advantage of his short-term employment. At mealtime, he ran up the studio bills with his passion for steak dinners. When the studio balked at this, Morrison stood up for Bond and the other players. A one-time collegiate athlete himself, Morrison understood that things would not always be so good for them; he was also well aware of their enormous appetites. Consequently, he was willing to put his job on the line for men who were not even friends of his at the time. There have been countless stories about the generosity of Duke Morrison—soon to become John Wayne—once he was a great star, but he was just as generous when he had hardly anything to give.

Having "tasted" the sweet part of moviemaking, Bond decided that it was a valid excuse for remaining in California. Since he did not think of himself as an actor, he was willing to remain in extra roles. He returned to Fox and worked in *Words and Music* (1929), in a part less noticeable than the one in *Salute*. Morrison had another bit, as did a girl named Frances Dee. (Twenty-five years later, Dee would play Bond's wife in her last film.) Other minuscule parts followed. Only when one considers that Bond had briefly studied medicine, and got a degree in engineering from USC in 1931, do these parts seem like a waste of time. Obviously, he was drawn to the "fun" aspect of moviemaking, especially the Ford sets. Ford used him again in *Born Reckless* (1930) and *The Brat* (1931), the first of Bond's sympathetic cop roles. He also led his first of many wagon trains in Fox's super-production *The Big Trail*, the wide-screen epic that launched John Wayne. (*The Big Trail* was not a success, and Wayne was blamed; after that, his days at the studio were numbered.)

Though Wayne and Bond were often situated at the same studio, the two would only work together two more times in the '30s. That would all change, afterwards.

In those early Depression days, there were many classes within the motion picture community. Everyone was hungry for work and there was a distinction, however fine, between being an extra, a dress extra or a bit player; this distinction was particularly important in the salary department. Thanks to Ford, Bond quickly became a bit player with dialogue but he soon found he had nowhere to go from there. Casting directors had their choice of too many people with genuine acting credentials, to bother raising someone like Bond to the position of "featured player." Bond soon began making the rounds of other studios. Ford gave him bits in films he made at other studios: *Arrowsmith* (1931) at Goldwyn and *Air Mail* (1932) at Universal. When the director was working on the MGM film *Flesh* (1932), he decided that Bond was ready to play an important scene and cast him as an arrogant wrestler who quickly gets what he deserves in an encounter with Wallace Beery, a newly arrived German wrestler. This did not cause any immediate upswing in Bond's career. More typical of this era were his roles in the 1932 Fox films *Rackety Rax*, a fight story starring Victor McLaglen, and *Trial of Vivienne Ware* with Joan Bennett in the lead. His entire part in the latter consisted of running into a courtroom, giving a piece of information to lawyer Donald Cook and then hurrying out.

Bond found his steadiest employment at Columbia, when the Harry Cohn outfit was still way down on the Hollywood totem pole. Columbia made scores of action films with people like Jack Holt, Buck Jones and Tim McCoy, and Bond got his first featured work as either villain or hero's friend in these inexpensively made B's. (John Wayne, who preceded Bond to the studio, also worked on films with those stars, until he ran afoul of Cohn and left.) Bond worked in more than 35 Columbia films in the 1930s. One of his first was as a buddy of cab driver Pat O'Brien in *Virtue* (1932), which also starred Carole Lombard. Others who picked up bits at the studio, occasionally crossing Bond's path, were Lucille Ball, Walter Brennan, Andy Devine and J. Carrol Naish.

While Bond's name appeared in the credits of most of his Columbia films, he continued to work *un*credited in other studios' product. In 1933, he did three at Warners, all directed by William Wellman: *Heroes For Sale*, *Wild Boys of the Road* and *College Coach*, the latter reuniting him with Wayne, who was temporarily under contract there. His large 1934 output provided him with better parts in two prestigious films on his own lot. He was cast in the two Frank Capra Columbia films released that year: as a bus driver in *It Happened One Night* and as a villainous henchman in *Broadway Bill*. During the making of the former, he struck up a friendship with star Clark Gable, who shared his love for hunting. Becoming a crony of one of the biggest stars in Hollywood did not hurt; Gable helped Bond secure bits in important MGM pictures, beginning with his own *Chained* (1934). Over the next few years, Bond worked on the Culver City lot in films starring Joan Crawford, Robert Taylor and Spencer Tracy.

The majority of Bond's early roles could be categorized under the three B's: brief, brawny and brainless. Anyone needing a big, dumb lug for a single scene need look no further than Bond. He was considered too stupid and too insignificant in those days to be a gang leader. The more films he made, the more he became typecast as the tough but dumb guy. By the time he was 30, he had worked for every important studio in Hollywood, so if nothing else, he was familiar to all the casting people. He began appearing in more Warner Brothers pictures, opposite stars like James Cagney and Paul Muni and three supporting actors whose careers were picking up: William Gargan, Barton MacLane and Lloyd Nolan. In 1936, he married Doris Sellers Childs.

The bigger the studio, the smaller the role he was given. At MGM, he was an objector in director Fritz Lang's American debut film *Fury* and an officer in Clarence Brown's *The Gorgeous Hussy*. He did no better at Paramount; RKO at least gave him roles in which the character had a name. Columbia still provided the biggest roles: as Charles Bickford's marine buddy in *Pride of the Marines* and the loyal henchman who finds that his old gangland boss (Ralph Bellamy) has had a facial and character transformation in *The Man Who Lived Twice*. He was also reunited that year with John Wayne, this time at Universal, for *Conflict*, about corruption in the prizefighting game. Bond was that film's chief heavy, a boxing champ who exploits newcomer Wayne. (Wayne was still in the category of action star of hour-long programmers.)

By now, every studio seemed to have a uniform that fit Bond perfectly. The maturing actor now began landing roles as authority figures, either military or police, sharing these parts with such little-known actors as Wade Boteler, Edgar Dearing, James Flavin and William Haade. (Like Bond, Haade had the kind of face which looked right on either side of the bars of a jail cell.) If a viewer blinked his eye, he would have missed Bond standing at a newsstand in *The Case Against Mrs. Ames* (1936) or as a prison guard in *The Accusing Finger* at Paramount. That studio delivered an even crueller blow when they cut his scene from their super-spectacular *Souls at Sea* (1937). At this late date, Bond still was the expendable bit player.

Bond was quite noticeable in William Wyler's *Dead End* (1937) as the doorman of an exclusive apartment house, constantly razzed by the Dead End Kids (their screen debut). In 1938, Columbia put him in their year's top film, *You Can't Take It With You*, but unlike his previous Capra film appearances, his role as a detective here was quite small. He was also dropped into one of the studio's B films, *Penitentiary*, to do a one-scene joke as a prison barber who was sent up by the man he is now shaving, new warden Walter Connolly. The studio used to do better by him; it was obvious that his days there were numbered.

In 1938, Bond added a new standard role to his repertoire. As a motorcycle cop, he made such stars as Cary Grant, Harold Lloyd and Dick Powell pull over to the side of the road. He returned to the studio where it all started, now called 20th Century–Fox, to play a dumb fighter in *Mr. Moto's Gamble* (1938). He was also reunited with John Ford, who cast him in a routine service film, *Submarine Patrol*. But this was just a prelude to what was to come in 1939, a year that marked a turning point in both the Ford and Bond careers.

That was the year the director decided that John Wayne was ready to star in big films and he began the year with *Stagecoach*. (Bond was not in that classic film, but he accompanied his friends to the location site.) The year did not begin so promisingly for Bond, who was toiling away in another clutch of bit parts. At Warner Brothers, he was particularly active, promoting John Garfield for a small-time fight in *They Made Me a Criminal* and then grappling with Garfield in the back of a box car in *Dust Be My Destiny*. He was on the wrong side of the law of the Old West, riding for Humphrey Bogart (*The Oklahoma Kid*) or Bruce Cabot (*Dodge City*); was an American Legionnaire sounding off against the Nazi bund in *Confessions of a Nazi Spy*; and did another punchy fighter bit in *The Kid from Kokomo*. Thanks to hunting buddies Gable and director Victor Fleming, he joined the lengthy cast list of the year's most talked-about picture, playing a Yankee captain in *Gone with the Wind*.

It was at Fox, late in the year, that Bond had his first chances to play more than the usual one-dimensional part. The two films were directed by Ford, had Henry Fonda in the lead and gave Bond the opportunity to play characters essential to the plot. First came *Young Mr. Lincoln*, one of the truly outstanding Fonda films and performances. Concentrating on Honest Abe's early days as a lawyer, it is done in Ford's simple, unpretentious style. The basic plot involves Lincoln's defense of two brothers accused of a killing actually committed by J. Palmer Cass (Bond). Fonda's cross examination of the actual culprit is a masterpiece; Lincoln ruffles the man (who has just admitted that his friends sometimes call him Jack) by calling him "Jack Cass." Eventually, Lincoln unmasks Cass, who was never any match for him. Audiences were able to enjoy the way the actors played off one another as well as the depiction of the seeds of greatness that we associate with the sixteenth president of the U.S.

Close on the heels of this film came *Drums Along the Mohawk*. This is a fairly straightforward account of early American settlers in the Mohawk Valley, plagued by Indians. Claudette Colbert and Fonda play newlyweds who suffer through the attacks; the film was one of the most spectacular Technicolor films made up to that time. Bond had his largest part to date as pioneer Adam Helmer, sharing some comic scenes with Edna May Oliver. He was still billed way down (twelfth place) in the cast listing, but for the first time his performance in a major film was mentioned favorably by *The New York Times*. Two of John Ford's biographers, Joseph McBride and Michael Wilmington, recognize that Ford was establishing Bond as an authority figure, the role he would later excel at. "He is the one who explodes with joy and runs the Star and Stripes up the flagpole at the end of *Drums Along the Mohawk*," they wrote.

Critics were becoming aware that Ford had his own repertory group of actors. And, true to the repertory concept, Bond went from important character role to bit player. He was back in uniform as a policeman in one of the great director's greatest films, *The Grapes of Wrath* (1940), which also starred Fonda. The actor also worked in several low-grade Fox films of the same year (*Heaven with a Barbed Wire Fence*, *Sailor's Lady* and *The Cisco Kid and the Lady*) and in two Errol Flynn Civil War films (*Virginia City* and *Santa Fe Trail*) at Warners. He menaced Jack Benny for laughs in *Buck Benny Rides Again* at Paramount and played a Nazi in *The Mortal Storm* at MGM. From then on, the actor would choose to play only one of two nationalities, American or Irish.

Before the year was out, Ford came through with another major role for Bond, that of Yank in one of his most beautiful films, *The Long Voyage Home*. Like *Stagecoach*, this film was scripted by Dudley Nichols and produced by Walter Wanger for United Artists release. The story was based on several one-act plays by Eugene O'Neill and told of the camaraderie between a group of sailors serving on a private cargo ship, circa World War I. The film offered rich roles to its leading players, particularly Thomas Mitchell, who is even better here than he was in his Academy Award–winning part in *Stagecoach*. John Wayne, in perhaps the most uncharacteristic role of his career, is effective as a dumb Swede protected by the rest of the crew; also good are Barry Fitzgerald, Mildred Natwick, John Qualen and Ian Hunter, who plays the ship's introverted loner. Bond had his warmest characterization to date and, with other actors around to handle the lighter moments, he was allowed to be reasonably intelligent. He, like Wayne, really proved himself to Ford in *The Long Voyage Home*. If nothing else, this film solidified the lifelong relationship between the three—quite appropriate in view of its theme of brotherhood among men.*

Bond was so sure of Ford's good judgment that he again played a bullying oaf in the director's workmanlike adaptation of the long-running play *Tobacco Road* (1941). Wayne had also developed some clout with producers and began recommending Bond for parts in his films. The first two were still stereotypes: the moronic killer in *A Man Betrayed* (1941) at Republic and the Ozark bully in *The Shepherd of the Hills* (1941) at Paramount. Bond also retained his standing at Fox and Warners. He was in the latter studio's two biggest hits of 1941, Howard Hawks' *Sergeant York*, as one of Gary Cooper's hillbilly pals, and John Huston's *The Maltese Falcon* as Detective Polhaus, Sam Spade's friend. (Polhaus was also the last name of one of the boyhood pals of Dashiell Hammett, who wrote *The Maltese Falcon*.) Bond's part was not big, but he did have the last word, typically a bewildered "Huh?" to Humphrey Bogart's famed "The stuff that dreams are made of" description of the black bird. The film was almost immediately successful for Huston, so he used practically the entire cast in unbilled cameos in his second directorial effort, *In This Our Life* (1942). Only the sharpest-eyed movie buff can spot Bond,

---

*Both The Grapes of Wrath *and* The Long Voyage Home *were nominated for best picture of 1940 and both were ahead of* Gone with the Wind *in the National Board of Review Listings.*

along with Bogart, Mary Astor, Peter Lorre, Sydney Greenstreet and Barton MacLane, among the patrons at a roadhouse.

Bond made less movies each year in the early '40s, an indication of his growing prominence as a featured player. Bond also went on prolonged hunting trips and indulged in a new interest, motorcycling with various filmland cronies. When the extravagant Bond bought a beautiful new shotgun, John Wayne was jealous. There are many stories circulating about the Wayne-Bond-Ford friendship that are obviously tall tales, but several sources have verified that when "Duke" Wayne asked Bond if he could use that shotgun, the curt reply was "Over my dead body." Some two decades later, Wayne was willed the very same shotgun.

After Pearl Harbor, naval officer Ford went overseas to make documentaries for the War Department, but members of his "stock company" did not find themselves out of work. In 1942, Bond played the brainless, hulking brute Moose Malloy in *The Falcon Takes Over* at RKO. It was particularly degrading because that character, as created by Raymond Chandler in *Farewell, My Lovely*, could be quite interesting; lesser actors like Mike Mazurki (*Murder, My Sweet*, 1944) and Jack O'Halloran (*Farewell, My Lovely*, 1975) proved it so in legitimate versions of the story. Bond also inherited a "Big Boy" Williams part in Warners' *Manpower* (1941) with Edward G. Robinson, George Raft, and Barton MacLane, in a smaller role. The director was Raoul Walsh, who had given Bond one of his earliest parts. Because of Walsh's feisty Irish ways and his proficiency with masculine adventure films, some dubbed Walsh the poor man's John Ford. One of Walsh's next films focused on the rise of the great heavyweight fighter Jim Corbett, climaxing with his defeat of the world's champion, John L. Sullivan. Errol Flynn was fairly excited (he never got over-enthused) about playing the Corbett role. The film was to be called *Gentleman Jim*, so that Flynn could emphasize the dandyish quality that Corbett brought to the boxing world, as well as the man's Irish brashness. For the role of the bare-knuckle fighter Sullivan, Walsh chose Bond as much for his measurements as for his acting ability. (Bond had previously been lost in a number of Flynn epics.) Flynn and Bond may not have been the physical matches for the two fighters in their prime, but few quarreled with their performances. What Flynn lacked in depth, he made up for in charm. And Bond here gave undoubtedly his finest performance outside of a John Ford picture as the loudmouth Sullivan, who proves to be a good loser.

The final scene is described succinctly by authors James Robert Parish and Don E. Stanke in their book, *The Swashbucklers*. They write that Bond as Sullivan was so good that his presentation of the championship belt to Corbett at a victory party after the decisive ring battle is poignant for even the most seasoned moviegoer. Though eighth-billed, Bond got the best reviews. When the film was released in the fall of 1942, it almost immediately raised his asking price per picture and the parsimonious Warner Brothers, instead of offering a contract, did not employ him for eight years; then began hiring him again when independent producers like the Cagney brothers and Wayne requested him.

Immediately after *Gentleman Jim*, Bond landed his first and only starring role in a movie, Producers Releasing Corporation's *Hitler— Dead or Alive* (1943), one of wartime's most flagrant bits of exploitation. The incredible plot had an American financier placing a bounty on the head of Adolf Hitler, which three gangsters set out to collect. They die trying, but before the leader does, he forcibly shaves off Hitler's mustache and the dictator is shot by his own men! Hollywood's perennial Hitler impersonator, Robert Watson, played Der Fuhrer, Bond played the gangster leader, and his henchmen were Warren Hymer (a specialist in dumb gangster roles, and the king of the field up until a few years earlier) and Paul Fix. Fix, who went from weasely gangsters in the '30s to solid citizens in the '70s, had incredible longevity in the industry. An old stage buddy of Clark Gable, he was also a good friend of John Wayne and managed to be in more of his pictures than Bond. He would later become well-known as the marshal in *The Rifleman*, the Chuck Connors TV series.

Because of the shortage of males in WWII Hollywood, actors Bond's age and older were getting bigger parts. But Fox, where he was still making most of his films, didn't get the message. In 1942–1943, they were still casting him in such pictures as *Ten Gentlemen from West Point*, *Hello Frisco, Hello* and *They Came to Blow Up America* in the same kind of roles he played prior to *The Long Voyage Home* and *Gentleman Jim*.

His first picture at MGM in several years was a forgettable Lana Turner comedy, *Slightly Dangerous* (1943). But he was soon back on the lot when another old director pal Victor Fleming asked for him for a picture to be called *A Guy Named Joe* (1943). Fantasies were being well-received during the war and the idea of a special Heaven for dead pilots seemed to appeal to a lot of people. Bond was delighted with the part he was to play, the well-rounded character of Al Yackey, best pal of star Spencer Tracy. Bond, like practically every other actor in the business, idolized Tracy. Bond had only played bit parts in a couple of his movies; here he would share most of his scenes with the actor. His part was so big that he was given fourth-billing after stars Tracy, Irene Dunne and Van Johnson. When the film was released, one of the names below his was the studio's grand old man, Lionel Barrymore, who had been brought in to play a cameo as the dead pilots' commander. To come before a Barrymore at Metro meant something and Ward Bond knew it.

In the film, combat pilot Tracy is in love with Dunne. After he is shot down, fellow pilot Bond (who silently loves her also) looks after her. When she falls in love with younger pilot Johnson, there is the usual concern about whether she will be hurt again. But no one alive knows that Tracy's ghost has been given permission to watch over her and he returns to Dunne in the end. Had a lesser director, cast or technical crew worked on it, *A Guy Named Joe* would have turned into mush. But MGM had the best and the film went on to be named one of the ten best of 1944 by *The Film Daily*, which conducted an annual poll of the country's leading film critics. Bond, like everyone else in the cast, reaped benefits from this moneymaker. Ironically, the man responsible for the scenario that gave him the most screen time in a major film in his entire 14-year film career was Dalton Trumbo. A few years later, Trumbo and the rest of the Hollywood Ten would come to represent everything Bond despised.

Considering his conservative viewpoint, it seems a shame that Bond did not secure a regular berth at MGM, whose chief Louis B. Mayer was a diehard Republican. As his own affluence increased, Bond seemed to swell with increased patriotic feelings, not a strange way to think in time of war. His best friends in the industry seemed to feel the same way, but they were not as "ornery" as Bond. Bond joined with a number of friends to form the Motion Picture Alliance for the Preservation of the American Ideal. This came out of a number of discussions in which it was decided that the lingering war was demoralizing many Americans. These people looked to films as a means of finding some solace, and film people were concerned that the right messages were being put across. Actors were becoming cognizant of certain trends they didn't like growing; there seemed to be an inordinate amount of Hollywood films about the valiant Russians.

The heroes of these films seemed far more idealized than the more familiar American G.I. stereotype. This minor carping was actually symptomatic of the great divisiveness among members of the motion picture community. In the '30s, when craftsmen fought for and won the right to have a union, it was the old struggle between labor and management. But in the '40s, as individuals from both camps changed sides, the lines were drawn between liberals and conservatives. Eventually, the name calling deteriorated into what were considered epithets of the day: Communists or Fascists.

It was in this climate of growing uneasiness that a group of conservatives formed the Motion Picture Alliance in February 1944. There was a huge turnout for the first meeting, at the Beverly Wilshire Hotel. Only a handful present, such as Adolphe Menjou, had read enough about Communism to know what they were talking about, but they had so magnified the effects of Karl Marx's teachings that their arguments were too exaggerated. Few at those first meetings could direct themselves to the issues as they affected their community. Nevertheless, the association was convincing enough to win some strong support, including some top producers. Big names seemed to dominate the group in all but one area. Most of the foremost movie writers seemed to be against them. And it was in 1944 that actors began to scrutinize any scripts submitted to them a little more closely. With screenwriters now giving him more to say, Bond was one who wanted to make sure that what he said was the right thing. Though it was a small part, he played a Naval officer who brings the news of the death of five brothers who served together on the same ship, in Fox's *The Sullivans* (1944); the film had the type of propaganda of which he approved. On the home front, he and his wife Doris split up after eight years of marriage in 1944.

Bond brought his friend John Wayne to the meetings. Wayne was apolitical, not feeling that he knew enough about the issues to take any stand. But after a meeting at the home of MGM executive producer James Kevin McGuinness, Wayne began to feel that he owed it to the country to continue attending. Around this time, Bond made three films in a row with his friend. He was the chief villain in RKO's *Tall in the Saddle* (1944) and Republic's *Dakota* (1945). In the former, he was the conniving Judge Garvey, and he and the Duke engage in a convincing climactic fight scene. In the latter, he was even more evil as Jim Bender, but he is done in by henchman Mike Mazurki, probably so Wayne could meet the challenge of fighting an even bigger adversary. In both films Bond was allowed to look prosperous for a change, wearing only business suits as he went about his nefarious business.

The third film was their reunion with John Ford, back from the war: *They Were Expendable* (1945). This was a major MGM production dedicated to the men who manned the Navy's PT boats during World War II. Wayne was co-starred with a real naval officer, Robert Montgomery; another, retired lieutenant commander Frank "Spig" Wead, wrote the script. A flyer in the first war, Wead was paralyzed in an accident and had forged a successful career as the author of many films and plays about flying. The script for *They Were Expendable* was not particularly good; there were some high spots but the film as a whole resembled too many war dramas that had preceded it. Bond's small part as "Boats" Mulcahey turned out to be his first as an older character man; he certainly looked older than Montgomery, who was 41 at the time. Bond was a very old-looking forty.

Bond ended his association with the liberal Zanuck-controlled Fox with Ford's *My Darling Clementine* (1946). The actor had already appeared in an earlier film (*Frontier Marshal*, 1939) which dealt with events leading up to the legendary gunfight at the O.K. Corral, but there he had played an ineffectual lawman. Here he was Morgan Earp, who with his brother Wyatt (Henry Fonda) survives the final shootout. He even gets to gun down Walter Brennan, who as Pa Clanton was playing one of his occasional mean old man roles. As Doc Holliday, Victor Mature gave one of his best performances.The film has grown in status over the years, admired by critics for its grim realism as opposed to the flashier treatment director John Sturges gave the same story in *Gunfight at the O.K. Corral* (1957).

Bond's diminishing film output was further slowed in January 1946: He was hit by a car while crossing Olympic Boulevard in Los Angeles and although he wasn't laid up for very long after, he had to hobble around on crutches for months. It did not keep him from going to meetings or social functions like Wayne's second wedding (his first marriage ended in divorce around the same time as Bond's did). He was back in action in the Frank Capra classic *It's a Wonderful Life* (1946), playing the same type of role he had played for Capra in the '30s. Yet Bond admired the director so much that as late as 1950, he was willing to reprise his old role in *Broadway Bill* in the Capra musical remake *Riding High*. It didn't call for much work, since he only had a few new lines to match up with the old scenes shot 16 years earlier. By then, Bond was used to blackening his hair and shaving off his mustache to make himself look younger. (His new mustache became an asset in most of his films. The "bulldog" face was becoming almost distinguished.)

The mustache was right for *The Fugitive* (1947), a John Ford rarity in that the director did extensive location work outside of the U.S. (the story was set in Mexico). RKO thought that they would repeat the success of their earlier Ford film *The Informer* (1935), also about an outcast in a foreign land; that was why he was working with Graham Greene's *The Power and the Glory*, which this film was based on. But even a proven combination like Ford and Henry Fonda, who played a Catholic priest hunted by a Mexican government that was anti-clergy, had to strike out some time. The story was far too philosophical for the director's more sentimental tendencies. Also, the only American in the film was Bond's character, a badman known simply as "El Gringo," who performs one noble gesture to help Fonda in his plight. The inclusion of players Dolores del Rio, Pedro Armendariz and Leo Carrillo, authentic Mexicans, would have worked better if the lead role had not been miscast; the usually more than competent Fonda was just too American to be convincing as a Mexican priest.

Ford redeemed himself (particularly at the box office) by pairing Fonda and Wayne in his next RKO film, the immensely popular *Fort Apache* (1948). The first of his famed "cavalry trilogy," this film had what may be the quintessential Ford cast. Besides the two stars and Bond, it had Victor McLaglen, Pedro Armendariz, George O'Brien, Anna Lee, Grant Withers and Mae Marsh, plus Shirley Temple and her then-husband John Agar in the juvenile roles. It was even shot in the director's favorite location, Monument Valley, Utah. Fonda had a strong role, cast against type as the martinet fort commander Thursday, whose Apache policies get his troop massacred. Wayne, as Fonda's more understanding second officer, allows the colonel (killed by the Indians) to be glorified as a national hero, though he personally disliked the man. Bond plays the veteran sergeant-major who bravely accompanies his commander to his foolhardy death. He was conspicuously absent from *She Wore a Yellow Ribbon* (1949) and *Rio Grande* (1950), the other two films in the "cavalry trilogy." It didn't matter that he had been killed in the first; McLaglen also got killed and was in the other two films.

If there was one particular role Ford saw Bond as just about perfect, it was as a father figure to a community of settlers. Later in 1948, this type appeared in Ford's *Three Godfathers* under the name Sheriff "Buck" Sweet. The film was Ford at his sentimental worst and its history is more interesting than the finished product. On September 21, 1947, the veteran actor Harry Carey died. He had been Ford's first star three decades earlier and the man John Wayne most admired and emulated. Determined to give him a proper tribute, they decided to do a new version of one of the Carey silents, based on a story called "The Godchild," about three outlaws redeemed by their efforts to save the life of an infant in the desert. Since Ford had last utilized the property, there had been two sound versions (Universal's *Hell's Heroes*, directed by William Wyler and MGM's *Three Godfathers*, directed by Richard Boleslavski) and the story was not wearing well. MGM still held the literary rights and they were delighted when the director and star of the successful *They Were Expendable* approached them with a ready-made package. They agreed to distribute the film, which was actually produced by Argosy Pictures, a company Ford and Merian C. Cooper had formed. Wayne, Pedro Armendariz and Harry Carey, Jr. (who was elevated from bit player to complete the tribute to his father), played the title roles. The previous MGM version (1936) ended with the last outlaw (Chester Morris) bringing the baby into a church and then collapsing. Ford decided such an ending was too abrupt and grim after the grueling story of survival, and what was needed was some of the old-fashioned Ford comedy relief. So he prolonged the picture with a lot of nonsense featuring comic judge Guy Kibbee, townswoman Jane Darwell and Bond, as the crotchety lawman who will take the child while Wayne goes off to prison for a short spell. This anti-climactic epilogue disjoints the effective scenes that come before. (Critics have tried to alibi Ford by calling these sequences part of a religious parable.) The result was one of Ford's weakest films, a less than fitting tribute to Carey. If for nothing else, the film can be remembered as the one that established Bond in the kind of part he would play best in other Ford films over the next decade as well as his hit TV series *Wagon Train*, the tough guy–born leader who has a warm heart.

Bond's work in action films made him a natural for epics by other major producers. He worked in such color spectacles as Cecil B. DeMille's *Unconquered* (1947). He did three for Walter Wanger: *Canyon Passage*, 1946, *Joan of Arc* and *Tap Roots*, both 1948. In the latter, he had a particularly good role as the head of a Mississippi plantation family in Civil War times. (The *Times* gave his performance a rare knock, saying he was way over his head in his final mad scene.)

Bond next became involved in theatrical endeavors. (He had been one of a handful of movie actors who had never had any stage experience.) When things were not going so well for John Wayne in the mid-'30s, he was asked to perform in a play written by his friend Paul Fix. But the only way Wayne could get himself to go on stage and speak lines was to get completely soused before the performance. Bond felt pretty much the same way. In the late '40s, a group of film actors gave some of their time to the La Jolla Playhouse, which was designed to give Hollywood performers an opportunity to play stage roles. They performed a variety of well-known classics, each play usually having a one- or two-week run. The performers included Gregory Peck, Robert Ryan, Jose Ferrer and Mel Ferrer, all actors with whom Bond had a good professional relationship. Bond occasionally cast a jaundiced eye at certain production choices (too many foreign plays were produced to his way of thinking).

His most substantial stage appearance was in Maxwell Anderson and Lawrence Stallings' famed World War I comedy-drama *What Price Glory?* with Bond as Sgt. Quirt and Pat O'Brien as his nemesis, Capt. Flagg. Because it was for charity, two of Hollywood's biggest stars, Peck and Wayne, took bit parts as soldiers. Bond did well as Quirt in the production, which ran nine days.

Bond played with James Cagney in two of his personal productions, *The Time of Your Life* (1948), as an argumentative hardhat, and *Kiss Tomorrow Goodbye* (1950). In the latter, a Warner Brothers release, the two cops from *The Maltese Falcon*, Bond and Barton MacLane, are again plainclothes detectives, but with a decided difference. Bond is now top dog with MacLane his back-up man and both are thoroughly crooked here. Trying to shake down brutal hoodlum Cagney, they wind up his confederates in an ever-expanding organization. Their robbery plans go awry when Cagney is killed by his moll, Barbara Payton. Based on a Horace McCoy story, *Kiss Tomorrow Goodbye* was perfectly timed to begin a new decade that reflected a new cynicism, with a whole spate of films about dishonest law enforcement officers. Cagney was portrayed as a vicious killer, but his "respectable" associates were far more frightening for what they represented. The two upholders of the law are such greedy men that their very entrance, clad in the prerequisite hats and overcoats all detectives were supposed to wear, was a harbinger of some danger afoot. In the old days, the screen softened the image of the bad cop, either by redeeming him or having a good cop around to offset him. Bond and MacLane were not balanced here and may be the first movie law enforcement officers to be rightfully referred to, using a latter-day epithet, as "pigs."

His other notable 1950 film was Ford's RKO film *Wagonmaster*. The hero role went to ex-stuntman Ben Johnson, who had been built up in several previous Ford films. Bond portrayed the leader of a wagon train of Mormons plagued by ruthless outlaws. This was the first of the films in which he played what some called "the warrior-cleric," a religious man leading a beleaguered group of people. The film was rather straightforward and simple in plotting and one can only wonder why Ford didn't use this opportunity to star his old friend Bond, who did have the title role, rather than elevate untried actor Johnson.*

It is ironic that the actor's greatest success (*Wagon Train*) was in the role of a wagonmaster, *sans* the religion. Ford may have supplied the inspiration, but he certainly hadn't explored all the possibilities.

In the early '50s, Bond averaged about three films a year, most of which were made by Warner Brothers or Republic. Wayne had a new production deal with the former studio and Bond joined him for the first effort, *Operation Pacific* (1951). A World War II naval story, it allowed Bond the rare opportunity to play an officer, a submarine commander who for once outranked Wayne. It also allowed him to engage in heroics, sacrificing his life so that his vessel, endangered by the Japanese, can submerge quickly. Significantly, he was nicknamed "Pop" in this film, while Wayne sported his own nickname "Duke." At the same studio, he worked in another Cagney production, produced by William Cagney though without brother James as star. *Only the Valiant* (1951) was a Western ancestor of *The Dirty Dozen*, with incorrigible soldiers sent to man a deserted fort against hordes of Indians (and dying as required). As one of the troublesome soldiers, Bond lasted longer and had a few good moments as he maddeningly stands on the fort's parapet, demanding the savages come and get him. Gordon Douglas, who previously directed Bond in *Kiss Tomorrow Goodbye*, did his usual workmanlike job and used several cast members from the earlier film: Neville Brand, Steve Brodie, Herbert Heyes, Dan Riss and leading lady Barbara Payton.

---

*Wagonmaster *did nothing for Johnson's career. Ford never used him after 1950, except for a bit in* Cheyenne Autumn *(1964). He gradually returned to prominence, winning a Best Supporting Actor Oscar for* The Last Picture Show *(1971).*

Bond's name usually topped the supporting casts of major motion pictures or was billed equally with the stars of such lesser programmers as *Hellgate* and *Thunderbirds*, both 1952 products. *The Quiet Man* (1952) would end Wayne's almost two-decade commitment to Republic, which had always given him security when he needed it. He brought John Ford to the studio, which could have never afforded a director of his caliber and jumped at the chance to at least distribute some of his films. In the case of *The Quiet Man*, they got more than they could have expected.

The Quiet Man could be called Ford's "valentine to Ireland." Unlike his own films *The Informer* and *The Plough and the Stars*, as well as most of the other pictures about that country, this is not concerned with the "troubles" that have long plagued that country. Also unlike those films, this one was actually filmed in the Irish countryside in beautiful Technicolor. It was a typical Ford family affair, since he and partner Merian C. Cooper were answerable to no studio; their Argosy Productions footed the bill. His favorite scripter of the period, Frank Nugent, adapted the warm and witty story. The director's older brother, Francis, had a part in the film, as did leading lady Maureen O'Hara's two brothers. Siblings Barry Fitzgerald and Arthur Shields, who Ford had first used when they were members of the famed Abbey Players, made a rare appearance in the same film. Even four of John Wayne's children were given bit parts. The story is almost inconsequential: Wayne plays a prizefighter who has returned from America a withdrawn individual because he caused an opponent's death. He loves O'Hara and eventually resolves to stand up to her and her bullying brother, wonderfully played by Victor McLaglen (his best Ford role in many years). Bond as the local Catholic priest, Father Lonergan, is again a community leader. Speaking the narration as well, he gets some of the film's wittiest lines, done with a brogue. The film was almost universally applauded; it was the National Board of Review's top picture of the year and it won Ford another Oscar as Best Director. It may not be thought of as one of his best directional jobs today, but *The Quiet Man* remains one of his best-loved films.

With film production beginning to taper off due to the inroads of television, Bond found himself with more leisure time on his hands. Boating had become his first love; his frequent vacationing buddies were not usually top stars. They were Frank McGrath and Terry Wilson, stunt doubles who worked frequently in Hollywood action films, including the Fords. They also did extra work, thereby

The more benevolent Ward Bond of *The Quiet Men* (1952).

often filling several roles within the same film. Bond enjoyed the company of Wilson and McGrath, which would one day stand them in good stead. Bond lost one of his best outdoors buddies (as well as one of the more conservative directors in Hollywood) when Victor Fleming died soon after directing him in *Joan of Arc*.

After almost a decade of bachelorhood, Bond chose to marry again. He was pushing 50 when he chose Mary Lou May as his second wife. He had known her for some time, since May was secretary to Wayne's business manager. The new bridegroom was ready to settle for a more tranquil domestic life and their residence in Encino provided a perfect "home base" for the most successful years of his career. After his marriage, he began doing more anthology work on television, which got him home a lot earlier than location shooting ever did.

His three 1953 films were all distributed by Warners, two of them shot in the three-dimension process which flourished briefly in Hollywood during the early '50s. Both were Westerns; *Hondo* was a popular offering of Wayne's production company, notable for its Mexican location shooting. During production, Wayne courted Pilar, the woman who became his third wife. The less lavish *The Moonlighter* with Barbara Stanwyck and Fred MacMurray was a second feature; the *Herald Tribune* was derisive about the final showdown, in which Stanwyck bested Bond with rifles at 50 yards. Stanwyck was also one of the stars of *Blowing Wild*, a more contemporary western, which also starred Gary Cooper, Anthony Quinn and Ruth Roman. In a plot stolen from earlier Warner pictures like *They Drive by Night*, Cooper is put out of business when his truck is wrecked and partner Bond wounded by bandits in Mexico. He goes to work for an old buddy, oilman Quinn, whose predatory wife Stanwyck creates the subsequent trouble. The picture did well, but it was a shame that such major performers were given recycled material to work with.

In MGM's *Gypsy Colt* (1954), Bond was definitely the male star, but not so you'd notice. It is a time-worn theory that no matter how seasoned the actor, he cannot hope to compete with children and animals and here he was co-starring with one of each. This partial remake of *Lassie Come Home* (1943) changed the collie to a horse and a little boy into a girl (Donna Corcoran), but not much else. Bond, like Donald Crisp in the earlier film, had to sell the colt to pay off his farm's debts, but in true family film style, all ends happily. At least it was a new experience for him to be playing a warm, loving father figure, but the picture was just designed as a second feature. After its completion, Frances Dee, who played the child's mother, completely retired from the screen.

Bond returned to Republic for what turned out to be one of that studio's big moneymakers, *Johnny Guitar* (1954). Westerns were enjoying a revitalization period and that had encouraged the usually stingy production chief Herbert J. Yates to allow a higher budget and select a top star, Joan Crawford, for the lead. The Nicholas Ray film became one of the most fondly remembered Westerns of the period—and somewhat unusual, in that the main protagonists, valiant Crawford and villainous Mercedes McCambridge, were women who invaded a man's world. Most of the male characters (including Sterling Hayden, deceptively cast in the title role) were props for these women. Bond, as a leading citizen of the community, was completely dominated by the incredibly evil McCambridge. If the fireworks on screen weren't enough, the two ladies developed a mutual dislike and everyone else steered clear.

By comparison, Bond's next venture was a breeze, Allied Artists' *The Bob Mathias Story* (1954). He entered the territory lately reserved for either Charles Bickford or Lloyd Nolan as the coach-mentor of the famed Olympic track star, who proved quite likable as himself. It was always good for an untried actor to have a pro like Bond around and since this pro also happened to be one who had gotten into films because of his own athletic prowess, he was quite willing to give Mathias all the help he could.

His next stop was at Columbia, the studio that had kept Bond going during the dark days of the '30s. Although their friend Wayne had a long-standing (and justified) grudge against studio boss Harry Cohn, John Ford and many of his regulars were involved in the production of *The Long Gray Line* (1955), at Cohn's studio. In many ways, this underrated film is as loving a tribute to Ireland as was *The Quiet Man*, even though the entire film is set in the United States. Based on an autobiographical work by Martin Maher, Irish immigrant–staff sergeant at West Point military academy who shepherded many a future military leader over a period of many years, the film is not perfect. The leading character is an over-sentimentalized version of the old schoolmaster, Mr. Chips. What saves the character of Maher and therefore the film that hangs upon it is the wonderful performance of Tyrone Power in the lead. Although not Ford's first choice for the role, Power invests it with such a rich amount of humanity that the viewer happily ignores many of the clichés. It is regrettable that the star and the director never got together earlier, considering both had lengthy tenures at Fox. Maureen O'Hara and Donald Crisp were cast as Maher's wife and father. Bond had the role of Capt. Koehler, one of several West Point commandants during the time the film depicts. This was Bond's first film in Cinema-Scope, a process that Ford did not like and avoided using unless absolutely necessary. The early use of the process was awkward and this is one of the many films that suffers on its television showings. In scenes with a star like Power, Bond (who had been visible in the movies) suddenly became an off-screen voice.

Almost immediately after filming was completed, Ford, Bond and other *Long Gray Line* cast members (Betsy Palmer, Phillip Carey, Harry Carey, Jr., Marty Milner and young Patrick Wayne) were off to Hawaii. The project they were to work on was another special in CinemaScope and color, the film version of the stage hit *Mister Roberts*. It is an incongruity that a film which ultimately gave so many people so much pleasure should have been so trouble-ridden.

When Henry Fonda left Hollywood after *Fort Apache*, he went into the Mister Roberts role, in the play authored by his old friend Joshua Logan and Thomas Heggen. Fonda received much acclaim for playing the decent Naval lieutenant forced to do battle with his commanding officer rather than the Japanese and went from there into such prestigious plays as *Point of No Return* and *The Caine Mutiny Court Martial*. By not returning to Hollywood after his first stage hit, Fonda was written off by the town. Even Josh Logan, who had hoped to make his solo directorial debut with the *Roberts* film, was willing to go with the then-hot Marlon Brando, who had expressed interest in the starring role.

That situation changed when John Ford entered the picture. Given his track record, Ford seemed the ideal director for the job. However, when he had been in New York to see the play, he had called it "homosexual." Nevertheless, Ford was known to be rather iconoclastic even about his own films, so no one took the remark seriously. Jack Warner, who had bought the film rights to the play, was delighted at the chance to finally get the great director in his studio. It was generally understood that Ford was doing the film to work with Fonda again. (Josh Logan was disappointed, but producer Leland Hayward promised that they would be true to the original play.) As it turned out, Fonda and Leland Hayward were the only people connected with the show who were involved in the same capacity. And both were powerless to stop the Ford steamroller.

Probably the reason the film is remembered primarily as a comedy is that Ford siphoned off much of the play's sentimentality, which he hadn't really understood. One cannot fault his casting of Jack Lemmon as Ensign Pulver and William Powell as Doc, because they were both excellent. As for James Cagney, as the Captain, his interpretation was highly entertaining, but it threw off the balance of the play. On stage, the captain was mostly an unseen menace, discussed in fearful tones by members of the crew. The casting of a star like Cagney required the building-up of the scenes he appeared. As nasty as his portrayal was, the more he was seen, the less monstrous and more amusing he became. His portrayal was not the one Logan and Heggen had envisioned.

As for Bond, he pulled double duty on the film. Besides playing the sixth-billed role of Chief Petty Officer Dowdy, he found himself put into the position of assistant director. It appeared he was the only one Ford would trust to keep the cameras rolling when he himself was incapacitated (the director drank quite a bit on this location). Much of the Frank Nugent script had been shot when the bottom fell out. While drunk, Ford asked Fonda what he thought of the film so far and the star gave an honest reply. Ford got angry and knocked Fonda down, ending one of Hollywood's finest professional relationships. The team that had made *The Grapes of Wrath* and *Young Mr. Lincoln* would never collaborate again. Ford had to be taken off the picture because there was too much of Fonda already shot for him to be replaced, but not enough for the film to be finished without him. Besides, Ford was physically fatigued. A standard statement about his "ill health" was released and Mervyn Leroy was brought in to complete the film, with Josh Logan plugging up some of the holes (and given a phony credit as Nugent's collaborator on the script). Although he received no screen credit at all for performing in the capacity of director, the fact remains that Bond did direct some part of one of the '50s' biggest moneymakers.

Aside from the Fonda-Ford split, practically everyone benefitted from *Mister Roberts*. Lemmon won an Oscar as Best Supporting Actor and was on his way to film stardom. William Powell retired immediately afterward, with a hit exit film. Fonda was once again a movie commodity. And Logan, by not being called upon to direct the film, was free to direct the film version of another play he had directed, the same year's *Picnic*, and did a beautiful job of it. As for Ford, the reasons for his being relieved from duty were not widely known and his career continued to flourish. In fact, his very next film, which Warners also released, is considered by many to be his greatest of all. *The Searchers* (1956) is undeniably his greatest western.

In 1955, Bond assumed the presidency of the Motion Picture Alliance for which he had worked so hard all these years. He had resisted the chance for years, standing aside to let his friend Wayne serve. He had felt that the organization would be better served by having an admired star as president. It didn't matter that much because by this time Bond was known and greatly disliked for his vehement "anti–Red" stand. During the height of the blacklist, when not performing in front of the camera, he was one of the Hollywood people who would pressure studios not to employ those suspected of communist sympathies. (His *Hondo* co-star Geraldine Page was suspect merely due to her "New York acting background.") Even given the times, there could be no valid excuse for such reprehensible behavior and even the town's "closet conservatives" were as appalled as were Bond's victims. Whatever one's political beliefs, no one has the right to deny a man his livelihood. Some of those who were not dismissed had to compromise their principles by signing ill-conceived loyalty oaths prepared by studio attorneys. Other "suspects" escaped any compromise due to their importance to a studio or sometimes their images (usually comic performers). One could say it was a time of great hypocrisy, but while one could say many things about Bond, he was not a hypocrite. To be fair about it, there is no known instance of his having personally profited by the dismissal of another actor. In other words, he did not take these actions to improve his status in the movie industry; he did these things because he actually believed they were the right things to do.

In the years since his death, Bond has become a popular whipping boy for what happened to the movie industry during the McCarthy era. In his 1979 memoirs, producer-turned-monotonous character actor John Houseman singled the actor out for criticism. While it is understandable to read these things in a book by a former black-listee, Houseman was at his height as an MGM producer during this period and did not suffer for lack of work. His stance is therefore as a belated defender of less fortunate friends. Earlier in the book, he recalled producing the RKO film *On Dangerous Ground* (1951), in which Bond was cast, "prophetically, as the villain." In fact, Bond played a hard-nosed rural sheriff, unsympathetic but not particularly villainous. It should be remembered that during those years there were still liberals in hiring positions who would have died sooner than give Bond a job. Had Bond lived through the more permissive '60s, one wonders how many directors, except for Ford or Wayne, would have used him in a theatrical film. Houseman's comments prove that old grudges linger for many years.

Continuing to work in television, Bond did several of *Ford Theater* half-hours, including a memorable episode with William Bendix in which Bond played a cop who subdues a "temporarily incensed" henpecked husband. When John Ford made his television debut as director, disciples Bond and Wayne were on hand. The occasion was a unique anthology series called *Screen Directors' Playhouse*, on which Hollywood notables turned in short stories. The 1955-56 TV season was notable as the first one in which the major studios became active in the new medium; what better time for the movies' most-honored director to get his feet wet? Since baseball films were pretty well out of favor in the '50s, Ford chose that sport as the backdrop for two of the three telefilms he directed. One was called "Rookie of the Year" and it presented Wayne as a newspaper sports writer who takes an interest in a promising young rookie (played by his son Patrick). While doing a story about him, he discovers that the boy's father, played by Bond, was a former ballplayer thrown out of baseball for taking a bribe during a Black Sox–type scandal. Wayne must then decide whether to write the whole story or not. Of course, the reporter chooses not to allow the sins of the father to cast a shadow on the career of the son. It was a curious denouement when one considers the political stance of the director and his two leading actors: The story negated the validity of the public's right to know in favor of personal freedom at the same time they, as private citizens were ferreting out deep dark secrets about colleagues in the same industry. Perhaps Ford did not see the connection, but then he was one director who had never allowed politics to stand between him and a good story.

Many would disagree with the above statement and would say the film Ford was making at the same time as "Rookie of the Year" espoused his reactionary views. A number of cast members of *The Searchers* (the two Waynes, Bond and Vera Miles) went directly from the film into this teleplay. And for Wayne and Bond, the film represented the pinnacles of their respective careers. Although critics marvel at what seemingly was a Ford resurgence, many believed that the director had gone as far right as he could. His casting of Wayne as the Indian-hating Ethan Edwards seemed to condone bigotry, just as his casting him as opponent to the bigoted Henry Fonda in *Fort Apache* seemed to say the opposite. Even those who praise the technique used in *The Searchers* still don't understand the basic plot.

Based on a novel by Alan LeMay, *The Searchers* is the story of a Civil War veteran (Wayne) who has a brief reunion with his brother's family before most of them are massacred by Indians. The simple story details the search by Edwards and a half-breed young man (Jeffrey Hunter) who was raised by the family to find the little girl who was taken alive. The search lasts several years, during which time Edwards' niece grows up. She has become a true squaw, so that when her uncle discovers this, he almost does what he planned to do from the first: kill her. But he relents and takes her back to "civilization," establishing himself as a tragic figure rather than a hateful, vengeful man. Yet people who thought that Wayne could only play the good guy with the white hat dismissed his performance, saying that the role was shaped to Wayne's specifications, when actually the reverse was true. He had developed the real maturity to play a man of depth; he had been merely interesting in *Red River* and *She Wore a Yellow Ribbon* in which he had relied on the makeup man rather than his own ability to provide character. Here he relied on himself and he was great, reaching a height he would never again attain.

Captain Reverend Sam Clayton is Bond's best Ford part because it combines all the elements of characterization the two men had been developing over the years. Clayton is a warrior-cleric—a Texas Ranger officer as well as a minister—and the actor plays him to the hilt. He is a man who relishes both positions of authority and he is a human being who can make mistakes (and does). Some of the film's most subtle moments are his. As Clayton drinks his coffee while standing in the home of Edwards' brother, through an open doorway he spots the lady of the house (Dorothy Jordan) dusting off her brother-in-law's coat in an affectionate manner. Bond does a beautifully discreet turn which suggests not only someone not wishing to intrude on this tender moment, but also a man of God who has heard a silent confession and has filed it away forever within him. All the while, he has continued to do nothing more than sip a cup of coffee. Yet this is a very important moment because, outside of the use of sentimental music, this is Ford's only on-screen suggestion of the love between Edwards and his sister-in-law, which has a great deal of bearing on his subsequent hunt for her captured child. Here is a prime example of economy in both acting and direction being perfectly in tune.

Of course, Ford was not above using Bond in comic moments, always loving to burst his characters' egos. Late in the picture, an overeager young cavalry lieutenant (Patrick Wayne) has to be constantly warned by Clayton where to keep his saber, since this argument against nepotism in the military will be riding at his side when they come up against a Comanche war party. In the final scene, in a break from the sentiment, we see Clayton lying on his stomach and a surgeon administering to his backside. When asked whether it was arrow or bullet that did the deed, Clayton bellows "No!," and we know that young Wayne's saber has done its work and this reverend is merely "turning the other cheek." Somehow, because Bond is so good, this last shot does not diminish the character's dignity.

Fortunately, the fine performances were backed by first-class production values. Ford and Merian C. Cooper ended their professional partnership with a winner. It wasn't Warners but rather the backing of millionaire C. V. Whitney which allowed them to have everything their own way. Besides a return to Ford's favorite location, Monument Valley, the budget allowed them to shoot the exteriors for the searchers' winter trek in Alberta, Canada. And rather than be saddled with the studio's usual Warner color and CinemaScope, Ford asked for and got Technicolor and the Paramount-processed, less obtrusive VistaVision. One has only to see one of his great doorway shots from this film to realize what a longer, narrower screen would have done to them.

During this period, Bond appeared in a slew of additional westerns. He played a disabled lawman in Republic's *A Man Alone* (1955), which was directed by its star, Ray Milland. In two 1956 films, Universal's *Pillars of the Sky* and Republic's *Dakota Incident*, he played, respectively, another minister and a politician with "eccentric" notions that he can mediate peacefully with attacking Indians; this of course results in his death. These movies were made at the tail end of the "you-must-kill savages" period. Bond also died in United Artists' *The Halliday Brand* (1957), playing an autocratic cattle baron and father of Joseph Cotten, who in reality was about a month younger than Bond.

As a respite from all these heavy roles, Ford cast him as film director John Dodge in *The Wings of Eagles* (1957); there was no doubt that Ford was the prototype for this character. Who but Bond would have been able to imitate the traits of his longtime friend and mentor, providing many an in-joke? The film was a long-planned tribute to Frank "Spig" Wead, with Wayne in the lead role and Maureen O'Hara once more epitomizing Ford's perfect wife. The film emphasized the lighter side of Wead's life, depicting him first as a rollicking young Navy flier during World War I. It only briefly concentrates on the disabling injury (he fell down a flight of stairs when his child cried out at night) that ended his military career. After his rehabilitation, he is persuaded by director Dodge to put some of his

Naval experiences on the screen. Although Wead really wrote some screenplays for Ford, his early work in Hollywood included Frank Capra's *Dirigible* and George Hill's *Hell Divers*, both 1931. (Since Ford made *The Wings of Eagles* at MGM, he utilized a scene of Wallace Beery and Clark Gable in *Hell Divers*.) Therefore, though Bond was made up to look like the man behind the camera, a fictitious name was used. However, Wead was not so well-known to so many people that Ford could not play fast and loose with the facts. The film was designed primarily as a piece of entertainment, and it achieved its purpose. Every few years, Ford, who had nothing more to prove to anyone, chose to make a fun movie. He considered it an in-joke to cast the ex-football player he had turned into an actor, as himself (Ford). Ironically, this would be the last Ford motion picture to feature Bond, although they did work together once more in another medium.

By this time, the actor had become so proficient as a character man that only rarely was that leathery toughness of his properly utilized. All that was about to change when he got his most popular role. By 1957, the Western movie had reached a new peak, helped along by more adult stories. Television was also filled with them, so much so that nearly every time the career of a movie western star faltered, he was given a TV series in which he did not have to remove his cowboy duds. There were shows featuring the likes of Rory Calhoun, Rod Cameron, Joel McCrea, George Montgomery, Audie Murphy and John Payne all over the airwaves. In 1955, CBS asked John Wayne to star in the TV version of their radio hit *Gunsmoke*. He refused, but recommended a young actor he had been bringing along in his films, James Arness, and filmed a personal introduction for the first show. Arness played Marshall Matt Dillon for 20 years. The following season, ABC and Warner Brothers inaugurated the first successful hour-long westerns, *Cheyenne* and *Maverick*. NBC, which was looking for shows that could spotlight the RCA color they had at their disposal, was determined to introduce the most spectacular TV western to date and for the next five years, they introduced a whole slew, culminating with *The Virginian*, the first 90-minute western series. But the program that started it all and one of the best was *Wagon Train*.

At the time, Universal utilized a television subsidiary called Revue, which mainly produced half-hour situation comedies. But many large-scale Western films with stars like James Stewart and Jeff Chandler were being filmed on the Universal lot. NBC decided to ask the studio to apply the same energy, and more importantly the same budget used for a moderately priced horse opera, to produce a weekly hour-long series. The studio eagerly drew from its large stable of what they considered "second string craftsmen" who were still drawing their salaries though the market for B pictures was grinding to a halt. A star salary did not fit into the plans. Once the *Wagon Train* concept was decided upon, it was reasoned that two leading actors who were not big names should be cast, while the glitter would be provided by strong guest stars. (The concept of having guests of such caliber on any regular series was fairly new.) However, the "staying" power of the show would be largely dependent upon audience interest in the two regular stars.

For the younger of the two, trail scout Flint McCullogh, Robert Horton, was chosen. A contract player at MGM, he had been cast in a number of colorless second leads. It seems that Universal did not want to tie up any of its own stable of young men with a series, since movies were still more important. The McCullogh character would provide a change of pace from the episodes back at the wagons; he would often become involved in some separate plot in the course of his scouting. Since the format provided that each episode title would include the name of the guest star's character, in McCullogh's episodes, the guest would be either in town or somewhere along the trail—not necessarily a wagon train passenger. But the drama of the train and the pioneers who signed abroad was the show's main quality and holding it all together would be the strong, tough wagonmaster, Civil War veteran Major Seth Adams. Cantankerous but sturdy as a rock, Adams seemed to step out of a John Ford movie. So who was better suited for playing him than Bond? The actor, who felt more at home in cowboy clothes and had never lost his affinity for the western genre, signed up.

Although he had been in demand in motion pictures for years, the deals he made were the standard kind usually afforded character actors. But every movie actor who took on a regular TV series was treated as royally as possible, considering the budget. The shooting schedule was rough, but not that much for this grizzled veteran of countless quickies from the 1930s. However, Bond learned that as a series star, he could enjoy some privileges of rank. When it was decided that two other regular roles were to be cast, Bond decided to get his pals Frank McGrath and Terry Wilson. This way he would work with buddies. Since McGrath's trail cook Charlie Wooster and Wilson's assistant wagonmaster Bill Hawks were originally conceived as bit parts used to tie scenes together, it didn't seem to matter that they had had little real acting experience. As it turned out, short, bearded McGrath and tall, balding Wilson became the only performers who appeared regularly on *Wagon Train* for its whole eight-year span. Their roles kept expanding, to the point that whole episodes were eventually built around them, with Major Adams and Flint McCullogh relegated to a small role in that particular hour (if they were seen at all).

Some of the best people in the business guested on the show. It is amazing that, with such a lengthy career in films, it wasn't until Bond got his own TV series that he got a chance to play scenes with the likes of Bette Davis and Charles Laughton, to name two of the illustrious people who took on title roles in the usually excellent scripts prepared for the show. It seemed that any name performer who did television in those days, had to do at least one *Wagon Train*; it became something of a status symbol. This had a lot to do with the popularity of the adult western, which allowed a greater range in the writing. Some episodes, usually comedies or tearjerkers, went by without one shot being fired. Western purists criticized this, saying that writers were just taking modern-day stories and changing the setting to the Old West. But *Wagon Train* quickly rose to the top of the ratings charts and became a permanent fixture on NBC every Wednesday night at 7:30, where it remained during its whole life on that network (five years).

Bond settled into the Major Adams character so quickly that the month of its network debut, an article "written" by him, "Riding the Wagon Train," appeared in the *New York Herald Tribune*. Much of it concerned his love of the western form and his long association with John Ford. It was basically just publicity for the show and had little of the depth of later articles written about him. Before its first season had ended, the show did a two-part episode *sans* big name guests. Titled "The Major Adams Story," it told, via flashbacks, the life of his character from Civil War service through an ill-fated romance and culminating in his becoming the wagonmaster. It had the sort of a story that devoted fans of a series love; it established a "life story" not only for Bond, but also for McGrath and Wilson. In that 1957-58 TV season, the greatest change of all came into Bond's career. He was no longer known as the bit-playing tough guy or even the relentless Red baiter; he was primarily a strong, warm father figure to a lot of novice pioneers and one of the most important TV personalities of the era. In short, he was a star.

Due to his strong new image, he would only appear in two feature film roles once the series got underway.* A guest star bit in Bob Hope's *Alias Jesse James* (1959) merely utilized him, in his Major Adams get-up, as one of the sharpshooters who comes to Hope's rescue in the finale. In Frank Borzage's *China Doll* (1958), he played another understanding cleric, a chaplain stationed in WWII China who counsels pilot Victor Mature about his relationship with a Chinese girl. Inspired by the success of pictures like *Sayonara*, many films of the late '50s revolved around affairs between American or British servicemen and Oriental women, but the professionalism of this one made it more palatable than most. Then came Howard Hawks' *Rio Bravo* (1959). As one of John Wayne's most entertaining and best-liked films, it was fitting that Bond's film career should end with this film.

Rio Bravo is not a powerful adult western like *The Searchers* or even Hawks' own *Red River*. There has been some talk in recent years that Wayne purposely made this film as a criticism of *High Noon* (1952), in which Gary Cooper is the marshal deserted by the entire town in time of need. In this film, Wayne's Sheriff Chance holds off against an even larger group of men with only minimal help from others. Comparisons aside, *Rio Bravo* can be looked at as a very well-directed and -acted, fun picture. It helped establish Dean Martin, as a reformed alcoholic deputy, as a serious actor, gave Angie Dickinson her first leading role in an important picture, and probably contains the ultimate Walter Brennan performance. As the grizzled old deputy Stumpy, the veteran award-winning actor uses every trick in his proverbial bag in portraying an old man who wants to prove to the man he admires that he is just as necessary in time of crisis as he was in time of tranquility.

Bond as the lawman's old friend, trail boss Pat Wheeler, is first sighted riding into town, looking as if he'd just left his TV location. Because he had to begin shooting a new season of *Wagon Train*s, his part was short. Before Wheeler can help Sheriff Chance, he is gunned down by the villains, making this his smallest part in years—the type of role that usually went to someone like Paul Fix. However, when Dave Garroway visited the location of the movie on his Sunday afternoon NBC-TV show *Wide, Wide World*, Bond was present and seemed to be in good spirits, among friends on a movie set.

Both films were shot during his first year's hiatus from Wagon Train *and naturally he was cast in a totally sympathetic light.*

During *Wagon Train*'s second season, Bond agreed to be interviewed by *TV Guide*. The finished product appeared in the April 11, 1959, issue, coming about a month following the release of *Rio Bravo*. This story and another *TV Guide* article, written shortly before his death, constitute the only times the public got to know the private Bond.

"Well, it's a great business we're in," Bond said. "I love it. I'll do another year of *Wagon Train*. He then added that he originally signed a five-year contract. When pressed about the rigors of doing a weekly show, he admitted, "It takes a lot out of you, this television." Later, he discussed his physical condition: "My weight crawls up to around 233 and I have to go on a diet and get it down to 225." He also made the proud admission that he'd cut down from four to two packs of cigarettes a day. (When the second article appeared, a little over a year and a half later, Bond had been dead for two weeks.)

During those final years of TV stardom, Bond tried to keep a low profile politically. But in September 1959, he was so angered by the fuss made over visiting Soviet Premier Khrushchev in Hollywood that he flew his American flag at half mast at his house in Encino during the Russian's visit to the film capital. When Khrushchev made some comments at 20th Century–Fox during the shooting of *Can Can*, Bond gave out news stories of his own free will. He got some coverage, not so much for his vehement anti–Communism, but primarily because he was a TV star and it made an interesting story for reporters. He saw this whole thing as a symbol that the pendulum was swinging from right to left. If the visit by the Soviet head of state did not exactly mark such a happening, it can be said that around 1959, films began getting more liberal in their views and many of the battle-scarred McCarthy victims of the movie colony began inching their way back.

Bond did not personally cast people in *Wagon Train*, but he was always happy to see people like Richard Arlen and Evelyn Brent, stars when he was starting out, given small character parts. A large number of the guests had co-starred with him at least once; they included William Bendix,* Ernest Borgnine, John Carradine, Linda Darnell, Andy Devine, Henry Hull, Marjorie Main, George Montgomery, Cesar Romero and Barbara Stanwyck. The guests (sometimes doubled up on shows) also included such disparate types as Judith

---

*Bendix later got into a feud with "the *Wagon Train* crowd" and even knocked Bond, but the latter kept out of the fracas, which after all was non-political.

Anderson and Lou Costello, who made his one endeavor into dramatics on this program shortly before his death. One of Bette Davis' several appearances had her playing the widowed mother of a large brood who fears for her family's survival in the West. Her scenes with the understanding wagonmaster made this episode one of the series' best and the playing of both performers was exceptional. In the days when Davis was the "Queen of Warner Brothers," the only way Bond could have shared a scene with her was if the script called for her to receive a traffic ticket. But the series had finally granted him the opportunity to play opposite the great actress and he did not waste the moment. And Davis enjoyed the experience enough to sign up for the following season, playing a change of pace role. The next time around, she portrayed the not-so-proper chaperon of a group of nubile young ladies whose purposes in travelling west are quite obvious.

At the beginning of the show's third season (fall 1959), the TV western was bigger than ever. Although NBC dropped their hour-long Saturday night failure *Cimarron City*, they brought in the colorful *Bonanza*, giving it an early evening spot. Sunday night began with *Riverboat*, which some people labelled "a floating *Wagon Train*." The Tuesday night 7:30 slot was filled with *Laramie*, a more youth-oriented western about the operators of a stagecoach relay station. Over at CBS, *Wagon Train*'s most successful imitation, *Rawhide*, became a big hit on Friday nights. There wasn't a night when one station did not air a western show. Possibly the only "harm" the large-scale models did was to the old half-hour cowboy shows. Little shows like *Buckskin* and *Johnny Ringo* folded up and the 30-minute oaters that remained, *Gunsmoke* and *Tales of Wells Fargo*, had to take on the longer form. Only ABC's *The Rifleman* made it into the '60s without expanding.

Despite the early concept that Major Adams would just back up the guest stars, viewers had taken to his character so much that they wanted to see more about him. (It was also felt that it was unrealistic for a new guest to suddenly appear out of nowhere on the wagon train, when the treks westward sometimes took a year or more. The third season increased the workload of all the regulars. In one show, a smooth-talking stranger (Noah Beery, Jr.) comes between the Major and his closest friend Bill Hawks, who leaves the train with the schemer. Eventually, Hawks learns what the man is really like but not before he almost kills the Major. The interplay between Bond and Terry Wilson was always realistic, mainly due to their real-life friendship. In fact, some of the best shows involved differences of opinion among the principals in matters of survival. And the Major was not always right, even in those days of almost God-like TV heroes. Some of those season's shows even took him out of his usual setting, such as the episode where Major Adams investigates the mysterious death of a friend's wife and learns all about her past through flashbacks. These changes of pace were welcome.

Few critics could complain that *Wagon Train* glamorized the West; the pioneers were often depicted as stupid, cowardly, bigoted or just mercenary. Indian attacks were usually sporadic, caused by stray renegades rather than enormous war parties studding an entire mountain. Death more than likely came from the fever, a bad encounter with the elements or from a fellow passenger, rather than from an arrow in the chest. It was this quality that set the program apart from most of its contemporaries, and the reason it was thought highly of by people in the business.

When John Ford agreed to squeeze an episode of *Wagon Train* into his schedule, the TV producers did not realize that he would bring his own people. But there was no one willing to give Ford an argument. The show was called "The Colter Craven Story," and in that role he cast character actor Carleton Young, who had been in his last three films. Other leads were taken by actors like Paul Birch, Willis Bouchey and Anna Lee, all from the Ford stock company. The title character, Craven, was a disillusioned alcoholic travelling on the wagon train, unable to practice medicine because he cannot forget a tragic blunder in his past. Major Adams tells Craven the story of another alcoholic, a man considered a failure by his own family, who became General of the U.S. Army and eventually President: Ulysses S. Grant. Ford handled this story-in-a-story in a low-key manner, which prevented the moralizing from becoming too thick. In the Civil War sequence, an actor named Michael Morrison played the bearded Gen. Sherman; John Wayne took time from the massive job of editing his own film *The Alamo* to play this bit for old time's sake.

The airing of "The Colter Craven Story" was scheduled for the fall of 1960, early in the program's fourth season. This seemed to call for another *TV Guide* article on Bond and his long-time association with Ford. In that article, the actor told of his great respect for his friend, something these men usually kept to themselves because being sentimental about another male was not considered macho. The piece was prepared for the November 19 issue of the magazine, since the Ford show was to appear that week, on Thanksgiving Eve, November 23.

Bond had finally begun to be receptive to requests for him to make personal appearances in his Major Adams garb; western stars were particularly popular at rodeos. He was delighted to make an appearance during halftime at a Dallas Cowboys–Los Angeles Rams football game at the Cotton Bowl in Dallas; this was a game he personally wanted to see. On Saturday, November 5, 1960, word came out that Ward Bond had collapsed and died of a heart attack in a motel not far from the stadium. It was the same week that John F. Kennedy was elected president.*

Within a few hours of Bond's death, his old hunting pal Clark Gable was stricken and rushed to the hospital. Eleven days later, "The King" was dead, also of heart failure. The '60s had just begun, but Gable's death marked the end of an era.

Bond's death was, of course, a shock to the network and his studio. So important had he become to the success of his program that it was hard to imagine *Wagon Train* without Major Adams. He had filmed enough episodes to last through January, so no snap decision was made about replacing him. Many of Bond's old tough-guy contemporaries were considered, including his old cohort Barton MacLane, who had just begun a regular run in NBC's newest western series *The Outlaws*. It was quickly decided that whoever came into the show would be a totally new character, allowing Major Adams to die with the actor so strongly identified with him. The last Bond episode was called "The Weight of Command," in which almost everyone disagrees with the Major about the route to be taken by the train. When he imposes his strong will, he becomes a pariah, in a sort of parallel to Wayne's *Red River*. Only in the last minutes of the program is it shown that Major Adams was right and his unpopular decision saved the lives of the people in his care. It seemed a fitting finish to the saga of Major Adams.

In the end, it was decided to cast a different type of actor as the new wagonmaster. In view of the fact that the show ran until 1965, this was a wise decision. The new character, Chris Hale, was more outwardly sympathetic and appeared more vulnerable than the rocklike Major, and veteran character actor John McIntire was cast in

---

A man of completely opposite political views, Kennedy would nevertheless soon stand up to the Russians in a way that even a conservative like Bond would have admired. He would also die in Dallas, a little over three years later.

the role. An actor developed in the old days of radio, McIntire underplayed his role, always deferring to guest performers as Bond had rarely done. He was introduced as a stunned man whose entire family had been massacred by Indians when he is picked by the train. Hale uses his experience to take over the wagon train when the appointed wagonmaster (Lee Marvin) turns out to be a sadistic brute who terrorizes the passengers. Eventually, Robert Horton left the series and two young scouts, Robert Fuller and Scott (Denny) Miller, joined the cast around the time the show moved to ABC in 1962. For one season, all episodes were 90 minutes long. The only constants that remained were Frank McGrath and Terry Wilson. During these last years, the old episodes with Bond were put into syndication with the new title *Major Adams—Trailmaster.**

Besides the posthumous cover story in *TV Guide*, a letter highlighting his long film career appeared in *Films in Review* a month after he died. Had it included a film index approximating anywhere near the accurate amount, it would likely have eliminated the space for any other letters for that issue.

Because Ward Bond was allowed into people's living rooms as Major Adams every Wednesday night, his untimely death was mourned by people who had never even heard of the Hollywood blacklist. The two men closest to him, Ford and Wayne, were admired by far more people, but their deaths in the 1970s came after long lingering illnesses, well-publicized. Bond's death was shocking in its suddenness. Although no screen acknowledgment was given, the very next film begun by Ford was dedicated to his late friend. *The Man Who Shot Liberty Valence* (1962) was his first black-and-white western in over a decade. Supporting stars James Stewart and Wayne was a galaxy of Ford veterans: Vera Miles, John Carradine, Andy Devine, Anna Lee, John Qualen, Woody Strode and Carleton Young. The picture's theme (the disparity between truth and legend) harks back to earlier Ford films like *My Darling Clementine* and *Fort Apache*. In the midst of this big reunion, one remark stood out. It went uncredited, but could have been said by anyone there. It was simply this: "I sure wish Ward Bond were here." Then things would have been like they always had been.

---

*A quarter of a century later, they reverted to their original title showings on CBN Cable (later The Family Channel).

The Films of Ward Bond

Bond made well over 200 films. Many of his early roles were non-speaking bit parts in films like *Arrowsmith* (1931), *Affairs of Cellini* (1934) and *The Gorgeous Hussey* (1936). His small part was deleted from *Souls at Sea* (1937). He was an unbilled guest star in *In This Our Life* (1942) and *Alias Jesse James* (1959). Films in those categories have been omitted.

1. *Salute.* Fox 1929. John Ford. George O'Brien, Helen Chandler, Frank Albertson, Stepin Fetchit, William Janney, Joyce Compton, Duke Morrison (John Wayne). WB debuts as a football player in the Army-Navy game.

2. *Words and Music.* Fox 1929. James Tinling. Lois Moran, Helen Twelvetrees, David Percy, Elizabeth Patterson, William Orland, Duke Morrison (John Wayne), Frances Dee.

3. *The Big Trail.* Fox 1930. Raoul Walsh. John Wayne, Marguerite Churchill, Ian Keith, Tyrone Power, Sr., El Brendel, Tully Marshall, David Rollins. A vehicle for Wayne that didn't quite work out. WB is a wagon train passenger, a precursor of later roles.

4. *Born Reckless.* Fox 1930. John Ford. Edmund Lowe, Marguerite Churchill, Lee Tracy, Frank Albertson, Catherine Dale Owen, Warren Hymer, Mike Donlan. World War I veterans turn away from their criminal past. WB is a soldier.

5. *The Brat.* Fox 1931. John Ford. Sally O'Neill, Alan Dinehart, Frank Albertson, Virginia Cherrill, June Collyer, J. Farrell MacDonald. WB is a sympathetic precinct cop.

6. *High Speed.* Col 1931. D. Ross Lederman. Buck Jones, Loretta Sayers, Wallace MacDonald, Mickey McGuire (Rooney).

7. *White Eagle.* Col 1932. Lambert Hillyer. Buck Jones, Barbara Weeks, Robert Ellis, Jason Robards, Jim Thorpe.

8. *The Trial of Vivienne Ware.* Fox 1932. William K. Howard. Joan Bennett, Donald Cook, Zasu Pitts, Skeets Gallagher, Lillian Bond, Alan Dinehart, Herbert Mundin, Jameson Thomas. WB is an aide to defense attorney Cook.

9. *Virtue.* Col 1932. Edward Buzzell. Carole Lombard, Pat O'Brien, Mayo Methot, Shirley Grey, Edward LeSaint, Jack LaRue, Willard Robertson. WB is cab driver O'Brien's buddy.

10. *Hello Trouble.* Col 1932. Lambert Hillyer. Buck Jones, Lina Basquette, Wallace MacDonald, Spec O'Donnell, Ruth Warren, Frank Ricci.

11. *When Strangers Marry.* Col 1932. Clarence Badger. Jack Holt, Lillian Bond, Arthur Vinton, Gustav von Seyffertitz, Barbara Barondess, Paul Porcasi, Harry Stubbs, Rudolph Anderson, Charles Stevens.

12. *Sundown Rider.* Col 1932. Lambert Hillyer. Buck Jones, Barbara

Weeks, Wheeler Oakman, Bradley Page, Pat O'Malley, Niles Welch, Frank Larue.

13. *Unknown Valley.* Col 1932. Lambert Hillyer. Buck Jones, Cecilia Parker, Carlotta Warrick, Wade Boteler, Frank McGlynn, Gaylord (Steve) Pendleton.

14. *Air Mail.* Univ 1932. John Ford. Ralph Bellamy, Pat O'Brien, Frank Albertson, Gloria Stuart, Slim Summerville, Russell Hopton, David Landau, Francis Ford, James Donlan, Lew Kelly, Louise MacIntosh, Wade Boteler. WB works at an air mail outpost.

15. *Rackety Rax.* Fox 1932. Alfred Werker. Victor McLaglen, Greta Nissen, Alan Dinehart, Nell O'Day, Allen Jenkins, Arthur Pierson, Vince Barnett, Marjorie Beebe, Ivan Linow. WB is a gangster.

16. *Flesh.* MGM 1932. John Ford. Wallace Beery, Ricardo Cortez, Karen Morley, Jean Hersholt, John Miljan, Herman Bing. German wrestler Beery makes short work of loudmouth American opponent (WB) outside the ring.

17. *Heroes for Sale.* WB 1933. William A. Wellman. Richard Barthelmess, Aline MacMahon, Loretta Young, Gordon Westcott, Berton Churchill, Robert Barrat, Charles Grapewin, Grant Mitchell, James Murray. Strong depiction of one man's life, from the end of the World War through the depression. WB is one of the homeless men Barthelmess meets.

18. *Police Car 17.* Col 1933. Lambert Hillyer. Tim McCoy, Evalyn Knapp, Wallis Clark, Harold Huber, Edwin Maxwell, DeWitt Jennings. WB is a cop.

19. *The Poor Rich.* Univ 1933. Edward Sedgewick. Edward Everett Horton, Edna May Oliver, Leila Hyams, Andy Devine, Thelma Todd, John Miljan.

20. *Wild Boys of the Road.* WB 1933. William A. Wellman. Frankie Darro, Dorothy Coonan, Edwin Phillips, Arthur Hohl. Sterling Holloway. Early juvenile delinquent film. WB is a guard brutalized by the title kids.

21. *Straightaway.* Col 1933. Otto Brower. Tim McCoy, Sue Carol, William Bakewell, Francis McDonald, Samuel S. Hinds, Arthur Rankin. WB is a race car driver.

22. *College Coach.* WB 1933. William A. Wellman. Dick Powell, Pat O'Brien, Ann Dvorak, Arthur Byron, Lyle Talbot, Hugh Herbert, Arthur Hohl, Guinn Williams, Nat Pendleton, Donald Meek, John Wayne. Back where he started, WB is assistant to O'Brien's title character.

23. *Frontier Marshal.* Fox 1933. Lewis Seiler. George O'Brien, Irene Bentley, Ruth Gillette, George E. Stone, Frank Conroy, Edward LeSaint, Russell Simpson. WB is a troublesome cowboy.

24. *Obey the Law.* Col 1933. Ben Stoloff. Leo Carrillo, Lois Wilson, Dickie Moore, Gino Corrado, Ed Gargan. WB is a bully who preys upon immigrant shopkeepers.

25. *It Happened One Night.* Col 1934. Frank Capra. Clark Gable, Claudette Colbert, Walter Connolly, Alan Hale, Roscoe Karns, Jameson

Thomas, Charles Wilson, Wallis Clark, Arthur Hoyt, Blanche Frederici, Eddy Chandler. WB's first Capra, as one of the bus drivers.

26. *Voice in the Night.* Col 1934. Charles C. Coleman. Tim McCoy, Joseph Crehan, Billie Seward, Francis MacDonald, Kane Richmond, Guy Usher. WB is a shady type in another modern-day McCoy vehicle.

27. *The Wrecker.* Col 1934. Albert Rogell. Jack Holt, Genevieve Tobin, George E. Stone, Sidney Blackmer, Irene White. WB is a member of Holt's construction crew.

28. *Here Comes the Groom.* Par 1934. Edward Sedgewick. Jack Haley, Mary Boland, Neil Hamilton, Patricia Ellis, Lawrence Grant, Isabel Jewell, Sidney Toler, E. H. Calvert, Arthur Treacher.

29. *Whirlpool.* Col 1934. Roy William Neill. Jack Holt, Jean Arthur, Lila Lee, Allen Jenkins, Donald Cook, Arthur Hohl, John Miljan.

30. *The Human Side.* Univ 1934. Edward Buzzell. Adolphe Menjou, Doris Kenyon, Reginald Owen, Charlotte Henry, Joseph Cawthorne, Betty Lawford, Dickie Moore. WB works for theatrical producer Menjou.

31. *Death on the Diamond.* MGM 1934. Edward Sedgewick. Robert Young, Madge Evans, Ted Healy, Paul Kelly, Nat Pendleton, David Landau, DeWitt Jennings, Mickey Rooney, Robert Livingston. WB is a guard.

32. *The Defense Rests.* Col 1934. Lambert Hillyer. Jack Holt, Jean Arthur, Raymond Walburn, Donald Meek, Nat Pendleton. WB is a police officer.

33. *Man's Game.* Col 1934. D. Ross Lederman. Tim McCoy, Evalyn Knapp, DeWitt Jennings, Robert Kortman, Wade Boteler, Alden (Stephen) Chase. WB is the uniformed son of a fire chief.

34. *Most Precious Thing in Life.* Col 1934. Lambert Hillyer. Jean Arthur, Richard Cromwell, Donald Cook, Anita Louise, Jane Darwell, Ben Alexander, Mary Forbes.

35. *Men of the Night.* Col 1934. Lambert Hillyer, Bruce Cabot, Judith Allen, Charles Sabin, Matthew Betz, Walter McGrail.

36. *Broadway Bill.* Col 1934. Frank Capra. Warner Baxter, Myrna Loy, Walter Connolly, Helen Vinson, Lynne Overman, Raymond Walburn, Douglass Dumbrille, Clarence Muse, Margaret Hamilton, Paul Harvey, Irving Bacon, Charles Lane. WB is a gambler's henchman—the same role he would play 16 years later in Capra's *Riding High.*

37. *Grand Old Girl.* RKO 1935. John Robertson. May Robson, Fred MacMurray, Mary Carlisle, Alan Hale, Gavin Gordon, Ben Alexander, Edward Van Sloan, Etienne Girardot. WB is an athlete who needs tutoring.

38. *Devil Dogs of the Air.* WB 1935. Lloyd Bacon. James Cagney, Pat O'Brien, Margaret Lindsay, Frank McHugh, Helen Lowell, John Arledge, Robert Barrat, William Davidson. WB is an air corps flight instructor.

39. *Justice of the Range.* Col 1935. David Selman. Tim McCoy, Billie Seward, George (Gabby) Hayes, Guy Usher. WB is an outlaw.

40. *Black Fury.* WB 1935. Michael Curtiz. Paul Muni, Karen Morley,

William Gargan, Barton MacLane, John Qualen, Vince Barnett, Tully Marshall, J. Carrol Naish, Mae Marsh, Henry O'Neill, Joseph Crehan, Akim Tamiroff, Willard Robertson. WB is a mine worker.

41. ***Fighting Shadows.*** Col 1935. David Selman. Tim McCoy, Geneva Mitchell, Robert Allen, Frank Rice, Si Jenks. WB is an outlaw.

42. ***Western Courage.*** Col 1935. Spencer Gordon Bennet. Ken Maynard, Cornelius Keefe, Geneva Mitchell, Betty Blythe, Rene Whitney.

43. ***Murder in the Fleet.*** MGM 1935. Edward Sedgewick. Robert Taylor, Jean Parker, Jean Hersholt, Ted Healy, Una Merkel, Arthur Byron, Mischa Auer, Donald Cook, Frank Shields. WB is a sailor.

44. ***Little Big Shot.*** WB 1935. Michael Curtiz. Robert Armstrong, Glenda Farrell, Sybil Jason, Edward Everett Horton, Jack LaRue, J. Carrol Naish, Edgar Kennedy. In this "poor man's *Little Miss Marker*," WB is a hood.

45. ***She Gets Her Man.*** Univ 1935. William Nigh. Zasu Pitts, Helen Twelvetrees, Hugh O'Connell, Warren Hymer, Bert Gordon. WB is a mug.

46. ***Guard That Girl.*** Col 1935. Lambert Hillyer. Florence Rice, Robert Allen, Elizabeth Risdon, Barbara Kent, Arthur Hohl. WB is a detective.

47. ***Last Days of Pompeii.*** RKO 1935. Ernest B. Schoedsack. Preston Foster, Basil Rathbone, Dorothy Wilson, Alan Hale, Louis Calhern, David Holt, Zeffie Tilbury, John Wood. Lowly blacksmith Foster's rise to patrician is stymied by, among others, gladiator WB.

48. ***Waterford Lady.*** Mascot 1935. Joseph Santley. Ann Rutherford, J. Farrell MacDonald, Purnell Pratt, Frank Albertson. WB is a henchman.

49. ***His Night Out.*** Univ 1935. William Nigh. Edward Everett Horton, Irene Hervey, Jack LaRue, Robert McWade, Willard Robertson. WB is a gangster.

50. ***The Leathernecks Have Landed.*** Rep 1936. Howard Bretherton. Lew Ayres, James Ellison, Isabel Jewell, J. Carrol Naish, James Burke, Clay Clement, Paul Porcasi. WB is a marine.

51. ***The Bride Walks Out.*** RKO 1936. Leigh Jason. Barbara Stanwyck, Robert Young, Gene Raymond, Ned Sparks, Helen Broderick, Billy Gilbert, Vivian Oakland. WB is a mover.

52. ***Too Tough to Kill.*** Col 1936. D. Ross Lederman. Victor Jory, Sally O'Neill, Thurston Hall, Johnny Arthur, Robert Gleckler, George McKay, Robert Middlemass. WB is one of the workmen at a labor camp who mistrusts newcomer Jory.

53. ***Muss 'Em Up.*** RKO 1935. Charles Vidor. Preston Foster, Alan Mowbray, Ralph Morgan, Margaret Callahan, Maxie Rosenbloom, Molly Lamont, Robert Middlemass, John Carroll. WB is a hired thug.

54. ***The Case Against Mrs. Ames.*** Par 1936. William Seiter, Madeleine Carroll, George Brent, Alan Baxter, Beulah Bondi, Arthur Treacher, Edward Brophy, Esther Dale, Scotty Beckett. WB is a man at a newsstand.

55. *Pride of the Marines.* Col 1936. D. Ross Lederman. Charles Bickford, Florence Rice, Robert Allen, Billy Burrud, Thurston Hall, Joseph Sawyer, George McKay. WB is one of a group of marine buddies.

56. *Cattle Thief.* Col 1936. Spencer Gordon Bennet. Ken Maynard, Geneva Mitchell, Sheldon Lewis, Roger Williams, Glenn Strange. WB is an outlaw.

57. *The Man Who Lived Twice.* Col 1936. Harry Lachman. Ralph Bellamy, Marian Marsh, Isabel Jewell, Thurston Hall, Ann Doran, Nana Bryant. WB is a loyal henchman of a gangster who gets a personality change.

58. *Without Orders.* RKO 1936. Lew Landers. Sally Eilers, Robert Armstrong, Charles Grapewin, Francis Sage, Frank M. Thomas. WB is the co-pilot of an airliner.

59. *They Met in a Taxi.* Col 1936. Alfred Green. Chester Morris, Fay Wray, Lionel Stander, Raymond Walburn, Henry Mollison, Kenneth Harlan. WB is a policeman.

60. *Crash Donovan.* Univ 1936. Jean Negulesco and William Nigh. Jack Holt, Nan Grey, John King, Eddie Acuff. WB is a motorcycle cop.

61. *Conflict.* Univ 1936. David Howard. John Wayne, Jean Rogers, Tommy Bupp, Eddie Borden, Harry Woods. Wayne exposes fight promoter WB.

62. *Legion of Terror.* Col 1936. Charles C. Coleman. Bruce Cabot, Marguerite Churchill, Crawford Weaver, Charles Wilson, John Hamilton. WB is killed by the Klan-like organization he belonged to.

63. *The Devil's Playground.* Col 1936. Erle C. Kenton. Richard Dix, Chester Morris, Dolores Del Rio, Pierre Watkin, George McKay, Francis McDonald, John Gallaudet, Ann Doran. WB is a member of a diving team.

64. *You Only Live Once.* UA 1937. Fritz Lang. Sylvia Sidney, Henry Fonda, Barton MacLane, William Gargan, Jean Dixon, Chic Sale, Jerome Cowan, Margaret Hamilton, Guinn Williams, Warren Hymer, Jonathan Hale, Wade Boteler. WB is a prison guard.

65. *Park Avenue Logger.* RKO 1937. David Howard. George O'Brien, Beatrice Roberts, Willard Robertson, Bert Hanlon, Gertrude Short, Hal K. Dawson. WB almost married the woman whose logging operation he has tried to sabotage.

66. *23½ Hours Leave.* Grand National 1937. John Blystone. James Ellison, Arthur Lake, Ruth Terry, Ray Walker, Murray Alper. WB is a sergeant.

67. *Night Key.* Univ 1937. Lloyd Corrigan. Boris Karloff, Warren Hull, Jean Rogers, Hobart Cavanaugh, Alan Baxter, Samuel S. Hinds. WB is one of the gangsters trying to use Karloff's skills in a robbery.

68. *Topper.* MGM 1937. Norman McLeod. Constance Bennett, Cary Grant, Roland Young, Billie Burke, Eugene Pallette, Alan Mowbray, Hedda Hopper, Arthur Lake, Virginia Sale, Hoagy Carmichael. WB is a chauffeur.

69. *The Go Getter.* WB 1937. Busby Berkeley. George Brent, Anita Louise, Charles Winninger, John Eldredge, Henry O'Neill, Joseph Crehan,

Gordon Oliver, Eddie Acuff, Willard Robertson, Helen Valkis. Disabled war veteran Brent shows his mettle against tough guys like WB.

70. ***The Wildcatter.*** Univ. 1937. Lewis D. Collins. Scott Colton, Jean Rogers, Jack Smart, Russell Hicks, Suzanne Kaaren. WB is an oilman.

71. ***Dead End.*** Goldwyn-UA 1937. William Wyler. Sylvia Sidney, Joel McCrea, Humphrey Bogart, Wendy Barrie, Claire Trevor, Gabriel Dell, Leo Gorsey, Huntz Hall, Billy Halop, Allen Jenkins, Marjorie Main, Bernard Punsley, Minor Watson. Doorman WB is a favorite victim of razzing by the neighboring Dead End Kids.

72. ***They Gave Him a Gun.*** MGM 1937. W. S. Van Dyke. Spencer Tracy, Gladys George, Franchot Tone, Cliff Edward, Charles Trowbridge, Mary Treen, Edgar Dearing, Gavin Gordon, Joseph Sawyer. WB is a cop.

73. ***Marry the Girl.*** WB 1937. William McGann. Mary Boland, Frank McHugh, Hugh Herbert, Mischa Auer, Carol Hughes, Allen Jenkins, Alan Mowbray, Hugh O'Connell, Teddy Hart. WB is a motorcycle cop.

74. ***Escape by Night.*** Rep 1937. Hamilton McFadden. William Hall, Anne Nagel, Steffi Duna, Dean Jagger, Murray Alper, George Meeker, Charles Waldron, Anthony Warde. WB is a member of a gang on the lam.

75. ***Hawaii Calls.*** RKO 1937. Edward Cline. Bobby Breen, Ned Sparks, Warren Hull, Irvin S. Cobb, Gloria Holden, Pia Lani. WB is an officer on a steamship.

76. ***Over the Wall.*** WB 1937. Frank McDonald. Dick Foran, June Travis, Joan Litel, Dick Purcell, George E. Stone, Veda Ann Borg, Tommy Bupp, Raymond Hatton, John Hamilton. WB is a prison guard.

77. ***Penitentiary.*** Col 1938. John Brahm. John Howard, Walter Connolly, Jean Parker, Robert Barrat, Arthur Hohl, Marc Lawrence, Marjorie Main, Ann Doran. WB is a convict-barber.

78. ***Of Human Hearts.*** MGM 1938. Clarence Brown. Walter Huston, James Stewart, Beulah Bondi, Charles Coburn, Guy Kibbee, John Carradine, Gene Reynolds, Ann Rutherford, Charley Grapewin, Gene Lockhart, Leatrice Joy Gilbert. WB is a troublemaker.

79. ***Mr. Moto's Gamble.*** 20th 1938. James Tinling. Peter Lorre, Keye Luke, Lynn Bari, Dick Baldwin, Douglas Fowley, Maxie Rosenbloom, Jayne Regan, Harold Huber. WB is a slow-witted fighter.

80. ***Born to Be Wild.*** Rep 1938. Joseph Kane. Ralph Byrd, Doris Weston, Robert Emmett Keane, Charles Williams, Bentley Hewlett. WB is a trucker.

81. ***The Law West of Tombstone.*** RKO 1938. Glenn Tryon. Harry Carey, Tom Holt, Evelyn Brent, Allan Lane, Tom Tyler, Clarence Kolb, Jean Rouverol, Bradley Page, Paul Guilfoyle. WB is a gunslinger.

82. ***Bringing Up Baby.*** RKO 1938. Howard Hawks. Katharine Hepburn, Cary Grant, Charles Ruggles, May Robson, Barry Fitzgerald, Walter Catlett, Fritz Feld, Jonathan Hale, Leona Roberts, Jack Carson. WB is a motorcycle cop.

83. ***Reformatory.*** Col 1938. Lewis Collins. Jack Holt, Bobby Jordan,

Charlotte Wynters, Grant Mitchell, Sonny Bupp. WB is a disciplinarian working at a reform school.

84. *The Amazing Dr. Clitterhouse.* WB 1938. Anatole Litvak. Edward G. Robinson, Claire Trevor, Humphrey Bogart, Donald Crisp, Allen Jenkins, Gale Page, Maxie Rosenbloom, John Litel, Henry O'Neill, Vladimir Sokoloff, Curt Bois, Bert Hanlon. WB is a member of a gang of crooks.

85. *Professor Beware.* Par 1938. Elliot Nugent. Harold Lloyd, Raymond Walburn, Phyllis Welch, William Frawley, Lionel Stander, Etienne Girardot, Montagu Love, Cora Witherspoon, Thurston Hall, Sterling Hollaway, Mary Lou Lender. WB is a cop.

86. *Submarine Patrol.* 20th 1938. John Ford. Richard Greene, Nancy Kelly, Preston Foster, George Bancroft, Slim Summerville, John Carradine, Joan Valerie, Warren Hymer, Henry Armetta, Douglas Fowley, Charles Trowbridge, Robert Lowery. WB plays a World War I–era sailor in this film, reuniting with Ford after their longest professional separation (six years).

87. *You Can't Take It With You.* Col 1938. Frank Capra. Jean Arthur, Lionel Barrymore, James Stewart, Edward Arnold, Mischa Auer, Spring Byington, Samuel S. Hinds, Halliwell Hobbes, Donald Meek, Ann Miller, H. B. Warner, Lillian Yarbo, Eddie Anderson, Harry Davenport, Mary Forbes, Charles Lane, Dub Taylor. WB is a detective.

88. *Going Places.* WB 1938. Ray Enright. Dick Powell, Anita Louise, Louis Armstrong, Allen Jenkins, Ronald Reagan. WB is a security guard.

89. *Pardon Our Nerve.* 20th 1939. H. Bruce Humberstone. Lynn Bari, June Gale, Michael Whalen, Guinn Williams. WB is a punchy fighter.

90. *They Made Me a Criminal.* WB 1939. Busby Berkeley. John Garfield, Claude Rains, Gloria Dickson, May Robson, Leo Gorcey, Huntz Hall, Billy Halop, Bobby Jordan, Ann Sheridan, Robert Gleckler, Barbara Pepper, John Ridgely, Gabriel Dell. WB is an amateur fight promoter.

91. *Made for Each Other.* UA 1939. John Cromwell. Carole Lombard, James Stewart, Charles Coburn, Lucile Watson, Eddie Quillan, Alma Kruger, Esther Dale, Louise Beavers, Donald Briggs. WB is a pilot dispatcher.

92. *The Oklahoma Kid.* WB 1939. Lloyd Bacon. James Cagney, Humphrey Bogart, Rosemary Lane, Donald Crisp, Harvey Stephens, Hugh Sothern, Charles Middleton, Edward Pawley, John Miljan. WB is a member of Bogart's gang.

93. *Dodge City.* WB 1939. Michael Curtiz. Errol Flynn, Olivia de Havilland, Ann Sheridan, Bruce Cabot, Frank McHugh, Alan Hale, John Litel, Henry O'Neill, Henry Travers, Gloria Holden, Victory Jory, Guinn Williams, William Lundigan, Bob Watson. WB is a member of Cabot's gang.

94. *The Kid from Kokomo.* WB 1939. Lewis Seiler. Pat O'Brien, Wayne Morris, Joan Blondell, May Robson, Jane Wyman, Sidney Toler. WB is a fighter.

95. *Mr. Moto in Danger Island.* 20th 1939. Herbert Leeds. Peter Lorre, Jean Hersholt, Amanda Duff, Warren Hymer, Leon Ames, Douglass Dumbrille, Richard Lane, Robert Lowery. As in his previous *Moto* picture, WB is a dense prizefighter (though with a smaller bit).

96. ***Girl from Mexico.*** RKO 1939. Leslie Goodwins. Lupe Velez, Leon Errol, Donald Woods, Linda Hayes, Elizabeth Risdon, Donald MacBride, Edward Raquello. In the first of the sorry *Mexican Spitfire* series, WB is Mexican Pete.

97. ***Confessions of a Nazi Spy.*** WB 1939. Anatole Litvak. Edward G. Robinson, Francis Lederer, Paul Lukas, George Sanders, Henry O'Neill, Lya Lys, James Stephenson, Sig Rumann, Grace Stafford, Dorothy Tree, Joe Sawyer. WB is an American Legionnaire who speaks out against Nazism.

98. ***Return of the Cisco Kid.*** 20th 1939. Herbert Leeds. Warner Baxter, Lynn Bari, Cesar Romero, Kane Richmond, Robert Barrat, Henry Hull, C. Henry Gordon, Chris-Pin Martin, Adrian Morris. WB is a Western thug.

99. ***Young Mr. Lincoln.*** 20th 1939. John Ford. Henry Fonda, Alice Brady, Marjorie Weaver, Richard Cromwell, Arleen Whelan, Eddie Collins, Donald Meek, Pauline Moore, Eddie Quillan, Spencer Charters, Milburn Stone. WB is a suspect-witness in a murder trial in which Abe Lincoln (Fonda) is the defense counsel.

100. ***Trouble in Sundown.*** RKO 1939. David Howard. George O'Brien, Rosalind Keith, Cy Kendall, Chill Wills, Earl Dwire. WB is another henchman.

101. ***Waterfront.*** WB 1939. Terry Morse. Gloria Dickson, Dennis Morgan, Marie Wilson, Larry Williams, Sheila Bromley, Aldrich Bowker, Frank Faylen. Troublesome WB brawls with Morgan.

102. ***Dust Be My Destiny.*** WB 1939. Lewis Seiler. John Garfield, Priscilla Lane, Frank McHugh, Alan Hale, John Litel, Charles Grapewin, Billy Halop, Bobby Jordan, Stanley Ridges, Henry Armetta, Victor Kilian. WB brawls with Garfield on the back of a boxcar.

103. ***Frontier Marshal.*** 20th 1939. Allan Dwan. Randolph Scott, Nancy Kelly, Cesar Romero, Binnie Barnes, John Carradine, Edward Norris, Tom Tyler, Eddie Foy, Jr., Lon Chaney, Jr. WB is a crooked lawman.

104. ***Drums Along the Mohawk.*** 20th 1939. John Ford. Claudette Colbert, Henry Fonda, Edna May Oliver, John Carradine, Eddie Collins, Jessie Ralph, Arthur Shields, Dorris Bowden, Robert Lowery, Roger Imhof, Kay Linaker, Francis Ford. WB is an eighteenth century American pioneer.

105. ***Gone with the Wind.*** Selznick-MGM 1939. Victor Fleming. Clark Gable, Vivien Leigh, Leslie Howard, Olivia de Havilland, Hattie McDaniel, Laura Hope Crews, Jane Darwell, Harry Davenport, Victor Jory, Evelyn Keyes, Thomas Mitchell, Ona Munson, Carroll Nye, Barbara O'Neill, Oscar Polk, Ann Rutherford, Rand Brooks, Butterfly McQueen, George Reeves. In the second half of this classic, WB is Gable's Yankee captain pal.

106. ***The Grapes of Wrath.*** 20th 1940. John Ford. Henry Fonda, Jane Darwell, John Carradine, Charles Grapewin, Dorris Bowden, Russell Simpson, John Qualen, Eddie Quillan, Frank Sully, Zeffie Tilbury, Darryl Hickman, Shirley Mills, Grant Mitchell. WB is one of the California policemen with whom a family of Oklahoma migrants comes in contact.

107. *Heaven with a Barbed Wire Fence.* 20th 1940. Ricardo Cortez. Jean Rogers, Glenn Ford, Marjorie Rambeau, Raymond Walburn, Nicholas (Richard) Conte, Eddie Collins, Irving Bacon, Kay Linaker. WB is a ruffian among a group of homeless wanderers. Ford and Conte's first film.

108. *Virginia City.* WB 1940. Michael Curtiz. Errol Flynn, Miriam Hopkins, Randolph Scott, Humphrey Bogart, Frank McHugh, Alan Hale, John Litel, Guinn Williams, Douglass Dumbrille, Moroni Olson. WB is in uniform again, stopping travellers during the Civil War.

109. *Little Old New York.* 20th 1940. Henry King. Alice Faye, Fred MacMurray, Richard Greene, Brenda Joyce, Andy Devine, Henry Stephenson, Fritz Feld, Robert Middlemass, Virginia Brissac, Theodore Von Elitz. WB is a ruffian who makes trouble for steamboat company founder Fulton (Greene).

110. *Buck Benny Rides Again.* Par 1940. Mark Sandrich. Jack Benny, Ellen Drew, Eddie "Rochester" Anderson, Virginia Dale, Dennis Day, Andy Devine, Phil Harris, Don Wilson, James Burke, Morris Ankrum. Tough cowboy WB menaces showoff dude Benny.

111. *The Mortal Storm.* MGM 1940. Frank Borzage. Margaret Sullavan, James Stewart, Robert Young, Frank Morgan, Bonita Granville, Robert Stack, Irene Rich, Maria Ouspenskaya, William T. Orr, Gene Reynolds, Esther Dale, Dan Dailey, Jr., Russell Hicks, William Edmunds, Granville Bates. WB is a German storm trooper in Young's command.

112. *Sailor's Lady.* 20th 1940. Allan Dwan. Nancy Kelly, Jon Hall, Dana Andrews, Joan Davis, Larry "Buster" Crabbe, Mary Nash, Katherine Aldridge, Peggy Ryan. WB is a shore patrolman.

113. *The Cisco Kid and the Lady.* 20th 1940. Herbert Leeds. Cesar Romero, Marjorie Weaver, George Montgomery, Virginia Field, Robert Barrat, Chris-Pin Martin, Harry Green. WB is another troublesome cowboy.

114. *Kit Carson.* UA 1940. George B. Seitz. Jon Hall, Lynn Bari, Dana Andrews, Harold Huber, Renie Riano, C. Henry Gordon, Clayton Moore, Charles Stevens, William Farnum, Raymond Hatton, Edwin Maxwell, Harry Strang. WB is a saddle buddy of Carson (Hall).

115. *The Long Voyage Home.* UA 1940. John Ford. John Wayne, Thomas Mitchell, Ian Hunter, Barry Fitzgerald, J. M. Kerrigan, Wilfred Lawson, Mildred Natwick, John Qualen, Joseph Sawyer, Arthur Shields, Douglas Walton. WB is an American among Eugene O'Neill's melting pot crew of a ship carrying munitions. This was his best Ford film to date.

116. *Santa Fe Trail.* WB 1940. Michael Curtiz. Errol Flynn, Olivia de Havilland, Ronald Reagan, Raymond Massey, Alan Hale, Van Heflin, William Lundigan, Gene Reynolds, Alan Baxter, Henry O'Neill, Guinn Williams, John Litel. WB is a Civil War soldier.

117. *Tobacco Road.* 20th 1941. John Ford. Charles Grapewin, Gene Tierney, Marjorie Rambeau, Dana Andrews, Elizabeth Patterson, Grant Mitchell, Russell Simpson, Charles Halton. WB is a slow-witted bumpkin.

118. *A Man Betrayed.* Rep 1941. John H. Auer. John Wayne, Frances

Dee, Edward Ellis, Wallace Ford, Alexander Granach, Harold Huber, Barnett Parker, Tim Ryan, Harry Hayden, Russell Hicks. Lawyer Wayne gets involved with crooked politicos trying to solve a murder committed by WB.

119. ***Doctors Don't Tell.*** Rep 1941. Jacques Tourneur. John Beal, Florence Rice, Edward Norris, Douglas Fowley, Grady Sutton, Joseph Crehan, Paul Porcasi. WB is a cop.

120. ***The Shepherd of the Hills.*** Par 1941. Henry Hathaway. John Wayne, Betty Field, Harry Carey, Beulah Bondi, James Barton, Marjorie Main, Samuel S. Hinds, Marc Lawrence, John Qualen. WB is a backwoods family member.

121. ***Manpower.*** WB 1941. Raoul Walsh. Edward G. Robinson, Marlene Dietrich, George Raft, Alan Hale, Barton MacLane, Frank McHugh, Eve Arden, Walter Catlett, Egon Brecher, Joyce Compton. WB is a power lineman co-worker of Robinson and Raft.

122. ***Sergeant York.*** WB 1941. Howard Hawks. Gary Cooper, Walter Brennan, Joan Leslie, Noah Beery, Jr., Dickie Moore, Stanley Ridges, George Tobias, Margaret Wycherly, Erville Alderson, Clem Bevans, David Bruce, Harvey Stephens. WB is one of York's (Cooper) "down home" pals.

123. ***The Maltese Falcon.*** WB 1941. John Huston. Humphrey Bogart, Mary Astor, Peter Lorre, Gladys George, Barton MacLane, Sydney Greenstreet, Lee Patrick, Jerome Cowan, Elisha Cook, Jr., Charles Burke, Walter Huston (unbilled). WB is Sam Spade's (Bogart) police officer friend.

124. ***Swamp Water.*** 20th 1941. Jean Renoir. Dana Andrews, Anne Baxter, Walter Brennan, Walter Huston, Virginia Gilmore, John Carradine, Eugene Pallette, Mary Howard, Guinn Williams, Joseph Sawyer. WB is one of the backwoods toughs making trouble for Andrews.

125. ***Wild Bill Hickok Rides.*** WB 1941. Ray Enright. Constance Bennett, Bruce Cabot, Warren William, Betty Brewer, Howard Da Silva, Faye Emerson, Russell Simpson. WB is a flunky of villainous William.

126. ***Ten Gentlemen from West Point.*** 20th 1942. Henry Hathaway. Maureen O'Hara, George Montgomery, Laird Cregar, John Sutton, John Sheppard (Shepperd Strudwick), Victor Francen, Harry Davenport, Douglass Dumbrille, Ralph Byrd, Tom Neal, Blake Edwards. WB is a troublemaker, victimizing the first military cadets at West Point.

127. ***The Falcon Takes Over.*** RKO 1942. Irving Reis. George Sanders, Lynn Bari, James Gleason, Allen Jenkins, Anne Revere, Helen Gilbert, Hans Conried, Turhan Bey. A disguised version of Raymond Chandler's *Farewell, My Lovely*, with WB as a hulking hood seeking his missing girl.

128. ***Sin Town.*** Univ 1942. Ray Enright. Broderick Crawford, Constance Bennett, Patric Knowles, Leo Carrillo, Andy Devine, Anne Gwynne, Hobart Bosworth, Arthur Aylesworth, Ralf Harolde, Jack Mulhall, Oscar O'Shea, Bryant Washburn. WB, one of the crooks preying on a modern western town, is defeated by reformed con man Crawford.

129. ***Gentleman Jim.*** WB 1942. Raoul Walsh. Errol Flynn, Alexis Smith, Jack Carson, Alan Hale, John Loder, William Frawley, Minor Watson, Rhys

Williams, Arthur Shields, Dorothy Vaughn, James Flavin. WB's best performance in a non–Ford picture as outgoing champion John L. Sullivan.

130. *Hitler—Dead or Alive.* PRC 1943. Nick Grinde. Dorothy Tree, Warren Hymer, Paul Fix, Russell Hicks, Felix Basch, Robert Watson, Bruce Edwards. WB is one of three men who set out to kill the Nazi leader.

131. *Slightly Dangerous.* MGM 1943. Wesley Ruggles. Lana Turner, Robert Young, Walter Brennan, Dame May Whitty, Eugene Pallette, Alan Mowbray, Ray Collins, Florence Bates, Bobby Blake, Ann Doran, Millard Mitchell. WB is a department store detective.

132. *Hello Frisco, Hello.* 20th 1943. Bruce Humberstone. Alice Faye, John Payne, Jack Oakie, Lynn Bari, Laird Cregar, June Havoc, George Barbier, Aubrey Mather, John Archer, Frank Orth, George Lloyd, Frank Darien. WB is a nemesis of Barbary Coast wheeler-dealer Payne.

133. *They Came to Blow Up America.* 20th 1943. Edward Ludwig. George Sanders, Anna Sten, Sig Ruman, Dennis Hoey, Robert Barrat, Ludwig Stossel, Charles McGraw. WB is an American naval officer.

134. *A Guy Named Joe.* MGM 1943. Victor Fleming. Spencer Tracy, Irene Dunne, Van Johnson, Lionel Barrymore, James Gleason, Barry Nelson, Don DeFore, Henry O'Neill, Esther Williams, Addison Richards, Charles Smith, Mark Daniels, William Bishop, Mary Elliott, Walter Sande. WB is the best friend of pilot Tracy, who dies in battle but whose spirit returns.

135. *The Sullivans.* 20th 1944. Lloyd Bacon. Anne Baxter, Thomas Mitchell, Selena Royle, John Campbell, James Cardwell, George Offerman, Jr., Edward Ryan, Trudy Marshall, Roy Roberts, Bobby Driscoll, Mae Marsh, John Alvin, Addison Richards. WB is a Naval recruiting officer who handles the enlistment of the Sullivan brothers. The five actors playing the title roles are insufferable.

136. *Home in Indiana.* 20th 1944. Henry Hathaway. Walter Brennan, Jeanne Crain, June Haver, Lon McCallister, Charlotte Greenwood, George Cleveland, Willie Best, Charles Dingle. WB runs a horse breeding ranch.

137. *Tall in the Saddle.* RKO 1944. Edwin L. Marin. John Wayne, Ella Raines, George "Gabby" Hayes, Audrey Long, Elisabeth Risdon, Paul Fix, Raymond Hatton, Emory Parnell, Russell Wade, Wheaton Chambers, Frank Puglia. WB, a corrupt Western judge, runs afoul of Wayne.

138. *Dakota.* Rep 1945. Joseph Kane. John Wayne, Vera Hruba Ralston, Walter Brennan, Ona Munson, Hugo Haas, Mike Mazurki, Grant Withers, Paul Fix, Robert Livingston, Olive Blakeney, Robert Barrat, Nicodemus Stewart, Paul Hurst, Olin Howlin, Pierre Watkin. Newlywed pioneer Wayne throws a crimp in the plans of WB, who's grabbing prime land for the oncoming railroad.

139. *They Were Expendable.* MGM 1945. John Ford. Robert Montgomery, John Wayne, Donna Reed, Jack Holt, Leon Ames, Donald Curtis, Paul Langton, Cameron Mitchell, Marshall Thompson, Arthur Walsh, Jeff York, Robert Barrat. WB is a veteran Navy man in World War II. Ford's first Hollywood picture since '41.

140. *Canyon Passage.* Univ 1946. Jacques Tourneur. Dana Andrews, Brian Donlevy, Susan Hayward, Patricia Roc, Hoagy Carmichael, Andy Devine, Rose Hobart, Stanley Ridges, Lloyd Bridges, Halliwell Hobbes, Ray Holden, Onslow Stevens, James Cardwell, Ray Teal, Erville Alderson. WB returns to brutishness as a pioneer community's chief troublemaker.

141. *My Darling Clementine.* 20th 1946. John Ford. Henry Fonda, Victor Mature, Linda Darnell, Walter Brennan, Cathy Downs, Tim Holt, John Ireland, Alan Mowbray, Grant Withers, Jane Darwell, Francis Ford, J. Farrell MacDonald, Roy Roberts, Russell Simpson. WB is Morgan Earp. This is a partial remake of the '39 film *Frontier Marshal,* also with Bond.

142. *It's a Wonderful Life.* RKO 1946. Frank Capra. James Stewart, Donna Reed, Lionel Barrymore, Thomas Mitchell, Henry Travers, Beulah Bondi, Frank Faylen, Gloria Grahame, Samuel S. Hinds, Todd Karns, Mary Treen, H. B. Warner, Frank Albertson, Sheldon Leonard, Lillian Randolph, Charles Williams. Classic film with WB as Stewart's policeman friend.

143. *The Fugitive.* RKO 1947. John Ford. Henry Fonda, Dolores del Rio, Pedro Armendariz, J. Carrol Naish, Leo Carrillo, Robert Armstrong, John Qualen, Fortunio Bonanova, Chris-Pin Martin, Miguel Inclan. WB is an American outlaw who sacrifices himself for a fellow fugitive, priest Fonda.

144. *Unconquered.* Par 1947. Cecil B. DeMille. Gary Cooper, Paulette Goddard, Boris Karloff, Howard Da Silva, Cecil Kellaway, Henry Wilcoxon, C. Aubrey Smith, Katherine DeMille, Virginia Grey, Porter Hall, Mike Mazurki, Gavin Muir, Alan Napier, Jane Nigh, Victor Varconi, Robert Warwick, Lloyd Bridges. WB is a Revolutionary War era pioneer (and friend of Cooper).

145. *Fort Apache.* RKO 1948. John Ford. John Wayne, Henry Fonda, Shirley Temple, Pedro Armendariz, John Agar, Guy Kibbee, Anna Lee, Victor McLaglen, George O'Brien, Irene Rich, Dick Foran, Francis Ford, Miguel Inclan, Mae Marsh, Jack Pennick, Grant Withers. WB is a dedicated Cavalry sergeant-major whose son (Agar) has become an officer.

146. *The Time of Your Life.* UA 1948. H. C. Potter. James Cagney, William Bendix, Jeanne Cagney, Broderick Crawford, Wayne Morris, Gale Page, Tom Powers, James Barton, Paul Draper, Richard Erdman, Howard Freeman, Natalie Schafer. WB is a construction worker who likes barroom arguments.

147. *Tap Roots.* Univ 1948. George Marshall. Van Heflin, Susan Hayward, Boris Karloff, Richard Long, Julie London, Whitfield Conner, Arthur Shields, Griff Barnett, Sondra Rogers, Ruby Dandridge. Mississippi family patriarch WB goes mad because of pressures in the Civil War South.

148. *Three Godfathers.* MGM 1948. John Ford. John Wayne, Pedro Armendariz, Harry Carey, Jr., Mildred Natwick, Guy Kibbee, Jane Darwell, Mae Marsh, Ben Johnson, Dorothy Ford, Hank Worden. Overly sentimental Ford remake of worthier films with WB as the first of several sympathetic lawmen.

149. *Joan of Arc.* RKO 1948. Victor Fleming. Ingrid Bergman, Jose

Ferrer, Hurd Hatfield, John Ireland, Francis L. Sullivan, George Coulouris, Cecil Kellaway, Gene Lockhart, J. Carrol Naish, Richard Ney, Irene Rich, Selena Royle, Shepperd Strudwick. WB is a French soldier.

150. *Singing Guns.* Rep 1950. R. G. Springsteen. Vaughn Monroe, Ella Raines, Walter Brennan, Jeff Corey, Barry Kelley, Rex Lease, Harry Shannon, Tom Fadden, Ralph Dunn, Jimmie Dodd, Billy Gray, Mary Eleanor Donahue. Sheriff WB learns that a Western outlaw (Monroe) is really a good-hearted soul.

151. *Riding High.* Par 1950. Frank Capra. Bing Crosby, Coleen Gray, Charles Bickford, William Demarest, Douglass Dumbrille, Frances Gifford, James Gleason, Oliver Hardy, Paul Harvey, Margaret Hamilton, Percy Kilbride, Charles Lane, Gene Lockhart, Marjorie Lord, Clarence Muse, Raymond Walburn. WB acted in some new scenes to match his footage from *Broadway Bill* (1934).

152. *Wagonmaster.* RKO 1950. John Ford. Joanne Dru, Ben Johnson, Harry Carey, Jr., Alan Mowbray, Charles Kemper, Jane Darwell, James Arness, Hank Worden, Jack Pennick. WB is the Mormon elder and leader of a wagon train besieged by a family of outlaws.

153. *Kiss Tomorrow Goodbye.* WB 1950. Gordon Douglas. James Cagney, Barbara Payton, Luther Adler, Helena Carter, Barton MacLane, Steve Brodie, William Frawley, Herbert Heyes, Robert Karns, John Litel, Dan Riss, Rhys Williams, Neville Brand. Crooked cops WB and MacLane become accomplices of sociopathic Cagney.

154. *The Great Missouri Raid.* Par 1950. Gordon Douglas. Macdonald Carey, Wendell Corey, Ellen Drew, Anne Revere, Bruce Bennett, Edgar Buchanan, Bill Williams, Barry Kelly. Another version of the legend of the outlaw James boys, with WB as the Pinkerton man tracking them.

155. *Operation Pacific.* WB 1951. George Waggner. John Wayne, Patricia Neal, Philip Carey, Scott Forbes, Paul Picerni, Bill Campbell, Kathryn Givney, Martin Milner, Cliff Clark, Jack Pennick, Virginia Brissac, Sam Edwards. WB is a Naval sub commander who sacrifices his life.

156. *Only the Valiant.* WB 1951. Gordon Douglas. Gregory Peck, Barbara Payton, Gig Young, Lon Chaney, Jr., Warner Anderson, Michael Ansara, Neville Brand, Steve Brodie, Jeff Corey, Herbert Heyes, Terry Kilburn, Hugh Sanders. WB is one of a motley crew of cavalrymen assigned to defend a fort from Indians.

157. *On Dangerous Ground.* RKO 1951. Nicholas Ray. Ida Lupino, Robert Ryan, Ed Begley, Charles Kemper, Cleo Moore, Anthony Ross, Olive Carey, Frank Ferguson. WB is a vengeance-seeking rural lawman.

158. *Hellgate.* Lippert 1952. Charles Marquis Warren. Sterling Hayden, Joan Leslie, James Arness, Robert J. Wilke, Peter Coe, Marshall Bradford, John Pickard, Richard Paxton. WB runs a federal prison in the Old West.

159. *Thunderbirds.* Rep 1952. John H. Auer. John Derek, John Barrymore, Jr., Mona Freeman, Gene Evans, Eileen Christy, Ben Cooper, Barton MacLane, Wally Cassell, Mae Clarke, Slim Pickens. Seasoned veteran WB guides new recruit flyers through the early days of World War II.

160. *The Quiet Man.* Rep 1952. John Ford. John Wayne, Maureen O'Hara, Barry Fitzgerald, Victor McLaglen, Mildred Natwick, Francis Ford, Eileen Crowe, Arthur Shields, James Lilburn, Jack MacGowran, Sean McClory, May Craig. WB is an understanding Catholic priest in a small Irish community.

161. *The Moonlighter.* WB 1953. Roy Rowland. Barbara Stanwyck, Fred MacMurray, William Ching, John Dierkes, Morris Ankrum, Jack Elam, Charles Halton, Norman Leavitt. Western bad guy WB meets some formidable competition (Stanwyck and MacMurray). Originally released in 3D.

162. *Blowing Wild.* WB 1953. Hugo Fregonese. Gary Cooper, Barbara Stanwyck, Anthony Quinn, Ruth Roman, Ian MacDonald, Richard Karlan, Juan Garcia. In Mexico, Cooper goes to work for Quinn's oil operation after his trucker partner WB is injured in an encounter with bandits.

163. *Hondo.* WB 1953. John Farrow. John Wayne, Geraldine Page, Lee Aaker, James Arness, Michael Pate, Rodolfo Acosta, Leo Gordon, Tom Irish, Paul Fix. WB's second, and last, 3D movie. He plays an old saddle buddy of the title character (Wayne). *Fort Dobbs* (1958) was an uncredited remake.

164. *Gypsy Colt.* MGM 1954. Andrew Marton. Frances Dee, Donna Corcoran, Lee Van Cleef, Larry Keating, Burt Mustin, Bobby Hyatt, Nacho Galindo, Jester Hairston. Struggling rancher WB is forced to sell his daughter's horse.

165. *Johnny Guitar.* Rep 1954. Nicholas Ray. Joan Crawford, Sterling Hayden, Mercedes McCambridge, Scott Brady, Ernest Borgnine, Ben Cooper, John Carradine, Royal Dano, Frank Ferguson, Paul Fix, Ian MacDonald, Robert Osterloh, Rhys Williams, Will Wright. WB is a leading citizen of a town under the thumb of vengeful McCambridge.

166. *The Bob Mathias Story.* Allied Artists 1954. Francis D. Lyon. Bob Mathias, Melba Mathias, Howard Petrie, Ann Doran, Paul Bryan, Diane Jergens. WB is the local coach who first sees the athletic prowess in Mathias.

167. *The Long Gray Line.* Col 1955. John Ford. Tyrone Power, Maureen O'Hara, Donald Crisp, Robert Francis, Betsy Palmer, Phil Carey, Harry Carey, Jr., William Leslie, Sean McClory, Peter Graves, Martin Milner, Erin O'Brien Moore, Milburn Stone, Patrick Wayne. Power wonderfully portrays Martin Maher, an Irish immigrant who becomes a sort of "Mr. Chips" of West Point. WB plays one of the commandants during Power's tenure as staff sergeant.

168. *Mister Roberts.* WB 1955. John Ford and Mervyn LeRoy (uncredited directors: Joshua Logan and WB). Henry Fonda, James Cagney, William Powell, Jack Lemmon, Betsy Palmer, Phil Carey, Harry Carey, Jr., Ken Curtis, Nick Adams, Frank Aletter, Fritz Ford, William Henry, Perry Lopez, Martin Milner, Patrick Wayne. Still entertaining version of the stage classic. WB is Chief Petty Officer Dowdy.

169. *A Man Alone.* Rep 1955. Ray Milland. Milland, Mary Murphy, Raymond Burr, Arthur Space, Alan Hale, Jr., Lee Van Cleef, Douglas Spencer, Tom Browne Henry, Kim Spalding, Minerva Urecal, Grandon

Rhodes. A fugitive from the law, Milland proves his decency to lawman WB, whose home he has used for refuge.

170. *The Searchers.* WB 1956. John Ford. John Wayne, Jeffrey Hunter, Vera Miles, Natalie Wood, Olive Carey, Harry Carey, Jr., Ken Curtis, John Qualen, Antonio Moreno, Henry Brandon, Dorothy Jordan, Walter Coy, Pippa Scott, Lana Wood, Hank Worden, Patrick Wayne. Ford's greatest Western and WB's best Ford role. He plays Sam Clayton, Texas Ranger captain and man of God.

171. *Pillars of the Sky.* Univ 1956. George Marshall. Jeff Chandler, Dorothy Malone, Keith Andes, Lee Marvin, Sydney Chaplin, Willis Bouchey, Michael Ansara, Olive Carey, Pat Hogan, Charles Horvath. WB is a kindly missionary who mistakenly believes he can quell an Indian uprising.

172. *Dakota Incident.* Rep 1956. Lewis R. Foster. Linda Darnell, Dale Robertson, John Lund, Regis Toomey, Skip Homeier, Whit Bissell, Irving Bacon, John Doucette, William Fawcett, Malcolm Atterbury. Politician WB tries to reason with marauding Indians.

173. *The Wings of Eagles.* MGM 1957. John Ford. John Wayne, Dan Dailey, Maureen O'Hara, Edmund Lowe, Kenneth Tobey, Ken Curtis, Sig Ruman, Henry O'Neill, Dorothy Jordan, Evelyn Rudie, Charles Trowbridge, James Todd, Barry Kelley, Willis Bouchey, Louis Jean Heydt. WB is crusty movie director John Dodge.

174. *The Halliday Brand.* UA 1957. Joseph H. Lewis. Joseph Cotten, Viveca Lindfors, Betsey Blair, Bill Williams, Jay C. Flippen, Chris Dark, Jeanette Nolan. Western patriarch WB's dominance is challenged by his family.

175. *China Doll.* UA 1958. Frank Borzage. Victor Mature, Li Li Hua, Bob Mathias, Stuart Whitman, Ann McCrea, Johnny Desmond, Elaine Curtis, Tige Andrews, Don Barry, Danny Chang. WB is an Air Force chaplain, lending advice and comfort to flyer Mature as he embarks on an interracial marriage.

176. *Rio Bravo.* WB 1959. Howard Hawks. John Wayne, Dean Martin, Ricky Nelson, Angie Dickinson, Walter Brennan, John Russell, Pedro Gonzalez-Gonzalez, Estelita Rodriguez, Claude Akins, Malcolm Atterbury, Harry Carey, Jr., Nesdon Booth. In his final film role, WB is the trail boss of a cattle drive who vainly tries to aid an old friend (sheriff Wayne) in his battle with the hired guns of a powerful cattleman.

Broderick Crawford

The scene is a fashionable dinner party for members of an American film company in Paris, France. The film's director, an egocentric phony, has just made a catty sexual reference about his hostess' daughter and has been punched in the stomach by the girl's date, the teenage son of a Paris cab driver. Watching all of this is the star of the film within a film, an aging American actor named Broderick Crawford. He applauds the boy, who, being a cinema buff, tells Crawford that it is the same kind of stomach punch that he once delivered to Ward Bond's mid-section in a picture called *Sin Town*. The actor, looking puzzled, asks the boy if he is sure it was Bond and not Richard Widmark he hit. The boy says he's sure, as well he might, since he is right.

The amusing incident is one of the few bright spots in George Roy Hill's *A Little Romance* (1979), which has otherwise very little to do with old Hollywood films. The star of the film was Laurence Olivier, in a Maurice Chevalier–type characterization of an aging French pickpocket helping two romantic adolescents. But the film's best casting decision was the actor who played the veteran Hollywood actor Broderick Crawford, the same person who won the Best Actor Academy Award the year after Olivier won for *Hamlet*. The critics who mentioned this performer in their reviews were in basic agreement. In the fairly small part he had, Broderick Crawford was perfectly cast as himself.

But reviewers have pretty much always felt that Crawford played himself; he is perhaps the least critically respected actor to have ever won the top Oscar. Such a comment about so lengthy a film career as his seems a bit unfair. The fast-talking son of an equally fast-talking actress, Crawford seemed earmarked for a career as a comic actor. Even a powerful stage role could not turn the tide. Only the

Broderick Crawford publicity shot from the early '50s.

intervention of World War II changed things around for him; he suddenly was taken seriously as a dramatic actor—temporarily at least.

He was born on December 9, 1911, in Philadelphia, Pennsylvania, the birthplace of his mother just 21 years earlier. Several record books give his birth name as William Broderick Crawford, but this was only because his father, whose real name was Pendergast, had adopted the stage name of Lester Crawford. The Broderick came from his mother, Helen Broderick. Broderick and Crawford had developed a vaudeville act and, although Philadelphia remained their home base, they spent much of the year touring the country. They did well enough to send their son to the best private schools, but when school was out, young Crawford was usually worked into the performance in some way. This was considered a youthful lark. Like most show business parents of the era, the Crawfords wouldn't consider anything as undignified as a performing career for their son.

In his youth, that kind of thinking was all right with Crawford. He grew up with a strong desire to prove himself without the help of his parents. This desire became even stronger when his mother's unique deadpan comedy delivery came to the attention of Broadway producers. His parents' act had dissolved so that Broderick could begin a successful stage career, primarily in musical revues. The highlight of her stage work was probably the 1931 production of *The Band Wagon* starring Fred and Adele Astaire. By that time, vaudeville was dead, so Crawford was grateful for his wife's success on Broadway and later in Hollywood, where she is best remembered for supporting Astaire and Ginger Rogers. Her son admired what she did, but he had no desire to imitate that.

Instead, he went through all the phases young men experience. He had his football period. Then he had his share of rough jobs, like being a stevedore. Having proven an ability to earn his way in life, Crawford (then in his early twenties) fell into the life of playboy with relative ease. Around the time his mother began appearing in movies, he began to make the rounds of the Broadway casting people. It seemed the natural thing to do; he had not picked up any particular skills, so why not go into the "family business" which at least would help him maintain a carefree lifestyle? The proud young man landed his first good part in the London company of *She Loves Me Not* (1932). He got the role himself, but it was general knowledge whose son he was. He was constantly asked the same question—whether he was as funny as his mother. Though he said no, his early stage work was in comedy, indicating producers' belief in his ability to be funny. By adopting the professional name Broderick Crawford, he was ensuring that the association with both parents would continue. This was mostly due to pride in the family name, not a desire to trade off it.

His work on Broadway brought him in contact with such names as Noël Coward and the Lunts, but garnered him little personal success. He was more of a standout in a formula comedy like *Sweet*

Mystery of Life (1935), which brought him to the attention of Warner Bros. director Lloyd Bacon. Bacon, who had cast Crawford's parents in their first talkie (*Fifty Million Frenchmen*, 1931), was about to direct the screen version of the play, musicalizing it as *Gold Diggers of 1937*. Circumstances prevented Bacon from casting Crawford in the film, but the director promised him a future part. He made his film debut for Samuel Goldwyn in a forgettable screwball comedy, *Woman Chases Man* (1937), with Miriam Hopkins and Joel McCrea. As he had done on the stage, he played a rough-and-tumble character for comedy, teamed here with singer Ella Logan, whose main success continued to be on the stage. That seemed to be Crawford's lot as well; his face didn't photograph well, his voice didn't record well. The new actor appeared quite unpleasant. A part in a Bacon film solved the problem of what to do with him: make him less visible and audible. In *Submarine D-1* (1937), Crawford was lost amidst the many sailors. The shooting was pleasant due to the director's skill and the friendliness of Pat O'Brien, George Brent and Wayne Morris, all of whom would work with Crawford again. Also in the film was young fledgling contractee Ronald Reagan.

Seeing no future for himself in Hollywood, Crawford decided to return to the stage. Fortunately for him, the veteran theatrical producer Sam Harris was looking for a young actor who was big and muscular for the important role of Lennie in a dramatization of the John Steinbeck novel *Of Mice and Men*. It was the break he needed to get away from the comedy roles he had been given because of his name. Harris picked him because there were few who could fit the role—a giant of a man with the mind of a child. Lennie had to tower over George, the friend who took care of him; George was to be played by Wallace Ford, hardly a diminutive, slight-of-built type, so having a big man like Crawford as Lennie was a necessity. There was not such a pronounced difference between the two men; Crawford, burly and rugged looking, merely seemed to be above-average height, which he certainly wasn't. (When the play was filmed in 1939, the two leading actors, Lon Chaney, Jr., and Burgess Meredith as Lennie and George respectively, fit the physical requirements much better.)

The play, staged by George S. Kaufman, opened on Broadway on November 23, 1937, to critical acclaim, with plenty of praise for the actors. It is the character of George who must convey the feeling between the two men and really move the audience. Ford succeeded at this and was greatly praised as George, just as Meredith would be in the film. This is a sound dramatic device, allowing the viewer to see one man's tragedy through the eyes of another. Crawford, pleased with the reception for his first serious stage acting role, remained with the play for most of its 207 performances.*

Playing Lennie on film might have served as a springboard to other important leads, like those he would play a decade later, but Crawford didn't land the part. Lon Chaney, Jr., also the son of a famous parent, had been appearing in minor roles throughout the '30s without getting anywhere. By the time producer Hal Roach and Director Lewis Milestone rushed *Of Mice and Men* into production, Crawford had already signed with Paramount and was committed to other films. *The New York Times*, in reviewing the film, said Chaney did not quite erase memories of Crawford's performance. Chaney would remain tied to his father's image and was continually cast in horror films throughout his long career. Whenever he and Crawford did a film together, it was always Crawford who had the better billing and the good-sized parts.

Crawford's stage success gave him confidence. Two months after the show's opening, he appeared with his mother on an NBC radio interview program—something that he once was too insecure to do. Helen Broderick was one of the last people to be convinced of her son's ability to handle a dramatic role. When they were both in Hollywood, she also meddled in his personal life. Whenever she was around her son and one of this dates, she would mimic the girls to make him break up. One of the girls at the time was a minor-league RKO contractee, Lucille Ball. Crawford's most serious involvement of the period, however, was with another screen newcomer, the lovely MGM player Rita Johnson, who was then thought to have great promise. For a while, the columnists wrote about an engagement; then suddenly the whole thing was called off. The papers got no further information; both married others within a year after the broken engagement.

On the movie front, work was steady. Paramount did not seem to know his strong points; they cast him as a sponging brother-in-law in *Sudden Money* (1939) and in three quickie adventure films that same year. When Crawford was cast as a bad guy, he would be

---

*It is alleged that one of director Kaufman's most famous comments was directed at Crawford. After viewing one of the actor's lesser nights as Lennie, he sent him a wire backstage: "Am sitting in the back row. Wish you were here." This may have been an act of revenge. Kaufman once told Helen Broderick that her slip was showing. She then referred to an ailing show of his with that classic rejoinder, "George, your show is slipping."

the henchman and never the brains of the gang. That was because, whether he was playing a villain or a friend of the hero, he was expected to play it one way—like the dimwitted ox he had played on stage. *Beau Geste* (1939), the first of two Gary Cooper films he made that year, was at least a major production. As one of the Foreign Legionnaires, he worked for the first time with Brian Donlevy, Ray Milland and Albert Dekker, three more actors who would turn up in other Crawford pictures. During production, there were a lot of pranks, most of them harmless and enjoyed by both prankster and victim. Crawford, whose sense of humor meshed well in this kind of atmosphere, made many friends among his fellow performers. But he disliked Paramount's treatment of him and asked for his release, hoping to find greener pastures elsewhere.

For his second Cooper picture, he returned to the scene of his first Hollywood experience, the Sam Goldwyn studio. In *The Real Glory*, Cooper and Crawford once more battled villainous native tribesmen, this time the Philippines' deadly Moros. Unlike the earlier film, Cooper survives, but Crawford this time is martyred.

During the shooting, a reporter asked Crawford for an interview. The actor talked about what a wonderful man Gary Cooper was. When pressed to say something about himself, he revealed very truthfully what some of the Hollywood hostesses thought of him. (Throughout his career, he would remain pretty contemptuous of the party scene in the movie capital.)

Producer Walter Wanger was responsible for Crawford's first really good screen roles when he signed him for two independent productions, *Eternally Yours* (1939) and *Slightly Honorable* (1940), both directed by Tay Garnett. In the former, he played a role close to himself, a playboy-type who loses his fiancée Loretta Young to magician David Niven. Just being cast as a man engaged to Miss Young seemed a step in the right direction. In the latter, he started out looking like just another slow-thinking sidekick, but in the surprise ending of this comedy-mystery-political corruption drama, his character proved to be more than met the eye. Garnett liked his work and used him again in his next 1940 film, *Seven Sinners*. (That film was made by Universal; Crawford had signed with that studio.) He played another lummox, loyal to sultry singer Marlene Dietrich. By this time, he had perfected this type of characterization.

The Universal deal represented a turning point in Crawford's career. He had not taken his work under Paramount's aegis seriously and still considered himself a stage actor in need of a play. But

Universal promised him bigger and better roles, and signing with them strengthened his ties with Hollywood. For the most part, the studio delivered, giving him good parts in action films, primarily westerns directed by veteran specialists like Allan Dwan and George Marshall. He still was assigned to play comical roles in serious films, sometimes coming off as a less lovable Andy Devine (an actor with whom he was often paired in those days). But his best roles during that period were those of fairly decent men driven to villainy after losing the heroine to the handsomer leading man. But Crawford was no loser in love in real life: In November 1940, he married radio singer Kay Griffith after a courtship more publicized than some of his movies.

Crawford and Devine played comic helpers of hero Franchot Tone in a tongue-in-cheek Western called *Trail of the Vigilantes* (1940), but in their two other Westerns together, *When the Daltons Rode* (1940) and *Badlands of Dakota* (1941), Crawford was strictly dramatic. Even Devine was serious as a sidekick of the Dalton brothers (Brian Donlevy, Stuart Erwin, Frank Albertson and Crawford) in the former; in that oater, the Daltons were driven into their lawless careers by far more evil men. Director George Marshall had purposely cast likable actors so as to garner as much sympathy as possible; only Donlevy had previously played an effective menace. Crawford starts off in the film as a decent upstanding law officer, the fiancée of Kay Francis. When he learns that she prefers the film's nominal hero, Randolph Scott, that (combined with some family travails) turn him bad and lead him and the others to their ultimate doom.* Crawford was a far more interesting character than those played by bigger names (Scott, Francis and Donlevy). *Badlands of Dakota* was a lesser film with a similar formula: Western bigshot Crawford sends his kid brother Robert Stack to pick up his future bride Ann Rutherford. Stack and Rutherford fall in love and Crawford becomes enraged. The results were predictable.

Crawford also supplied comedy in a so-called horror film, *The Black Cat* (1941), which had no connection (other than the presence of Bela Lugosi) to Universal's excellent 1934 fright film of the same name. This haunted house film also had nothing to do with Edgar Allan Poe, being more in the *Cat and the Canary* vein. Crawford

---

*A New York Times *critic wrote that the demise of all the Daltons prevented another film called* The Daltons Ride Again. *But Universal released a film with that title and a different cast five years later.*

then reteamed with Donlevy and Devine as South Seas adventurers in *South of Tahiti* (1941). The film was primarily a showcase for Maria Montez, a Dominican Republic beauty who had been plucked out of bit parts and surprisingly became one of the most enduring symbols of Universal in the '40s.

Crawford never got to work with the real studio queen of the period, Deanna Durbin, but his mother did in two films. Helen Broderick did most of her latter-day films for Universal; mother and son were working on the lot at the same time while she was shooting the 1941 Durbin film *Nice Girl?* As close as he remained with his mother, he tried to avoid discussing their mutual vocation. In real life, Broderick was not far removed from the sharp-tongued ego deflator she usually played on screen. In later years, Crawford revealed that both of his parents would always be ready with some criticism. He told an interviewer that they would call him about something they had seen him do the previous night on television; years after he had won the Oscar they were still telling him how to perform. The elder Crawfords had by that time given up active performing, but they had never retired from the practice of giving advice.

Crawford's two most famous screen roles would be as men who bulldozed their way into the American political arena. His first screen politician was a creation of Damon Runyon: In *Tight Shoes* (1941), playing a grafter who is literally undone by his big feet, he was only slightly smarter than his usual comic lugs. He was cast in another Runyonesque role the following year, playing one of the title characters in *Butch Minds the Baby.* In 1942, he enacted a like characterization on loanout to Warner Bros., working again with director Lloyd Bacon in *Larceny, Inc.* One of the best of the Edward G. Robinson gangster comedies, it also featured such fine performers as Jane Wyman, Jack Carson, Edward Brophy, Jackie Gleason, Vera Vague and another fugitive from Paramount second features, Anthony Quinn. The film hilariously detailed the efforts of three bumbling ex-cons who buy a luggage shop just so they can dig through to the bank next store. The comic highlights involve Robinson (as "Pressure," the brains of the gang) barking out orders to his dumb flunky Crawford and Robinson's reactions to the trouble he usually gets into when Crawford does something wrong. These two "serious actors" worked together like some of the best comedy teams, which was only surprising to those who forget that Robinson was a brilliant comic as well as dramatic actor. This film was

Robinson's last contract picture at the studio that had established him, although he would return over the years for individual films.

The parts seemed to be getting better at Universal. A new adaptation of the '20s play *Broadway* (1942) gave him the role of an immoral, brutal gangster without any of the redeeming qualities he usually had. George Raft played himself, recalling his days as a dancer in Prohibition era speak-easies, and Pat O'Brien played a cop. One of the girls Crawford has victimized finished him off in the end. His last released picture of 1942, *Sin Town*, was also his last film for a three-year period. He had the lead, playing opposite Constance Bennett, who was not the big star she had been a decade earlier, but still had enough class to make low-budgeters seem better than they were. Crawford played a con man who saves a small town from far worse crooks. (This was the film alluded to 37 years later in *A Little Romance*.)

Rather than allow himself to be drafted, Crawford chose the Air Force. He served with distinction from late 1942 through the end of the war. For a handsome leading man, those would have been vital years; for Crawford, it didn't seem to matter very much.

Returning to Hollywood after three years, Crawford might as well have been a newcomer making his first stab at movie success. He still had a contractual obligation to Universal, but they were in no hurry to have him honor it; he cooled his heels for seven and a half months before the studio called him in for a film, aptly titled *The Runaround* (1946). He was a private detective in this one and a policeman in his other 1946 release, *Black Angel*.

Crawford made his last picture for Universal in 1947, a few months after his mother made her last screen film appearance. Helen Broderick drifted into retirement after completion of the Deanna Durbin–Charles Laughton film *Because of Him* (1946). Crawford's final Universal, *Slave Girl*, was an Yvonne DeCarlo–starring adventure which made fun of the studio's own Maria Montez films (Montez was still at Universal). Crawford was once more the dumb sidekick, this time of George Brent. He saw no future in continuing with the studio and left (by mutual consent) to hit the freelance trail. The first film away from the home studio looked worse than anything done previously. In *The Flame* (1947), he was at Republic in the company of John Carroll and Vera Ralston, playing a blackmailer.

Crawford experienced several "dry" periods over the next two years. During that time, he contemplated returning to New York and live theater. On radio, he got his one chance to work opposite Ingrid Bergman, in *Anna Christie*, playing the role that Charles Bickford had played opposite Greta Garbo on film. Another successful radio excursion was his reteaming with Edward G. Robinson in an adaptation of *Blind Alley* on *Screen Guild Playhouse*. Crawford played a ruthless killer who is undermined by the psychiatrist whose home he has invaded. He was in fact better suited to the role than the actors who had played it on screen, Chester Morris and William Holden. His screen villains never had any of the psychological shading this role had, nor did any of his celluloid work up to that time allow him to act on a one-to-one basis with pros like Bergman and Robinson, so these broadcasts were particularly welcome by him. Performing live, even with a script in hand, would be the closest he would come to the theatrical experience until the 1970s, when he finally returned to the stage to tour in demanding roles like the coach in *The Championship Season*, a play requiring strong ensemble acting.

A strong ensemble piece of its day was William Saroyan's *The Time of Your Life* (1948); James Cagney's independent production cast Crawford as the loquacious cop. The well-constructed play made it easy for any competent actors to shine in the brilliantly realized Saroyan cameos, but Cagney and director H. C. Potter cast a fine actor in each part. Crawford once again squares off against Ward Bond here, but this time their conflict is strictly verbal, limited to a barroom argument about the state of the world.

Crawford continued appearing in A-productions, albeit of lesser quality than *The Time of Your Life*. *Sealed Verdict* (1948) returned him to the Paramount lot in the role of an American army officer in charge of security at the Nuremberg trials. Though that sounds like a weighty subject for a film, the script fell victim to the old truism about movies based on then-current headlines. *Sealed Verdict* quickly sank into melodrama; it would be 13 years before Stanley Kramer filmed *Judgment at Nuremberg*, the first meaningful film on the trials. Crawford's part descended into just another sidekick characterization, with the hero this time Army lawyer Ray Milland.

Crawford appeared in Warners' *Night Unto Night* in 1947, but this Don Siegel–directed film was a pretty somber affair and the studio withheld its release until early 1949, after new leading lady Viveca Lindfors was introduced in better fare. It's obvious what attracted him to this film: He was being given the rare opportunity to play an intellectual, the pipe-smoking friend of the hero, future

President Ronald Reagan.* Since the latter was suffering from epilepsy, no less, and involved with Lindfors, a neurotic war widow, there were a lot of opportunities for Crawford to dispense advice. As if to make up for this blatant act of miscasting, he was then assigned the role of a dumb mug in a Warner comedy called *A Kiss in the Dark* (1948), which starred Reagan's soon-to-be-ex-wife Jane Wyman and another frequent colleague of Crawford, David Niven. The latter inherits an apartment house full of "funny" tenants like Crawford. The poor quality of the script made the opportunities for laughs practically non-existent and he once more started to think that Broadway had to have something better to offer.

Columbia's *Anna Lucasta* (1949) was based on a play and his part was strong: heroine Paulette Goddard's boorish brother-in-law, who doesn't want her back in the family house because of the shady life she had been leading. This film, like *The Time of Your Life*, is unavailable for television airing; there was an all-black remake by the play's author, Philip Yordan, nine years later with Eartha Kitt and Frederick O'Neal in the role Crawford plays here. While on the Columbia lot, Crawford and another actor working on the same picture, John Ireland, tested for a new picture being prepared by writer-director Robert Rossen. Ireland, having been signed to a specific number of films for Columbia, seemed a likely candidate for a role, but Crawford, the outsider, had the edge.

The film was an adaptation of Robert Penn Warren's novel *All the King's Men*, dealing with "Willie Stark," a corrupt Southern politician. Most people know that Stark was actually Huey Long (1883–1935), the grass roots lawyer who rose to the position of Governor of Louisiana. He was said to have established the closest thing to an American dictatorship, one that continued even after he took a Senate seat. Long's attempts to change the politics of the nation (plus his assassination) made his story an ideal subject for filming, but in 1949, Hollywood was not at the point where they would tackle such a biography. So Warren's book, with all the characters possessing assumed names, seemed an ideal compromise. Nevertheless, Rossen wanted someone as physically like the stubby Long as was humanly possible; he had left a vivid legacy through newsreel films and was part of the country's recent history. This film was important to Rossen, whose credits up to this time were largely as a

---

*Reagan and Crawford reportedly relieved the boredom of shooting by teaching the Swedish-born Lindfors lewd American words and then watching others' reactions.

screenwriter of pictures like *The Roaring Twenties* (1939), and he wanted to prove himself as a director. Studio boss Harry Cohn would have preferred to borrow some name actor to play Willie Stark, but no star in Hollywood fit the description of the character and Rossen remained steadfast on that point. (Columbia made an overture to MGM for the loanout services of Spencer Tracy, but that studio's asking price was too steep.) Crawford and Ireland read for Rossen, and he chose them both. Ireland would play reporter Jack Burden and Crawford was signed for the role of Willie Stark. A skeptical Cohn accepted this, remembering that his studio's biggest hit of recent years, *The Jolson Story* (1946), had starred a previously unknown contractee, Larry Parks.

Still, the casting of Crawford was looked on with disapproval by those who felt he would give a B-picture quality to potentially exciting material. More importantly, there were those in the know who, having observed him throughout his career, felt that the role was beyond him. Aware of this, he and his director worked hard to prove that he was not just a physical presence and could display the Stark charisma that could win over both men and women. They succeeded to a great extent but unfortunately, in this writer's opinion, to the detriment of the picture as a whole. For the most part, the film was cast with shallow performers so that Crawford and Mercedes McCambridge, playing one of his loyal assistants, were made to seem more dynamic than was necessary, this helped them to win their Oscars as much as anything. It starts and ends like one of the '40s crime films; a documentary style might have been more apropos to such an important subject. Both the Academy and the New York Film Critics named *All the King's Men* the year's best picture, but both gave the best director nod to others.

Crawford's performance is still worthy of praise. Bosley Crowther of *The New York Times* was a major booster, saying he used tremendous energy in his portrayal of Stark. Crowther wrote, "He draws a compelling portrait, in two dimensions, of an egomaniac." However, opinions were divided; when the film reached England in 1950, critic Richard Winnington thought that Crawford failed to capture "the multi-facets of the character's changes" and opined that Crawford made Stark into "a stick figure." Despite these diverse opinions, he won the New York Film Critics best actor award and the Oscar.

Why was Crawford given a top accolade for a possibly once-in-a-lifetime performance in a non-commercial prestige film? The answer is relatively simple: Harry Cohn promoted him for the award. There were many insiders who believed that Cohn was the real model for Crawford's gruff politico and no one did anything to dispel that notion. One character that was thought to be even more like Cohn was Harry Brock, the ruthless junk dealer in Garson Kanin's play *Born Yesterday*. When *Born Yesterday* made it big on the stage, Cohn gleefully outbid his competitors for the film rights. He had initially planned to star the queen of the lot, Rita Hayworth, as Billie Dawn, but her marriage to Prince Aly Khan robbed her of a role that might have proven an interesting change of pace. Eventually it was decided that the studio would do best to go with the play's star Judy Holliday. And once *All the King's Men* had turned Crawford into a Columbia star, he was given the part of Brock over the stage original, Paul Douglas. (Douglas would have had to be borrowed from Fox anyway.)

There was a time lag before the Academy Awards ceremony for 1949 and the production of *Born Yesterday* and the studio had to keep their unusual new male star busy, so they cast him in two program pictures. There was very little thought put into either film. He was paired with John Ireland for a third straight film in *Cargo to Capetown* (1950), an already dated piece about two experienced seamen in love with the same woman (Ellen Drew). This program-filler only proved that these two good actors did not display any of the chemistry of such combos as Victor McLaglen and Edmund Lowe or Wallace Beery and Clark Gable. For the same year's *Convicted*, he put a tinge of gray in his hair, indicating that he was playing a more dignified character. In this third Columbia screen version of Martin Flavin's play *The Criminal Code*, he played the role previously enacted by Walter Huston and Walter Connolly, that of a district attorney turned prison warden who tries to help a young man he sent up. He even allows the con (Glenn Ford) to win his daughter, played by Dorothy Malone. This was the first of several films teaming Crawford with Ford, who was considered by Harry Cohn to be like "a son"—at least when the studio chief was in a sentimental mood.

Cohn's other honorary son, William Holden, was given the pivotal but thankless role of the reporter in *Born Yesterday* (1950), and it certainly added to Crawford's status that he would be billed above Holden, whose name would also bolster the box office. In the end result, it really didn't matter because the critics took little or no notice of the two actors' excellent work, saving their accolades for

Miss Holliday.* As Harry Brock, Crawford was even more ideally cast than as Willie Stark. Thanks to the direction of George Cukor, the kind of craftsman that Crawford rarely worked with, Brock was given a dimension beyond that of a bully. Cukor made him and Holliday into an updated extension of his famous screen team of the '30s, Wallace Beery and Jean Harlow in *Dinner at Eight* (1933). On the stage, Holliday was often intimidated by Douglas' erratic insecurity and when the two were actually angry with one another, that had an effect on their bickering scenes. In Crawford, she found a screen actor of many years' experience who knew what he had to do and did not give his co-stars hard times. Also notable is the scene where he exerts force to quell the attack of conscience felt by a longtime stooge, superbly played by Howard St. John. The point is made that Brock is not just a man who wants to wield power, but particularly prefers to dominate people who are, by virtue of their birth, better educated than he. It was a masterful performance, but many critics compared him unfavorably to Douglas.

Crawford continued to tackle tough guy roles, including a Western remake of Bogie's *Sahara*, called *Last of the Comanches* (1952). Before that came *The Mob* (1951), his first completely heroic role, as a law enforcement officer who goes undercover to smash a waterfront racket. There was nothing out of the ordinary about the film outside of the fact that it featured early screen appearances of Ernest Borgnine, Richard Kiley and Charles Buchinsky, who would again meet Crawford under the new name of Charles Bronson.

After Crawford completed *Scandal Sheet* (1951), in which he played a newspaper editor driven to murder, he was farmed out. He was starred with Clark Gable and Ava Gardner in *Lone Star* (1952), though as Hollywood's top star's romantic rival for Gardner, he did not stand a chance. At least he was not a real villain, his disagreement with Gable on the political destiny of Texas resolved by the same sort of fistfight that used to settle Gable's clashes with Wallace Beery. As if to cement Crawford's parallels to the late Beery, he chose the latter's longtime stand-in Harry Wilson to fill the same position for him. Crawford was a pretty rugged guy who did not really require a regular stand-in, but he knew that Wilson hadn't worked since Beery's death.

Next came a trip to Warner Bros., the studio which in the past

---

*In June 1965, Holden called Crawford on location in Spain to tell him of Holliday's death from cancer, since the three had become friends.

Judy Holliday, Broderick Crawford and William Holden in *Born Yesterday* (1950).

had only given him inconsequential supporting roles; now he would be starred. Unfortunately, he and Claire Trevor, the tough guy's best gal, were saddled with *Stop, You're Killing Me* (1952), an ill-advised remake of 1938's *A Slight Case of Murder*, which had been just about perfect in its original incarnation. It was made for two reasons: Warners paid Damon Runyon and Howard Lindsay $50,000 plus a percentage for the rights to their play and they rarely used a good script only once. And Runyon and Lindsay had now become even more popular, thanks to the great theatrical success of *Guys and Dolls* and *Life with Father*, respectively. But none of these facts, nor the direction of Roy Del Ruth (another veteran of Warners' heyday), could freshen material that had become dated over the years. The studio knew it had a lemon and the film wound up playing as a second feature with a more marketable Doris Day film, *April in Paris*.

In April 1952, Crawford made his television debut on CBS' *Video Theater* and for the next few years, did many of the half-hour anthology dramas. Back at Columbia, he followed up *Last of the*

Comanches with *The Last Posse* (1953), a Western with a better than average script. He played an honorable lawman, pretty much at the end of his career, who sacrifices his own life to see that tyrannical rancher Charles Bickford gets his for murdering the men he (Crawford) wanted to bring to trial. Acting for the first time with consummate pro Bickford, Crawford matched him with an equally strong performance. This was the third picture in which the studio expected him to prop up the callow juvenile John Derek and he was becoming annoyed with it. But he had one more picture to do for the studio.

The idea of *Human Desire* (1954) sounded promising, more so in comparison to the usual fare served up by Columbia. It was an Americanized remake of Jean Renoir's *La Bête Humaine* (1938), based on a story by Emile Zola. The director would be the legendary Fritz Lang. Crawford was to have co-starred with the studio's most popular romantic team, Rita Hayworth and Glenn Ford, but Hayworth couldn't make the picture. It was not her marriage to a prince this time (as it had been in the case of *Born Yesterday*); Hayworth had divorced Aly Khan and returned to the studio as a working actress. But after doing credible work in versions of *Salome* and *Miss Sadie Thompson*, she was not ready to return to the role of the heartless siren she had played in the '40s pictures like *Blood and Sand* and *The Loves of Carmen*. The script called for her, the adulterous wife of a violent brute (Crawford), to pursue an unwilling Ford, who is interested in another girl. This meant that there would be no torrid love scenes between Ford and Hayworth, something audiences expected. When she bolted the production, she was replaced by Gloria Grahame, a recent Oscar winner who had just been successful in another Lang film co-starring Ford, *The Big Heat* (1953). (Hayworth was also spared at least one on-camera ordeal: Perfectionist Lang had Crawford slap Grahame a record number of times for one take.) In the meantime, the production delays had caused Crawford to take another outside assignment.

Night People (1954) represented two firsts for him: his first work under the 20th Century–Fox banner and his first film made on actual European locales. That part pleased him greatly and he became an avid adherent of location work thereafter. This film, one of the few directorial works of famed writer-producer Nunnally Johnson, was one of several that Fox shot in Berlin in the '50s, beginning with the Paul Douglas film *The Big Lift*. Like that film, *Night People* dealt with American soldiers in post war Germany, focusing on the kidnapping of a young G.I. by Communists and the efforts to get the young man back. Crawford, once again portraying all that was wrong with blustery, self-made American millionaires, was the soldier's demanding father, badgering American intelligence officer Gregory Peck throughout the proceedings. His part was evidently not big enough to warrant equal billing with Peck, a man he had beaten out in the Oscar sweepstakes five years earlier. This was an early CinemaScope film, and in their scene together, Crawford was confined to one corner of the screen. In theaters not yet equipped for the width of this new process, and later on television, the actor was out of the picture completely, with only the distinctive Crawford voice to make audiences aware that he was even present.

If an untried director like Johnson did not do well by Crawford, an acknowledged great like Fritz Lang (*Human Desire*) was no more successful. Trying too hard to imitate the style of the earlier French version, with atmospheric shots of railroads and railroad yards, he stranded his actors in one-dimensional stereotypes. Two years earlier, he had shown in *Clash by Night* how well he could do a triangle drama, but the characters in *Human Desire* weren't comparable. Lang put Crawford back into the area of senseless brute, not allowing him the screen time Renoir gave Michel Simon to develop the character. It was all in all an unfortunate end to Crawford's association with Columbia, the studio that made him a name, but he realized that if he wanted to remain a name, he had better do some freelancing, choosing the parts that would be right for him.

His first work as an independent, *Down Three Dark Streets* (1954), a United Artists release, was the last film in which Crawford got to play an out-and-out hero. He played an FBI agent following up the strands of a few different cases left incomplete by the murder of a colleague. It was well-cast and professional and made no more of an impression than countless other FBI films shot during that period. Crawford next began a longtime association with the producer-director team of Clarence Greene and Russell Rouse. The role of larger-than-life crime boss Lupo in *New York Confidential* (1955) appealed to Crawford and he was given strong support by Richard Conte as the protégé who is out to topple his organization and Anne Bancroft as Lupo's thrill-seeking daughter. What was unusual about the film was that all the major characters were criminals; law-and-order figures and decent citizens were relegated to small supporting roles. Greene and Rouse worked independently and then found a studio to distribute their product; in this case, they gave those distribution rights to Warner Bros., the true "parent company" of gangster movies.

Crawford was then immediately asked to play another bad guy, one that made Lupo seem like a pillar of the community. In United Artists' *Big House, U.S.A.* (1955), he was a completely evil convict who leads a prison break, then plans a kidnapping. His gang includes Charles Bronson, Lon Chaney, Jr., and Ralph Meeker, the only one with even a glimmer of humanity in the bunch. Crawford could see that unless he changed his screen image, producers would continue to cast him in that mode. He hadn't left Columbia for that. He began rejecting scripts that required him to perform any acts of villainy.

His next two roles were new experiences: In both, he played men of medicine. On NBC's prestigious *Producers' Showcase*, he appeared as a doctor fighting yellow fever in turn-of-the-century Cuba in an adaptation of Sidney Howard's play *Yellow Jack*; he was credible in the part. By the time that telecast was aired in January 1955, he had been signed to appear in another release for United Artists, Stanley Kramer's big-budget *Not as a Stranger*. He played the relatively small part of Dr. Aarons, the head pathologist of a large medical college, and took fifth billing, his lowest since the pre–*All the King's Men* days. To prepare for the small but meaty role, Crawford did some research, going to see an actual autopsy so that he would look somewhat realistic when he confronted a cadaver on-screen. He watched for only a few minutes before the proceedings made him sick to his stomach. He portrayed Aarons as a fearsome authority figure, the terror who menaced mature-looking med students Robert Mitchum, Frank Sinatra and Lee Marvin; yet also a man who is the best at what he does. There was much fine acting in this film and it is to Crawford's credit that his major scenes, coming relatively early in a long film, were not overlooked by the critics, especially in comparison to the superb performances of Charles Bickford, as an aging general practitioner, Myron McCormick, an incompetent doctor, and Lon Chaney, Jr., in a poignant bit as Mitchum's alcoholic father.* In fact, the actors, more than any other factor, saved Kramer's first directorial effort from drowning in soap suds.

Wanting to solidify a reputation as a serious dramatic actor (and also looking for more jobs away from Hollywood), Crawford found

---

John Steinbeck's most famous Lennies made a total of four features and one short, the wartime Keeping Fit, *together.* Not as a Stranger *was their last.*

an opportunity to achieve both these goals. His disdain for the movie capital of the world had grown with the years. He felt that while the studio system had died, the cattiness and backbiting had not. He told one of his favorite jokes to let interviewers know why he didn't socialize with the movie crowd: "When people tell you they saw your last picture," he said, "well, the way they say it, it sounds like they hope it was." Since even the independent producers did not offer parts any more appetizing than Columbia had, he chose the most daring of the offers presented him, this one from the famed Italian director Federico Fellini.*

The trip to Italy taught Crawford a few things about shooting away from a Hollywood soundstage. Fellini had just finished making *La Strada* and was already being acclaimed as a genius. (Fellini was at his best in that film, but credit was also deserved by Giuletta Masina—Signora Fellini in real life—for her poignant Gelsomina, and by her two co-stars from America, Anthony Quinn and Richard Basehart.) After that, the director felt the need to put at least one American in every one of his films. Immediately after the successful *La Strada*, it seemed feasible to sign Crawford to star with Masina and Basehart in *Il Bidone*. The picture would be retitled *The Swindle* for U.S. release. Fellini cast his wife as the cohort of swindlers in *Il Bidone*, which tried to be very hard and resembled such contemporary American films as Stanley Kubrick's *The Killing* (1956), also about a group of marginal crooks who fail in their seemingly perfect plan. There were some humorous aspects to the film, but they were inspired more by the neo-realistic nature of the post war Italian cinema than by aspects of Fellini's own adaptation of his own story.

Up to that time, all of Crawford's death scenes had been played under controlled conditions on Hollywood soundstages. In this film, Crawford "died" in the streets of Rome, sharing this big scene with the voice of an irate local citizen who did not appreciate a film crew's interference with his business. Fellini recorded things that had nothing to do with his shooting script, and if they did not detract from the product, these extraneous sounds very easily could turn up in distributors' prints. All this was naturally disconcerting to Crawford, who wondered if he had been properly appreciative of the "controlled atmosphere" of the three Hollywood studios where he was under contract.

---

*His marriage, which had been feeling some strain as of late, began to come apart around this time. He and his wife Kay decided to try a separation period. Unfortunately, it did not make things work better for them.

Il Bidone suffered in comparison to Fellini's deeper or more flamboyant films, but it had its champions among critics. Nevertheless, it was not a commercial film and did not show up in the U.S. for seven years, when (as *The Swindle*) it played briefly in art houses. The good reviews garnered by the cast therefore did them no good. But Crawford had not been turned off by his foreign filmmaking experiences, and would return to Italy for other pictures, generally cheap adventure films.

His absence from the country for a few months had done nothing to strengthen Crawford's marriage. He and his wife decided around this time to make their separation more permanent; their two sons Kim and Kelley were considered old enough to understand that their parents were no longer happy together. (Kim Crawford was adopted as an infant in 1947 with club feet that were eventually corrected; Kelly was born to them in 1950.) Ironically, Crawford's public statements of the period indicated some desire to prolong the marriage; even when the final divorce decree was pending, he would still refer to their "separation." He did not marry until seven years after the split.

With a failed marriage and a disappointing film behind him, it didn't seem that 1955 was his year. And yet he now embarked on a project that he is remembered for as much, and probably more, as any of his major films. For a while, he had been on the list of performers who were considered good bets as television series stars. Of course, any movie name was a commodity at this point and now Crawford saw that it would be wise to accept one such offer while he still could trade on his name. The syndicated series' title was *Highway Patrol* and it began on NBC on October 24, 1955: It became familiar to thousands of viewers in one time period, 7 P.M. on Monday nights, a rarity for syndicated shows which are always being reshuffled into new time periods. This program was one of the few series not designed for prime time that developed a cult status.

Like many popular TV shows, *Highway Patrol* was based upon a simple premise. Crawford was cast as highway patrol Chief Dan Matthews, who each week barked out orders to his men on the way to solving whatever crime that episode involved. Even though it was set in California, the show's publicity stressed the idea that Matthews and his men were guardians of all the nation's highways. Regular viewers fondly recall Matthews' familiar hat and coat and his regular sign-off after talking to a colleague on his car radio, the famous code numbers "10-4." It was the Crawford personality, however, that brought the character to life; his lopsided walk, his gruff exterior and his rapid-fire barking of orders were the things that "made" Dan Matthews. He quickly learned that TV acting mostly was based on being yourself. And by doing that week after week, he became well-known to many people who had no idea of the number of movies he made.

It was during the run of the show that Crawford became popular with comic impersonators. When a young small part actor named Frank Gorshin began doing impressions, the swaggering Crawford was one of his first targets. Other mimics followed suit, but the subject didn't mind; it did not hurt to be impersonated on top-rated series like *The Ed Sullivan Show*.* He got used to this just as he had long ago accepted harsh criticism of his acting. After all, he was in his mid-forties and still received some of his toughest reviews from his retired parents. Helen Broderick and Lester Crawford now saw their son once a week and they usually came through with some complaints about his emoting.

Crawford intended to continue working in motion pictures and, during his first hiatus from *Highway Patrol*, he took on some film work. The team of Greene and Rouse had done well by him in *New York Confidential*, so he signed up with them for *The Fastest Gun Alive* (MGM, 1956), in which he would co-star with his old Columbia buddy Glenn Ford. At the peak of his generally underrated career, Ford was dividing his time up between Columbia and MGM; he managed to pick up some of the best parts available on both lots, and was coming to this film right from a trio of excellent Metro dramas (*Blackboard Jungle*, *Trial* and *Ransom*.) Like those films, this unpretentious Western was photographed in black and white. In the *High Noon* tradition, this film has Ford playing a respected small-town businessman who thought he buried his gunslinger past, until Crawford and his gang arrive on the scene. Ford's friends shy away from helping him as he goes to face the big showdown. The third-billed Crawford's role was on the smallish side, possibly due to his heavy television schedule at the time, but the film was interesting and the plot not as hackneyed as it would become in a few short years, with every Western star in Hollywood doing at least one film in which he stood alone without the aid of his town.

Crawford had been good enough in real life to attain the rank

---

Even his name was poked fun at: Cartoonist Al Capp called an Indian Broderick Crofoot in his Li'l Abner *comic strip.*

of Air Force sergeant, but his few military roles in films were typically officers. As the sadistic Army officer Waco Grimes in 20th Century–Fox's *Between Heaven and Hell* (1956), he was no credit to that branch of the service. Grimes is a certifiable mental case who has created a virtual kingdom for himself while his company is billeted on a South Pacific island. The Japanese move in and Grimes and his stooges are killed, leaving clean-cut young lieutenant Robert Wagner to come out the hero. Once again Crawford's footage is limited, which is a shame since his scenes are the ones that spark this Richard Fleischer–directed film. The early part, concentrating on Wagner's civilian life and his romance with Terry Moore, looks like a totally different movie, but such sequences were prerequisites for war films of the day.

Crawford was next to have starred with Sal Mineo in a Warner Bros. film tentatively called *Teenage Tragedies*, another one of the many films inspired by those classics of juvenile delinquency as *Blackboard Jungle* and *Rebel Without a Cause*. However, after initial planning and casting (including some real-life street kids), it was realized that the market for such films was already petering out. So Warners shelved the film, which Crawford would have made during his second hiatus from his TV show. Because of this, 1957 was the first year since he returned from the war in which he was not featured in at least one motion picture. But in April 1957, he proved that he had arrived as a TV star: He was profiled in *TV Guide* in an interview that seemed to concentrate on the sweet, gentle qualities of Broderick Crawford. It was not exactly an in-depth story, mainly concerned with publicity for his series.

Despite its success, *Highway Patrol* remained a low-budget affair, as dictated by its time period and lack of regular sponsorship. Crawford was surrounded by mostly unknown actors, some just starting out. One actor who made frequent appearances was Stuart Whitman, and he and Crawford became quite friendly. In 1958, when Andrew L. Stone was casting his MGM thriller *The Decks Ran Red*, Crawford and Whitman were given the heavy roles. Crawford achieved a new low in heinous acts as he and Whitman played seamen who murdered their fellow sailors so they could have the freighter all to themselves. Writer-director Stone and his wife Virginia specialized during that period in this type of "panic" film in which an unproven hero, this time ship's captain James Mason, tests his mettle against an unexpected disaster. However, this 1958 film did not go anywhere but to the bottom half of the double bill; it did not enjoy the popularity of the Stones' *Julie* and *The Last Voyage*, which dealt respectively with such proven cliffhangers as landing airliners without pilots and rescuing shipwreck victims.

Whitman went from this film to a Fox contract, and Crawford remained friendly with the younger actor over the years. Crawford would later guest in the role of a prison warden in *Convicts 4* (1962), in which Whitman was one of the stars. Ironically, during the four years in which the latter's career had developed so well, Crawford had not appeared in one American-made picture. In the late sixties, he would also do a guest shot on Whitman's TV series *Cimarron Strip*. This particular working relationship would extend into the 1980s, including an episode of the CBS series *Simon and Simon* which had Whitman as a has been cowboy star accused of murdering Crawford, a producer who had taken advantage of him.

Highway Patrol should have done better by its star, considering the show's enduring popularity. The cameras stopped rolling on the series in the late '50s, but many fans did not realize it since it was being broadcast for years after the shooting stopped. Less than ten years after winning the Oscar, Crawford appeared to have lost a lot of the respect of his peers. His appearance in Dan Matthews' rumpled outfit invoked laughter and many (including the producers who did the hiring) stopped thinking of him as the serious actor he was.

Even with residuals due him, the veteran performer had to work. Crawford returned to Italy and Spain; unfortunately, he was not invited this time by the likes of Signor Fellini. Italian producers were now concentrating on production of "sword and sandal" epics and they usually got one American actor for their international market. If such Americans as Bruce Cabot or Cameron Mitchell were busy, they took Edmund Purdom, who along with Belinda Lee seemed to be at the forefront of the British contingent in Rome. Crawford was considered ideal for all the mad emperor roles and was thrown into a piece of junk called *Goliath and the Dragon* (1960), in which he menaced the hero. He did not even rate Steve Reeves, the American strongman whose Hercules films had started this abominable trend; a poor man's version, Mark Forest, gave the degenerate Crawford his comeuppance. Fortunately, Crawford did not get mired in this artistic quagmire and, though he would continue to do films in both Italy and Spain, his work would encompass different genres. He seemed more at home as a villain of a spaghetti Western than as the crazed ruler of some ancient empire. When he did play the latter, in the Spanish-made *The Castilian*, he at least had the consolation that other exiles from the U.S., Frankie Avalon and Cesar Romero, were also trapped in this production. Thanks to the cast, Warner Bros. gave the film a better than average distribution in the U.S. in 1963.

Crawford's low professional period following the demise of *Highway Patrol* was matched by a period of discord in his private life. Saddest of all was the death of his mother in September 1959. In later years, he would acknowledge how great her influence was on his life, even going so far as appearing on talk shows just to tell stories about her. He showed Helen Broderick to be a woman with a great sense of humor, much like the characters she portrayed in 30 talkies. His favorite story about her involved another legendary performer from the old days, actor and monologist DeWolf Hopper. Helen was the daughter of Hopper's old colleague Bill Broderick, and she once introduced herself to Hopper. The disinterested Hopper said to send his regards to her father, to which an angered Helen said, "You're going to see him first, so say hello for me, because he's been dead for 20 years." Crawford also described falling asleep in front of the television and suddenly hearing the voice of his mother, lecturing with the waspish tongue he knew so well. He opened his eyes, ready to comply with her wishes, and discovered he had not been dreaming. His mother was indeed in the room ... appearing in an old TV movie.

By the early '60s, Crawford had wearied of travelling from one country to another making films in a sporadic manner. He packaged a syndicated series for himself, *King of Diamonds*. In this half-hour show, he portrayed John King, an international adventurer who takes all kinds of tough jobs. Like most adventure series with middle-aged heroes, he had a good-looking young assistant (Ray Hamilton). The series did not have that much to offer and many stations around the country opted for proven older shows, including *Highway Patrol*. They knew of Dan Matthews' enduring appeal, while John King remained an unknown quantity. Some of the major markets picked up *King of Diamonds* for the 1961-62 season (in New York, ABC aired the show on Friday nights at seven). One of the few notable things about this series was the one episode in which William Gargan, mute after throat cancer surgery, made his final acting appearance. But the new series failed to rack up the numbers and no new episodes were made after the initial batch.

He also made news of another kind with his marriage to actress Joan Tabor, a beautiful blonde young enough to be his daughter. She had been appearing in various TV shows for a few years. He claimed it was her superior skill as a bowler (she was better than him) that attracted him. His wittiest statement to the press at the time of the marriage: "I've got her where she wants me." From then on, whenever he appeared with his wife on some TV game show, there would be snide remarks about his taking degrading work just to favor Tabor's career. Coming at this rather unsettled point in his career, this interlude did little more than give gossip columnists something to write about him. His May-December union was soon shunted aside by the more celebrated ones of Cary Grant and Dyan Cannon or Frank Sinatra and Mia Farrow. By comparison to those, Crawford and Tabor lasted an eternity, just barely past the mid-'60s. Nineteen sixty-two was also the year of Lester Crawford's death. He was discussed less by Broderick, who was aware of his father's resentment at having a more famous wife and son. But a deep affection was felt by the two of them.

Crawford continued to be professionally active, dividing his time between Hollywood and abroad. Even an accident did not slow him down for too long a time. During that period, he walked into a glass partition at an airport, causing minor though painful injuries. The papers picked this up and, because he was an actor, there were intimations that he was drunk. His injuries had no effect on his career; he had already acquired the odd way of walking that latter-day audiences recognized as his alone, as well as his bloated and puffy appearance. The playboy of a quarter century earlier, who could have suffered serious career reversals if he had damaged his appearance, was long gone. (A car accident in the late '60s did further facial damage; he allegedly was not the driver.)

One of his last foreign pictures was released in this country by MGM in 1963 under the title *Square of Violence* and is notable only because it was probably the last film for many years to require any sort of characterization from him. Co-starring with two celebrated actresses (Sweden's Bibi Andersson and Italy's Valentina Cortesa), Crawford played a doctor who commits acts of sabotage against the oppressors of his homeland (a country not identified in the screenplay, but probably Yugoslavia under Nazi occupation). The routine way the subject matter was handled negated much of the good in the film and its star was only directed to be Broderick Crawford. Yet, compared to the villainies he was required to perform in later pictures made in other countries (such as the 1966 releases *Kid Rodelo* and *The Texican*, routine Westerns), this role had more than its share of validity.

His American film work of the '60s was nothing to rave about, either. Old friends from the past decade, Clarence Greene and Russell Rouse, came through with a couple of small guest star roles in *A House Is Not a Home* (1964) and *The Oscar* (1966). In the former, a "biography" of New York madam Polly Adler (Shelley Winters), he played a politico who frequented her establishment; in the latter, he was a small town sheriff who busts up Stephen Boyd's operation. Both required only a few days' work. In the case of *The Oscar*, the reason for the casting of Crawford, Ernest Borgnine, Walter Brennan, James Dunn and several others was obvious: All these actors had won Oscars.

That film may have brought back memories for him, being made at Paramount, his first "Hollywood home" (now being taken over by Gulf and Western). The old Hollywood was dead and the actors who were part of it were not exactly in demand. So it was only a matter of time until Crawford made his contribution to one of A.C. Lyles' Paramount Westerns. Just like William Bendix, Brian Donlevy and Barton MacLane, he joined the swelling ranks of movie veterans with *Red Tomahawk* (1967), a standard cowboys and Indian film in which he played a seasoned cavalry scout. He soon found that once an actor fell into the image of has-been or just "an old-timer," it was a difficult thing to shake. In the late '60s, there were new studios cropping up that were the modern equivalents of the old Poverty Row outfits, and some, like Independent International, were stocking their films with many of Hollywood's elder citizenry. Crawford tried to steer clear of features that appeared to be hiring actors based on the wrinkles on their face, but occasionally, over the next few years, he did do some, such as *The Fakers*. *Terror in the Wax Museum* (1973) was one of several features he made with his old co-star Ray Milland, who was also forced to tread this B-picture path. It said something about the overall value of these epics that very few of them received wide release; they usually became second features at drive-ins.

Crawford decided that the TV guest star circuit was more promising than the films he was being offered. In the mid–'60s, he increased his television output with guest roles on Hollywood-based anthology series like *The Bob Hope Theater*. He also worked on shows featuring former co-workers from the old movie days, guesting on David Niven's *The Rogues*, Robert Wagner's *It Takes a Thief* and at least three different segments of Robert Stack's *The Name of the Game*. During this period, he and Tabor were divorced; their differences irreconcilable. The second Mrs. Crawford died of an undisclosed illness a little more than a year after their divorce, on December 18, 1968. She was only 35.

Crawford became a bit of a hermit after the marriage broke up. He now seemed to welcome isolation, moving into a house somewhere outside Tucson. Staying there for any length of time required more domestic work, which meant more television. On September 25, 1970, he was seen for the first time as Dr. Peter Goldstone on the Friday night CBS-TV series *The Interns*. Based on two popular Columbia movies of the '60s, it cast the veteran actor as the mentor of a group of neophytes at one of those ever-popular "large metropolitan hospitals." The role was modelled after Dr. Riccio, a character portrayed by Telly Savalas in the feature films, but fans familiar with *Not as a Stranger* were reminded of Dr. Aarons, the gruff but decent medical college instructor Crawford had played 15 years earlier. Medical series had come back into vogue the prior season with the success of *Marcus Welby, MD*, *Medical Center* and *The Bold Ones*, but like most trend followers, *The Interns* had a short life. Having the doctors alternate on different cases gave the program a more realistic approach, but when the older star of the series has more charisma than the younger ones, the fans work up little interest.

The short-lived series served other purposes. It brought him back to the scene of his greatest cinematic successes, Columbia Pictures; it got him another *TV Guide* interview; and he enjoyed working with the young actors who co-starred: Mike Farrell, Stephen Brooks, Hal Frederick, Elaine Giftos, Sandra Smith and Christopher Stone. Crawford's two sons were grown by this time and he could identify with the problems of the young. He told *TV Guide* in the March 6, 1971, issue. "I believe in [the kids]. They got a helluva beef. National Guard on campus! Kids bleeding in the streets." Although much of this was foreign to ideals he had when growing up, he had obviously developed an understanding of a newer generation. His warm feelings for Kim and Kelly Crawford came through in just a few brief words: "If they weren't my sons, they'd be the best friends I had." The Dwight Whitney article was a vast improvement over the piece in the same magazine 14 years earlier, revealing not only an improvement in the quality of writing but also a new softness emanating from an old tough guy.

He continued to do TV guest star work, including a rare chance to use his gift for comedy in a spoof of *The Treasure of the Sierra Madre* on *Get Smart*. Much of his TV work of the early '70s returned him to Universal, another earlier Hollywood home; there he played series roles in *Banacek*, *Jigsaw* and *Night Gallery*. He also got into the new TV trend of making 90-minute telefilms by appearing in *The Challenge* (1970), as an American general involved in a unique version of World War III, *The Tatt0ered Web* (1971), as a derelict accused of murder, and the *Adventures of Nick Carter* (1972), as a turn-of-the-century New York tycoon. His next "TV movie" *Forbidden Knowledge*, is actually no movie at all, just pasted-together episodes of Anthony Quinn's *Man and the City* teleseries from the 1971-72 series. It is worth mentioning because his entire performance runs little more than ten minutes but it is probably the most sensitive and moving performance Crawford ever gave in the medium. Using his father's surname Lester, he played a construction tycoon who was imprisoned years earlier when his work was found to be unsafe. Although he had always protested his innocence, he now confesses his guilt to save his grown son (Dack Rambo) from facing similar, but false, charges. Parental sacrifice is a tried-and-true theatrical device, but it was a new kind of role for Crawford.

After that came another European jaunt, the highlight of which were the few good moments he picked up as the security chief at the American Embassy in Beirut, Lebanon, in *Embassy* (1972). It had a good cast, including Ray Milland as the Ambassador, but just as had been the case for these two actors a quarter century earlier in *Sealed Verdict*, they were in the wrong topical spot at the wrong time. During this period, it was not an acting role that brought him satisfaction; it was his third marriage. His 1973 union with Mary Alice Mitchell brought him the mature relationship and the tranquility he had long desired in his personal life.

On his return to the U.S., he found that he was getting more leisure time, thanks to the diminishing size of his parts. With the 1974 TV movie *The Phantom of Hollywood* and the 1976 theatrical film *Won Ton Ton, the Dog that Saved Hollywood*, he and other screen veterans were shoe horned into ill-fitting roles. This was done presumably to generate interest in these irreverent tributes to the movie colony, but in Crawford's case, it seemed the rule in practically all his domestic roles of the mid- to late-'70s. He and Milland met again in not one but two 1976 TV movies of dubious quality. The only plus in either *Look What's Happened to Rosemary's Baby*, a disgraceful sequel to Roman Polanski's fine 1968 film, or the mini-disaster *Mayday at 40,000 Feet* was that neither required Crawford's presence during the entire shooting time.

The one exception among his film roles of that period was *The Private Files of J. Edgar Hoover*, a starring role in a biographical study of the recently deceased FBI chief. Once again, the cast was studded with many names from the past (dependable performers Dan Dailey, Jose Ferrer, June Havoc, Celeste Holm and Lloyd Nolan), but he would share the lead with James Wainwright, who played the FBI chief as a younger man. Crawford, although no double for Hoover, was just the type for the role. But exhibitors saw only one thing: The film had a has-been star in an unflattering portrayal. They were not convinced that a film revealing the nefarious activities of the FBI would win box office approval, and they were probably right. In trying to soften the man, the script painted surprisingly uncomplimentary pictures of John and Robert Kennedy (William Jordan, Michael Parks), Lyndon Johnson (Andrew Duggan), Martin Luther King (Raymond St. Jacques) and Richard Nixon, insultingly played by his supposed look-alike, non-actor Richard Dixon.

Crawford went on the publicity trail for *Hoover*. Many stars have hosted NBC's popular *Saturday Night Live* since its 1975 premiere, so it was not surprising to see him in his *Highway Patrol* role when a satire of his two decades–old TV series was called for; the star wore his familiar hat and trenchcoat. A nice touch was a "cinema verité" tour of New York streets, with the camera following Crawford past areas he had known as a struggling young actor in the '30s, all the while being greeted by well-wishers. Near the end of the show, he appeared as FBI chief Hoover receiving a late night caller (then–President Nixon, brilliantly impersonated by Dan Aykroyd). The sketch was basically just another one of their Watergate-related satires, but the image of Crawford calming the upset Nixon one minute and returning to bed with his teddy bear will not soon be forgotten. It was amusing to know that he had just played the same character in a serious film dealing with Hoover's fear of women and a columnist's intimations about his relationship with his longtime henchman Clyde Tolson.

In subsequent years, Crawford turned up in his Dan Matthews guise doing commercials for motor oil and being pulled over by the motorcycle patrolmen on *CHiPs*. Playing himself in *A Little Romance* was essentially more of the same. He interspersed those self-mocking roles with some straight stage acting during the late

'70s. He began with the difficult role of the bigoted old basketball coach in Jason Miller's *The Championship Season*. In many spots during his lengthy tours of his play, it was his name that brought in people who had never heard of the prize-winning play. The play enabled him to once again get the feel of a live audience as well as to travel; he went with it to England and Australia. In the latter country in 1979, he looked up his old *Born Yesterday* co-star William Holden, who was shooting a picture there. An occasional drinking buddy, Holden was interested in playing the coach in the movie version of the play. (He was set for the role when he died in 1981; Robert Mitchum played the role in the 1982 film.) Usually while on tours in other countries, Crawford found time for a small film role, so it was not surprising that he turned up in an Australian suspense film called *Harlequin* (1980). In the U.S., his theatrical work consisted mostly of performing "in the round" in dinner theaters. He took a much lighter role in a play called *The Second Time Around*, which hadn't made it on Broadway with the reliable Hans Conreid in his part, that of an elderly widower who finds a new romantic partner his own age and gets flack from his grown children. This new type of comedy offered a break from typecasting, for touring companies sometimes took whoever was available and did not consider whether they fit or not. But Crawford surprised them, using some of his own personal experiences with his children from his first marriage to identify with the part. If this performance had been in front of a wider audience, critics might have been surprised to find that the actor was not only capable of playing "himself."

Crawford was a once popular TV performer, so the neglect he received from that medium is appalling. After the *Saturday Night Live* appearance, TV producers ignored his comedic gifts. Although he reached the age of 70 in December 1981, he still appeared capable of more than just cameo roles on two of TV's most abysmal series, *Vega$* and *Fantasy Island*. As an island shopkeeper on the latter, he was required to be called "old man" and shoved around by a gang of pseudo-toughs, allowing the heroics to be performed by the slightly younger Claude Akins. Crawford also made a guest appearance on the PBS senior citizen–oriented series *Over Easy*.

The last of the second string tough guys died of complications from a series of strokes on April 26, 1986. He died within weeks of two other 1940s Best Actor Oscar winners. One was his old friend Ray Milland and the other was James Cagney. (It could be said that the latter was the last of the "first-string tough guys.") These two passings seemed to signify the end of an era. The words attributed to him in what was possibly his last interview were typical of the man: "The 'take the money and run' days never end. Oscar winner. Big deal. Cukor wants you. Fritz Lang, Fellini ... and still you spend a life waiting for another phone call. To pay the rent and keep your face up there, you do TV. Hell, if they're stupid enough to pay you for that junk, that's their problem." He also said how glad he was his sons chose not to be actors, and that his mother was better off dead, and out of the rat race.

So why, feeling as he did, did he continue acting when so many of his contemporaries had resigned themselves to living off Social Security and investments? One should remember that he was the son of a show business family—vaudevillians, no less. Vaudevillians were possibly the most resilient, flexible entertainers around. They put up with bad billing, poor accommodations and the derision of their Broadway counterparts. Somehow they survived, even though their art form did not. This was the source of Crawford's toughness as he survived on schlocky TV series and soap pad commercials. It certainly may not have been Shakespeare, but Crawford had as much tradition in his blood as did any member of Britain's National Theater.

The Films of Broderick Crawford

1. ***Woman Chases Man.*** Goldwyn-UA 1937. John Blystone. Miriam Hopkins, Joel McCrea, Charles Winninger, Ella Logan, Erik Rhodes, Alan Bridge, Leona Maricle. BC's debut, as an unconventional butler.

2. ***Submarine D-1.*** WB 1937. Lloyd Bacon. Pat O'Brien, George Brent, Wayne Morris, Doris Weston, Frank McHugh, Henry O'Neill, Dennie Moore, Regis Toomey, Veda Ann Borg, John Ridgely, Ronald Reagan. BC is briefly seen as a sailor.

3. ***Start Cheering.*** Col 1938. Albert Rogell. Jimmy Durante, Walter Connolly, Joan Perry, Charles Starrett, The Three Stooges, Gertrude Niesen, Hal LeRoy, Louis Prima, Ann Doran. Late entry in the college musical sweepstakes has a movie star going to college and being given a hard time by classmates like BC.

4. ***Sudden Money.*** Par 1939. Nick Grinde. Charles Ruggles, Marjorie Rambeau, Joyce Matthews, Evelyn Keyes, Richard Denning, Billy Lee, Philip Warren, Mary Parker, James Burke. BC is a sponging in-law of Ruggles.

5. ***Ambush.*** Par 1939. Kurt Neumann. Gladys Swarthout, Lloyd Nolan, William Henry, Ernest Truex, William Frawley, Antonio Moreno,

Richard Denning, Raymond Hatton, Polly Moran. BC is a member of a bankrobbing gang.

6. *Undercover Doctor.* Par 1939. Louis King. Lloyd Nolan, J. Carrol Naish, Heather Angel, Janice Logan, Robert Wilcox, Richard Carle. A J. Edgar Hoover–sanctioned tale with BC as another hood.

7. *Beau Geste.* Par 1939. William Wellman. Gary Cooper, Ray Milland, Robert Preston, Brian Donlevy, Susan Hayward, J. Carrol Naish, Albert Dekker, Heather Thatcher, James Stephenson, G. P. Huntley, Jr., Harold Huber, James Burke, Charles Barton, Henry Brandon, Donald O'Connor. BC is an American in the Foreign Legion.

8. *The Real Glory.* Goldwyn-UA 1939. Henry Hathaway. Gary Cooper, David Niven, Andrea Leeds, Reginald Owen, Kay Johnson, Vladimir Sokoloff, Henry Kolker, Roy Gordon, Russell Hicks. BC, an American soldier in the Philippines after the Spanish-American War, is a casualty in a battle with Moro natives.

9. *Island of Lost Men.* Par 1939. Kurt Neumann. Anna Kay Wong, J. Carrol Naish, Anthony Quinn, Eric Blore, Ernest Truex, Richard Loo, Rudolph Forster. BC is an overseer on a remote island outpost.

10. *Eternally Yours.* UA 1939. Tay Garnett. Loretta Young, David Niven, Hugh Herbert, Billie Burke, C. Aubrey Smith, Zasu Pitts, Virginia Field, Eve Arden, Raymond Walburn, Ralph Graves, Hillary Brooke. BC's fiancée Young becomes interested in magician Niven.

11. *Slightly Honorable.* UA 1940. Tay Garnett. Pat O'Brien, Edward Arnold, Ruth Terry, Eve Arden, Janet Beecher, Phyllis Brooks, Alan Dinehart, Clare Dodd, Douglass Dumbrille, Douglas Fowley, Evelyn Keyes, Bernard Nedell, Ernest Treux. O'Brien investigates political corruption and murder with the help of his old pal BC.

12. *I Can't Give You Anything But Love, Baby.* Univ 1940. Albert Rogell. Peggy Moran, Johnny Downs, Gertrude Michael, John Sutton, Jessie Ralph, Warren Hymer, Horace MacMahon. BC is a "mama's boy" gangster.

13. *When the Daltons Rode.* Univ 1940. George Marshall. Randolph Scott, Kay Francis, Brian Donlevy, George Bancroft, Stuart Erwin, Andy Devine, Frank Albertson, Harvey Stephens, Mary Gordon, Edgar Buchanan. BC is the most responsible of the law-abiding Dalton brothers, forced by circumstances to lead his family into a life of crime.

14. *Seven Sinners.* Univ 1940. Tay Garnett. Marlene Dietrich, John Wayne, Mischa Auer, Albert Dekker, Reginald Denny, Billy Gilbert, Oscar Homolka, Anna Lee, William Bakewell, James Craig, Vince Barnett, Samuel S. Hinds, Antonio Moreno. BC is the dumb but loyal sidekick of chanteuse Dietrich.

15. *Trail of the Vigilantes.* Univ 1940. Allan Dwan. Franchot Tone, Warren William, Mischa Auer, Andy Devine, Peggy Moran, Porter Hall, Samuel S. Hinds, Charles Trowbridge, Max Wagner. Dude newspaperman Tone gets a crash course in the cowboy way from BC and Devine.

16. ***The Texas Rangers Ride Again.*** Par 1940. James Hogan. Akim Tamiroff, Ellen Drew, John Howard, May Robson, Anthony Quinn, Charley Grapewin, John Miljan, Robert Ryan. BC is a bad guy in the modern West.

17. ***The Black Cat.*** Univ 1941. Albert Rogell. Basil Rathbone, Bela Lugosi, Gladys Cooper, Hugh Herbert, Gale Sondergaard, Anne Gwynne, John Eldredge, Claire Dodd, Alan Ladd, Cecilia Loftus. Typical mystery-comedy about a family brought together to await the inheritance of a dying relative. BC is a bumbling crime solver.

18. ***Tight Shoes.*** Univ 1941. Albert Rogell. Binnie Barnes, John Howard, Anne Gwynne, Leo Carrillo, Samuel S. Hinds, Shemp Howard, Richard Lane, Edward Gargan, Sarah Padden. Crooked politician BC is undone by a pair of ill-fitting shoes in this Damon Runyon tale.

19. ***Badlands of Dakota.*** Univ 1941. Alfred E. Green. Robert Stack, Richard Dix, Frances Farmer, Ann Rutherford, Hugh Herbert, Lon Chaney, Jr., Andy Devine, Donald Driggers. Successful westerner BC entrusts the well-being of his future bride to his younger brother—and regrets it.

20. ***South of Tahiti.*** Univ 1941. George Waggner. Brian Donlevy, Maria Montez, Andy Devine, Henry Wilcoxon, H. B. Warner, Armida, Abner Biberman. BC is Donlevy's pearl-diving buddy.

21. ***North to the Klondike.*** Univ 1942. Erle C. Kenton. Lon Chaney, Jr., Evelyn Ankers, Andy Devine, Keye Luke, Stanley Andrews, Willie Fung, Jeff Corey. BC battles for possession of an Alaskan gold mine.

22. ***Larceny, Inc.*** WB 1942. Lloyd Bacon. Edward G. Robinson, Jane Wyman, Jack Carson, Anthony Quinn, Barbara Jo Allen, Edward Brophy, Harry Davenport, Joseph Downing, Jackie Gleason, George Meeker, John Qualen, Andrew Tombes. BC is Robinson's dumb ox henchman who is given the task of digging a tunnel to the bank vault next door to their newly purchased luggage shop.

23. ***Butch Minds the Baby.*** Univ 1942. Albert Rogell. Virginia Bruce, Dick Foran, Porter Hall, Richard Lane, Grant Withers, Shemp Howard, Rosina Galli. Runyonesque lug BC becomes a sitter for Bruce's baby.

24. ***Broadway.*** Univ 1942. William Seiter. George Raft, Pat O'Brien, Janet Blair, Marjorie Rambeau, Anne Gwynne, S. Z. Sakall, Iris Adrian, Edward Brophy, Gus Schilling, Arthur Shields, Ralf Harolde, Abner Biberman. BC is a ruthless Prohibition-era gangster eventually killed by girlfriend Gwynne.

25. ***Men of Texas.*** Univ 1942. Ray Enright. Robert Stack, Jackie Cooper, Ralph Bellamy, Anne Gwynne, Leo Carrillo, Jane Darwell, John Litel, William Farnum, Janet Beecher, Kay Linaker, Joseph Crehan. BC is involved in an internal battle in post Civil War Texas.

26. ***Sin Town.*** Univ 1942. Ray Enright. Constance Bennett, Patric Knowles, Anne Gwynne, Leo Carrillo, Andy Devine, Ward Bond, Hobart Bosworth, Rolf Harolde, Arthur Aylesworth. BC's best lead to date, as a shady but intelligent character fighting for control of a town.

27. ***The Runaround.*** Univ 1946. Charles Lamont. Rod Cameron, Ella

Raines, Frank McHugh, Samuel S. Hinds, Joan Fulton (Shawlee), George Cleveland, Dave Willock, P.I. BC attempt to find a runaway heiress.

28. ***Black Angel.*** Univ 1946. Roy William Neill. Dan Duryea, June Vincent, Peter Lorre, Constance Dowling, Wallace Ford, John Phillips, Hobart Cavanaugh, Freddie Steele. Police captain BC keeps an eye on a woman who is trying to exonerate her husband, convicted of murder.

29. ***Slave Girl.*** Univ 1947. Charles Lamont. Yvonne DeCarlo, George Brent, Albert Dekker, Andy Devine, Lois Collier, Carl Esmond, Arthur Treacher, Philip Van Zandt. BC is the sidekick of adventurer Brent.

30. ***The Flame.*** Rep 1947. John H. Auer. John Carroll, Vera Ralston, Robert Paige, Henry Travers, Constance Dowling, Hattie McDaniel, Blanche Yurka, John Miljan, Victor Sen Yung, Harry Cheshire, Jeff Corey. BC is a blackmailer involved in ne'er-do-well Carroll's plot to gain an inheritance.

31. ***The Time of Your Life.*** UA 1948. H.C. Potter. James Cagney, William Bendix, Wayne Morris, James Barton, Ward Bond, Jeanne Cagney, Paul Draper, Jimmy Lydon, Gale Page, Tom Powers, Natalie Schafer, Howard Freeman, Pedro deCordoba. BC is a talkative cop who likes to argue with Bond.

32. ***Sealed Verdict.*** Par 1948. Lewis Allen. Ray Milland, Florence Marly, John Hoyt, John Ridgely, Ludwig Donath, Dan Tobin, Norbert Schiller, James Bell, Frank Conroy. BC is an American officer at Nuremberg.

33. ***Bad Men of Tombstone.*** AA 1948. Kurt Neumann. Barry Sullivan, Marjorie Reynolds, Julie Gibson, Guinn "Big Boy" Williams, Fortunio Bonanova, Harry Cording, Robert Barrat, Morris Ankrum, Douglas Fowley. Outlaw leader BC leads his men on the road to destruction.

34. ***A Kiss in the Dark.*** WB 1948. Delmer Daves. David Niven, Jane Wyman, Victor Moore, Wayne Morris, Maria Ouspenskaya, Joseph Buloff, Curt Bois, Raymond Greenleaf, Percival Vivian. Concert pianist Niven acquires an apartment house in which he encounters, among others, BC as an angry tenant who hates noise.

35. ***Night Unto Night.*** WB 1949. Don Siegel. Ronald Reagan, Viveca Lindfors, Rosemary DeCamp, Osa Massen, Craig Stevens, Erskine Sanford, Art Baker, Ross Ford, Ann Burr, Lillian Yarbo. Made in 1947. BC cast against type as an intellectual friend of ailing scientist Reagan.

36. ***Anna Lucasta.*** Col 1949. Irving Rapper. Paulette Goddard, Oscar Homolka, William Bishop, John Ireland, Whit Bissell, Will Geer, Lisa Golm, Gale Page, Mary Wickes. Boorish BC tries to use the return home of his prodigal sister-in-law Goddard for his own financial ends.

37. ***All the King's Men.*** Col 1949. Robert Rossen. Joanne Dru, John Ireland, John Derek, Mercedes McCambridge, Shepperd Strudwick, Walter Burke, Ralph Dumke, Raymond Greenleaf, Grandon Rhodes, Anne Seymour, Katherine Warren, Will Wright. BC's Oscar-winning role as grass roots politician Willie Stark, based on Louisiana's Huey Long.

38. ***Cargo to Capetown.*** Col 1950. Earl McEvoy. John Ireland, Ellen

Drew, Edgar Buchanan, Ted DeCorsia, Leonard Strong, Gregory Gay, Peter Mamakos. Ship's captain Ireland hires friendly enemy BC as his engineer.

39. *Convicted.* Col 1950. Henry Levin. Glenn Ford, Dorothy Malone, Millard Mitchell, Carl Benton Reid, Ed Begley, Frank Faylen, Will Geer, Roland Winters, Whit Bissell, Henry O'Neill. D.A. turned prison warden BC tries to help convict Ford, who he had originally sent up.

40. *Born Yesterday.* Col 1950. George Cukor. Judy Holliday, William Holden, Howard St. John, Frank Otto, Larry Oliver, Barbara Brown, Grandon Rhodes, Charles Cane, Claire Carleton. BC is a superb Harry Brock, an uncouth, self-made millionaire throwing his weight around Washington, D.C.

41. *The Mob.* Col 1951. Robert Parrish. Richard Kiley, Betty Buehler, Otto Hulett, Neville Brand, Ernest Borgnine, Charles Buchinsky (Bronson), Matt Crowley. Undercover cop BC tries to bring in waterfront racketeers.

42. *Scandal Sheet.* Col 1951. Phil Karlson. John Derek, Donna Reed, Rosemary DeCamp, Henry (Harry) Morgan, Henry O'Neill, Griff Barnett, Regis Toomey, Ida Moore, James Millican, Jonathan Hale, Pierre Watkin. After accidentally killing his ex-wife, news editor BC tries to steer his reporter protégé away from the truth.

43. *Lone Star.* MGM 1952. Vincent Sherman. Clark Gable, Ava Gardner, Lionel Barrymore, Beulah Bondi, Ed Begley, James Burke, William Conrad, William Farnum, Lowell Gilmore, Moroni Olsen, Russell Simpson. BC is a Texas politician who favors a treaty with Mexico, and clashes with Gable over that issue and Gardner.

44. *Last of the Comanches.* Col 1952. Andre DeToth, Barbara Hale, Lloyd Bridges, Martin Milner, John War Eagle, Johnny Stewart, Mickey Shaughnessy, George Matthews. Cavalry sergeant BC and men face extinction.

45. *Stop, You're Killing Me.* WB 1952. Roy Del Ruth. Claire Trevor, Virginia Gibson, Bill Hayes, Charlie Cantor, Margaret Dumont, Sheldon Leonard, Louis Lettieri, Henry (Harry) Morgan, Howard St. John. BC back in Runyon territory as an ex-bootlegger striving for legitimacy.

46. *The Last Posse.* Col 1953. Alfred Werker. John Derek, Charles Bickford, Wanda Hendrix, Henry Hull, Warner Anderson, Skip Homeier, James Bell, Tom Powers, Raymond Greenleaf, Will Wright. Veteran lawman BC takes a courageous stand against ruthless rancher Bickford.

47. *Night People.* 20th 1954. Nunnally Johnson. Gregory Peck, Anita Bjork, Rita Gam, Walter Abel, Buddy Ebsen, Casey Adams, Jill Esmond, Peter Van Eyck. In post war Berlin, American millionaire BC pressures the military to locate his kidnapped soldier son.

48. *Human Desire.* Col 1954. Fritz Lang. Glenn Ford, Gloria Grahame, Edgar Buchanan, Kathleen Case, Dan Seymour, Grandon Rhodes, Peggy Maley. BC is an insanely jealous husband who believes Ford is his wife's lover.

49. *Down Three Dark Streets.* UA 1954. Arnold Laven. Ruth Roman,

Martha Hyer, Marisa Pavan, Casey Adams, Kenneth Tobey, Gene Reynolds, Claude Akins, Harlan Warde, Alan Dexter. Fed BC seeks a colleague's killer.

50. *New York Confidential.* WB 1955. Russell Rouse. Richard Conte, Anne Bancroft, Marilyn Maxwell, J. Carrol Naish, Onslow Stevens, Mike Mazurki, Barry Kelley, Herbert Heyes, Steven Geray, Celia Lovsky, Ian Keith. BC is a powerful crime boss brought down by those close to him.

51. *Big House, U.S.A.* UA 1955. Howard W. Koch. Ralph Meeker, Charles Bronson, Lon Chaney, Jr., Reed Hadley, William Talman, Randy (Felicia) Farr, Willis Bouchey, Roy Roberts, Peter Votrian. BC is a scheming convict.

52. *Not as a Stranger.* UA 1955. Stanley Kramer. Robert Mitchum, Olivia de Havilland, Frank Sinatra, Gloria Grahame, Charles Bickford, Myron McCormick, Lon Chaney, Jr., Lee Marvin, Jesse White, Harry Morgan, Virginia Christine, Whit Bissell, Mae Clarke. BC has another change of pace as the brilliant medical school teacher of Mitchum, Sinatra and Marvin.

53. *The Swindle.* Lopert 1955. Federico Fellini. Giuletta Masina, Richard Basehart, Franco Fabrizi, Sue Ellen Blake, Giacamo Gabrielli. BC is an Italian-based crook tripped up by his own cohorts.

54. *The Fastest Gun Alive.* MGM 1956. Russell Rouse. Glenn Ford, Jeanne Crain, Russ Tamblyn, Leif Erickson, Allyn Joslyn, John Dehner, Rhys Williams, J. M. Kerrigan, Noah Beery, Jr., Chris Olsen. Variation on *High Noon* with gangleader BC looking for the title character.

55. *Between Heaven and Hell.* 20th 1956. Richard Fleischer. Robert Wagner, Terry Moore, Robert Keith, Buddy Ebsen, Skip Homeier, Brad Dexter, Mark Damon, Harvey Lembeck. WWII officer BC runs his company like a kingdom.

56. *The Decks Ran Red.* MGM 1958. Andrew Stone. James Mason, Dorothy Dandridge, Stuart Whitman, Katherine Bard, Jack Kruschen, Joel Fluellen. BC and Whitman are crewmen on a freighter who embark upon a murderous plot to collect salvage on their vessel.

57. *Goliath and the Dragon.* AIP 1960. Vittorio Cottafavi. Mark Forest, Gaby Andre, Bruce Cabot, Leonora Ruffo. BC is a despotic tyrant. (Italian title: *La Vendetta de Ercole.*)

58. *Convicts 4.* AA 1962. Millard Kaufmann. Ben Gazzara, Stuart Whitman, Ray Walston, Sammy Davis, Jr., Vincent Price, Rod Steiger, Dodie Stevens, Naomi Stevens, Jack Kruschen, John Kellogg, Carmen Phillips, Timothy Carey, Tom Gilson. BC has a cameo as a prison warden.

59. *The Castilian.* WB 1963. Javier Seto. Cesar Romero, Frankie Avalon, Alida Valli, Spartaco Santony, Fernando Rey, George Rigaud, Teresa Velasquez. BC is another tyrant, this time in Spain.

60. *Square of Violence.* MGM 1963. Luca Bercovici. Valentina Cortesa, Bibi Andersson, Anita Bjork, Branko Plesa, Dragomir Felba, Bert Sotlar, Victor Starcic. Filmed in Yugoslavia in 1961. BC is an anti–Nazi doctor.

61. ***A House Is Not a Home.*** Embassy 1964. Russell Rouse. Shelley Winters, Robert Taylor, Cesar Romero, Ralph Taeger, Kaye Ballard, Mickey Shaughessy, Jesse White, Roger C. Carmel, Connie Gilchrist, Raquel Welch, Edy Williams, Allyson Ames, Hayden Rorke. BC is a crooked politician.

62. ***Up from the Beach.*** 20th 1965. Robert Parrish. Cliff Robertson, Red Buttons, Irina Demich, Marius Goring, Francoise Rosay, James Robertson Justice, Slim Pickens. BC is seen briefly as an American officer on the beach at Normandy shortly after the invasion.

63. ***Kid Rodelo.*** Par 1965. Richard Carlson. Don Murray, Janet Leigh, Richard Carlson, Miguel Castillo, Jose Nulo. BC is one of a group of people seeking a fortune in gold in this Western lensed in Spain.

64. ***The Oscar.*** Par 1966. Russell Rouse. Stephen Boyd, Tony Bennett, Milton Berle, Joseph Cotten, Eleanor Parker, Elke Sommer, Jill St. John, Edie Adams, Ed Begley, Ernest Borgnine, Walter Brennan, James Dunn, Jean Hale, Peter Lawford, Jack Soo. BC is a small town sheriff, one of many to come into contact with ambitious actor Boyd.

65. ***The Texican.*** Col 1966. Lesley Selander. Audie Murphy, Diana Lorys, Luz Marquez, Antonio Casas, Antonio Perel, Molino Rogo, Aldo Sambrell. Seeking his brother's killer, Murphy comes up against outlaw BC.

66. ***Red Tomahawk.*** Par 1967. R. G. Springsteen. Howard Keel, Joan Caulfield, Wendell Corey, Scott Brady, Richard Arlen, Ben Cooper, Tom Drake, Donald Barry. BC is a seasoned cavalry scout lending a hand during an Indian uprising.

67. ***The Vulture.*** Par 1967. Lawrence Huntington. Robert Hutton, Akim Tamiroff, Diane Clare, Phillip Friend, Patrick Holt, Annette Carrell, Edward Caddick. BC is one of the targets of mad scientist Tamiroff.

68. ***Mutiny at Fort Sharp.*** Medallion 1967. Fernando Cerchia. Elisa Montes, Julio Pena, Marisol Valdermin, Nando Angelini. BC is a fort commander.

69. ***Hell's Bloody Devils.*** Independent-International 1968. Al Adamson. Scott Brady, John Gabriel, Keith Andes, John Carradine, Robert Dix, Jack Starrett, Kent Taylor, Vicki Volante. BC is a mobster in this mélange about gangs of lowlifes battling one another. Also known as *The Fakers*.

70. ***How Did a Nice Girl Like You Get Into This Business?*** Independent 1970. Will Tremper. Barbi Benton, Hugh Hefner, Jeff Cooper, Robert Morley, Lionel Stander, Hampton Fancher, Klaus Kinski, Max Nosseck, Jose Luis de Villalonga. An unnecessary ripoff of *Candy* (1968), about sexy Benton's encounters in the big bad world. BC makes a mercifully brief guest appearance, as a benign aging lecher.

71. ***The Yin and the Yang of Mr. Go.*** Ross International 1971. Burgess Meredith. James Mason, Jeff Bridges, Irene Tsu, Alec McCowen, Peter Lind Hayes. Confused tale of international arms trading. BC narrates sequences that were added without director Meredith's participation.

72. ***Embassy.*** Helmdale 1972. Gordon Hessler. Max Von Sydow, Richard Roundtree, Chuck Connors, Ray Milland, Marie Jose Nat, David

Bauer, Karl Held, Sarah Marshall, David Healy. BC is a security chief at a U.S. embassy.

73. ***Terror in the Wax Museum.*** Cinerama 1973. Georg Fenady. Ray Milland, John Carradine, Maurice Evans, Louis Hayward, Patric Knowles, Elsa Lanchester, Shani Wallis, Mark Edwards, Lisa Lu, Steven Marlo, Nicole Shelby. BC is a wealthy prospective buyer of the title establishment, whose previous owner (Carradine) has been killed.

74. ***The Private Files of J. Edgar Hoover.*** AIP 1976. Larry Cohen. Ronee Blakely, Dan Dailey, Howard Da Silva, Jose Ferrer, June Havoc, Celeste Holm, William Jordan, John Marley, Lloyd Nolan, Michael Parks, Raymond St. Jacques, Rip Torn, James Wainwright, Jack Cassidy, Andrew Duggan. BC is the older Hoover in this exploitative biography.

75. ***A Little Romance.*** WB 1979. George Roy Hill. Laurence Olivier, Diane Lane, Thelonious Bernard, Arthur Hill, Sally Kellerman, David Dukes, Andrew Duncan, Anna Massey, Claudette Sutherland, Peter Maloney. BC, as himself, is seen as the star of a movie being shot in France.

76. ***There Goes the Bride.*** Vanguard 1979. Terence Marcel. Tom Smothers, Twiggy, Jim Backus, Hermione Baddeley, Martin Balsam, Phil Silvers, Sylvia Syms, Michael Witney. This British farce about a wedding day tries to appeal to American audiences with guest shots by Crawford et al.

77. ***Harlequin.*** Australian 1980. Simon Wincer. David Hemmings, Robert Powell, Carmen Duncan, Gus Mercurio, Alan Cassell, Mark Spain, Sean Myers, Alyson Best, Mary Simpson, Bevan Lee. BC is in charge of security for politician Hemmings. Also known as *Dark Forces*.

78. ***Liar's Moon.*** Filmways 1981. David Fisher. Matt Dillon, Cindy Fisher, Hoyt Axton, Maggie Blye, Christopher Connelly, Yvonne DeCarlo, Susan Tyrell, Mark Atkins, Molly McCarthy. BC is the wealthiest man in a small town in Texas shortly after World War II.

79. ***Upper Crust.*** 1985? Peter Patzak. Frank Gorshin, Nigel Davenport. This film may not have been released.

80. ***Ransom Money.*** 1986? Dewitt Lee. Rachel Roman, Gordon Jump. This film may not have been released.

BC was one of the many veterans appearing in cameos in *Won Ton Ton—The Dog That Saved Hollywood* (Paramount, 1976). He provided an off-screen voice for *The Candidate* (WB, 1972) and was in the short *Keeping Fit* (Universal, 1942). He also appeared in these made-for-television movies: *The Challenge* (1970), *A Tattered Web* (1971), *Adventures of Nick Carter* (1972), *The Phantom of Hollywood* (1974), *Mayday at 40,000 Feet* (1976) and *Look What's Happened to Rosemary's Baby* (1976).

Brian Donlevy

During World War II, Brian Donlevy got a taste of stardom—not usual for the second-string tough guy. In all his films of the early '40s, he either shared top billing or had it all to himself in films that for the most part were major products. More importantly, the range of parts was extremely wide for an actor who had already spent five years or so establishing a certain film image. During the good years, he played some shady politicians, an immigrant, gamblers and gangsters, lawmen, officers in various branches of service, pioneers and Western outlaws, musicians and even the ghost of a former president. Although these were years when there was a shortage of competent leading men, Donlevy played a variety of roles denied to bigger stars even in peacetime.

That five-year period should be stressed, because without them, Donlevy's 40-year film career would be rather undistinguished. His tough guy of the '30s was particularly indicative of the era, but his later character work had few high spots. He may have not been physically suited for a starring career, but he was a lot more muscular than George Raft, who was more famous but could never have played most of the roles listed above. Raft had the advantage of a reputation as a lover, but a comparison of the two would clearly indicate that Donlevy was no less convincing when holding a young lady in his arms. A less fortunate trait shared by these performers was the ability to reject roles that might have given their film careers a shot in the arm. Like Raft, Donlevy appeared in a version of a Dashiell Hammett story, but missed out on a chance to play a basic Hammett hero: Raft rejected *The Maltese Falcon* while a projected film of *Red Harvest* for Donlevy was shelved before he could change his mind about doing it. And both actors had a shot at the role in *Double Indemnity* before a light comedian named Fred MacMurray

Brian Donlevy's westerns of the late '30s sometimes found him as the dude villain (obviously about to get his just desserts).

came along and made the character of Walter Neff forever his. At that time, Donlevy and Raft were obsessed with playing good guys.

Whenever Donlevy worked for one of the great directors, he responded to the guidance and turned in a fine performance. But the majority of Hollywood craftsmen could not always find the time to work with an actor who needed help and Donlevy's could almost match his wooden performances up with the quality of the particular director. Perhaps his movie success turned him into an introvert, on-camera as well as off. His early ambition to become a writer had been a lot stronger than any desire to perform. Like a great many actors of his generation, he had taken his vocation just as a means of survival and as the years went by, he became even more passive about it. All the good and bad that overtook him was not the result of any particular effort on his part.

He was that rare bird, an all–American tough guy not born in the U.S. Waldo Bruce Donlevy was born in Portadown, a village in County Armagh, Ireland, although by the time he was a year old, the family had immigrated to the U.S. They settled in Sheboygan Falls, Wisconsin. There is confusion as to the exact dates involved in Donlevy's early life. His date of birth was February 9, but the year has been reported in various sources as 1899, 1901 and 1903, with the middle year mentioned most frequently. It is further verified by the story that Donlevy ran away from home at age 15, to become a bugler with Gen. Pershing's U.S. Expeditionary Forces on their famous hunt for Pancho Villa in Mexico. That campaign took place in 1916. He was also said to have served as a pilot in the Lafayette Escadrille at the tender age of 16 and it has never been verified; possibly this was a creation of some over-zealous press agent in later years. Donlevy certainly could be the perfect model for the American fighting man he was to portray many times in later years.

Whatever his experiences in the first World War, he did attend St. John's Military Academy, although sources once again vary on whether he graduated from there in 1921. He then entered the U.S. Naval Academy with every intention of becoming a pilot (if he really had the experience in France, that should have helped), but he dropped out in less than a year. He had already become interested in writing and had a portfolio filled with poems and a play, which he took to New York with him. No one was interested, but he found work through a meeting with an artist he admired. The first wide public exposure to be afforded the Donlevy countenance was in his job as male model for the Arrow Collar company.

Around this time, Donlevy dropped the names Waldo Bruce (which he hated) and took the name Brian. Once he found that models were often picked for silent picture work, he decided to try it. In 1923, he made his first screen appearance in a short called *James-*

town. The following year, he had a bit part in *Monsieur Beaucaire* starring Rudolph Valentino. All his film roles of that era were so minute that he went virtually unnoticed.

It was the theater that brought Donlevy his first success as an actor. The story of how he won the part of Corp. Gowdy in the acclaimed comedy-drama *What Price Glory?* may also be apocryphal. He supposedly got drunk with the star of the play, Louis Wolheim, who promised him a part. Although Wolheim supposedly did not remember this promise when sober, he kept his word. The brawling duo of Capt. Flagg and Sgt. Quirt was created by Wolheim and William Boyd (the latter later changed his name to William "Stage" Boyd to avoid being confused with the movie star of the Hopalong Cassidy pictures). The play was a hit (433 Broadway performances). With a regular paycheck coming in, Donlevy had more opportunity to write. He took a creative writing course at Columbia University, but his professor did not think he had any talent. Although he never made a dime as a writer, he did not lose his enthusiasm and in the latter part of his life, when acting jobs were less frequent, he continued to turn out short stories.

Donlevy occasionally played bit parts in films during his first decade as an actor, but he concentrated more on the Broadway stage. He landed in a number of musicals (*Hit the Deck* and *Rainbow*), signed for his growing competence as a comic actor rather than for any musical ability. He continued to pick up extra income as a model for a variety of products in newspaper ads. Although *Rainbow* was not one of the top shows of 1928, Donlevy felt financially secure enough to marry Yvonne Grey in October of that year. Between shows, he picked up some film work in the New York area, securing his biggest part in an early talkie called *Mother's Boy* (1929); the film was designed to establish Morton Downey as a sort of "Irish Al Jolson," but failed in that attempt.

In the early '30s, Donlevy branched out into another medium with frequent roles on radio dramas. His stage appearances were numerous, but only three were unqualified hits: *Up Pops the Devil*, *Three-Cornered Moon* and *The Milky Way* were popular enough to be purchased by Paramount. (He did not get to recreate any of his theatrical parts in the film versions.) It was his flashy champion fighter in *The Milky Way* that attracted the movie scouts, but before he headed west, he had one more stage success in 1934, supporting future *Wizard of Oz* stars Bert Lahr and Ray Bolger in the musical revue *Life Begins at 8:40*. Once again he was acclaimed for his comic acting. What he did not know was that he was embarking on a new career that almost never required him to be funny again.

Donlevy's first noticeable film roles were villainous characters; these evil men were allowed an occasional evil smile, but they were essentially humorless. He was very noticeable as Edward G. Robinson's henchman Knuckles in Howard Hawks' *Barbary Coast* (1935); its producer Samuel Goldwyn "rewarded" him with another heavy role in the Eddie Cantor musical of the following year, *Strike Me Pink*. Paramount followed up his slimy henchman role in *Mary Burns, Fugitive* (1935) with a part on the right side of the law (a federal agent posing as a brain surgeon) in *13 Hours by Air* (1936). (At the same time, that studio was filming *The Milky Way* with a better-known screen personality, William Gargan, in Donlevy's stage role. In the remake *The Kid from Brooklyn*, Steve Cochran had the part of the fighter.) He had a larger-than-usual part in *Another Face* (1935), an RKO B-picture in which he played a gangster who gets plastic surgery and decides to crash the movies, which proves his undoing.

His first steady film work came with a player contract at 20th Century–Fox, which was trying to develop a good secure feature unit. But this break came too late to affect his marriage, which came to an abrupt end soon after his arrival in Hollywood. Although the breakup of his seven year, four month marriage left him somewhat bitter, he did not remain single for very long. Within ten months of his divorce from Yvonne Grey, he married nightclub singer Marjorie Lane just before Christmas 1936. Although an extrovert, the new Mrs. Donlevy soon adapted to her husband's disinterest in public socializing.

Donlevy was quickly starred in a succession of low budget but well-made programmers, usually playing reporters and detectives. His leading ladies ranged from the demure Rochelle Hudson and Gloria Stuart to the more hardened Glenda Farrell and Claire Trevor. He came off well as a tough hero in these films, especially in comparison to his roles in some of Fox's bigger films. In these films, he was called upon to menace pretty boys Tyrone Power and Robert Taylor and there was little chance for him to simulate brutality when being bested by these non-rugged heroes. Nevertheless, *This Is My Affair* (1937) with Taylor and *In Old Chicago* (1937) with Power were basically good entertainment and Donlevy was seen by people who rarely stayed for second features. Perhaps that was why he preferred to make these roles as sympathetic as possible—he did not want to be identified with such parts. Refusing to indulge in overt acts of villainy may have cost him some points; in *In Old Chicago*, he balked at performing some unseemly act upon the dead body of Don Ameche. The size of his part dropped, as did his billing. He was less reluctant in his next Power picture, *Jesse James* (1939), which had the same director, Henry King. Donlevy was cast as a villainous railroad hireling who blows up the James boys' farm (and their mother with it). He pulled out all the stops to make his character the ultimate in evil only to have Power, in the title role, gun him down relatively early in the film. But for hissing audiences, it didn't happen a moment too soon.

But before this picture, Fox had given Donlevy the opportunity to play comedy on screen. Ever since Edmund Lowe had left Fox, it seemed as though they didn't know what to do with Victor McLaglen. The indelible impression the two had made in the film version of *What Price Glory?* had put them in good stead for a decade after. But now they didn't know what kind of picture to cast him in, especially without another tough male who could be counted on to make a fool out of him. Even McLaglen's favorite director, John Ford, had him playing straight for *Wee Willie Winkie* star Shirley Temple in 1937, two years after his Oscar win for *The Informer*. That same year, he was cast as Donlevy's henchman in *This Is My Affair* and the two played well together. Since Donlevy had been playing the same type of leads that Lowe used to play, it was decided to try McLaglen and him as a team.

They didn't exactly set the screen ablaze as a pair of rough conventioneers in *Battle of Broadway* (1938), in which Raymond Walburn, as their bombastic boss, stole the show. Director George Marshall gave this trivial film a great deal of pace, which helped. Then the studio sent their new team to England, where many of the majors were trying to set up production. The film was called *We're Going to Be Rich* and they co-starred with the very popular British performer Gracie Fields. Her husband, former comic Monty Banks, directed. Donlevy, the only American in the cast, did some of his broadest playing in the role of a pubkeeper in England. However, Fields, who never quite caught on with American audiences, appeared a bit too mature for Donlevy to be brawling with McLaglen over, especially considering the more youthful leading ladies he appeared with in the States. There were no subsequent ventures for this male duo, which was just as well.

Not entirely satisfied with their B-picture unit, Fox allowed

Donlevy to do outside work. In 1939, he was a villain in no less than five big budgeted films and also squeezed in a potboiler at Columbia, *Behind Prison Gates*, playing the same kind of hero's role he'd been playing at Fox. Cecil B. DeMille's *Union Pacific* and William A. Wellman's *Beau Geste* began his successful career at Paramount. Although he was still unhappy about playing the menace, he was now matched against the industry's more rugged stars: Gary Cooper, Joel McCrea, Randolph Scott, Jimmy Stewart and John Wayne all took cinematic swings at him within a two-year period. Their presence gave his villainous acts greater credibility.

While it never hurt to be a villain in a DeMille epic, it was *Beau Geste* that really lifted him out of the category of just another tough guy. Robert Preston, then a screen newcomer, was in both these films and would become a good friend of Donlevy, but it reportedly was not easy on the set of *Beau Geste*. Recognizing the great opportunity offered by the role of the evil Russian-born Sgt. Markoff, the actor began living the part on and off the set. The results speak for themselves: Donlevy etched one of the screen's most unforgettable portraits of villainy, while at the same time showing this monster to be a superb military man. His positioning of dead Legionnaires in the Fort's parapets as a way of duping the attacking tribesmen is a classic scene. It is far superior to the 1926 version, in which Noah Beery was defeated by his silent gesticulating as well as a death which came too early in the film. In the 1966 version, Telly Savalas played the parallel role like a coldly efficient robot. The excellence of Donlevy's performance was acknowledged with an Academy Award nomination as Best Supporting Actor of 1939, no small accomplishment in that golden year.

The film's heroes, the Geste brothers, were played by Gary Cooper, Ray Milland and Robert Preston and the superb cast also included J. Carrol Naish, Susan Hayward, Broderick Crawford and Albert Dekker. All were resigned to letting Donlevy walk away with the acting honors, but were put off by his nasty manner between takes. Director Wellman, who had the reputation of manipulating his actors' emotions to get the best results, allowed Donlevy to go as far as he could. Milland, not as easygoing as his co-stars, began to feel the same way about Donlevy as his character felt about the sergeant. In the scene where Cooper lies dying, Donlevy searches his person and steals a valuable jewel. Milland comes upon this and, when Cooper trips Donlevy, Milland runs the hateful sergeant through with his bayonet. To get Wellman's realistic effect, Donlevy was heavily padded for the occasion, but not covered under his arms, where Milland thrust the bayonet's point. Beneath that cruel veneer, Donlevy was still a softie and at the first sight of his own blood, he collapsed. Years later, Wellman was still telling this anecdote and Milland gleefully recounted the episode in his autobiography, *Wide-Eyed in Babylon*. Even the victim has verified this occurrence; Donlevy mentioned it over 20 years later while being interviewed on the TV program *Here's Hollywood*. He may have wanted to show he had no malice when he claimed it was an accident, but since he later appeared with Milland in other films, maybe he never got the joke. After Donlevy's death, Hollywood would learn this was one of the town's legends that was not apocryphal.

This incident was rare, because Donlevy usually made friends, not enemies. Younger actors such as Preston and William Holden liked him very much, and he became popular with some directors. George Marshall, for whom he had done *Battle of Broadway*, summoned him to Universal in 1939 for a film that turned out to be the surprise hit of the year, *Destry Rides Again*. His role of Kent was more like his typical villainous parts, a suave heel who is attractive enough to have had a prior liaison with heroine Marlene Dietrich, who in her classic role of Frenchy reforms enough to take the bullet Kent means for Destry (James Stewart). Familiarity with the plot has diminished the film's overall value down through the years but there are still many moments of enjoyment, especially for the first time viewer.

After completing this film and the W. C. Fields classic *You Can't Cheat an Honest Man*, Marshall had one more film to do for Universal under his three-picture deal with them. He invited Donlevy in on this project since they were both in the same position, having been signed by Paramount, a studio that did not have their next projects lined up. One night Donlevy, Broderick Crawford and some other performers were invited to Marshall's house where they were introduced to an old codger who claimed to be the last surviving Dalton brother, member of the notorious outlaw gang of more than a half-century earlier. Several of the remaining Western badmen had become technical advisors or bit players in early Hollywood, so this was not too surprising. The Daltons had started out as lawmen and Marshall was interested enough to have a script prepared. This script adhered more closely to the motion picture theme of "crime doesn't pay," so the Dalton stories were hardly transferred verbatim. Typically, Donlevy was cast as the meanest brother (Grat), with burly Crawford,

Sergeant Brian Donlevy confronts Legionnaire Gary Cooper in *Beau Geste* (1939); Donlevy received an Oscar nomination for his performance.

mild-mannered comic actor Stuart Erwin and the eternal kid brother Frank Albertson rounding out the unusual sibling gang. Like other movies focusing on real-life outlaws, when the Dalton's rode sympathies were with them and all the blame was placed on the shoulders of the scheming businessmen who drove them into lives of crime. Just as in the previous year's *Jesse James*, Randolph Scott played the sympathetic lawman entrusted with the task of bringing in the outlaws he really likes. This would be a role that Donlevy would soon become familiar with: He played a variation of the lawman character the following year in *Billy the Kid*. Throughout his career, he would appear in pictures about many infamous badmen; besides the films featuring the James and Dalton boys and Billy Bonney, he would later portray, in two separate films, the mercenary guerrilla leader of the Civil war, Quantrill. In fact, as he grew older, he was seen more frequently in the Old West than in the modern-day big city.

His contractual obligation to Fox came to an end with *Brigham Young* (1940), another Tyrone Power epic. He played Angus Duncan, a Mormon who almost wrecks the chances of his sect to establish themselves in Salt Lake City, Utah, due to his in-fighting with Dean Jagger, who has the title role. Next came Preston Sturges' *The Great McGinty* (1940). Had Sturges, a successful playwright-turned-screenwriter, been able to film his original story "The Vagrant" when it was first written seven years earlier, Donlevy would have lost out. But the author's earlier film about the rise and fall of a man in contemporary America, *The Power and the Glory* (1933), had not made money, so Sturges put aside this story. After penning many successful scripts for Paramount, they were willing to give him a chance as director, though on a limited budget. That meant a low-salaried star—namely Donlevy. Like most directors who cast Donlevy in pivotal roles, he was apprehensive about Donlevy's abilities but later came to trust him.* The sardonic humor Donlevy had used mostly on stage came in handy for McGinty, the bum who is made governor by the machinations of political boss Akim Tamiroff. What may have prevented the film from becoming a really outstanding political satire was the problem that blighted Sturges' career: the lack of discipline that turned potentially serious moments into wild comic frenzy. Nevertheless, the reviews could not have been better had *The Great McGinty* been considered an A-product rather than a low-budgeter (under $350,000) made in three weeks. Bosley Crowther (*The New York Times*) wrote that both Donlevy and Tamiroff "catch the satiric points in their roles with consistent brilliance." Sturges' original screenplay won an Oscar.

Still unsure about what leads Donlevy was suited for, the studio next cast him as flight instructor to Ray Milland, William Holden and Wayne Morris in *I Wanted Wings* (1941), one of the more popular pre–Pearl Harbor service dramas. In the musical *Birth of the Blues* (1941), as a trumpeter, he seemed to be having a good time throughout. His contract allowed him considerable leeway in obtaining outside work, so much so that he became essentially a contractee at MGM and Universal through a good part of the '40s. At the former studio, he paid Robert Taylor back for *This Is My Affair* by rather reluctantly gunning him down in *Billy the Kid*. His last release of 1941 was Universal's *South of Tahiti*, the first of the Maria Montez

---

*Sturges feared a confrontation when requesting Donlevy shave his mustache for the role but the actor readily agreed.

island melodramas. His buddies were his old compatriots from the Dalton picture, Broderick Crawford and Andy Devine.

The following year was his most productive of all. Only one of his eight films relegated him to a supporting role. In William Wellman's *The Great Man's Lady*, he was billed below the title and the stars Barbara Stanwyck and Joel McCrea, who had served the same capacity in *Union Pacific*. He played a gambler who paid court to Stanwyck, while she remained true to trailblazing but neglectful McCrea. It was his last role for some time that did not seem tailored for him and he was allowed to be honorable about his wooing of Stanwyck, not a trait the old Donlevy would have displayed. His three other 1942 Paramount releases gave him top billing and more depth. The first was *The Remarkable Andrew*, which provided another opportunity to combine bluster with wry comic timing. As the ghost of the seventh U.S. president Andrew Jackson, he leads a gang of illustrious ghosts in an attempt to exonerate government clerk William Holden. In true Frank Capra style, the young man has been framed by the city fathers, the real crooks. Unfortunately, director Stuart Heisler was no Capra and this blend of fantasy and political comedy isn't too effective. This time Donlevy was billed over Holden, unlike *I Wanted Wings*. (Holden's longtime valet Byron Fitzpatrick was initially Donlevy's; supposedly Donlevy lost him to Holden in a poker game.)

It had to give Donlevy satisfaction to be starred in *A Gentleman After Dark* at United Artists. The script was just a rehash of an old Paramount property (*A Whiff of Heliotrope*) which had been utilized by those very dignified gentlemen Clive Brock and Herbert Marshall, the latter playing the role now inherited by Donlevy. Donlevy played a kind-hearted gangster with a vicious wife; playing that part, and billed below him in the credits, was Miriam Hopkins. She had been the star of his first Hollywood film *Barbary Coast*, so here was solid evidence of how far he had risen in seven years. Once a temperamental screen star, Hopkins had all but given up films for stage work, save for some stunning character work, so the billing here was understandable.

Donlevy and an old New York acting compatriot, Pat O'Brien, shared star billing in Columbia's *Two Yanks in Trinidad*, a bit of patriotic fluff that set no sparks off at the box office. But his next two Paramount films were definitely among his biggest successes. First up was *Wake Island*, possibly the most topical war film ever made, as it was released within months of the real-life event. He

sank his teeth into the meaty role of the courageous Major Caton.*
The film's topicality paid off, winning director John Farrow the top
accolade from the New York Film Critics for the year; the film itself
was Oscar-nominated. Many of the war films that followed tried to
capitalize on its success, using a currently renowned battle zone for
its title, usually to prop up a hackneyed story. *Wake Island* was the
first and, except for the slightly more moving Tay Garnett film
Bataan, remained the best.

Since Fred MacMurray and Ray Milland were still primarily
involved in comedy, Donlevy found himself Paramount's top mature
leading dramatic actor. The studio felt secure in casting younger
actors like Preston, Holden and Macdonald Carey in his company.
(Years later, Preston expressed gratitude for having actors like Donlevy around early in this career, and Holden thought enough of Donlevy to ask him to be his best man when he eloped with Brenda
Marshall.) Two other Paramount newcomers who worked well with
Donlevy were Alan Ladd and Veronica Lake, who had just had a
successful teaming in *This Gun for Hire*. The studio reteamed them
in *The Glass Key*; Donlevy was top-billed but Ladd got the most
footage. Ladd had the role George Raft played in the 1935 version
of Dashiell Hammett's story, bodyguard and friend to the McGinty-like political boss played by Donlevy. As far as the fan magazines
were concerned, Donlevy might not have been in the picture at all.
Even William Bendix, riding high due to his success in a much better part in *Wake Island*, drew more attention in the small role of a
brutish thug. Donlevy's large output during this period did not
always guarantee him the meatiest role, but he brought authority to
this film.

Donlevy reportedly told his bosses that he only wanted to play
"he-men roles—rough, tough and realistic." He had little faith in his
versatility, though some directors knew he was capable of more. Universal's 1942 *Nightmare* filled his specifications; it was an unpretentious little film compared to his Paramount fare. The actor would
thereafter refer to the part of fast-talking gambler Daniel Shayne as
his favorite. His leading lady in this tale of Nazis and murder was
the unfortunate Diana Barrymore. Donlevy's affection for this character would spill over into other mediums; in the radio and TV series

---

*A pseudonym for Major Devereaux, the commanding officer on Wake Island, who had been reported missing while the film was in production. Bosley Crowther of The New York Times *wrote that Donlevy's characterization was "a credit to the corps, not to mention the acting profession."*

Dangerous Assignment, he played a similar type named Steve Mitchell, and it's easy to see a similarity between Mitchell and Shayne. His preference for this character type over the much more brilliantly executed Sgt. Markoff may reveal why his career sank as fast as it did. Soon after this, Paramount put him on suspension when he chose not to play Walter Neff in *Double Indemnity*.

He kept up his status at MGM with *Stand By for Action* (1942). He shared stellar billing with Robert Taylor and the formidable Charles Laughton, strangely cast as an American admiral. Donlevy, as Lt. Taylor's immediate superior, proved as adept in a naval uniform as he had been in other branches of the service. His next film was a setback and the first Donlevy performance that can be termed wooden. As the Czech doctor who kills the Nazi Heydrich in Fritz Long's *Hangmen Also Die!* (1943), he was miscast and not because of his nationality, since he is out-acted by such non–Czechs as Walter Brennan, Anna Lee and Dennis O'Keefe. (Donlevy was completely turned off by the domineering Lang.) During the early days of TV, before the major studios sold out, the independently-made *Hangmen Also Die!* was (unfortunately) the Donlevy film most frequently telecast. Nineteen forty-three also marked the birth of daughter Judith Ann.

In 1944, he completed two brief chores at Paramount. He and Akim Tamiroff reprised their *Great McGinty* characterizations in Preston Sturges' *Miracle of Morgan's Creek*; it was a short but amusing cameo in a film that was far bigger box-office than the earlier film. (He played McGinty once more in a 1955 *Lux Video Theatre* adaptation of the original film.) He narrated the short *The City That Stopped Hitler—Heroic Stalingrad*, a documentary made by the Soviets. He then embarked upon what was probably his most taxing film role. The film was King Vidor's *An American Romance* (1944), made at MGM. It was originally planned for Spencer Tracy, who decided against doing it, so Donlevy was recruited. The director envisioned the film as the reaffirmation of the American dreams, as he showed the rise of an illiterate immigrant to a powerful executive position. Donlevy played the lead with proper zest, sprinkling his good humor into a film that was otherwise heavy-handed in its approach. *New York Times* critic Bosley Crowther felt that Donlevy's performance was "in the thick style of dialect comedy." The film was much too long and, even after MGM cut it, it still ran 122 minutes and the star was on screen for just about every one of them. To his credit, he played it as though he was totally unaware that it was already a stereotype; Paul Muni, Edward G. Robinson and some lesser actors had done variations on the industrious immigrant's success in American industry. Vidor, aware of Donlevy's contribution, called him "a splendid actor, in his way," perhaps still feeling that Tracy would have made his film more profound. But even if the film had been better, it was far too specialized to enjoy a wide appeal with wartime audiences. Donlevy retained a special fondness for the film with good reason: It was his last really worthwhile leading role.

He continued to turn down roles offered by Paramount, preferring to spend his time working around his Brentwood estate and playing with his baby daughter. He used his few suspension periods to turn his home into a farm, raising chickens and growing crops. His ten years of success in the movie industry had made it possible for him to indulge in various new interests. He collected great works of art, a common practice among the Hollywood crowd. Like Charles Bickford, he also purchased mines and sometimes drove out to the Mojave Desert to see how work progressed on them.

He was reunited with Alan Ladd and William Bendix in *Two Years Before the Mast*, which was actually filmed in 1944, soon after Ladd got out of the service. Ladd, by now one of the most popular stars in the business, assumed top billing. The studio had decided to space the releases of his film and this one was not seen by the public until 1946. Second-billed Donlevy played the author of the piece, Richard Henry Dana, serving as a narrator while on-screen and involved in the action onboard ship. The film was exciting and made money, but its delayed release did not help him at the studio. As the war was coming to an end, actors returned from the service; the actors who had filled the void in their absence *and* the newly returned stars combined were a glut on the market. The major studios responded by terminating those contract players considered the least popular. Donlevy gradually slipped back into something closely resembling his pre-war status.

In 1945 he did a guest stint in Paramount's all-star *Duffy's Tavern* and worked again with Ray Milland (sans weapon) in a light comedy called *The Trouble with Women*, which had such a delayed release that Donlevy was no longer under contract to them when it finally hit theaters. Donlevy saw that this was no time to be selective and his last two Paramount films indicate this. He took his first villainous role in years, playing Trampas in a 1946 color remake of *The Virginian*. In the earlier 1929 version, Walter Huston could not do much with this sneering man in black, and Donlevy was no

Huston. His last work on the Paramount lot was in *Our Hearts Were Growing Up* (1946), playing a comic bootlegger in support of Diana Lynn and Gail Russell, who were so good as Emily Kimbrough and Cornelia Otis Skinner in the earlier film *Our Hearts Were Young and Gay* that a sequel was called for.

Donlevy did not feel the crunch immediately as he still owed both MGM and Universal some pictures. Universal's *Canyon Passage* (1946) was a particularly fine production, colorful and well-paced by director Jacques Tourneur. Second-billed Donlevy played a banker who loses girlfriend Susan Hayward to his best friend (top-billed Dana Andrews), and then loses his life due to his gambling weakness. Ward Bond was the chief menace in this western. Far less noteworthy was Universal's *Song of Scheherezade* (1947) in which he played a Russian naval captain whose ship is becalmed in an eighteenth century Middle Eastern seaport. Allegedly a comic spoof, it usually found Donlevy and his fellow actors reaching for laughs that were not there.

Metro put him into some class films before his obligation to them ended. *The Beginning or the End* (1947) was an expensive and detailed study about the events leading up to the preparation of the atomic bomb, culminating with the bombing of Hiroshima and Nagasaki. Fortunately, the studio bigwigs resisted the temptation to have big stars play the scientific, political and military higher-ups involved; Donlevy and Robert Walker, as the officers in charge of the Manhattan Project, are the biggest names involved with a supporting cast of character actors impersonating Einstein, Oppenheimer, Roosevelt and others. In our modern era, when the term "docu-drama" has been given new meaning by countless TV movies, this film takes on added significance, especially since it involves an act that is still being debated today. As for Donlevy, he had to behave in an exemplary manner since, just as in *Wake Island*, he was playing a real-life character, Gen. Leslie Groves.

His last three pictures for Metro offered him negligible roles. In *Killer McCoy* (1947) he played a gambler who buys up the contract of fighter Mickey Rooney, only to find that Rooney is romantically involved with his daughter Ann Blyth. The film, designed to present a more adult Rooney, was a remake of Robert Taylor's *The Crowd Roars*; just as in *The Glass Key*, Donlevy was playing a role first played by Edward Arnold. In *A Southern Yankee* (1948), he did for Red Skelton what he had done for Eddie Cantor in the '30s and would do for Jerry Lewis in the '60s: play straight man. This was one of Skelton's more inventive comedies, helped by the sight gags devised by Buster Keaton. *Command Decision* (1948) was a top quality film with a splendid cast (Clark Gable, Walter Pidgeon and Van Johnson). But Donlevy, as an Air Force general forced to replace his outspoken friend Gable, never seemed to get too involved in the action. In *Kiss of Death* (1947), made by his old studio Fox, Donlevy was the least critically praised of the stellar performers. His straightforward playing of Deputy D. A. D'Angelo just couldn't compete with the strong performances of stars Victor Mature and Richard Widmark.

Donlevy and wife Marjorie split in 1947; their mutual love for their daughter Judy was no longer enough to keep them together. He gave her the Brentwood house and moved to Malibu,* and the settlement allowed both equal time with their child. During this period of renewed socializing he served as an escort to Joan Crawford, who had been divorced from actor Phillip Terry in 1946. A negative by-product of the divorce was a marked increase in his "social drinking" and his waistline.

Because he had tasted stardom, it took Donlevy longer to switch to character work. He began working almost exclusively for secondary studios, playing his last romantic hero roles in three United Artists productions. In *Heaven Only Knows* (1947), *The Lucky Stiff* (1949) and *Impact* (1949), he looked too old for his leading ladies. *The New York Times* described his work in the latter film as having "all the animation and charm of an automaton." After that, Donlevy was more likely to be seen as the girl's "much older" husband. Such was the case in Universal's *Shakedown* (1950), where he is a reformed ex-gangster double-crossed by a scheming photographer (Howard Duff) who wants his younger wife (Anne Vernon). Another Universal release of 1950, *Kansas Raiders,* found him playing a vile Quantrill whose young wife Marguerite Chapman found more to admire in Jesse James (Audie Murphy).

He again played Quantrill in Republic's *The Woman They Almost Lynched* (1953), the last of four pictures he did for that studio. Fortunately, Republic was spending more on pictures in those days and Donlevy worked with such old Fox compatriots as Claire Trevor, J. Carrol Naish and director Allan Dwan, who had supervised

---

For a period, Donlevy held the honorary title of Mayor of Malibu Beach. Film stars were often selected by their neighbors as "chief executive" of the California community they resided in. The job required no particular administrative duties.

the filming of his very first starring roles in 1936. His worst picture of the era was not for Herbert Yates' small studio but for Howard Hughes' more prestigious one, RKO. Its title was *Slaughter Trail* (1951) and it may outrank the Japanese sci-fi film *Gammera, the Invincible* (1967) as the actor's worst. It was one of the most cliché-filled cavalry vs. evil white men pictures, made even more obnoxious by the then-popular habit of having some singer constantly wailing the events of the plot on the soundtrack. Donlevy was the fort commander and Howard Da Silva, the evil ship captain in *Two Years Before the Mast*, was the villain. When it became obvious that Da Silva was to be the next victim of the Communist witch hunt, the conservative studio fired him and reshot all his scenes with a miscast Gig Young assuming the role, thus making the events behind the scenes just as unpalatable as was the final product upon the screen.

Donlevy had remained a frequent performer on radio even after making it in Hollywood. Programs like the *Lux Radio Theatre* allowed him to recreate such roles as Major Caton in *Wake Island* for the airwaves, as well as tackling movie parts that others had played. But he did not headline his own series until 1950, when he starred in *Dangerous Assignment* for NBC. It was the kind of role he had always liked—a tough adventurer who comes to the rescue of those in trouble. Many name actors were headlining radio shows in those days, trying to save the medium from the onslaught of television. When Donlevy decided he would transfer the show to that new visual medium, he found he was making an unpopular choice. Many aging performers preferred a brief supporting role in a feature film to a starring role on TV, at least in the early '50s. But Donlevy still wanted stardom, wherever he could get it, and took the plunge.

One of the most memorable moments of TV in the early days was the regular opening of *Dangerous Assignment*. Donlevy would be seen walking down a dark street impeccably dressed for the evening, complete with top hat. Suddenly a knife would be thrown at him, missing his head by inches and lodging in the wall beside him as a symbol of the danger he was about to face. Unfortunately, the body of the show was never as exciting. It began in March 1952 and had a good run, with its reruns doing even better in syndication over the years. But even though the star was also the show's producer, he did not collect any residuals in later years. He had no particular business sense and, like many people, did not read the fine print in the contracts he signed.

If the series proved somewhat disappointing in the long run, there was one positive side to it. The show's bookkeeper was the fortyish Lillian Arch Lugosi, who for 20 years was the wife of the screen horror king, Bela Lugosi. From the time of the Bela-Lillian wedding in 1933, Lillian put up with her famous husband's erratic behavior, complete with practical jokes, temper tantrums and eventually drug addiction. She gave him a son, Bela, Jr., kept his house and (when things got rough for him in the movie business) she accompanied him on tours of summer theaters, where he recreated his famous role of Dracula. Eventually, things proved too much for her and she was in the process of obtaining a divorce when she and Donlevy first became acquainted. (Lugosi did not seek a cure to his drug addiction until after the divorce became final.) Having both been burned by their earlier marriages, Donlevy and the fortyish Lillian found solace in their quiet, mature companionship.

Donlevy left Malibu and moved to Palm Desert, intending to resume writing. He knew that there were few worthy acting roles awaiting him, but he found he could not completely forsake performing. Sometimes, the location of the filming played a large part of his decision. A desire to go to England figured in his acceptance of starring roles in a pair of science fiction films inspired by the popular *Quatermass* TV series of 1953. In Britain, these films were named for the Dr. Quatermass character, the part he essayed, but the U.S. distributor United Artists released them under the more exploitative titles *The Creeping Unknown* and *Enemy from Space*. They were lost among the plethora of other space invader films then glutting the market. Val Guest, who directed both films, would later comment about his star's drinking between takes and then having to be reminded of what was occurring in the scene, but he characterized Donlevy as a "great guy and great to work with." It was obvious that Donlevy was hired because an American name was needed to improve the films' box office prospects, a common practice at the time. Back at home, he found he also had to swallow his pride and play characters who were not exactly the center of attention. *The Big Combo* (1955) offered a fine role, an aged gangster who must do the bidding of younger Richard Conte, and he made the most of his good scenes. With his TV series now ended, he also returned to stage work.

Donlevy made short tours of various theaters in the round all over the country, acting in then-recent New York successes. The two roles he took were certainly diverse. He played a cartoonist in the light comedy *King of Hearts* and then turned around and played a once-great actor destroyed by alcohol in *The Country Girl*. (The role of Frank Elgin in the latter had been played superbly by Paul Kelly in its original Broadway incarnation.) In some ways, it may have been the most difficult part he ever took on. Donlevy, like Elgin, usually turned to drink when personal problems became too much to bear, but the real actor was able to set limits on his imbibing, thanks to the fairly constant work schedule he set for himself. But no matter where acting jobs took him, Donlevy always made sure that he was back at his California home in time for his daughter's annual stay with him. The knowledge that he still had the girl's love and devotion helped him over a lot of bad spots.

His screen roles were now divided into two categories: If it was a big-budgeter, he'd have a supporting role; if it was a quickie, he'd have one of the leads. Due to their similar introverted ways, Donlevy had remained friendly with his old Paramount co-star Alan Ladd. Through his Jaguar Productions at Warners, Ladd continued to use his former pals William Bendix, William Demarest, Frank Faylen and Lloyd Nolan (all former Paramount contractees) as costars in his films; by working for Ladd, Donlevy finally got a credit at Warners, the one major he had never worked for. Ladd did not appear in *A Cry in the Night* (1956), a suspenseful little B picture, with second-billed Donlevy as a police lieutenant who takes over the investigation of a girl's kidnapping. The girl (Natalie Wood) happens to be the daughter of Donlevy's superior, Edmond O'Brien. Veteran Paramount director Frank Tuttle was in charge, so working conditions were favorable. But with teenage rock 'n' roll movies now popular, some producers were reluctant to hire any older actors; the supply was now far greater than the demand for their services.

Donlevy filled in the drier periods with increased television work, guesting on two big western series, *Wagon Train* and *Rawhide*. And before the decade ended, he secured two good, though small, film roles. In Columbia's *Cowboy* (1958), a straightforward story of a cattle drive which starred Glenn Ford and Jack Lemmon, he had a sad cameo as a once-renowned gunfighter who is just another drover now that he has become old. He must have identified with it strongly, for his beautifully underplayed performance belies what many were saying about his "lost talent." In John Sturges' *Never So Few* (1959), his first for MGM in a decade, he was billed seventh and appeared relatively late in the proceedings. On the plus side, he got to play a general again, coming to the aid of unorthodox Capt.

Frank Sinatra, who is about to be crucified by the Army brass for gunning down our vicious jungle allies. On the less notable side were his parts in such minor fare as *Escape from Red Rock* (1958) and *Juke Box Rhythm* (1959).

Not many one-time stars get a chance to return to their place of great triumph, especially as head of the studio, but ironically Donlevy did. His first picture for Paramount after a 15-year absence found him as Mr. Paramutual, head of the studio, in Jerry Lewis' *The Errand Boy* (1961). Like Barton MacLane in the earlier *The Geisha Boy*, Donlevy was used by the star-director as a tough authority figure who could be turned into a stooge. His next picture, also for Paramount, was *The Pigeon That Took Rome* (1962), an abysmal comedy about the invasion of Italy. He was demoted in rank to colonel, dispatching Charlton Heston on a secret mission. Unfortunately, the mission was completed with an almost total lack of wit, proving that good budgets did not necessarily prevent stinkers. His best work in 1962 was as a down-and-out newspaperman in the opening segment of the short-lived TV series, *Saints and Sinners*, a worthwhile show produced by Four Star.

He acted on foreign soil in the films *Girl in Room 13* (1961), shot in Brazil, and the British-made *Curse of the Fly* (1964), respectively playing a private detective and a mad scientist. In this country, he accepted roles in such epics as *How to Stuff a Wild Bikini* (1965) and *The Fat Spy* (1965), having the dubious honor in the latter of playing the father of Jayne Mansfield. Donlevy and George Raft finally worked together in the foreign-made *Five Golden Dragons* (1967), playing (along with Dan Duryea and Christopher Lee) the "masked" rulers of the Hong Kong underworld. These four got to conceal their faces throughout most of the picture, while another veteran, Bob Cummings, had to expose his throughout the entire mess, since he was the hero. But even though Donlevy's face was concealed from view, the slurred quality of his latter-day voice was recognizable.

Donlevy even struggled through a commercial, though he was long past the time when he would have made a convincing TV pitchman. And in the summer of 1966, he once again stepped upon the stage for a brief summer run in Ruth Gordon's autobiographical play *Years Ago*, playing the father Clinton Jones (a role created on stage by Fredric March, on film by Spencer Tracy and on television by Robert Preston). Once again, renewed activity seemed inspired by Donlevy's personal life. In February 1966, he married his longtime friend and companion, Lillian Lugosi. Lillian, sharing many of his likes and dislikes, was the perfect mate for the introverted Donlevy. Besides his place in the desert, they took an apartment in Culver City, near the old MGM lot. It was obvious that he needed someone to stem the loneliness that came with advancing age; his daughter was now grown and he could not depend on her annual visits. He could not have chosen a better companion for his last years.

The actor continued in the TV guest star circuit, but the roles he received were clear indications that he was not in the forefront in this field. He played a retired general accused of murder on *Perry Mason* and a tycoon who passes himself off as one of his hirelings on a construction crew on *Family Affair*, one of the most hideously saccharine comedy series in the history of the medium. Yet he seemed to be enjoying himself in this hokey part. However, his last five years saw no humorous roles come his way. At least, they weren't intentionally humorous.

Returning to the Paramount lot, he followed William Bendix, Broderick Crawford, Barton MacLane and other old compatriots into the series of low-budgeted westerns produced by A. C. Lyles. Lyles' films were basically rehashes of the tried-and-true older westerns, but he gave work to some actors who were not in demand for any other kind of production. In deference to Donlevy's former standing, he was given equal billing with the male and female leads. He played a veteran gunfighter in *Waco* (1966) with Howard Keel and Jane Russell, a marshal in *Hostile Guns* (1967) with George Montgomery and Yvonne De Carlo and a mayor in *Arizona Bushwackers* (1968) with Keel and De Carlo. The bad thing about these films was the way they made some of the older actors appear. They were no longer up to learning lines quickly, as they had in their younger days, and the directors, stuck with speedy schedules, could offer no help. Thanks to his earlier investments, Donlevy was not as bad off as some of his co-stars, some of whom were damaging their fans' fond memories of them by doing inferior work just to pick up a few paychecks. His last Lyles picture was a modern-day private eye story, *Rogue's Gallery* (1968), but by this time, Paramount had no need for inexpensive second features and the film was not seen for five years, until ABC-TV bought it from the studio with a block of more desirable titles. The hero of *Rogue's Gallery*, Roger Smith, thereafter left acting to manage the career of his wife Ann-Margret. Playing a police detective, Donlevy made his next to last screen appearance.

Some of his contemporaries may have ended their film careers on a high note; Donlevy's ended with something called *Pit Stop* (1969)—an apt title since the film definitely was the pits. Running a speedway where race car drivers try out their vehicles left him little to do but constantly be looking at something. Like daredevil auto racers, it is difficult for actors to emerge from a film such as this unscathed. Only one *Pit Stop* performer did—an actress named Ellen McRae who later changed her name to Ellen Burstyn. *Pit Stop* brought Donlevy's 45 years as an actor to a screeching halt. The film itself only secured limited bookings, often as a grind house second feature.

During his last years, he was seen primarily on TV. While people in some areas were still viewing his commercial for a freezer, his voice in actuality was no higher than a whisper. He consulted a doctor only when he found himself unable to properly speak the smallest amount of dialogue. In 1971, with no career obviously ahead of him, he consented to having surgery performed on his throat. But there were no optimistic results—he had cancer and it was malignant. Now there was no time left, even to do the writing he had always longed to do in retirement.

He spent the last month of his life, March 1972, in the Motion Picture County Hospital in Woodland Hills. He died there on April 5. It had been his wish that he be cremated and his ashes scattered at sea. This was done. His widow Lillian lived another nine years, passing on in 1981.

Some fans remember with fondness some bits of his earlier characterizations. One of the best remembered scenes would have been the moment in *The Great McGinty* when the title character is reading a fairy tale to his small stepchildren. When his wife tells him that the children are asleep, Donlevy refuses to stop until he learns how the story turns out. The way he and Director Sturges pull it off, McGinty is neither the low comic buffoon or even the foolish illiterate he is in other segments of this screenplay. There is a decency of the human spirit that shines in this film and also, perhaps, in *An American Romance*: convincing portraits of men with no education and great sensitivity.

The Films of Brian Donlevy

Donlevy appeared in extra and bit parts in the mid- to late-20s in such pictures as *Monsieur Beaucaire* (1924) and *Gentlemen of the Press* (1929). Below are his speaking parts.

1. *Mother's Boy.* Pathé 1929. Bradley Barker. Morton Downey, Helen Chandler, Barbara Bennett, Osgood Perkins, Beryl Mercer, Lorin Raker, John T. Doyle, Jennie Moskowitz. BD is a show business hanger-on.

2. *Barbary Coast.* Goldwyn-UA 1935. Howard Hawks. Edward G. Robinson, Miriam Hopkins, Joel McCrea, Frank Craven, Walter Brennan, Harry Carey, Donald Meek, Otto Hoffman, Rollo Lloyd. BD is Robinson's henchman Knuckles.

3. *Mary Burns, Fugitive.* Par 1935. William K. Howard. Sylvia Sidney, Melvyn Douglas, Pert Kelton, Alan Baxter, Wallace Ford, Frank Sully, Charles Waldron, Norman Willis, Ann Doran. BD is a henchman.

4. *Another Face.* RKO 1935. Christy Cabanne. Wallace Ford, Erik Rhodes, Phyllis Brooks, Alan Hale, Molly Lamont, Hattie McDaniel. BD is a gangster who breaks into movies after getting plastic surgery.

5. *Strike Me Pink.* Goldwyn-UA 1936. Norman Taurog. Eddie Cantor, Ethel Merman, Sally Eilers, Parkyarkarkus [Harry Einstein], William Frawley, Jack LaRue, Helen Lowell, Gordon Jones, Edward Brophy. BD muscles in on an amusement park.

6. *13 Hours by Air.* Par 1936. Mitchell Leisen. Fred MacMurray, Joan Bennett, Zasu Pitts, John Howard, Alan Baxter, Ruth Donnelly, Fred Keating, Marie Prevost, Dean Jagger, Adrienne Marden. Phony doctor BD is a passenger on a hijacked airplane.

7. *Human Cargo.* 20th 1936. Allan Dwan. Claire Trevor, Alan Dinehart, Ralph Morgan, Rita Cansino (Hayworth), Helen Troy, Herman Bing, Morgan Wallace. BD's first hero role, as a reporter after smugglers of aliens.

8. *Half Angel.* 20th 1936. Sidney Lanfield. Frances Dee, Charles Butterworth, Helen Westley, Henry Stephenson, Sara Haden, Etienne Girardot, Gavin Muir, John Carradine, Paul Stanton. BD is a reporter championing the cause of a suspected murderess.

9. *High Tension.* 20th 1936. Allan Dwan. Glenda Farrell, Norman Foster, Helen Wood, Robert McWade, Joseph Sawyer, Theodore Von Eltz, Hattie McDaniel, Murray Alper. This film provided BD with his first top billing.

10. *36 Hours to Kill.* 20th 1936. Eugene Forde. Gloria Stuart, Douglas Fowley, Stepin Fetchit, Warren Hymer, Isabel Jewell, Julius Tannen, James Burke, Jonathan Hale, Romaine Callendar, Charles Lane. BD is a G-man on a long train trip.

11. *Crack-Up.* 20th 1936. Mal St. Clair. Peter Lorre, Helen Wood, Ralph Morgan, Thomas Beck, Kay Linaker, J. Carrol Naish, Lester Matthews, Earl Foxe, Oscar Apfel, Paul Stanton. BD is a pilot who sells out to foreign agents.

12. *Midnight Taxi.* 20th 1937. Eugene Forde. Frances Drake, Gilbert Roland, Alan Dinehart, Sig Rumann, Regis Toomey, Harold Huber, Lon Chaney, Jr. BD is a federal agent smashing a racket.

13. *This Is My Affair.* 20th 1937. William A. Seiter. Robert Taylor, Barbara Stanwyck, Victor McLaglen, Alan Dinehart, Douglas Fowley, Sig

Rumann, Sidney Blackmer, Robert McWade, Frank Conroy, John Carradine, Marjorie Weaver. Taylor is the government man who infiltrates BD's gang at the turn of the century.

14. *Born Reckless.* 20th 1937. Mal St. Clair. Rochelle Hudson, Barton MacLane, Robert Kent, Harry Carey, Chick Chandler, Pauline Moore, William Pawley, Francis MacDonald, Joseph Crehan. BD exposes a taxi cab racket.

15. *In Old Chicago.* 20th 1937. Henry King. Tyrone Power, Alice Faye, Don Ameche, Alice Brady, Andy Devine, Tom Brown, Phyllis Brooks, Sidney Blackmer, Berton Churchill, June Storey, Paul Hurst, Gene Reynolds, Tyler Brooke. BD is Faye's scheming saloon owner boss.

16. *Battle of Broadway.* 20th 1938. George Marshall. Victor McLaglen, Louise Hovick (Gypsy Rose Lee), Raymond Walburn, Lynn Bari, Jane Darwell, Sammy Cohen, Fay Holden, Hattie McDaniel, Esther Muir, Paul Irving. BD has a friendly rivalry with McLaglen as they try to get their boss out of a jam.

17. *We're Going to Be Rich.* 20th 1938. Monty Banks. Gracie Fields, Victor McLaglen, Coral Browne, Ted Smith, Charles Carson, Gus McNaughton, Syd Crossley, Hal Gordon, Alex Davies, Tom Payne. BD and McLaglen continue their rivalry, this time over Britain's biggest star of the era (Fields), in this English-made feature.

18. *Sharpshooters.* 20th 1938. James Tinling. Lynn Bari, Wally Vernon, John King, Douglass Dumbrille, C. Henry Gordon, Sidney Blackmer, Frank Puglia, Romaine Callendar. BD is a daredevil newsreel cameraman.

19. *Jesse James.* 20th 1939. Henry King. Tyrone Power, Henry Fonda, Nancy Kelly, Randolph Scott, Henry Hull, Slim Summerville, J. Edward Bromberg, John Carradine, Donald Meek, Jane Darwell, John Russell, Willard Robertson, Charles Tannen, Ernest Whitman. After destroying the James boys' farm and killing their mother, villainous railroad employee BD gets a swift comeuppance.

20. *Union Pacific.* Par 1939. Cecil B. DeMille. Barbara Stanwyck, Joel McCrea, Akim Tamiroff, Robert Preston, Lynne Overman, Anthony Quinn, Robert Barrat, Stanley Ridges, Henry Kolker, Francis McDonald, Evelyn Keyes, Regis Toomey, Willard Robertson, Lon Chaney, Jr. BD is Sid Campeau, employed by bigwigs to sabotage the title railroad (as opposed to his role in *Jesse James* where he was clearing land to build tracks).

21. *Behind Prison Gates.* Col 1939. Charles Barton. Jacqueline Wells (Julie Bishop), Joseph Crehan, Paul Fox, George Lloyd, Richard Fiske, Dick Curtis. BD is an undercover agent, posing as a convict.

22. *Beau Geste.* Par 1939. William Wellman. Gary Cooper, Ray Milland, Robert Preston, Susan Hayward, J. Carrol Naish, Broderick Crawford, Albert Dekker, James Stephenson, Heather Thatcher, G. P. Huntley, Jr., James Burke, Harold Huber, Henry Brandon, Donald O'Connor. BD copped his only Oscar nomination as the exceedingly cruel foreign legionnaire, Sgt. Markoff.

23. *Allegheny Uprising.* RKO 1939. William Seiter. Claire Trevor, John

Wayne, George Sanders, Wilfred Lawson, Robert Barrat, Moroni Olsen, Eddie Quillan, Chill Wills, Ian Wolfe, Olaf Hytten. BD continues his string of heinous acts, selling guns to pre–Revolutionary War Indians.

24. *Destry Rides Again.* Univ 1939. George Marshall. James Stewart, Marlene Dietrich, Charles Winninger, Mischa Auer, Jack Carson, Billy Gilbert, Irene Hervey, Samuel S. Hinds, Allen Jenkins, Warren Hymer, Una Merkel, Tom Fadden, Edmund MacDonald, Lillian Yarbo. BD is Kent, the town boss and Dietrich's lover.

25. *The Great McGinty.* Par 1940. Preston Sturges. Akim Tamiroff, Muriel Angelis, Allyn Joslyn, William Demarest, Steffi Duna, Thurston Hall, Louis Jean Heydt, Libby Taylor, Esther Howard, Arthur Hoyt. BD's most celebrated role, as a tramp who is made governor by a political machine.

26. *When the Daltons Rode.* Univ 1940. George Marshall. Randolph Scott, Kay Francis, Broderick Crawford, George Bancroft, Stuart Erwin, Andy Devine, Frank Albertson, Harvey Stephens, Mary Gordon, Edgar Buchanan. BD is the most hotheaded of the four Dalton brothers.

27. *Brigham Young.* 20th 1940. Henry Hathaway. Tyrone Power, Linda Darnell, Dean Jagger, Mary Astor, Jane Darwell, John Carradine, Vincent Price, Jean Rogers, Willard Robertson, Moroni Olsen, Ann Todd, Marc Lawrence. As Mormon Angus Duncan, BD opposes the leadership of Brigham Young (Jagger).

28. *I Wanted Wings.* Par 1941. Mitchell Leisen. Ray Milland, William Holden, Wayne Morris, Constance Moore, Veronica Lake, Harry Davenport, Phil Brown, Richard Lane, Willard Robertson, John Trent, Edward Fielding, Hobart Cavanaugh, Hedda Hopper, Addison Richards. BD is a tough flight instructor for fledgling pilots.

29. *Billy the Kid.* MGM 1941. David Miller. Robert Taylor, Ian Hunter, Gene Lockhart, Mary Howard, Henry O'Neill, Lon Chaney, Jr., Connie Gilchrist, Guinn Williams, Chill Wills, Ethel Griffies, Cy Kendall, Frank Puglia, Grant Withers, Olive Blakeney. BD is Jim Sherwood (a *nom de screen* for Sheriff Pat Garrett), reluctant killer of the title outlaw (Taylor).

30. *Birth of the Blues.* Par 1941. Victor Schertzinger. Bing Crosby, Mary Martin, Eddie "Rochester" Anderson, J. Carrol Naish, Carolyn Lee, Jack Teagarden, Warren Hymer, Horace MacMahon. BD is Crosby's trumpeter pal.

31. *South of Tahiti.* Univ 1941. George Waggner. Broderick Crawford, Maria Montez, Andy Devine, Henry Wilcoxon, H. B. Warner, Armida, Abner Biberman, Frank Lackteen. BD is one of three pearl divers.

32. *The Great Man's Lady.* Par 1942. William Wellman. Barbara Stanwyck, Joel McCrea, Katherine (K.T.) Stevens, Thurston Hall, Lloyd Corrigan, Damian O'Flynn, Lillian Yarbo, George Chandler, Charles Lane. BD is a gambler who spends a good part of his life in love with Stanwyck, the wife of heroic McCrea.

33. *A Gentleman After Dark.* UA 1942. Edwin L. Marin. Miriam Hopkins, Preston Foster, Harold Huber, Phillip Reed, Gloria Holden, Bill Henry, Douglass Dumbrille, Sharon Douglas. BD is a decent gangster whose only concern is his young daughter's welfare.

34. ***The Remarkable Andrew.*** Par 1942. Stuart Heisler. William Holden, Ellen Drew, Montagu Love, Gilbert Emery, Brandon Hurst, Rod Cameron, Minor Watson, Richard Webb, Spencer Charters. The ghost of Andrew Jackson (BD) leads a band of historical spirits that comes to the aid of small town clerk Holden in this Capra-esque fantasy.

35. ***Two Yanks in Trinidad.*** Col 1942. Gregory Ratoff. Pat O'Brien, Janet Blair, Donald MacBride, Roger Clark, John Emery, Frank Jenks, Veda Ann Borg, Frank Sully, Clyde Fillmore, Sig Arno. BD and O'Brien are underworld types who become patriotic during World War II.

36. ***Wake Island.*** Par 1942. John Farrow. Macdonald Carey, Robert Preston, William Bendix, Albert Dekker, Walter Abel, Mikhail Rasummy, Don Castle, Rod Cameron, Bill Goodwin, Barbara Britton, Frank Albertson, Phillip Terry. BD is the courageous Major Caton, commanding forces being decimated by the Japanese.

37. ***The Glass Key.*** Par 1942. Stuart Heisler. Veronica Lake, Alan Ladd, Joseph Calleia, Bonita Granville, Richard Denning, William Bendix, Frances Gifford, Donald MacBride, Moroni Olsen, Margaret Hayes, Dane Clark. BD is a political boss, framed for murder.

38. ***Nightmare.*** Univ 1942. Tim Whelan. Diana Barrymore, Henry Daniell, Gavin Muir, Arthur Shields, Hans Conreid, David Clyde, John Abbott, Stanley Logan. BD is a gambler-adventurer who becomes involved in a mystery with foreign spies.

39. ***Stand By for Action.*** MGM 1942. Robert Z. Leonard. Robert Taylor, Charles Laughton, Walter Brennan, Marilyn Maxwell, Henry O'Neill, Marta Linden, Chill Wills, Douglass Dumbrille, Richard Quine, Douglas Fowley, William Tannen, Tim Ryan. Pearl Harbor has left the service short of vessels, so WWI Navy veteran BD takes command of a ship from that earlier era.

40. ***Hangmen Also Die!*** UA 1943. Fritz Lang. Walter Brennan, Anna Lee, Gene Lockhart, Dennis O'Keefe, Margaret Wycherly, Alexander Granach, Nana Bryant, Jonathan Hale. BD is the Czech doctor who assassinates Nazi Commandant Heydrich.

41. ***Miracle of Morgan's Creek.*** Par 1944. Preston Sturges. Eddie Bracken, Betty Hutton, Diana Lynn, William Demarest, Porter Hall, Emory Parnell, Julius Tannen, Alan Bridge, Esther Howard, Akim Tamiroff. BD, a state's governor, reprises his role from *The Great McGinty*.

42. ***An American Romance.*** MGM 1944. King Vidor. Ann Richards, Walter Abel, John Qualen, Horace (Stephen) McNally, Mary McLeod, Jackie "Butch" Jenkins, Robert Lowell, Ray Teal. Originally two and a half hours long. Immigrant steelworker BD rises to a position of power.

43. ***The Virginian.*** Par 1946. Stuart Gilmore. Joel McCrea, Sonny Tufts, Barbara Britton, Fay Bainter, Tom Tully, Henry O'Neill, William Frawley, Bill Edwards, Marc Lawrence, Paul Guilfoyle, Vince Barnett. BD returns to villainy, as outlaw Trampas.

44. ***Our Hearts Were Growing Up.*** Par 1946. William D. Russell. Diana Lynn, Gail Russell, James Brown, William Demarest, Billy De Wolfe,

Bill Edwards, Mary Hatcher, Mikhail Rasumny, Frank Faylen, Sara Haden. Sequel to *Our Hearts Were Young and Gay* (1944) has the young Emily Kimbrough and Cornelia Otis Skinner becoming involved with benevolent bootlegger BD.

45. *Canyon Passage*. Univ 1946. Jacques Tourneur. Dana Andrews, Susan Hayward, Ward Bond, Patricia Roc, Hoagy Carmichael, Andy Devine, Rose Hobart, Stanley Ridges, Lloyd Bridges, Fay Holden, Halliwell Hobbes, Onslow Stevens. Western banker BD is ruined when he gambles with depositor's money.

46. *Two Years Before the Mast*. Par 1946. John Farrow. Alan Ladd, William Bendix, Barry Fitzgerald, Howard Da Silva, Esther Fernandez, Albert Dekker, Ray Collins, Roman Bohnen, Frank Faylen, Darryl Hickman, Duncan Renaldo, Luis Van Rooten. BD is author Richard Henry Dana, who based his book on his experiences as a seaman on a ship with a cruel captain shot in 1944.

47. *Song of Scheherezade*. Univ 1947. Walter Reisch. Yvonne De Carlo, Jean Pierre Aumont, Eve Arden, Charles Kullman, Phillip Reed, George Dolenz, Elena Verdugo, John Qualen, Richard Lane, Terry Kilburn. Curious mix of themes finds BD as a nineteenth century captain in the Russian Navy, dealing with a motley crew.

48. *The Beginning or the End*. MGM 1947. Norman Taurog. Robert Walker, Hume Cronyn, Joseph Calleia, Tom Drake, Victor Francen, Hurd Hatfield, Richard Haydn, John Litel, Barry Nelson, Godfrey Tearle, Audrey Totter, Beverly Tyler. BD is real-life Gen. Leslie Groves, who oversaw the Manhattan Project (the construction of the atomic bomb).

49. *The Trouble with Women*. Par 1947. Sidney Lanfield. Ray Milland, Teresa Wright, Rose Hobart, Charles Smith, Frank Faylen, Lewis Russell, Rhys Williams, Iris Adrian, Lloyd Bridges. Newspaper editor BD is out to get the goods on opinionated egghead Milland. This was released two years after it was made, well after BD's Paramount contract ended.

50. *Kiss of Death*. 20th 1947. Henry Hathaway. Victor Mature, Richard Widmark, Coleen Gray, Taylor Holmes, Karl Malden, Robert Keith, Howard Smith, Mildred Dunnock, Anthony Ross, Patricia Morison (scenes deleted). BD returns to Fox as New York D.A. D'Angelo.

51. *Heaven Only Knows*. UA 1947. Albert S. Rogell. Robert Cummings, Marjorie Reynolds, Jorja Cortright, Stuart Erwin, Bill Goodwin, John Litel, Gerald Mohr, Edgar Kennedy. Peter Miles, Lurene Tuttle. Western saloonkeeper BD becomes a personal project for angel Cummings.

52. *Killer McCoy*. MGM 1947. Roy Rowland. Mickey Rooney, Ann Blyth, James Dunn, Tom Tully, Sam Levene, Walter Sande, Mickey Knox, Gloria Holden, James Bell, Shelley Winters. BD is a big-time fight promoter.

53. *A Southern Yankee*. MGM 1948. Edward Sedgewick. Red Skelton, Arlene Dahl, George Coulouris, Lloyd Gough, John Ireland, Charles Dingle, Minor Watson, Joyce Compton, Art Baker, Reed Hadley, Arthur Space. Civil War profiteer BD uses bellhop Skelton as an innocent dupe.

54. *Command Decision*. MGM 1948. Sam Wood. Clark Gable, Walter

Pidgeon, Van Johnson, Charles Bickford, John Hodiak, Edward Arnold, Warner Anderson, Ray Collins, John McIntire, Cameron Mitchell, Richard Quine, Clinton Sundberg, Marshall Thompson. BD's General Garnet is forced to replace his good friend Gable as commanding officer of a U.S. air base in England during a period of heavy bombing raids.

55. *The Lucky Stiff.* UA 1949. Lewis R. Foster. Dorothy Lamour, Claire Trevor, Irene Hervey, Marjorie Rambeau, Warner Anderson, Robert Armstrong, Billy Vine. Lawyer BD defends accused murderess Lamour. The only picture produced by Jack Benny.

56. *Impact.* UA 1949. Arthur Lubin. Ella Raines, Charles Coburn, Helen Walker, Anna May Wong, Clarence Kolb, William Wright, Tony Barrett, Robert Warwick, Mae Marsh. BD is a wealthy businessman who escapes death at the hands of his wife's lover and is accused of killing the latter.

57. *Shakedown.* Univ 1950. Joseph Pevney. Howard Duff, Peggy Dow, Lawrence Tierney, Bruce Bennett, Anne Vernon, Stapleton Kent, Peter Virgo, Charles Sherlock, Rock Hudson. Photographer Duff instigates a gang war involving reformed mobster BD.

58. *Kansas Raiders.* Univ 1950. Ray Enright. Audie Murphy, Marguerite Chapman, Scott Brady, Anthony (Tony) Curtis, Richard Long, Richard Arlen, Richard Egan, Dewey Martin, James Best. During the Civil War, future outlaw Jesse James (Murphy) begins to question the leadership of his mentor Quantrill (BD).

59. *Fighting Coast Guard.* Rep 1951. Joseph Kane. Ella Raines, Forrest Tucker, John Russell, Richard Jaeckel, Steve Brodie, William Murphy, Martin Milner, Hugh O'Brian, Tom Powers, Morris Ankrum. BD, a Coast Guard officer, has personnel problems following Pearl Harbor.

60. *Slaughter Trail.* RKO 1951. Irving Allen. Virginia Grey, Gig Young, Andy Devine, Robert Hutton, Terry Gilkyson, Howard Da Silva (scenes deleted). Cavalry commander BD finds his greatest challenge from treacherous white men who provoke an Indian war.

61. *Hoodlum Empire.* Rep 1952. Joseph Kane. Claire Trevor, Forrest Tucker, Vera Ralston, Luther Adler, John Russell, Gene Lockhart, Grant Withers, Taylor Holmes, Roy Barcroft, Richard Jaeckel, William Murphy, Don Beddoe. Change-of-pace role has BD playing a senator conducting an investigation into organized crime.

62. *Ride the Man Down.* Rep 1952. Joseph Kane. Rod Cameron, Ella Raines, Forrest Tucker, Barbara Britton, Chill Wills, J. Carrol Naish, Jim Davis, Taylor Holmes, James Bell, Paul Fix, Jack LaRue. BD is involved in a range war for control of a large ranch after its owner's death.

63. *The Woman They Almost Lynched.* Rep 1953. Allan Dwan. John Lund, Joan Leslie, Audrey Totter, Ben Cooper, James Brown, Jim Davis, Ellen Corby, Minerva Urecal, Reed Hadley, Ann Savage. As in *Kansas Raiders*, BD again plays guerrilla leader Quantrill, meting out his own justice.

64. *The Big Combo.* AA 1955. Joseph Lewis. Cornel Wilde, Richard

Conte, Jean Wallace, Robert Middleton, Lee Van Cleef, Earl Holliman, John Hoyt, Helen Walker, Ted De Corsia, Jay Adler, Whit Bissell. BD is a hearing-impaired former racket boss kept on as an underling by big shot Conte.

65. *The Creeping Unknown.* UA 1955. Val Guest. Jack Warner, Margia Dean, Richard Wordsworth, David King Wood, Thora Hird, Harold Lang. Rocket scientist BD spearheads a project that ends in tragedy when an astronaut becomes a monster. (British title: *The Quatermass Xperiment.*)

66. *A Cry in the Night.* WB 1956. Frank Tuttle. Edmond O'Brien, Natalie Wood, Raymond Burr, Richard Anderson, Irene Hervey, Carol Veazie, Anthony Caruso, Peter Hanson, Mary Lawrence. BD is a police lieutenant trying to find his boss' kidnapped daughter. Made by Alan Ladd's production company Jaguar.

67. *Enemy from Space.* UA 1957. Val Guest. John Longden, Sidney James, Bryan Forbes, Michael Ripper, Vera Day, John Stuart, William Franklyn. Sequel to *The Creeping Unknown*, initially called *Quatermass II*. A later sequel substituted a real Brit in BD's professor role.

68. *Escape from Red Rock.* 20th 1958. Edward Bernds. Jay C. Flippen, Eilene Janssen, Gary Murray, Myron Healey, William Phipps, Nesdon Booth, Rick Vallin, Andree Adoree. Western outlaw leader BD is saddled with an innocent young fugitive.

69. *Cowboy.* Col 1958. Delmer Daves. Glenn Ford, Jack Lemmon, Anna Kashfi, Dick York, Victor Manual Mendoza, Richard Jaeckel, King Donovan, Vaughn Taylor, Donald Randolph, Eugene Iglesias, Strother Martin. A factual story about a cattle drive, with BD as a one-time lawman who signs on as one of the drovers.

70. *Juke Box Rhythm.* Col 1959. Arthur Dreifuss. Jo Morrow, Jack Jones, Karen Booth, Hans Conried, Marjorie Reynolds, Frieda Inescort, Fritz Feld, Earl Grant, The Treniers, George Jessel. BD is a record producer reunited with his ex-wife by their singing son.

71. *Never So Few.* MGM 1959. John Sturges. Frank Sinatra, Gina Lollobrigida, Peter Lawford, Steve McQueen, Richard Johnson, Paul Henreid, Dean Jones, Charles Bronson, Phillip Ahn, Robert Bray, Kipp Hamilton, John Hoyt, Whit Bissell, Ross Elliott. Crusty General BD rescues commando leader Sinatra from a World War II court-martial.

72. *Girl in Room 13.* American-International 1961. Richard Cunha. Andrea Bayard, Elizabeth Howard, Victor Merinow, John Herbert. Brazil-lensed detective film gives BD one last shot at playing hero.

73. *The Errand Boy.* Par 1961. Jerry Lewis. Jerry Lewis, Howard McNear, Dick Wesson, Robert Ivers, Iris Adrian, Isobel Elsom, Fritz Feld, Kathleen Freeman, Sig Ruman, Doodles Weaver, Leo Durocher, Dan Blocker, Lorne Green. BD (as a movie studio chief) must put up with Lewis, in the title role.

74. *The Pigeon That Took Rome.* Par 1962. Melville Shavelson. Charlton Heston, Elsa Martinelli, Harry Guardino, Salvatore Baccaloni, Marietto, Gabriella Palotta, Arthur Shields, Debbie Price, Rudolph Anders,

Renata Vanni. BD plays yet another military cameo, dispatching Heston on a mission to wartime Italy, in this weak comedy.

75. **Curse of the Fly.** 20th 1964. Don Sharp. Carole Gray, George Baker, Michael Graham, Jeremy Wilkins, Charles Carson, Rachel Kempson, Burt Kwouk. British-made sequel to *The Fly* with BD as another mad member of the Delambre family.

76. **How to Stuff a Wild Bikini.** AIP 1965. William Asher. Annette Funicello, Mickey Rooney, Buster Keaton, Dwayne Hickman, Harvey Lembeck, Jody McCrea, John Ashley, Beverly Adams, Bobbi Shaw, Frankie Avalon. BD descends further down the cinematic food chain. He plays an advertising bit shot.

77. **The Fat Spy.** Magna 1965. Joseph Cates. Phyllis Diller, Jack E. Leonard, Jayne Mansfield, Jordan Christopher, Johnny Tillotson, The Wild Ones, Toni Lee Shelley, Lance Berger. Another cultural monstrosity, with BD hamming it up as Mansfield's military man father.

78. **Waco.** Par 1966. R. G. Springsteen. Howard Keel, Jane Russell, Wendell Corey, Terry Moore, John Agar, Richard Arlen, Ben Cooper, Gene Evans, Fuzzy Knight, Jeff Richards, John Smith. BD, an old-time gunfighter, reunites briefly with some old buddies.

79. **Hostile Guns.** Par 1967. R. G. Springsteen. George Montgomery, Yvonne De Carlo, Tab Hunter, John Russell, Richard Arlen, James Craig, Robert Emhardt, Pedro Gonzalez-Gonzalez, Leo Gordon. BD is a U.S. marshal who oversees the transporting of convicts in a prison wagon.

80. **Gammera, the Invincible.** World Entertainment 1967. Noriaki Yuasa. Albert Dekker, John Baragrey, Diane Findlay, Eiji Funakoshi, Harumi Kiratachi, Dick O'Neill, Junichiro Yamashita. BD is an American general, plotting strategy against a giant turtle (another Japanese monster).

81. **Five Golden Dragons.** Anglo Amalgamated 1967. Jeremy Summers. Bob Cummings, Rupert Davies, Dan Duryea, Christopher Lee, Margaret Lee, Maria Perschy, George Raft, Klaus Kinski, Maria Rohm, Siegfried Rupp. BD is one of the masked title characters, the leaders of an international crime cartel.

82. **Arizona Bushwackers.** Par 1968. Lesley Selander. Howard Keel, Yvonne De Carlo, John Ireland, Marilyn Maxwell, Scott Brady, Barton MacLane, James Craig, Roy Rogers, Jr., Reg Parton; narrated by James Cagney. During the Civil War, BD is the mayor of a town ruled by villainous Brady.

83. **Rogue's Gallery.** Par 1968. Leonard Horn. Roger Smith, Farley Granger, Greta Baldwin, Dennis Morgan, Edgar Bergen, Mala Powers, Richard Arlen, Johnny Ray, Jackie Coogan. Producer A. C. Lyles switches from westerns to detectives. BD is a police officer.

84. **Pit Stop.** Distributors International 1969. Jack Hill. Dick Davalos, Ellen McRae (Burstyn), Sid Haig, Beverly Washburn, George Washburn, George Barris, Titus Moede. In his last film, BD puts on auto races.

BD also narrated Paramount's documentary *The City That Stopped Hitler—Heroic Stalingrad* (1943) and guested in their all-star *Duffy's Tavern* (1945).

Paul Douglas

A much-used show business term is the expression "a natural actor." It has been applied to everyone from small children to elderly people who begin performing after years engaged in other activities. Possibly the most natural was Paul Douglas. Many pigeonholed him in the same humorous mug roles as William Bendix and Broderick Crawford, and this was not surprising. They believed that he always played himself. But the life of the man belies that statement and makes it pretty evident that the Paul Douglas we saw on the screen for a relatively short time was the creation of a very talented performer.

He came equipped with years of experience as a radio announcer, during the era when they were of a more flamboyant variety. The young Douglas easily could have become another Graham MacNamee or Bill Stern, two of the top people behind the microphone during those days. From sports announcer, he graduated to nationally popular radio shows. Whether parrying comedy lines with Jack, George or Gracie, or hawking the sponsor's product, such men were encouraged to play broadly. Many announcers of the day tried to make it as straight actors, but never mastered screen acting as well as Douglas did. More recently, Ed McMahon has gone from *Tonight Show* announcer to straight actor and, mostly due to the nature of the business now, gone back to announcing. On those occasions, McMahon has cited Douglas as a role model. Douglas readily adapted to the film medium once he learned that while one must sell himself on screen, he must do it a lot more softly. His beefy appearance, together with a beautifully modulated speaking voice, may have made him one of the screen's true unclassifiables, but these traits carried him through 25 films in ten years.

New York Times film critic Bosley Crowther showed perception

A typical shot of Paul Douglas from the '50s.

in his review of Douglas' first starring role *Everybody Does It*: "Personally, we see Mr. Douglas as one of the most potential actors of the day; robust, experienced and oddly sensitive with serious as well as comic range. His peril, of course, is typecasting." Thanks to his work in the theater and even on television, Douglas avoided being typed to a certain extent, but did not quite succeed in living up to that statement. He came surprisingly close, but did not make it all the way to top stardom.

Paul Douglas was born November 4, 1907, in Philadelphia, Pennsylvania, where he grew up. He had the misfortune of losing both his parents relatively early in his life. To compensate for the sadness in his home life, he plunged into school activities. While attending West Philadelphia High School, he edited the school newspaper and served as secretary of the Shakespeare Club. From there he went to Yale University, where, although still studious, he found a great deal of time to spend on the football field. His parents had provided for him and he had little financial trouble staying in school, but he took an occasional odd job such as one in a candy factory.

Like with Bendix with baseball, Douglas might have found some career in pro football had it not been for the realities of the Depression era. When he returned to his hometown from college, he indulged himself and played locally with a team called the Frankford Yellow Jackets. In his early twenties, he was already the husky lug movie audiences would get to know some two decades later. Thereafter, he did his first acting with stock companies and married the first of five wives, a Nebraska girl named Elizabeth Farnsworth. Four of his five marriages ended in divorce because he did not sit still long enough to experience the joys of domesticity. He did not even father a child until his fourth marriage.

His first experience with radio, a medium he would be strongly identified with, came in Philadelphia in 1930. If he couldn't play football, he could at least report on it and quickly developed from a local announcer to national hookups. This led to other opportunities in the lucrative broadcasting field. Douglas had a voice that was a lot deeper and mellower than the average fast-talking sports commentator. He was therefore hired for a job where his voice would be put to perfect use: on some of the then-countless remote pickups of the big bands playing at various hotels. His soothing tones introduced many a late night melody. While always happy to find a way of augmenting his income, he remained true to his first love, sportscasting.

His first marriage had evaporated by this time, but he did not remain single for long. There is even less known about the second Mrs. Douglas, other than the name Sussie Welles, than there was about her predecessor. Even *The New York Times*, in the actor's obituary, seemed unaware of Miss Welles' existence, attributing only four marriages to him.

Douglas travelled constantly; without the benefit of coast-to-coast broadcasting, people like him had to go where the work was.

During the '30s, he also continued to branch out into other fields. He did some narration for the famed Fox Movietone newsreels, which are most closely associated with their most famous commentator, Lowell Thomas. In those days, even the ambitious Douglas probably never dreamed that he would someday be under contract to Fox as an actor. In 1935, he did take on an acting assignment, in a Broadway-bound play called *Double Dummy*. At the time, he did not consider it a springboard to any new career. Needless to say, the producers were not happy when he skipped a matinee to broadcast a football game. In spite of this, *Double Dummy* got him to Broadway, where it quickly joined the long list of flops that die early deaths each season. The brief sojourn of the young broadcaster went almost unnoticed in the trade papers. It's no wonder that, after he became a famous actor, Douglas preferred everyone to think that his next stage role was his New York debut.

In the late '30s, Douglas' radio reputation was such that he easily landed jobs on some of the better variety programs. He had a brief tenure as Jack Benny's announcer before Don Wilson became the Benny stalwart. He was then inherited by Benny's good friend George Burns, and worked for Burns and Allen for several years. After Douglas was no longer associated with the program, it fell into a slump and was only revitalized by the TV format. Unfortunately, the transcripts usually available are from the weaker '40s programs, not the ones with Douglas.

In 1938, he got his own program on NBC: *The Chesterfield Sports Column* was heard every weekday night. His third marriage, to Geraldine Higgens, was on solid ground when he was in New York with her, but fell by the wayside due to his constant trips to the West Coast, where most of his assignments were based. By the time he gave up being an announcer-stooge on several leading variety programs, it was too late to save his marriage. By then, he was in love with someone else.

After Pearl Harbor, Douglas went to work for the government, broadcasting for the Federal Office of Facts and Figures. And he chose for his fourth wife someone more well-known than he was. The beautiful and talented actress Virginia Field was born in London on November 9, 1917. She had come to the U.S. while in her teens to try to make it in American films. She was usually relegated to playing scheming second leads or colorless ingenues in male-oriented adventure films; a rare exception was the ballerina loyal to Vivien Leigh in *Waterloo Bridge* (1940). In the early '40s, she began to get a few leads, but they were in low-budgeters. Under contract to Fox for several years, she had just decided to try her luck on Broadway at the time of her marriage to Douglas, in April 1942. Since he was again becoming interested in acting, he felt lucky about this union with a woman whose aspirations lay in the same direction. She certainly gave him the class he always felt he needed, increasing his circle of friends in the theatrical world.

Field's splash on Broadway was somewhat limited; other performers got the showier roles. It was even more limited when she became pregnant. Douglas' first child was a daughter, Margaret, which was his wife's real name. This was Douglas' main accomplishment of the war years and even this didn't make married life any smoother. For the first time since his broadcasting career had begun, he seemed to be no longer branching out. To most people, he was still only the voice on the radio introducing something. It didn't matter how well-paid that voice was.

His break came in the midst of a social function. Also present was writer-director Garson Kanin, recently back from the service, and his celebrated wife, actress Ruth Gordon. Kanin had written a play and the leading role had just been cast with one of the biggest names in Hollywood, Jean Arthur. Arthur, usually cast as a self-sufficient woman, would be playing against type the illiterate mistress of a ruthless millionaire junk dealer who has used his wealth to buy himself some politicians. The problem was simply that the producers just could not think of the right actor for this powerful part. Unlike Hollywood, Broadway plays usually made do with only one big star and with lesser-known performers in the other major roles, since money was not backing the play so early in the planning stages. This is the reason that replacements in a show that are hits are often bigger names than their role's originator.

While Kanin was going on about this, the only thought on his mind, Ruth Gordon eyed Douglas. This theatrical couple had gotten to know him quite well over the last few years; they weren't at all snobbish about his being a radio personality. It occurred to Mrs. Kanin that Douglas could play the part. Never a particularly shy person, she expressed her opinion. And, using the old cliché, the rest is history.

The play was *Born Yesterday*, one of the most popular comedies in the history of the theater. But it never added any luster to the name of Jean Arthur. She hadn't worked on the stage in over a decade, and never in so demanding a part as Billie Dawn. She was overwhelmed by stage fright and began missing rehearsal sessions. Everyone made allowances for her, but it was soon apparent she was too ill to go on. There was no time to wait, so the search was on for a suitable replacement. This seemingly unfortunate series of events turned into one of the greatest success stories in show business, for this brought Judy Holliday to the show.

At the time, she was even more unknown than Paul Douglas, more unknown than her former partners in a nightclub act, Betty Comden and Adolph Green, who had recently soared to fame for their writing and performing in the musical hit *On the Town*. Before that, as members of a group called The Revuers, Comden, Green and Holliday had gone to Hollywood under contract to Fox. Only the latter lasted beyond the first film, in which their parts were cut down to nothing, but the studio gave up on her before the year was out. She didn't fit any preconceived notion of what a film actress should be like and her largest part was her few scenes in George Cukor's *Winged Victory* (1944),* as a flier's wife. Partnerless now, she made a hit on broadway as a supporting comedienne just when the part of Billie Dawn came her way.

Given the insecurity of two stars who had never before carried anything, let alone a major stage production, it was no wonder that Douglas and Holliday never mixed well backstage. There were rumors that sometimes he came on stage slightly intoxicated. She first appeared opposite him in his hometown of Philadelphia. While touring New England, she and the play got a mixed reception while Douglas garnered rave reviews. Holliday needed the crude character created by Douglas to play against. Because they were unfamiliar faces, audiences believed they "were" the people they played. Although Gary Merrill had the important role of the journalist who tutors Billie, audiences would concentrate upon and recall afterwards the confrontations between Billie Dawn and Harry Brock. Many would claim that all the actors and actresses that came after merely impersonated Douglas and Holliday.† They forget that prior to this play, both were like "unformed pieces of clay" that had to be molded into something workable. These characters would be the ones they would live with for what turned out to be two relatively short careers on stage and screen.

---

*Of the eight films subsequently made by Holliday, Cukor directed four of them.
†There were few replacements during that Broadway run of 1642 performances. Douglas stayed for two years, Holliday for three.

Unlike some "overnight successes" who develop a loathing for that one part that shapes their careers, Douglas never really lost his enthusiasm for Harry Brock. Even with a signed movie contract in his pocket, he remained doubtful about his ability to do anything else, especially on the movie screen. "How do I know I'm going to click?" he said in 1948, his first film already in the can. "If I don't, I won't be too worried. I can always fall back on *Born Yesterday* and play it on the road." He cited examples of other actors who had done the same with a particular property and he was perfectly serious about it. For his performance as Harry Brock, Douglas received the Donaldson Award as the year's best male newcomer and was awarded the Clarence Derwent annual trophy as best supporting actor. Although he had the male lead, Holliday was the undisputed star and that never seemed to bother him.

As the play's run continued through 1946 and into the 1947 season, he was more certain than ever that no actor but him could play the part. This helped precipitate yet another divorce in the life of Paul Douglas, caused by that old reason, "career separation." This time, it was the wife who went away. Miss Field had definitely not made the splash on Broadway her husband had and decided to return to Hollywood. Despite their child, things had grown strained between them and neither wanted a long distance relationship. Field's career continued in the "bitchy other woman" vein; a rare exception was her delightful cockney war bride in *John Loves Mary* (1949). But she soon found more solid contentment as the wife of film actor Willard Parker; it was one of the least publicized but most durable Hollywood marriages. And Douglas met Jan Sterling.

She was one of the many young blondes who followed Holliday into the Billie Dawn role—and had the capability to act rings around the character. With all due credit to Holliday, it was a role that could be played one-dimensionally and be great, while Sterling proved to be the possessor of a much wider range. Before Douglas made his screen debut, Sterling made an electrifying first impression in her film bow, *Johnny Belinda* (1948). As Stella, the girlfriend of the villain killed by deafmute Jane Wyman in self defense, she wins some sympathy for herself with a beautifully played, heart-rending courtroom admission scene.

She was born Jane Sterling Adriance in New York City on April 3, 1923. An early desire was to be an actress and in her teens she went to London to complete her studies. The war sent her home, but did not dampen her ambition. She had married at age 18 and was still married to the same man in her mid-twenties, when she first tested for *Born Yesterday*. She was accepted because she played the role the way it was expected to be played, an imitation of Judy Holliday. (Years after Holliday's death, actresses are still mimicking her in TV commercials; Sterling herself did "that voice" in at least one motion picture, 1950's *Caged*.) When she got the opportunity to play the part on the stage opposite Douglas, she was accepted as a carbon copy of the original star. There was little else Sterling could have done, short of altering the part. And if the male co-star noticed anything different about this Billie Dawn, he wasn't saying anything as of yet.

In 1948, Douglas relinquished the part of Harry Brock to John Alexander, the actor most remembered as the nut who thought he was Teddy Roosevelt and kept charging up the stairs in the stage and screen versions of *Arsenic and Old Lace*. (Anthony Quinn played Brock in the national tour.) Douglas had signed a contract with 20th Century–Fox and his first film role was ready. It didn't take him long to go Hollywood and he began bragging to reporters about an earlier offer from MGM, which he had turned down. He said he felt that he would have been "competing" with Clark Gable, Spencer Tracy and Walter Pidgeon for roles at that studio. "Then when Fox sent me the script of *A Letter to Three Wives*, I was crazy about it and I signed with them.... It's a good studio, especially for me. I'm only competing with Tyrone Power and Clifton Webb."

Douglas and his new employer could not have chosen a better part for his introduction to movie audiences. *A Letter to Three Wives* (1948) is one of the best films of the late '40s, a brilliant and biting satire of small town society with a script that in other hands would have played like a soap opera. In the hands of writer-director Joseph Mankiewicz, this *Cosmopolitan* serial became a classic. The story revolves around three marriages and the idea that each husband had a pre-marital involvement with the same woman, who has informed the wives (via the title letter) that she has gone away with one of the men. The stories of the marriages are told in flashbacks, though all the characters are involved in each other's lives, lessening the film's feeling of watching three separate episodes. Only the bitchy home wrecker is never seen, though Celeste Holm provides the ideal voice for her.

Douglas played Porter Hollingsway, a well-to-do store owner in love with Lora May (Linda Darnell), a poor girl only interested in his money. After their courtship and marriage, they remain at each other's throats. Although all the marriages seem shaky, it seems that

Porter is the most likely of the husbands to have gone back to his old girlfriend, which sets up the wonderfully ambiguous last scene. Ann Sothern and Kirk Douglas, as the radio writer and her teacher husband, had the best lines, but it was Darnell and Paul Douglas who made the biggest impression in their scenes together. This was because Mankiewicz and the story's adapter Vera Caspary created two basically intelligent people who were able to look at their own lives with a wryly humorous outlook. For this, Mankiewicz was deservedly awarded Oscars for his writing and direction. For many, Douglas' blustery good guy was the hit of a hit picture, as well as a completely unique character for moviegoers to identify with. His movie career was already on solid ground.

His contract called for two pictures a year for Fox and allowed him the option of one outside picture. Everyone assumed his first outside picture would be *Born Yesterday*, which Columbia had bought—everyone, that is, except Columbia boss Harry Cohn. He offered the Brock part to Humphrey Bogart, who was at the time making some independent pictures released by Columbia. But Bogart and Douglas had become friendly, even before Douglas came to Hollywood, and the movie star had assured him he had no designs on his part. In the meantime, Judy Holliday had made a favorable screen appearance in another 1949 hit, George Cukor's *Adam's Rib*, once again in a Garson Kanin role. It was a foregone conclusion that Cukor would direct Holliday in the *Born Yesterday* film, so Cohn was just following movieland tradition in seeking a box office name to co-star. Eventually he settled on two semi-names, both of them owing him pictures. Broderick Crawford, by virtue of his surprise smash in Columbia's award-winning *All the King's Men*, played Brock and William Holden was included in the still basically thankless role of the writer who redeems Billie. When the 1950 film was released, Holliday received the plaudits, while Crawford proved an excellent choice. But a strange thing had happened in this transformation: The camera highlighted the coarseness of characters that had been far more charming on stage. And Cukor's direction of the battles between Billie and Brock were somewhat reminiscent of the similar clashes he directed 17 years earlier, between Wallace Beery and Jean Harlow in *Dinner at Eight*, making Kanin's play seem more derivative of that great old George S. Kaufman–Edna Ferber play than it had been. Douglas' inability to land that film role was hardly the worst thing that could have happened to him. It was not to be his last shot at Harry Brock anyway.

Douglas went from fifth billing in his first film to third billing in the follow-up, his name coming immediately after Ray Milland and Jean Peters in *It Happens Every Spring* (1949). In this baseball comedy, Milland plays a chemistry professor who uses a formula that makes balls elude bats to turn himself into a top pitcher. Douglas is well-cast as the team's catcher who befriends him, and is completely dumbfounded by his talent. Just the sight of him in a baseball uniform made one aware of how good a Babe Ruth he would have been.

Douglas had joked about playing the romantic lead in *A Letter to Three Wives*, but he didn't have to joke about it in his next (*Everybody Does It*, 1949), for lead he was. He is again a well-to-do man, persuaded by operatic diva Linda Darnell that he could have a career in opera, though it is his wife Celeste Holm that has ambitions along those lines. Romantic complications arise, in a reversal of the *Letter to Three Wives* situation, where Holm was the woman who wanted to take him away from wife Darnell. They were backed by an excellent supporting cast, including Charles Coburn, Lucile Watson and Millard Mitchell. The film was a remake of *Wife, Husband and Friend* (1939), which starred Warner Baxter, Loretta Young and Binnie Barnes in the Douglas, Holm and Darnell roles. The newer version was far more lavish and Douglas was amusing, mouthing the words to the dubbed-in arias.

Bosley Crowther warned Douglas in his review of that picture about typecasting and it seemed the actor was worried about the very same thing. He let it be known to his Fox bosses that he was interested in dramatic roles and emphasized this by turning down a role in the Betty Grable musical *Wabash Avenue* (1950); Phil Harris eventually played it. Another proposed comedy that Joseph Mankiewicz was developing for Clifton Webb and Douglas, about a valet who goes to work for a gangster, was abandoned when the writer-director, who couldn't come up with a viable script, got involved with *All About Eve*. But studio execs took a liking to the idea of Douglas playing a comic gangster and started dusting off another old B comedy (*Tall, Dark and Handsome*, 1941) for him. Once again, they gave him an experienced director; veterans Lloyd Bacon and Edmund Goulding had lensed *It Happens Every Spring* and *Everybody Does It* respectively and oldtime comedy hand Alexander Hall was put in charge of the new one, *Love That Brute* (1950).

His first straight role was in *The Big Lift* (1950), the first of several early '50s Fox films shot in West Germany. This one concerned the Berlin airlift and he and Montgomery Clift played American servicemen. The latter was considered the movies' newest sensation, with three hit pictures under his belt, but his teaming with Douglas was hardly inspired. Like other rugged male co-stars of the brooding Clift, Douglas couldn't stand the seemingly unprofessional way the younger actor prepared for his scenes. (In Patricia Bosworth's biography, a complete description of Douglas' big flare-up against Clift is provided.) But the film itself had become tedious for those working on it and that is reflected on screen by the finished product. *The Big Lift* would have been far better as a documentary; the Clift-Douglas scenes were more intrusive than entertaining. To see these two fine performers, of completely different style and temperament, giving the most lifeless performances of their respective careers within the same film is certainly disconcerting.

He came off better in *Love That Brute*, though it was hokey comedy all the way. He played a soft-hearted gangster in the Chicago of the '20s, who locks up the gangland rivals he's supposedly killed in his cellar. He is completely reformed by the love of Jean Peters. An interesting point was that Cesar Romero, here playing a less redeemable gangster, had Douglas' part in *Tall, Dark and Handsome*. One trend in his typecasting did not cause any complaints by the actor: In practically all his films so far, he'd gotten the girl. He was soon to get the girl in real life.

Douglas had not entirely deserted radio and on Easter Sunday, 1950, he was in the cast of an all-star production of *Dinner at Eight*. Ironically, he played Dan Packard, the gruff ancestor of Harry Brock, while the film of *Born Yesterday* was still months away from release. Playing his wife Kitty, the Billie Dawn type, was Jan Sterling. She had come to Hollywood and was primarily playing floozies and gun molls. Signed by Paramount, she was seeing Douglas regularly. Judging by her first husband, John Merivale, the very distinguished son of Gladys Cooper, Sterling could not have gone farther afield than with the new man in her life. When marriage plans were announced, friends couldn't help being skeptical, but this time they were wrong.

His professional year ended on a positive note, with Fox scheduling him for several dramatic films. His first success in that field was Elia Kazan's *Panic in the Streets* (1950), in which he was paired with Richard Widmark. Widmark was a naval health officer teamed up with cop Douglas to find some carriers of a deadly plague who also happen to be fugitives from justice. Jack Palance and Zero Mostel played the hunted men. It was a suspenseful picture which benefited greatly from the interaction between Widmark and Douglas.

An even better part followed. Douglas again played a cop, a foot patrolman named Dunnigan, in *Fourteen Hours* (1951). This film contains what may be his finest serious acting. It takes the "good guy" characterization one step further: Here is a man who goes beyond the duties of his job in a desperate attempt to save the life of another human being. The story was inspired by a real-life happening, the 1938 suicide of a man who leapt from the fourteenth floor of New York's Gotham Hotel. The film's title refers to the length of time the man remains on the ledge. Here the character is a disturbed young man, played by Richard Basehart, while Douglas, the first cop on the scene, remains even after a more experienced police squad (headed by Howard Da Silva) arrives. The excellent cast also includes Barbara Bel Geddes as the would-be suicide's girlfriend and Agnes Moorehead and Robert Keith as his parents, both perfectly conveying the underlying causes for their son's nature. Even a subplot showing the budding relationship between two young bystanders, Debra Paget and Jeffrey Hunter, did not slow down the picture too much. This was largely due to Henry Hathaway's taut direction; he had already proven himself with other on-location New York stories like *The House on 92nd Street* (1945) and *Kiss of Death* (1947). *Fourteen Hours* was one of his best, and also the last of that type; unfortunately, the advent of CinemaScope tossed Hathaway back into the big-budget adventure film area where he began. As for the top-billed Douglas, though he reached his peak here, he was largely unappreciated, though the film was popular enough to land on several ten best lists. When it was redone in 1955 for TV's *Twentieth Century–Fox Hour*, reverting to the original story title "Man on the Ledge," William Gargan played Dunnigan.

Richard Basehart was named the year's best actor by the National Board of Review for his work in *Fourteen Hours*. The best actress award that year went to Jan Sterling for her finest dramatic opportunity thus far, opposite the other Douglas, Kirk, in Billy Wilder's searing drama *The Big Carnival*. Paramount had been wasting her in undistinguished second leads and she had only played the part of the venal wife of a trapped miner because no name actress would consider it. The impression she made immediately persuaded the studio to give her a lead opposite Ray Milland in a whimsical baseball story. *Rhubarb* (1951), about a cat that is willed a baseball team is pretty lame comedy. As a lark, Douglas made a gag appearance in the final scene with his wife and Milland, which made the film unique in one respect. Although they performed together on stage, TV and radio, this one scene represents the only instance in which Paul Douglas and Jan Sterling ever appeared together on the motion picture screen. And while it looked like her star was rising, her career in films quickly peaked and her best work from then on would be in supporting roles, albeit in some really fine films.

Fox now seemed more than willing for Douglas to take some of those outside commitments his contract allowed. Unfortunately, before he did, he made a film for them called *The Guy Who came Back* (1951), which seemed like a B-picture after all the first class products he had been cast in. It was the last of three teamings with Linda Darnell (they had proven a popular duo), and Joan Bennett had the other female lead, but the story of an ex–football star who cannot find the same kind of glory in any other profession looked more like a TV film. Thanks to television, the big studios were not renegotiating too many contracts and the front office had decided that the Douglas novelty had worn off. People who had been at the studio for as long as they'd been in Hollywood (Dana Andrews, June Haver, Gene Tierney and the aforementioned Darnell) were suddenly being encouraged by Darryl Zanuck's people to take on more "outside work." Douglas had not been at the studio long enough to become attached to it, so quickly caught on to the methods of freelancing.

He signed a non-exclusive deal with MGM, the first studio that had bid for his services. Ironically, two actors he had expected to be in competition with, Gable and Tracy, had already refused the first role he was given. Once again, the film was a comedy about the great American pastime. *Angels in the Outfield* (1951) promoted Douglas to manager of the Pittsburgh Pirates, who are on an incredible losing streak until they get some heavenly assistance. Some of the plot stickiness is alleviated by veteran Metro director Clarence Brown's straightforward approach to the fantasy and by Douglas' performance as the tough-talking manager who is somewhat "reformed" by the miracles that occur. Again, he was allowed a romantic interest, though young Janet Leigh was a little too sweet and innocent for the part. MGM's production values were still in evidence and such studio stalwarts as Keenan Wynn and Lewis Stone were on hand to lend support.

Clarence Brown next directed Douglas as a hard-boiled guy softened by a dose of religion (à la *Angels in the Outfield*). *When in*

Rome (1952) was set in that Italian city, with Douglas disguised as a priest for his own nefarious reasons (to shield him from the law). Even the presence of Van Johnson as a genuine clergyman didn't help; his box office value had dropped and the studio was placing him in moderately priced B pictures. The film was in black and white, so the actual location shooting did not soak up the beauty of Rome. Brown's direction was tasteful, but he was a few pictures away from retirement.

Although Douglas had more commitments with MGM, he worked elsewhere for the next two years. Jerry Wald* and Norman Krasna, who had an independent production company which released through RKO, next signed him to appear in a screen adaptation of Clifford Odets' play *Clash by Night* (1952), directed by Fritz Lang. The shooting script was so altered to meet the demands of the Production Code that the film wound up resembling a combination of *Anna Christie* and *They Knew What They Wanted* rather than the Odets play. The original denouement (one of the male leads kills another, who had been having an affair with his wife) was altered and a contrived happy ending was tacked on. Douglas, in a role created on stage by Lee J. Cobb, played a good-natured fisherman who marries a woman with a past (Barbara Stanwyck in Tallulah Bankhead's stage role). She then becomes involved with her husband's best friend, a self-centered movie projectionist well-played by Robert Ryan. (Ryan had appeared in a small role in the 1941 stage production, in which Joseph Schildkraut played the projectionist.) Another cast member, Marilyn Monroe, also received her share of attention. In fact, the cast came off better than the melodramatic script, with Odets getting a lot of criticism. Douglas was lauded for portraying the most decent character in the film; here he was sympathetic to begin with and didn't have to be reformed.

He completed his contract with Fox with a role in *We're Not Married* (1952), an omnibus film which failed to capture the style of *A Letter to Three Wives*. Douglas' name came after such non-contractees as Fred Allen and Eve Arden, an indication that he was leaving the studio none too soon. This comedy, about five couples who are informed that they were not legally married, is much too short to give its large cast anything in the way of depth and the individual episodes are uneven. Allen and Ginger Rogers have some amusing

---

*Wald also produced three of Sterling's best: Johnny Belinda, Caged, *and* The Harder They Fall.

lines as a bickering radio couple and Louis Calhern is superb as a millionaire who finds he won't have to pay grasping wife Zsa Zsa Gabor any alimony. The Eddie Bracken-Mitzi Gaynor segment lasts too long, considering the skimpy material. But the most disappointing sketch teams Douglas and Eve Arden. Bored with suburban domesticity, Douglas dreams of himself as a lady killer for a few minutes before deciding to take the vows all over again, without leaving his easy chair. This was a rather lackluster exit from the studio that had made him a leading man only a few short years earlier.

His last film of 1952, RKO's *Never Wave at a Wac*, gave him his most "normal" leading man role. It was the type of part normally played by Fred MacMurray or Robert Cummings, the ex-husband of Rosalind Russell who hangs around waiting for her to forget her foolishness and return to him for the fadeout. This wasn't even a good Russell vehicle, inspired by a TV play she had done. She played a Washington socialite who is taught a lesson when she's cajoled into joining the Wacs. As soon as the film was in the can, Russell was headed for Broadway, to appear in what would become her first stage success, *Wonderful Town*.

Douglas' planned return to Broadway in 1953, as replacement for Tom Ewell in the hit comedy *The Seven Year Itch*, was stymied when he came down with a bladder ailment. He also had no new film in release for a year following the release of *Never Wave at a Wac*. This was due to the usual delay in release of films made in other countries. Douglas had gone to England to work in a film directed by Alexander MacKendrick, right after that director's popular success *The Man in the White Suit* was released in the U.S. in 1952. The film they made was called *The Maggie* and was released in America in 1954. Douglas played a tough American businessman completely outwitted by a canny Scotsman, who is transporting his valuable cargo on a rickety boat, "The Maggie." The film (also known as *High and Dry*) is slight but amusing, particularly in the way it contrasts the American's practicality with the easygoing Scottish way of doing things. The finished product was played off as a second feature in the U.S.; American critics especially were rather intolerant of Hollywood actors who made films in other countries. It was just naturally assumed that these performers could no longer find work on their home ground.

Douglas had no such trouble, just preferring to diversify. He often found work at the same studio at the same time as Jan Sterling. Unfortunately, Mrs. Douglas had been placed in the niche of

"Queen of the Bs" at Paramount, turning out such pedestrian fare as *Pony Express* (1953) and *Alaska Seas* (1954). The studio gave her husband a classier role, a Broadway producer in *Forever Female* (1953). The witty script, though nowhere near the quality of *All About Eve*, made some amusing comments about theatrical people. He once again played a man who wins back an ex-wife (top-billed Ginger Rogers) after she considers a fling with a young playwright, (William Holden). Douglas had some of the best lines and critics, having not seen him in a year, had some kind words for him. He also acquired a new drinking buddy, Holden.

His next picture, also with Holden, brought him back to MGM. This was *Executive Suite* (1954), one of the most dramatically effective films about big business. This is the story of a battle for proxy power of a major corporation after the death of the company's president. The MGM policy of casting big names was adhered to by director Robert Wise, who reasoned that the best people would make audience identification with their problems easier. Because of this, Douglas received seventh billing, his lowest in any film, but no shame because the names above his were William Holden, June Allyson, Barbara Stanwyck, Fredric March, Walter Pidgeon and Shelley Winters, each of them a top-liner in other pictures. Practically all of them, as well as Louis Calhern, Dean Jagger and Nina Foch, had their chance to shine in some sequences. Not all the best scenes took place in the company's boardroom. One scene finds March as the scheming Loren Shaw learning that Douglas, as womanizing executive Josiah Dudley, is having an adulterous tryst with secretary Winters. We know that Shaw will do anything to get another executive to back him for the presidency of the company and is not above blackmail. Thanks to Ernest Lehman's script and to the playing of the actors, the significance of this moment is perfectly conveyed. Those who doubt Douglas' ability should take a look at that scene and how he handles himself in a few moments of film with one of this country's greatest actors, Fredric March. Arthur Knight in *The Saturday Review*, liked the way Hollywood handled a difficult book, lauded March and Foch for their inspired performances and said that Holden, Douglas and Calhern were excellent.

With leading roles not coming his way in Hollywood, Douglas looked to the stage for career sustenance. However, his visits to New York usually involved meetings with old cronies at Toots Shor's restaurant. He finally did return to the stage, in the familiar Harry Brock role, in a tour of *Born Yesterday*. His wife played Billie Dawn and a fast-rising Paramount contractee, Charlton Heston, played the writer. All three were not making anywhere near their motion picture salaries, but all were committed to continuing to do stage work. That year, he also increased his output of work in the TV anthology field. Television was not new to him. His first work in the medium dated back to May 1946, when he appeared on the premiere of an hour-long variety show called *Hour Glass*, probably the first of its kind. TV, with its great number of half-hour comedies and dramas, gave him the opportunity to play a wider variety of roles.

One property that might have been ideal for Douglas was a projected film about famed silent comedy director Mack Sennett and his star Mabel Normand. Paramount wanted him to play Sennett, with Betty Hutton as Normand, but then Hutton's sugar-coated musical biographies began to bomb. The studio dropped Hutton and the whole deal fell through. As the '50s progressed, Douglas developed more of his well-known outspokenness. While haggling with a film producer about money, the producer began mentioning his tax problems. He said that if he paid Douglas more, the government would only take more. To which Douglas replied, "Let me be the one to give it to them, not you." He, like other actors, was becoming increasingly bitter about his treatment at the hands of Hollywood's big shots. He knew that contracts were being terminated all over and the studio bosses were insuring that the people who worked on various films could not be paid residuals for subsequent television showings.

Only a studio commitment could have made Douglas do a picture like *Green Fire* (1954) for MGM. A colorful but woefully routine adventure film, this film gave him third-billing after Stewart Granger and Grace Kelly,* who three years earlier had begun her film career with a bit part in *Fourteen Hours*. He played Granger's partner in an emerald-hunting venture in Colombia, and there was a great deal of friction between the two until they unite against the villainous bandits and save Kelly's plantation. It was this kind of film that indicated that he had better look for work in other media.

Jan Sterling's career had temporarily picked up in 1954, thanks to a Best Supporting Actress Oscar nomination for her fine work in *The High and the Mighty*, but her other pictures that year were cheapies for Allied Artists. Yet she continued to work constantly and was set to play the wife of their friend Humphrey Bogart in a film

---

*Douglas had been friendly with Grace's father back in Philadelphia.

when she discovered she was pregnant. Although she was 32 and this was her first child, Mrs. Douglas took no special precautions and had three films ready for release in 1955. In October of that year, the baby (Adam Douglas, later a NASA programmer) was born in the Douglas home.

In the mid-'50s, Douglas tackled two of Bogart's most celebrated roles. He first starred in a mini-version of *Casablanca* on *Lux Video Theatre*, but his interpretation of cafe owner Rick was nowhere near Bogart's original. Douglas may have been able to play romantic parts under certain conditions, but these weren't the ones. However, the role of Capt. Queeg in the play *The Caine Mutiny Court-Martial* seemed an ideal choice. Queeg is not the biggest part in the play; he does not have to remain on stage throughout the play's action, as do the lawyers and judges. But his big scene on the stand, where he completely breaks down, is one of the most difficult in theatrical history. For an actor whose only stage experience was the enacting of a basically comic role, an uncouth junk dealer, the challenge would be enormous. Since this was a tour rather than a cold opening on Broadway, Douglas felt more secure. Other actors in the tour were Wendell Corey, who played defense attorney Greenwald, and Robert Lowery. Producer Paul Gregory had taken a special interest in this production, which was travelling through much of the deep South. But his hopes for success were suddenly dashed by his Capt. Queeg.

Not far into the tour, a reporter for a North Carolina newspaper made the mistake of asking Douglas what he thought of the South. The actor replied, "The South stinks. It's a den of sow belly and segregation." Members of the company were shocked; Wendell Corey quickly tried to apologize on his behalf, saying that Douglas didn't know any more about the South than what he'd seen from his train window. But no one really understood what had prompted the remark and Douglas was saying no more. The '50s' Civil Rights movements had made Southern officials more thin-skinned than ever and Douglas' remark reflected unfavorably upon the tour. After considering the replacement of Douglas with William Bendix, Gregory ended the tour instead. The actor "at fault" was given a year's suspension by Actor's Equity, which meant that he could not perform in a play anywhere in the U.S. for that period of time.

Douglas wasn't just a liberal, he was an outspoken liberal. He had a right to express his views, especially in 1955 when the country seemed to be getting out from under the McCarthy domination. But doing it the way he did it makes one wonder whether he was using this as a means to extricate himself from a difficult assignment. Curiously, Douglas would always say or do things that could hurt him whenever he was preparing for a stage role other than *Born Yesterday*, as if he had a subconscious desire to stop himself from having to go on. Of course, he was a marked man now; any reporter wishing for a newsworthy item would go out of his way to seek him out. And if Douglas was drinking at Toots Shor's at the time, so much the better.

Douglas plunged back into film production. He signed to make two films for Columbia's British outlet, the first one made simultaneously with his wife's picture *1984* (1956), an unsuccessful adaptation of the George Orwell novel. The closeness of the couple was strengthened by their determination, not only to work at the same studio, but in the same country at the same time. Douglas' first film there was *Joe MacBeth* (1955), a gangster version of the Shakespearean classic with the usually underrated Ruth Roman as Lady MacBeth. Douglas got a rare chance to play a straight tough guy and, more typically perhaps, a man whose weakness for a woman brings about his downfall. It would have been a better performance, but the script went little beyond the good original idea. The second feature, *The Gamma People*, released in the U.S. almost a year after *Joe MacBeth*, was completely confused. It was unusual to find him as the hero of a horror film, but whether the film was meant to be dramatic or comic, no one can be sure. Certainly, Douglas did not appear to be taking his role seriously. While in England, he also filmed a series of half-hour dramas for British television. He served as host-narrator for these, which were packaged under the title of *Adventure Theater* and telecast in the U.S. as a 1956 summer replacement. The same episodes were repeated the following summer.

In the summer of 1956, Douglas could also be seen on theater screens in Paramount's *The Leather Saint*. As a fight manager "handling" an incognito priest (John Derek), he had a part that he undoubtedly could have played in his sleep. But there was nothing wrong with his next film role, an adaptation of the George Kaufman–Howard Teichmann play *The Solid Gold Cadillac*. This 1956 film was his first work directly under Columbia boss Harry Cohn, the man who supposedly hadn't wanted him for *Born Yesterday*. He was finally getting a chance to play in a film with Judy Holliday, and the film's amusing narration was spoken by none other than his old radio boss, George Burns.

Douglas played Edward McKeever, a successful company president who is stepping down to take a job with the government. His greedy successor and the board of directors change many of his policies to suit themselves, until a small stockholder (Holliday) exposes them. She also becomes romantically involved with McKeever (an Abe Burrows alteration of the original play, in which the two leads were elderly people). But the result was certainly entertaining and even informative—how many moviegoers get a chance to see the way a stockholder's meeting is conducted? Holliday's Columbia film career was somewhat checkered and this film was a definite plus. For those who thought their original pairing was just a once in a lifetime success, this film proved conclusively that the chemistry could work just as well in a different kind of team effort.

Judy Holliday might have done the TV version of *Born Yesterday* with Douglas, but by the time it was planned, she was starring in the Broadway musical smash *The Bells Are Ringing*. So when NBC's *Hallmark Hall of Fame* mounted their production, Mary Martin was Billie Dawn. The Broadway musical star had become a TV great, thanks to *Peter Pan* and her Ford special with Ethel Merman, but she also was a fine actress. On Sunday night, October 28, 1956, Douglas played Harry Brock for the last time, and for the largest audience to which he had ever performed the role. The playing of Douglas and Martin was superb, with the only possible complaints being that the 90 minutes allotted for the play telescoped the action. Douglas' portrayal of the ruthless and coarse Brock still seemed fresh, a decade after he originated it.

There was nothing particularly significant about some of Douglas' next parts. In Paramount's *Beau James* (1957), he played Tammany Hall boss Nolan, who supposedly pulled the strings during the regime of New York Mayor Jimmy Walker (Bob Hope). Douglas' partially fictitious role was a colorless stereotype. He then joined one of his *Beau James* co-stars, Alexis Smith, in an episode of TV's *Twentieth Century–Fox Hour* called "The Heffernan Family." This was an adaptation of the old Fox film *Chicken Every Sunday*, with Douglas in the Dan Dailey role of a likable ne'er-do-well who jeopardizes his family's well-being due to his various money making schemes. This was aired in the spring of 1957.

Douglas wound up these California-based projects as fast as possible, in the fall of 1956, so that he could come east for rehearsals for a new play. The Equity ban had been lifted and he was ready to take on a major challenge. This was to be the first role created by him in a Broadway show since *Born Yesterday*. The project began when a comedy-drama by Arnold Shulman, *The Heart's a Lonely Hotel*, appeared on television a year earlier. Edmond O'Brien played the lead, a widowed Miami hotel owner trying to make a life for himself and his young son despite numerous problems. When that play was revised by its author for Broadway in the 1956-57 season, Douglas came into the picture. The play's warm humor seemed to be right up his alley.

When one considers the trepidation with which Douglas approached all post–Harry Brock stage roles, it is not surprising what happened next. When an actor signs a contract to do a play, the amount of time and any leave of absences desired are specified so that the producers may plan their schedule. But the actor assigned the leading role in *A Hole in the Head* (the play's new title) signed to do a film for MGM in the late fall of 1956, just when rehearsals were to begin. Douglas, true to form, seemed to have found another way of shirking a stage role. His contract could have easily been torn up since his action eventually caused the Broadway show opening to be delayed for close to six months. But this time, he was not tossed out, because everyone connected with the production, including its original director (Douglas' old friend Garson Kanin) really wanted him and no one else.

The film *This Could Be the Night* (1957) released in the spring of that year, shortly before *Beau James*, contains one of his best characterizations: Rocci, a reformed gangster operating a small New York night club. Once again he was directed by Robert Wise, whose ability to create individual sequences that were gem-like here made a seemingly trivial plot into what the New York *Daily News* terms a "sleeper" (a surprise hit). The film revolved around schoolteacher Jean Simmons, forced by circumstances to moonlight as Rocco's secretary. The tough mug soon succumbs to her charms, but decides to step aside, allowing her to be paired with his young partner (Anthony Franciosa). The film is basically comic but Douglas' best scene is quite moving, as he expresses a realistic attitude about the differences in age between the young teacher and himself after being accused of having an un-fatherly interest in her. Helping to move along this Joe Pasternak production was a group of excellently etched secondary characters: Neile Adams as an aspiring entertainer, Joan Blondell as her stage mother, J. Carrol Naish as the club's chef and Julie Wilson as the club's singer. But the film really belongs to Douglas, and, though it may not have been the only time that his depiction of a lovable tough guy so dominated a film, *This Could Be the Night* would be the last time that would happen.

The next part he played, the one he could have lost by doing this film, was another one that contained a tremendous amount of warmth and charm. *A Hole in the Head* opened on Broadway in March 1957 and won exceptional reviews. His portrayal of the unreliable but loving father Tony Mannetta was well-received. It was a comfortable part; the audience was behind him 100 percent. There was none of the ambiguity of a Capt. Queeg or even of Brock.

An actor in a Broadway success makes good copy, especially one who made a controversial remark two years earlier. Another "duty" of a Broadway star in those days was to make an appearance on TV's *The Ed Sullivan Show*, if only from the audience. The nature of *A Hole in the Head* made Sullivan want a scene recreated on the show. Shortly before he was to appear, Douglas made a statement to the press. He did not mince words as he took a swipe at television, a medium he seemed no longer to need due to his renewed stage success. One sentence raised a number of hackles, but it reflects Douglas' style: "There will always be an audience of slobs for Arthur Godfrey and Ed Sullivan." By the time the story was circulated, many thought he had called the two TV stars "slobs" rather than their viewers. Douglas later said he did not recall mentioning Sullivan at all. Again, his motivations remain cloudy. There was always some truth in his remarks, though in 1957, television still had many fine dramatic shows; it was not nearly the wasteland it was to become. He himself appeared in a great diversity of parts in the medium and this statement did not prevent him from picking up choice guest roles thereafter.

It may have been a streak of self-destructiveness and not just a big mouth that spurred Douglas to make such remarks. Besides being a popular TV host, Ed Sullivan was one of New York's most influential newspaper columnists. He had been known to save a foundering play with just a few kind words in the paper. Although he did not come out against the star or the play itself, he made little mention of *A Hole in the Head*. Its audience seemed to evaporate with the coming of the warm weather, always a make-or-break time in the theater. *A Hole in the Head* was an appealing sentimental comedy and, although it did not enjoy a lengthy run, it didn't lose money, thanks to the motion picture sale: In 1959, the part was rewritten for a third medium and a third performer, Frank Sinatra, in the successful Frank Capra film version.

In August 1957, Douglas signed for his first foreign-language film. He co-starred with Giuletta Masina (whose sensational *La Strada* was playing all over the U.S. at the time) in a film called *Fortunella*. Masina had a great deal of success when paired with such American actors as Richard Basehart, Anthony Quinn and Broderick Crawford, but this had occurred in the films of her husband, Federico Fellini. *Fortunella* did not have him as director, and the strolling street players in this film did not really invoke the poignancy of the travelling sideshow people of *La Strada*. Douglas was incongruously cast as a drunken professor (complete with a beard) who joins their tour and has a strange relationship with Masina. The film was picked up by Columbia and given the English title *The Princess* but it did not even get released.

The actor who had come out publicly against television did all his domestic work in that medium during the 1957-58 season. Opposite his wife, he played a Mafia character in an episode of the suspense series *Suspicion*. On *Alcoa Playhouse*, he played a farmer whose daughter (Patty McCormack) has to chain him up because he fears that he has been infected by a rabid skunk. He got to play himself on *I Love Lucy*, somewhat recalling his days as an announcer-stooge on the radio. In this hour-long episode, Douglas makes the mistake of picking Lucy Ricardo as his girl Friday on a new morning TV show. The episode proved that he had not lost the ability to play straight man. One of his most interesting television roles was in the *Playhouse 90* production "The Dungeon," a filmed drama that was screened in April 1958. In an uncharacteristic role, Douglas played a deranged millionaire who imprisons in a dungeon under his house several people who have been acquitted of crimes in courts of law. His malevolent performance helped the melodramatic plot to seem more believable. As usual with that fine program, he was backed by a strong cast, including Agnes Moorehead, Patty McCormack, Dennis Weaver, Julie Adams and Thomas Gomez.

In May 1958, the Douglases journeyed to London. Jan Sterling's motives were to visit with the celebrated mystery writer Agatha Christie, from whom she had optioned the rights to present on Broadway an adaptation of her *The Spider's Web*. In the meantime, Douglas went into rehearsal for a BBC production of *The Caine Mutiny Court-Martial*. The play and the actor were well-received when it was aired on June 1.

Douglas decided that, with no movie starring roles coming his way, he would become his own producer. He formed Renalda

Productions and relied on his wife to option properties for him, as she had the Christie play. From London, they travelled to the Berlin film Festival, since international contacts were necessary in the late '50s movie business. While in Berlin, Douglas became ill. The pneumonia he acquired did not last long, but caused him to be unable to report for production at Fox for Leo McCarey's *Rally 'Round the Flag Boys* (1958). This was the first time illness had caused him to relinquish a film role and it can truly be called a blessing in disguise. Director McCarey had lost his touch and this alleged comedy was atrociously lacking in wit; some of the jokes about rockets and rock 'n' roll were as dated at the time of release as they were decades later. Douglas would have played a total idiot, a bumbling Air Force captain, a role which defeated even a fine comedian like Jack Carson, who inherited the part from Douglas.

While laid up Douglas seriously considered doing a TV series for his own company. Many middle-aged actors were regaining or attaining popularity through weekly television exposure. Two ideas he considered were series based on the experiences of columnist Bob Considine and stories dealing with "psychic phenomena." But when he was better, he went into another movie role, much better than the one he missed out on, but still a supporting role. He played Pa Larkin, a farmer who doesn't pay his taxes in the MGM comedy *The Mating Game* (1959) and did well as an eccentric. More of the footage in this well-paced film naturally went to Debbie Reynolds, as his daughter, and Tony Randall, as the tax man who falls in love with her. The basic plot similarity to *You Can't Take It with You* did not hurt.

The suggested projects of the Douglas family had not engendered much interest yet, so they continued making the rounds of the television series field. For *Playhouse 90*, Douglas reentered the world of big business boardrooms similar to those in *Executive Suite* and *The Solid Gold Cadillac*. The teleplay, called "The Raider," was aired in February 1959 and co-starred Frank Lovejoy as a rival and Donald Crisp as the company's grand old man. Live dramatic series, especially 90-minute ones like this, enabled Douglas to take on strong dramatic roles, which he never got a chance to play on the stage. Douglas was an intimate type of actor, so the TV camera was ideal for him. Whatever his feelings about the medium, he never seemed to give less than his best in television appearances, whether a poorly conceived anthology series episode or an early Oscar telecast, when he was merely a commercial spokesman for Oldsmobile. (He had once hosted this prestigious program on radio in 1950.)

When Billy Wilder asked Douglas to play the womanizing executive J. D. Sheldrake, he agreed. The picture was *The Apartment*. He had never worked in a Wilder film, but his wife had had one of her best roles in *The Big Carnival* with that director. He would be third-billed to two of the biggest stars of the new generation, Jack Lemmon and Shirley MacLaine. But the film's schedule was delayed; for one thing MacLaine was working on *Can Can* through the summer of 1959. In *The Apartment*, she was to play an elevator operator who is almost destroyed by an affair with her married boss, the part Douglas was assigned. Lemmon was the ambitious employee who supplies the apartment for his superior's romantic trysts.

While waiting for production to begin, Douglas continued to take roles on television. He donned a baseball uniform once again for a Rod Serling *Twilight Zone* episode called "The Mighty Casey," scheduled for the fall of 1959. On September 11, a few minutes after getting out of bed, he collapsed, the victim of a heart attack. Before an ambulance could get there, Paul Douglas died. He was 51 years old. Fred MacMurray replaced him in *The Apartment* (1960), which went on to win the Oscar. For once, Douglas had been unable to play a role and it had not been of his own choosing.

Since his screen career lasted only slightly more than a decade, and practically none of the TV dramas from the '50s turn up in the rerun market, it would be understandable if Paul Douglas was hardly remembered today. Despite the inner reticence he seemed to possess, which prevented him from taking on heavier challenges, he had a widely varied career which enables different people to remember him for different things. A few people might even consider him a tough guy, in the accepted sense.

"Paul Douglas was a burly, big-mugged actor whose appearances in most films somewhat improved them," wrote David Shipman, when he surprisingly included Douglas in his book *The Great Movie Stars: The International Years*. Shipman continued, "He wasn't a supporting actor because he always had star billing, yet he wasn't exactly what is called a leading man, and he wasn't a character actor because he invariably played himself, a gruff, gravel-voice middle-aged man. If he wasn't exactly box office attraction, audiences liked his way with a line and his genial personality."

As an epitaph for a man who took almost everything too seriously, with the exception of himself, that seems highly sufficient.

The Films of Paul Douglas

1. ***A Letter to Three Wives.*** 20th 1948. Joseph L. Mankiewicz. Jeanne Crain, Linda Darnell, Kirk Douglas, Ann Sothern, Jeffrey Lynn, Barbara Lawrence, Connie Gilchrist, Florence Bates, Hobart Cavanaugh, Thelma Ritter, Patti Brady, the voice of Celeste Holm. In his screen debut, PD is the self-made department store tycoon Porter Hollingsway, partner in a stormy union with Darnell.

2. ***It Happens Every Spring.*** 20th 1949. Lloyd Bacon. Ray Milland, Jean Peters, Ray Collins, Ted De Corsia, Jessie Royce Landis, Ed Begley, Alan Hale, Jr., Debra Paget, Mae Marsh. Chemistry professor Milland becomes a big league baseball pitcher to test a theory and rooms with catcher PD.

3. ***Everybody Does It.*** 20th 1949. Edmund Goulding. Linda Darnell, Celeste Holm, Charles Coburn, Lucile Watson, Willard Mitchell, George Tobias, John Hoyt, Leon Belasco, Geraldine Wall, Tito Vuolo, Mae Marsh. Businessman PD scoffs at wife Holm's operatic ambitions until it is discovered that he is the one with "the voice."

4. ***The Big Lift.*** 20th 1950. George Seaton. Montgomery Clift, Cornell Borchers, O. E. Hasse, Bruni Lobel, Danny Davenport, Capt. Dante V. Morel, Capt. John Mason, Capt. Gail Plush. On-location shooting takes center stage as U.S. G.I.s Clift and PD become involved in the Berlin airlift.

5. ***Love That Brute.*** 20th 1950. Alexander Hall. Jean Peters, Cesar Romero, Keenan Wynn, Joan Davis, Arthur Treacher, Peter Price, Jay C. Flippen, Barry Kelley, Leif Erickson, Charles Lane, Edwin Max. Prohibition era gangster PD hides his soft heart well until an orphan comes into his life.

6. ***Panic in the Streets.*** 20th 1950. Elia Kazan. Richard Widmark, Barbara Bel Geddes, Walter (Jack) Palance, Zero Mostel, Dan Riss, Alexis Minotis, Tommy Cook, Guy Thomajen, Lewis Charles, Tommy Rettig, H. T. Tsiang, Lenka Peterson. New Orleans police captain PD helps Navy doctor Widmark find a pair of fugitives who are potential plague carriers.

7. ***Fourteen Hours.*** 20th 1951. Henry Hathaway. Richard Basehart, Barbara Bel Geddes, Howard Da Silva, Martin Gabel, Jeffrey Hunter, Robert Keith, Agnes Moorehead, Debra Paget, Jeff Corey, Frank Faylen, Grace Kelly, David Burns, Ossie Davis. In a brilliant performance, PD is police officer Dunnigan, who sets out to save the life of a potential suicide (Basehart).

8. ***The Guy Who Came Back.*** 20th 1951. Joseph M. Newman. Linda Darnell, Joan Bennett, Don DeFore, Zero Mostel, Billy Gray, Edmon Ryan, Ruth McDevitt. Football great PD tries to adjust to middle age, almost losing his family.

9. ***Angels in the Outfield.*** MGM 1951. Clarence Brown. Janet Leigh, Keenan Wynn, Donna Corcoran, Lewis Stone, Bruce Bennett, Spring Byington, Marvin Kaplan, Ellen Corby, King Donovan, John Gallaudet, Don

Haggerty. PD is the grumpy Pittsburgh Pirates manager, whose slumping team is saved by divine intervention. Unlike the Disney remake of the '90s, this film never shows these angels.

10. *When in Rome.* MGM 1952. Clarence Brown. Van Johnson, Joseph Calleia, Mimi Aguglia, Carlo Rizzo, Tudor Owen, Dino Nardi. Fugitive PD dons a priest's clothes to escape detection in Rome, and is reformed in the process.

11. *Clash by Night.* RKO 1952. Fritz Lang. Barbara Stanwyck, Robert Ryan, Marilyn Monroe, J. Carrol Naish, Keith Andes, Silvio Minciotti, Julius Tannen, Bert Stevens, Diane and Deborah Stewart, Mario Siletti. Fisherman PD is cuckolded by wife Stanwyck and his best friend Ryan.

12. *We're Not Married.* 20th 1952. Edmund Goulding. Ginger Rogers, Fred Allen, Eve Arden, Eddie Bracken, Louis Calhern, Zsa Zsa Gabor, Mitzi Gaynor, Marilyn Monroe, Victor Moore, David Wayne, Jane Darwell, James Gleason, Lee Marvin, Paul Stewart. PD is a bored husband in one of the five vignettes that comprise this comedy.

13. *Never Wave at a WAC.* RKO 1952. Norman Z. McLeod. Rosalind Russell, Marie Wilson, Arleen Whelan, William Ching, Leif Erickson, Hillary Brooke, Frieda Inescort, Louise Beavers, Regis Toomey. A Washington socialite learns humility after being forced to join the WACs. PD is her ex-husband, who eventually wins her back.

14. *Forever Female.* Par 1953. Irving Roper. Ginger Rogers, William Holden, Pat Crowley, James Gleason, Marjorie Rambeau, Jesse White, George Reeves, King Donovan, Vic Perrin, Marian Ross, Richard Shannon. Aging stage star Rogers has a fling with younger playwright Holden, while her producer PD (again cast as a star's ex) watches with amusement.

15. *Executive Suite.* MGM 1954. Robert Wise. William Holden, June Allyson, Barbara Stanwyck, Fredric March, Walter Pidgeon, Shelley Winters, Louis Calhern, Dean Jagger, Nina Foch, Tim Considine, William Phipps, Lucille Knoch, Edgar Stehli, Mary Adams. In an all-star cast, seventh-billed PD still scores as the sales director of a furniture company forced into a fight for control of the business by blackmailing fellow executive March.

16. *High and Dry.* Ealing 1954. Alexander MacKendrick. Alex MacKenzie, James Copeland, Abe Barker, Tommy Kearins, Hubert Gregg, Geoffrey Keen, Dorothy Allison, Russell Waters. PD is an American tycoon who learns a lesson from the Scottish captain and crew transporting his goods. Also known as *The Maggie.*

17. *Green Fire.* MGM 1954. Andrew Marton. Stewart Granger, Grace Kelly, John Ericson, Murvyn Vye, Jose Torvay, Robert Tafur, Charlita, Joe Dominguez, Nacho Galindo. PD and Granger search for diamonds in Colombia.

18. *Joe MacBeth.* Col 1955. Ken Hughes. Ruth Roman, Bonar Colleano, Sidney James, Gregoire Aslan, Harry Green, Robert Arden, Minerva Pious, Bill Nagy, Nicholas Stuart. The first of two gangster versions of the Shakespearean play ('91's *Men of Respect* was the second), with PD in the title role.

19. ***The Leather Saint.*** Par 1956. Alvin Ganzer, John Derek, Jody Lawrence, Cesar Romero, Ernest Truex, Richard Shannon, Yvette Dugay, Ricky Vera, Lou Nova, Tom Browne Henry. Fight manager PD is unaware that the boy (Derek) he is handling is a priest.

20. ***The Solid Gold Cadillac.*** Col 1956. Richard Quine. Judy Holliday, Fred Clark, John Williams, Hiram Sherman, Neva Patterson, Arthur O'Connell, Ray Collins, Ralph Dumke, George Burns (voice), Richard Deacon, Marilyn Hanold, Harry Antrim. PD gives up a corporate presidency for a job in Washington, only to learn from small stockholder Holliday about the dishonest tactics of his successor.

21. ***The Gamma People.*** Col 1956. John Gilling. Eva Bartok, Leslie Phillips, Walter Rilla, Phillip Leaver, Martin Miller, Michael Caridia, Jackie Lane, Rosalie Crutchley. American journalist PD uncovers a Communist plot to turn people into robots.

22. ***This Could Be the Night.*** MGM 1957. Robert Wise. Jean Simmons, Anthony Franciosa, Julie Wilson, Neile Adams, Joan Blondell, J. Carrol Naish, Rafael Campos, Zasu Pitts, Tom Helmore, Murvyn Vye, Frank Ferguson, James Todd. PD gives a terrific performance as Rocco, who runs a New York night club.

23. ***Beau James.*** Par 1957. Melville Shavelson. Bob Hope, Vera Miles, Alexis Smith, Darren McGavin, Joe Mantell, Horace MacMahon, Walter Catlett, Richard Shannon, Willis Bouchey, Jack Benny, Jimmy Durante, George Jessel, Walter Winchell (voice). PD is the Tammany Hall leader who "arranges" things for New York Mayor Jimmy Walker (Hope) during the '20s.

24. ***Fortunella.*** Col 1958. Eduardo de Filippo. Giuletta Masina, Alberto Sordi, Aldo Silvano, Mimmo Poli, Franca Marzi, Carlo Dapporto, Carlo Delle Piane, Piera Arico, Nando Bruno, Eduardo de Filippo, Guido Celano. A bearded Italian professor (PD) is a friend and confidante of waiflike Masina. Also known as *The Princess*.

25. ***The Mating Game.*** MGM 1959. George Marshall. Debbie Reynolds, Tony Randall, Fred Clark, Una Merkel, Philip Ober, Philip Coolidge, Charles Lane, Trevor Bardette, Donald Losby, Addison Powell, Bill Smith. Randall is assigned by the Internal Revenue department to investigate PD, a farmer who has neglected to pay his taxes.

PD also guest starred in wife Jan Sterling's film *Rhubarb* (Paramount, 1951) and appeared with other top names in the same year's religious short *You Can Change the World*.

William Gargan

To those who remember William Gargan well, it may seem odd to classify him as a tough guy. And it is particularly ironic that we don't remember him raising his voice. For in the last two decades of his life, he did not have the power of speech, so important to an actor. An act of courage which saved his life and proved his inner strength ended a long career as a performer. Yet it didn't surprise those who had watched him on screen for so many years; they knew he had courage.

If he was tough, he sprinkled that quality with a lot of Irish cockiness. He had the kind of face that always seemed to be smiling even when he didn't. It was easy for some to write him off as a performer because of the mostly inconsequential roles that seemed to come his way. When cast as a priest or policeman or kindly father, it always seemed to be in a film with a budget that could not afford a Pat O'Brien. Unlike the other tough guys mentioned in this book, he was never called upon to play someone completely unsympathetic and the worst you could say about any Gargan character was that he was "hard-boiled." He was taken for granted and shamelessly typecast in countess low budgeters. And some have had the temerity to claim that he only had three important roles in his entire career. In one of these, his underplaying was so effective that he stole scenes from one of the world's greatest actors, Charles Laughton, and Gargan received his only Academy Award nomination for that film. Most of his films required little more of him than dependability, and that was a quality he possessed in great abundance. At least he was brash and tough enough to keep from playing colorless juveniles.

William Dennis Gargan was born July 17, 1905, in Brooklyn, New York. His brother Edward, born three years earlier, was everything a boy could want in a big brother and young Bill seemed to

William Gargan publicity shot from the thirties.

walk in his shadow. The boys got some early exposure in film shorts and Bill worked with a more experienced and older street kid named Paul Kelly. But these were not the strangest of the boy's summer jobs. Most of the year, he was a pretty good student at St. Francis Xavier grade school. But every August, the Gargans went to Saratoga, New York, and stayed for the month of horse racing. From the age of six until he was 15, Bill was the youngest bookmaker at the Saratoga racetrack. He did this every year for nine years at a time when the child labor law enforcers were cracking down on those who employed minors in even less sordid occupations. The Gargan family's financial situation improved a great deal due to Bill's "August job." Extra work in movies seemed like peanuts by comparison. He was 12 years old when he appeared in his first feature film, Vitagraph's *Mother's Darling* (1917).

Show business success may not have been the initial goal of the Gargan brothers, but most of the jobs they had in their formative years required a kind of acting flair. Bill Gargan was barely out of St. James High School when he began working as a salesman. Ed's big, booming voice got him temporarily employed in the chorus of the Metropolitan Opera, which might surprise movie fans who remember his mangling of the English language in his many films. Bill got his first crack at stage acting with a part in an already hoary old play called *Aloma of the South Seas* in 1925. The part didn't pay much, so the enterprising young man doubled as assistant stage manager. His behind-the-scenes work led to jobs with national touring companies. But being appreciated for something other than performing did not sit well with young Gargan; he began to realize that he was a "ham." When he wasn't touring, the theater provided barely enough to keep him fed and he still had to take outside jobs. He even had a brief stint as a private detective, a portent of things to come.

In January 1928, one of the longest and most successful show business marriages began when 22-year-old William Gargan married Mary Kenny. (Early in their marriage, she worked as a dancer, becoming one of the first Rockettes when Radio City Music Hall opened.) Like everyone else who worked on the stage, Gargan needed to originate one memorable Broadway role in order to "make it" but, as the country moved towards its worst financial period, that break did not come. Everyone liked Gargan and admired his dependability, but no one could get really enthused about his talent.

Like other young Broadway actors, Brian Donlevy and Barton MacLane included, Gargan took bit roles in New York–based films between stage assignments; he made his talking picture debut in Tiffany's *Lucky Boy* (1929). The star was George Jessel, who did not live up to the title role; his attempt to make up for not doing the film *The Jazz Singer* failed and he never became a movie name as did his friends Eddie Cantor and Al Jolson. Gargan got the smallish part after appearing with Jessel in the short-lived Broadway play *War Song*, which also featured young newcomers Shirley Booth and

Raymond Guion (a.k.a. Gene Raymond, who became Gargan's friend for life). In 1929, Gargan was back on Broadway in a play called *Headquarters* which seems his first time in a milieu that would become very familiar to him: detective fiction. He then picked up more bit parts at Paramount's Astoria Studios, including *Follow the Leader* (1930), which did as much for the movie career of star Ed Wynn as *Lucky Boy* had done for Jessel. It didn't seem to hurt two young girls in the cast; both Ethel Merman and Ginger Rogers had been signed for the new George Gershwin show *Girl Crazy* and the rest is, of course, Broadway history.

While that show became a classic, Gargan's next play at least got a lot of publicity. Its press was largely based on controversy and not because the show was particularly good. Committed to doing works of substance, the Theater Guild was producing a Russian play about bigotry called *Roar China!* A future member of the Hollywood Ten, Herbert Biberman, directed the large cast. The obviously propagandist piece was about the death of a white man in China; two Chinese coolies are chosen by lot to be executed, even though the death had been an accident. Gargan appeared as an American exporter in a cast that was primarily Oriental. When it opened in New York in October 1930, critics devoted most of their reviews to its political implications, giving little or no mention to the players. Had those connected with the project realized there might be one day a backlash against those associated with plays such as these, they might not have imported this one.

Gargan was becoming increasingly disillusioned about the course his career was taking. When Paramount offered a screen test, he saw no reason why he shouldn't follow in the footsteps of more celebrated actors who "went Hollywood." For the time being, his "Hollywood work" continued to be in Astoria, Queens. His parts were slightly bigger in a pair of Claudette Colbert films, but Paramount did not follow through with a contract, preferring to use actors like him only when they needed them. It was the insecurity that was nurtured in those days that resulted in Gargan's total willingness to do a screen test for just about any part, even when his reputation was well established. That habit garnered him a nickname imposed by his colleagues: "Test Me Again, Gargan." This would at least make him widely known for his cooperative nature, if for nothing else.

One of the most successful playwrights of the period was Phillip Barry, who could be considered the Neil Simon of his day in that every season, Broadway saw a hit Barry comedy. In his early 30s, he hit his peak, turning out the plays *Paris Bound* and *Holiday* during a period when such sophisticated comedies proved very marketable, even in Hollywood. Barry remained true to the theater, usually letting fellow playwrights like Donald Ogden Stewart (*Rebound*) do screen adaptations of Barry's plays. The play that proved to be one of the greatest of his prolific period was not one of his longest runners. *The Animal Kingdom* with Leslie Howard opened on Broadway on January 12, 1932, and stayed around for just 183 performances (a short run by Barry standards). Howard played Tom Collier, a wealthy young man torn between his selfish wife and the girl he really loves, and it was made to order for his brand of understated acting.

There was a role in *The Animal Kingdom* not originally considered major, an ex–football-playing friend of the hero who has become his valet. Comedy writers of that period and beyond often employed athletic types as muscle bound jerks—targets for some of the lead's wittier cracks. But this character, Red Regan, emerged from Barry's pen as an individual, an outspoken sort who was completely sure of himself, which was not always the case with the upper class types surrounding him. Had not the right actor come along, Red Regan might have remained a minor player in Barry's chess game. A few seasons earlier, Howard had directed Gargan in a flop play called *Out of a Blue Sky*, so he was aware of the personality the actor projected, a decisive factor in his selection of Gargan to play Regan. (The contrasting natures of the characters Tom Collier and Red Regan was just as important as the play's romantic complications and Howard had a say in the casting. His influence had certainly led to the replacement of the actress playing his true love Daisy, after a less than pleasant pre–Broadway engagement in Pittsburgh in late 1931. The inadequate actress who was fired was Katharine Hepburn.) At the same time, 26-year-old Bill Gargan's relative youth was never found to be detrimental, though he was playing a contemporary of Howard, then pushing 40. Gargan appreciated the part's value, but even he was not prepared for an opening night audience reaction that was almost unprecedented. Gauging the response, the generous Howard broke with tradition and stepped aside so that the younger actor could stand alone on stage and receive his own ovation. Gargan would never forget this kindness.

Almost immediately, RKO bought the screen rights to the play; they had a director (Edward H. Griffith) and an actress (Ann Harding) who had done well by Phillip Barry in the studio's versions of his *Paris Bound* and *Holiday*. Howard would recreate his stage role and Myrna Loy won the selfish wife part.* Howard championed the stage Red Regan for the role and met little resistance. Producer David O. Selznick was impressed enough with Gargan to offer a standard contract and the actor felt that would give him the kind of security his previous film work had not. RKO did not have anything for him when *The Animal Kingdom* ended its Broadway run in June and the film was not yet ready to go. So Gargan went elsewhere for his first Hollywood credit, though it should have been called a "Catalina credit." That island was the primary location for filming of Lewis Milestone's *Rain* (1932).

At the time, the role of Marine Sgt. O'Hara was considered quite a plum for a newcomer who would be billed third after stars Joan Crawford and Walter Huston (playing, respectively, Sadie Thompson and Rev. Davidson). This was the first sound version of the Somerset Maugham story, which had been adapted by others into a play that required "extreme" histrionics on the part of the two leading players. Gargan did not have to overact as the Marine who causes Crawford to consider respectability after a life of whoring. He was not the first choice for the role and Paul Kelly would have gotten the part if not for recent controversy in his personal life. The plot of *Rain* was considered controversial enough. So Gargan got the part that had been played in the 1928 version *Sadie Thompson* by the film's director Raoul Walsh and in the later 1953 version by Aldo Ray. The critics were kind to him, saving their merciless barbs for Crawford. Even Gargan felt that the star was in way over her head with this part and said so. However, many still remembered the legendary Jeanne Eagels in the stage play and there were few other actresses of the period who could have measured up. Crawford did have some effective moments, indicating an ability to break away from the flapper roles she had been playing, but when so many people began knocking her performance, she herself got on the bandwagon, saying "I just gave a lousy performance." It is doubtful whether she truly believed it.

The experience of filming *The Animal Kingdom* (1932) was far more felicitous for the actor. It preserved for posterity the fine

---

*Loy had played a similar role in RKO's 1931 film of Donald Ogden Stewart's Rebound and these films proved a tremendous boost to a career then filled with mostly slanty-eyed villainesses. Animal Kingdom was shown at a tribute to Loy at Carnegie Hall in January of 1985.

interplaying between Howard and Gargan. The acting was what mattered and this was proven when Warner Bros. shot a remake, *One More Tomorrow*, 14 years later. In the remake, with the exception of Jack Carson, whose interpretation of Gargan's role was effective in a different way, no one in *One More Tomorrow* was right for the parts they played. Because RKO gave up the literary rights to Warners at the time, their version of *The Animal Kingdom* was never televised until a recent Turner Classic Movies airing. At the time, the film gave RKO some of the prestige it wanted.

Unfortunately for Gargan, David Selznick left RKO early in 1933 for his father-in-law Louis B. Mayer's studio. Gargan had already learned what the lot of a contract player was. Unlike a stage actor, he found that he was unable to concentrate on one part at a time, having to share the period he played Red Regan for the cameras with the character he played in a Joel McCrea starrer called *The Sport Parade* (1932). The stage-trained actors who had gone to Hollywood tried to reconcile this practice by likening it to being in a theatrical repertory company where someone played a different part each night. But there was a vast difference in the quality of the work. Gargan found this out also, as he was shunted into more typical RKO quickies as *Lucky Devils*, *Emergency Call* and *Headline Shooters*, all 1933 films. He felt at first that by playing leads or near-leads, he was making film audiences more familiar with his face. Actually, he was setting the stage for his entire film career.

RKO didn't mind using him much the same way they used Robert Armstrong; Gargan became primarily a back-up for fading silent screen stars like William Boyd and Charles Farrell. Armstrong was a similar type of performer who did not take full advantage of his fantastically successful role of Carl Denham in *King Kong*. Gargan had pretty much made up his mind not to remain with RKO when he got what seemed to be the next big break of his career, a call from Selznick at MGM. He was wanted for a role in the all-star production *Night Flight* (1933), based on the Antoine de Saint-Exupéry story of the men who fly the mail. He did not have to think twice about accepting, especially after learning he would be appearing with John and Lionel Barrymore, Clark Gable, Helen Hayes, Myrna Loy and Robert Montgomery. But despite all the talent used here, including that of Metro's skillful director Clarence Brown, critics called *Night Flight* a bore. At that time, MGM was so determined to be considered the best that they continually stuffed their films with stars. While it worked with *Grand Hotel* and Selznick's own *Dinner at Eight* that same year, it did not work in a film where shots of planes were as important as the acting. People expected more of Gable and Montgomery, so once again Gargan fared better than the bigger names. *London Film Weekly* critic John Gammie said the film contained only one sequence of genuine human interest: a scene between Gargan and Loy. The following year, Selznick established Loy as a leading lady by casting her opposite Gable and William Powell in *Manhattan Melodrama*, taking her out of the "second woman" category. He was not able to award similar success to Gargan, although there is evidence that he wanted to.

Selznick's personal unit had already started work on a big, splashy musical called *Dancing Lady* and Gable was expected to jump out of his cockpit and play a Broadway dance director opposite Joan Crawford. Gable had no particular affection for Selznick (this feeling endured through the making of *Gone with the Wind*) and felt he was being treated shabbily by being assigned to Selznick. When told by his doctor that he needed an appendectomy, the star was almost delighted to have an excuse to get some time off between the two Selznick pictures. The producer in turn decided this was an opportunity to replace Gable with an actor he had high hopes for, Bill Gargan. Selznick almost convinced the front office, who wanted a film that would duplicate the success of Warners' musicals; they felt that Crawford's name was enough to carry a picture. But he could not convince Crawford herself. She knew all too well what Gargan had said about her performance in *Rain* and did not want to leave herself open for that again. Besides, she was so in love with Gable that she welcomed any opportunity to appear with him, though he effortlessly stole every one of their co-starring vehicles. So the production stopped and they waited for Gable. (Two of the film's specialty performers, Fred Astaire and Nelson Eddy, would soon be ideal leads in their own rights. And the film's "other man" Franchot Tone would become, within two years, the husband of Joan Crawford.) As for Gargan, he received no further offers from Selznick, who was beginning to do more period pictures. But he still severed his contractual ties with RKO.

The next stop for the now freelancing actor was Paramount, where his brother Ed picked up a great deal of character work. Once again, the first film, *The Story of Temple Drake* (1933), seemed to have prestige written all over it. But he was to be disappointed once again. William Faulkner's novel *Sanctuary* was well-received by the critics and, years later, a portion of the book was turned into a play called *Requiem for a Nun*. But it was a total flop both times it was filmed. Its controversial subject matter didn't help; the people who made these films proved too timid to make them true to the source. What really went on between Miriam Hopkins (as Temple Drake) and Jack LaRue (as Popeye) was merely hinted at, with Gargan as a Southern defense attorney not picking up any of the information that a real lawyer would. When released in late 1933, the film was called *The Story of Temple Drake* so that the people who were appalled by *Sanctuary* might not recognize it. The new Production Code was already breathing down Hollywood's neck and Gargan could see there was much less to complain about in this finished product than there had been in *Rain* the previous year. Nevertheless, *The Story of Temple Drake* was less widely distributed than the average Paramount feature of the day.

Gargan played one of the two male leads opposite Claudette Colbert in Cecil B. DeMille's *Four Frightened People* (1934); the dependable Herbert Marshall had no trouble winning Colbert's affections away from the brasher Gargan. Since this was a fairly unspectacular DeMille epic, the actors were not overshadowed. Like the simultaneously filmed Paramount musical *We're Not Dressing*, *Four Frightened People* was a variation on James M. Barrie's *The Admirable Crichton*, which DeMille had done as a silent called *Male and Female*. This time he did not concentrate on the original's class distinctions between those stranded on an island; instead of a butler proving himself superior to his master in a difficult situation, here a plain spinster teacher and a henpecked husband come through in a crisis better than the braggart-adventurer (Gargan) who would be considered their natural leader. Colbert's metamorphosis from Plain Jane to alluring woman required her to shed some of her starchy clothing, making her attractive enough for the two men to compete for. Reaction to *Four Frightened People* was so minor that it was the last DeMille picture without a huge cast and under 90 minutes in length.

Paramount again had no further use for Gargan; like Preston Foster, Edmund Lowe and especially Charles Bickford, he remained one of the transient second stringers who might be called on when a part proved too insignificant for their premier tough guy George Raft. Gargan did another picture for RKO, *Strictly Dynamite* (1934), and then hit the freelance trail. Brother Ed, three years older, had already settled down to a comfortable career of playing cops in countless films for all the majors. William also thought that some of his too honest remarks about people like Joan Crawford had backfired.

There were, however, some people who either respected his acting ability or just liked having him around. Leslie Howard qualified on both counts and had been looking for a role for Gargan in another of his films. The two recent hits *Berkeley Square* (1933) and *Of Human Bondage* (1934), both "very British," would not have suited him, but when Howard saw a brash American role in the script of the Warner Bros. film *British Agent* (1934), he recommended Gargan. The film was about Russia in the last days of the Czar and a group of people from varying nations caught up in the turmoil. The role he got was not too important, but he did receive third billing below Howard and Kay Francis, two enormous stars. And the film's director was the flamboyant Michael Curtiz. In the hands of almost any other house director, *British Agent* would have been nothing more than drivel, but Curtiz could create more mystery and foreign intrigue on well-worn studio sets than many directors could with actual location shooting. Curtiz liked Gargan enough to think of him for a better part in his next film, one that would star the studio's greatest actor, Paul Muni. When an actor made one film for a studio and was considered for another, contracts were usually the next step. Warners seemed to be the ideal place for him to work, but he was not going to make any rash decisions.

Following the completion of *British Agent*, Howard returned to England to film *The Scarlet Pimpernel*, one of his greatest successes. Before that project was completed, Howard received an offer to star in Robert E. Sherwood's new Broadway play *The Petrified Forest*. It was not until he returned to the United States and became completely caught up in the play that he thought of Gargan for the still uncast role of gang leader Duke Mantee. Unmindful of the possibility of having more scenes stolen from him (*à la The Animal Kingdom*), Howard once again began pulling the strings for Gargan. But this time the actor refused the role. He was already filming *Black Fury* (1935) for Warners, a newly signed contract in his pocket. Gargan had established comfortable roots on the West Coast; it just didn't pay for a performer to go east and work hard on something that might only last for one night in some New York theater. With all that in mind, he said no. Using that old cliché, the rest was history. The role of Mantee went to Humphrey Bogart who had played a few minor tough guy roles in films and was considered a fading juvenile in theatrical circles. Howard, not especially familiar with Bogart's past work, was completely bowled over by Bogart's performance. When Warners planned to film *The Petrified Forest* within months of its successful debut in early 1935, Howard supported another actor's right to recreate his stage role with the same zeal he had utilized on Gargan's behalf a few years earlier.

The problem encountered by Gargan at Warner Bros. was obvious: There were too many similar-type actors there. The subtle caste system that existed took little notice of his prior credits. His role in *Black Fury* was an example of the type available to good but inconsequential second string performers. This was a strong, controversial film in its day, dealing with labor problems among coal miners. Paul Muni had one of his showiest parts as Joe Radec, an uneducated immigrant worker used as an innocent dupe by those elements wishing to foment a large-scale strike to further their own ends. In the screenplay (which somewhat resembles a modern day version of Victor Hugo's *The Hunchback of Notre Dame*), Radec turns against everyone who has abused him, holding out against the authorities and the other miners. By this time, the melodrama had completely engulfed any social message originally set down by the authors and the thing that survives today is Muni's bravura performance. He was given strong support by Karen Morley (who had also played his mistress in *Scarface*), John Qualen, Henry O'Neill, J. Carrol Naish, Mae Marsh, Barton MacLane and Ward Bond. MacLane, also just beginning his studio tenure, was particularly outstanding as a brutal company cop. In contrast, Gargan, third-billed, was made to be a little too bland as a more sympathetic officer whose main function in the story is as the real love interest of Muni's girl Morley. This was a problem that marred many a '30s film; Hollywood felt the need to have one decent all–American type written into any kind of script, no matter what squalor surrounded him. The message was clear: all company cops were not bad; and if small, foreign-looking Muni had lost his girl, he couldn't have asked for a better replacement than the dependable, ever-smiling Gargan.

Once again, Gargan had to get used to the hefty workload of a studio contractee. Warners top-billed him for the first time in the programmer *Night at the Ritz*, released in March 1935 (the same month as *Black Fury*). He was paired with teenager Patricia Ellis in this time-filler which inexpensively chronicled the events that occur in one night at an exclusive hotel. To compare it to the great model of the genre *Grand Hotel* would be ridiculous; at best, it could be called a bargain basement version of Warners' own *Wonder Bar*, though the cross-section of characters were not nearly as interesting. What was most evident about this picture was its cost; by Warners standards it wasn't even a B film. A month later, Gargan was again on the screen in another mildly good-humored role in *Traveling Saleslady*, playing unobtrusively against the then-popular team of Joan Blondell and Glenda Farrell. The men who appeared in films that starred these talented ladies were usually serviceable and forgettable; Gargan gave them just what they wanted.

The only thing the last two films brought Gargan was the all-too-rare opportunity to be the top male performer in a picture. The next quartet of films did not afford him this luxury. Only one of them, *Broadway Gondolier*, approached the big budget category, yet in all of the films he could not manage anything higher than fourth billing. In *Don't Bet on Blondes*, also a 1935 release, he was not even allowed a real name, appearing only in the comic role of "Numbers," a gambling crony of Warren William. (At least, he was billed over another Warners newcomer, a young man named Errol Flynn, but Flynn was to become a star with his very next film.) *Bright Lights*, an August 1935 release, was one of the non-musicals Warners allowed Busby Berkeley to direct. Gargan played the amiable Daniel Wheeler, who offers solace to Ann Dvorak when her vaudevillian husband Joe E. Brown temporarily lets success go to his head. Needless to say, he makes the grand gesture and steps aside for the finale; Brown had started to inject more pathos into his films, but he wasn't about to lose the girl in the end. At least the making of the film was enjoyable, which could not be said for *Man Hunt*, which was released early in 1936. This was a definite "C" picture with Gargan fourth-billed after Ricardo Cortez, Marguerite Churchill and Chic Sale, all of whom were past their best days. This was a good example of the way Warners used him mainly to plug in holes in various projects. Warners liked to spotlight the actors they themselves had discovered and gave as many breaks as possible to such second stringers as Ross Alexander, Lyle Talbot and Donald Woods. Gargan was never really "theirs" and once all parties realized this, their contractual agreement was severed by mutual consent. The studio just had too many of what they considered "the same types."

Just about the time Gargan was making his last contract film, the studio was shooting *The Petrified Forest*. The screen version of the play was criticized for its staginess, but the performances, particularly those of Leslie Howard and Humphrey Bogart, were praised. Yet even the latter's outstanding characterization did not seem to excite the Warners people; they would continue to use him in secondary gangster roles for five years. Without Howard's intercession on his part, Bogart would never have been signed by the people who eventually made him a star. This was not forgotten and years after Howard's death (the plane he was on was shot down by the Nazis on June 1, 1943), Bogart and Lauren Bacall named their daughter Leslie after him. But this was not the first namesake of that fine actor. Leslie was also the name of the Gargans' second son, after William, Jr. Gargan never forgot a star's generosity.

After his unhappy experience with Warners, Gargan chose to freelance, never signing for more than three pictures at a time with any one studio. He returned to Paramount to appear with Harold Lloyd and Adolphe Menjou in *The Milky Way* (1936). It was certainly one of his better roles of the period, a brash fight champion who accidentally gets his comeuppance from milkman Lloyd. Unfortunately, this prime example of Gargan's comedic talent goes largely unseen by audiences: Samuel Goldwyn purchased the literary rights to the Lynn Root–Harry Clork play for his 1946 remake, *The Kid from Brooklyn*.

Gargan remained at Paramount for *Sky Parade* (1936), as one of the flyers in an air circus who raises a dead buddy's child. He got some parts at Columbia—probably ones that Ralph Bellamy, Richard Dix and Chester Morris thought were beneath them. The bulk of his work over the next couple of years was at Universal, which was going through a rather low period. Over this period, he made ten films for them, all programmers. While quality rarely varied, Gargan's on-screen professions did. Among those were newspapermen, detectives, horse trainers, fight managers, pilots and radio commentators, all of which were played with the usual doses of Gargan's breezy charm. His best picture of the period gave him (predictably) a supporting role. That was in *You Only Live Once* (1937), directed by Fritz Lang and produced by Walter Wanger for United Artists release. In this well-remembered story, a young man (Henry Fonda) is forced by circumstance into a life of crime and, along with his loyal wife Sylvia Sidney, comes to a tragic end. Barton MacLane had a rare sympathetic role as Sidney's old boyfriend who tries to help and Gargan was the kindly prison chaplain who also tries to rehabilitate Fonda. Probably the film's most famous, and most imitated scene, had Gargan attempting to tell Fonda he's been pardoned and being inadvertently gunned down by the scared young convict in his break for freedom. The role was definitely Pat

O'Brien–ish; amusingly, in the Sylvia Sidney chapter of James Robert Parish's *The Paramount Pretties*, the author wrote that the role *was* played by O'Brien. For all of Gargan's pleasant smiling, most of his characters were venal at their worst and mildly selfish at best.

Films of the '30s were rarely shot on any location other than a sound stage, but *Fury and the Woman* (1937) was an exception (albeit a cheap one). Obviously an attempt to imitate Warners' colorful *God's Country and the Woman* and other lumber camp stories, its main distinction was that it was to be shot in Vancouver, British Columbia. A small production outfit, Rialto, signed Gargan, who turned out to be the only recognizable performer involved. The finished product was just more fodder for the same grind houses where his films usually played. Back at Universal, his roles were becoming more like his parts at Warners. He supported Alice Faye and George Murphy in *You're a Sweetheart* (1937), Ray Milland and Wendy Barrie in *Wings Over Honolulu* (1937) and Ralph Bellamy in *The Crime of Dr. Hallet* (1938). Paired with Paul Kelly, he sparred with Victor McLaglen in *The Devil's Party* (1938). *Some Blondes Are Dangerous* (1937) found him playing the tough manager of young prizefighter Noah Beery, Jr., in a rehash of *The Iron Man* (1931).

Another boxing story brought him back to MGM and into an A-product. It was *The Crowd Roars* (1938), that studio's entry in the pugilistic sweepstakes, fashioned by director Richard Thorpe as an opportunity for Robert Taylor to break away from his pretty boy image. As in his last quality film, *You Only Live Once*, Gargan again plays a good guy whose accidental death is caused by the hero of the piece. As a boy, Taylor idolized championship fighter Gargan, but years later when they meet in the ring, the young fighter does not know about Gargan's weakened condition and delivers a fatal beating to the worn-out older man. Gargan has taken the final match for the well-being of his family and he is given the typical sendoff, with Isabel Jewell as his tearful widow making an already morose Taylor feel considerably worse. Typically, Gargan shines in another small but well-written part, but is again overshadowed, primarily by the strong character acting of Frank Morgan as Taylor's alcoholic father (who proves to be even more self-sacrificing than Gargan was) and Edward Arnold as the hard fight promoter; both much bigger parts.* Nevertheless, other MGM parts followed.

In the 1947 remake, Killer McCoy, Gargan's character, now played by Mickey Knox, was even more inconsequential.

The year 1939 did not start off on a promising note: Gargan was appearing in films for his old employers, RKO and Warners. The RKO film *Three Sons* was just a remake of a 1933 film he had made for them, *Sweepings*; Gargan recreated the role of family friend that was trite the first time around. In Warners' *Women in the Wind*, he was Kay Francis' leading man, mainly because the studio was about to dump her anyway and didn't care how cheap her starring vehicles looked. MGM's *Broadway Serenade* offered Jeanette MacDonald a change to get away from Nelson Eddy, but little else to the rest of the cast, of which Gargan was a low member, billed below the studio's regular contractees. Later in the year came *Joe and Ethel Turp Call on the President*, an MGM film in which he, Ann Sothern and Lewis Stone essayed the title roles. This film was one of the oddities that studio's B-picture department occasionally turned out. The story of a decent American couple who champion the cause of their self-sacrificing neighborhood postman (Walter Brennan) was right up the Metro alley. They wanted audiences of the day to believe that any average citizen could bring relatively minor problems to the chief executive. Stone, the studio's wise "Judge Hardy," was Louis B. Mayer's idea of the perfect president, a lot more than FDR was in his political estimation. While the film was fairly lightweight, Sothern and Gargan played such well-developed characters that a series could have developed.

His next film and last release for the year gave him his best comedy role since *The Milky Way*. Maybe that was because he was teamed again with Adolphe Menjou, who had played his manager in the earlier film. *The Housekeeper's Daughter* was simply wacky comedy, understandable when one considers that the film was produced and directed by Hal Roach for his new production company at United Artists. The confused plot involving comic gangsters didn't make much sense, but what holds the film together is the witty repartee between sarcastic journalists, Menjou and Gargan, with dialogue that compared favorably with some of the material Ben Hecht and Charles MacArthur wrote for Walter Burns and Hildy Johnson in *The Front Page*, the prototypes for all film newsmen. The success of this project told Roach that this was the direction to take now that he was losing the services of Laurel and Hardy. He quickly brought back Gargan and Menjou, plus leading man John Hubbard, for the equally wacky *Turnabout* (1940). This was a fantasy based on a story by Thorne Smith, whose "Topper" had done very well for Roach; *Turnabout* concerned a husband and wife changing physical characteristics. But the writing wasn't at the level of *The Housekeeper's Daughter*, so the talented cast had less to work with. This was too bad because Gargan's comedic talents were perfect for the Roach lot. Although he was not much older than Hubbard or Dennis O'Keefe, he was so completely established as a character man that Roach wouldn't even think of him for the lead roles he gave those two.

Gargan's comedy roles became more and more negligible. He did a satirical portrait of a Darryl Zanuck–type producer in *Star Dust* (1940), not exactly a winning way for someone to begin an association with 20th Century–Fox. Universal squandered his comedic talents by making him straight man in a pair of Abbott and Costello pictures. But while he found no opportunity to be funny in the early '40s, his other histrionic abilities were put to good use.

RKO's *They Knew What They Wanted* (1940) is Gargan at his best, so much so that his peers who generally took him for granted gave him the nomination for Best Supporting Actor that year at Oscar time. The dated story of an Italian winegrower who lures a young bride to his California home by sending her a picture of his younger ranch foreman served Gargan much better than it did Charles Laughton. In his desire to make himself the ultimate Italian, the usually great actor took to chewing the scenery, and director Garson Kanin couldn't seem to control him. In contrast, Carole Lombard (the girl) and Gargan (the foreman) acted out their love-hate relationship with complete understatement, making the audience care more about them than the character playwright Sidney Howard meant us to care about, winegrower Tony. In fact, these two are vilified for the contemptible act (by 1940s standards) that they commit. But throughout the film, Gargan has been so decent to the buffoonish Laughton that we do not feel for the latter when he becomes enraged at the younger man (in a weak moment that he seems to regret, Gargan got Lombard pregnant). The Legion of Decency, of course, had to have their way, but when Gargan's Joe is thrown off his boss' property, he carries the audiences full sympathy. Even though the original play was a Pulitzer Prize–winner, it had gone through two earlier screen incarnations and was beginning to creak. This made Gargan's achievement all the more notable. (In other versions, including the Broadway musical *The Most Happy Fella*, Joe is portrayed more as a womanizing heel, his relationship with Tony is strictly employer-employee and his part is so minor that no one feels bad when he leaves the premises.) Critics may carp that the actor was using his typically pleasing personality to alter a role that would not have fitted him. But the fact that he could do this while an acting giant (Laughton) could not do what was required of him proved that Gargan had the skill when the right part came along.

Unfortunately, he did not win the Oscar; Walter Brennan won his unprecedented third Oscar for *The Westerner*. Had Gargan won, surely worthier roles would have come his way. Being relatively young, though over draft age, he could have stepped into leading roles the way Brian Donlevy did when the younger actors went into service in 1941 and 1942. But he continued pretty much in the same vein, usually picking up one meaty role a year amid the Universal programmers and unimportant character roles in major productions like Fox's *I Wake Up Screaming* (1941). The male star of that film was Victor Mature, who, two years earlier, had made a low-billed screen debut in *The Housekeeper's Daughter*, proving that not everyone's career stood still. Of course, Gargan had never been one to pose for "beefcake" stills, even in his *Aloma of the South Seas* days. He knew what he projected and what just would not have been right for him.

His next important parts were for United Artists, an independent which had to employ freelancers like Gargan. In *Cheers for Miss Bishop* (1941), he got to age some 40 years as the lifelong admirer of Midwestern schoolteacher Martha Scott. It was one of those films for which handkerchiefs were made. In this film and UA's *Miss Annie Rooney* (1942), he received second billing; in the latter he played the understanding widowed father of Shirley Temple, who had grown so much since her last film that it made Gargan suddenly seem middle-aged at 37. *Who Done It?* (1942) was the second of his two Abbott and Costello flicks. It boasted a better than average cast and one interesting aspect: as a police detective with a dumb assistant, he seemed to be doing Abbott to William Bendix's Costello. Perhaps Universal, already bothered by the skyrocketing team's demands, were trying to show the two of them they could be replaced, even by straight actors. Considering their talents, Bendix and Gargan would have been terrific.

Ralph Bellamy was a fine actor who had been wasted in many movies. To get parts in such films as *The Awful Truth* (1937) and *His Girl Friday* (1940), he had signed with Columbia. Although those films typecast him as the dumb other man, they were a lot better

William Gargan and Carole Lombard in *They Knew What They Wanted* (1940), for which he was Oscar-nominated.

than the parts Harry Cohn gave him in between those gems. After more than a decade in Hollywood, he wanted to get back to the stage. But Columbia had cast him in a film called *Ellery Queen—Master Detective* (1940) and a series evolved. Bellamy insisted that he would not renew his contract and, after three more series entries, his obligation ended and he kept his word. Columbia wanted to continue the series and, since they still had options on the services of Margaret Lindsay (who played Queen's Girl Friday) and Charley Grapewin (who played his police inspector father), they decided to get a new star. In the earlier Queen movies, he was portrayed as a sort of slumming socialite who solved murders. In view of the studio's new success with Chester Morris as Boston Blackie, it was decided to make Ellery Queen a tougher type. This change in attitude also followed in the wake of Lloyd Nolan's success as Fox's

Michael Shayne and was almost simultaneous with Humphrey Bogart's unforgettable one-shot portrayal of Sam Spade. Even though the market for tough guys had opened up again, it was surprising that the actor chosen (Gargan) was one who had only appeared in three undistinguished Columbia films, and nothing within the previous five years.

Gargan would star in only three Ellery Queen films, but as so often happens, he is remembered by more people for that role than for any other. There has always been a special cultish interest in the famous detective characters and the actors who played them. And this character, which originated as a pseudonym for a pair of authors who created a series of mysteries, seems to hold the record for number of portrayals. Besides Bellamy and Gargan, the character was played by Donald Cook and Eddie Quillan in earlier films and by Richard Hart, Lee Bowman, Hugh Marlowe, George Nader, Peter Lawford and Jim Hutton over a 25-year period on television. Gargan, a private investigator in his youth, was the only one who portrayed Queen the way audiences of today expect the "gumshoe" to behave, so he is best remembered for the role. It only seems to matter to the purists that the three he made (*Close Call for Ellery Queen*, *Enemy Agents Meet Ellery Queen* and *A Desperate Chance for Ellery Queen*, all 1942) had little to do with the Queen books, being mostly based upon original screenplays. They could have lasted through the war years, but the fact that he had no contractual obligation to a studio prevented Gargan from continuing in the role. With the new *Crime Doctor* and *Whistler* series ready to give new impetus to the careers of former stars Warner Baxter and Richard Dix, Columbia found it no longer required the services of Ellery Queen. So quickly was the series shelved that Margaret Lindsay and Gargan had to go on in an unrelated detective film, *No Place for a Lady* (1943), to make up for a Queen film that was cancelled. But even though Gargan had played an occasional private eye in the '30s, it was this handful of films which created an all-new image in the eyes of Hollywood's casting directors.

In 1943, he embarked upon another three-picture deal with MGM. The results were *Harrigan's Kid*, a sentimental racetrack yard, *Swing Fever*, a Kay Kyser musical with some prizefighting thrown in, and *The Canterville Ghost* (1944). The latter film, directed by Jules Dassin, was an enjoyable fantasy about a cowardly ghost in an English castle now occupied by a group of American G.I.s during World War II. Gargan, as the sergeant in charge of the billeted soldiers, is thereafter haunted by ghost Charles Laughton, the man he stole scenes from a few years earlier.* When one of Gargan's men, a Canterville descendant played by Robert Young, commits a brave deed, the tormented ghost is allowed a more tranquil afterlife.

At Christmas time 1943, Gargan embarked on a USO tour. With fellow film performers Paulette Goddard and Keenan Wynn, he spent several months visiting American bases in China. Of course, he was no song and dance man or comic, although he participated in comedy sketches. What was more important for the men in uniform who heard him were the quiet informal talks he gave. They were delivered in true Gargan style and the G.I.s responded. He found the entire experience (which continued past the first quarter of 1944) to be one of the most rewarding of his professional career. During that time, he wore the uniform of an Army major, because, as he was informed, the enemy never shot majors.

Gargan was probably not quite as eager as his compatriots on the tour to return to Hollywood. After all, Goddard was one of Paramount's top stars and, after bumping her head on the plane a few times, she was just as glad to go back as her studio was to *have* her back. Ironically, Wynn was wanted for his draft physical, but he also had an MGM contract. As a freelance performer, Gargan was returning to the same situation he had left, the same uncertainty about whether he would get any good roles from any of the majors. There were never any guarantees, but there were always what he called the "schlemiel" pictures. That was an adjective he picked up from some of the producers who were responsible for them.

Since Californians felt they had more reason for concern about a Japanese invasion than other Americans did, many changed their places of residence during the war years. The Gargans gave up their ranch and rented a house in the San Fernando Valley. It was immediately after his return from the overseas tour that he noted the type of parts he was being offered, due to the short-lived Queen series. More than half were low-budget affairs in which he would be starred as a cop, either public or private. But Gargan knew that "his public" would tire of him a lot faster if he only took one type of role. So he signed for two leading roles at Universal which he thought would offer a change of pace. Both were spoofs of more serious genres, unfortunately on the mild side. He was a member of his other

---

*Laughton was easier to work with this time, placated by a part and leading lady he liked, little Margaret O'Brien.

famous profession, a journalist, while Joan Davis played the detective in *She Gets Her Man* (1945), a kind of distaff version of *Destry Rides Again* with the comedienne as the inept daughter of a famous female detective and expected to be just as good. Her male lead merely stooged for her. The same year's *Song of the Sarong*, a terrible title to adorn any actor's list of credits, was a tongue-in-cheek variation on the Maria Montez–Jon Hall films that studio usually made. It paired him with the underrated Nancy Kelly, who was just as quick with a quip as he was. They made two more films together before Kelly deserted Hollywood for stage work, but even there she rarely got the parts she deserved.

They were much better served by their second teaming, *Follow That Woman* (1945), one of several films that each were contractually obligated to make for the William Pine–William Thomas second feature unit at Paramount.

The two low-budget producers (nicknamed "The Dollar Bills") had formed a partnership to turn out cheap action films and needed inexpensive stars, which meant someone like Gargan. *Follow That Woman* was one of their lighter efforts, using the popular storyline of the detective and the meddlesome wife who gets involved in her husband's case. It was the expert playing of Kelly and Gargan that made this usually hackneyed material seem entertaining. Ed Gargan made a rare appearance in one of his brother's films here. (Other screen teamings were *Miss Annie Rooney* [1942] and *Dynamite* [1948], the latter also for the Pine-Thomas unit.)

While most studios churned out B pictures with no connection from one to the next, Columbia Pictures made second features as if they were pilot films for potential series. When Gargan appeared as the star of their *Night Editor* (1946), it appeared that they were contemplating this as something along the lines of their successful *Whistler* series. Via those films, veteran star Richard Dix played ordinary, rather weak men propelling themselves towards some sort of doom. The "Night Editor," like the Whistler character, would merely relate to the audience the chain of events that engulfed the hero. Instead of playing a newspaperman, as the title probably indicated to some, Gargan played a policeman married to Jeff Donnell but involved in an affair with beautiful Janis Carter. During a furtive romantic moment, the two lovers witness a crime and Gargan must go against his sworn duty and ignore what he saw rather than reveal he was present. But Carter tries her hand at blackmailing the perpetrator of the crime, which eventually brings more grief to both of them. The doomed hero, popular in both A and B pictures of the '40s, did not manage to sell this series. Columbia's various methods of testing new films did not elicit a positive reaction to a "Night Editor" series, which might have given Gargan the same kind of popularity the Dix series had given its star during the waning years of his career. The studio went instead with another potential series that had a pre-sold radio popularity, the *I Love a Mystery* series, which proved to be a dismal failure and had a very limited run.

Gargan only made two really important films in the post-war period—both small parts for his old boss RKO and probably the only films of the era in which he didn't have to wear his "detective's hat." In director Leo McCarey's sequel to 1944's *Going My Way*, *The Bells of St. Mary's* (1945), he was the divorced father of one of the girls at Ingrid Bergman's convent school. His role of a veteran sergeant in Edward Dmytryk's *Till the End of Time* (1946) was just as brief. It was no wonder that he was losing practically all interest in film acting. In 1948, Pine-Thomas began making more expensive adventure films, usually with pirates or cowboys, and their old leading men like Richard Denning, William Eythe and Gargan were no longer needed. This coincided with Gargan's own wishes and he no longer sought movie roles. Though only in his early forties, he considered his film career to be virtually over.

Like most Hollywood actors, Gargan had made his share of radio appearances over the years. At one time, he had served as emcee of a variety interview show, imaginatively known as *Stars Over Hollywood*. In the '40s, when detective series were popular on the airwaves, it was decided that an actor who had played such roles countless times on film would easily adapt to the same thing on radio.* What sold Gargan on doing the *Martin Kane* series was that the character was much more well-rounded than the usual flatfoot he was called on to play. Whether in the station house or on undercover assignment, Gargan's movie cops had been steadily veering away from the tough cops and towards much more mellow individuals. Of course, radio had the ability to fake any number of things which would appear too graphic on the motion picture screen. In fact, fans of such radio characters as Sam Spade and Johnny Dollar expected to "hear" people being brutally beaten up. And they were used to hearing a seductive woman's voice making a veiled proposition to an extremely masculine hero. Radio also offered another

---

**An earlier program in that genre,* I Deal in Crime, *was not a success for Gargan.*

fringe benefit for him: Ever since his hair started graying while in his late twenties, he had had to work to keep it his old natural red color while on call for film roles. Now he had the luxury of allowing his hair to go white. He did not have to dye his hair for his family and friends, only working on it for an occasional public appearance.

Gargan was not really the orchestrator of any of the breaks he got in his career; he just took what came along and let things fall into place. He was pretty much of a conformist; after the war many a screen actor became more attracted to the broadcasting media. What basically attracted him to radio was that his friends were going into it, and if it was good enough for them, it was good enough for him. He was really sold when his longtime friend and fellow New Yorker Gene Raymond got a successful radio series called *The Amazing Mr. Malone*. If someone like Raymond, who had had a steady (though hardly spectacular) movie career, could be happy in front of a microphone, so could he. And Raymond and Gargan, by natural progression, became two of the first Hollywood people to move into television. Raymond first appeared as the host of *TV Reader's Digest* in 1950, but Gargan had beaten his friend to the punch. In 1949, Gargan came to television as *Martin Kane, Private Eye*.

Martin Kane, along with Ralph Bellamy's Mike Barnett and Roscoe Karns' Rocky King, can be considered the first of the TV tough guy detectives. Most of these shows were syndicated, sold to individual stations around the country rather than produced solely for the networks. They also had no specific guidelines concerning the amount of violence that could be shown. Some indulged in self-censorship while others took each script as it came. For the *Kane* series, the writers borrowed any number of traits that Gargan had portrayed in two decades of moviemaking. Like most celluloid private detectives, he usually kept his hat on, which only meant less application of the hair dye. An added affectation was Kane's puffing on a pipe, but it was not surprising when one considers the nature of broadcasting in those days. The sole sponsor of *Martin Kane, Private Eye* was the U.S. Tobacco Company.

Gargan played the role on NBC television for two years. Then the shoddiness of the product began to get to him. He had gotten used to the minimal sets, but could not adjust to the sameness of the scripts. The man who had never balked at doing anything in a quarter of a century of acting went to management to voice his objections. He asked for changes in plotlines—changes they were not prepared to make. The quickie way the episodes were turned out, coupled with the lengthy season, made Gargan's demands impossible to comply with. In the end, he asked for his release. He was replaced by another fine actor, Lloyd Nolan, whose "Martin Kane" was a lot like his "Michael Shayne." When Nolan's schedule forced him to bow out, Lee Tracy took over and Kane began talking a lot more rapidly, as this was Tracy's specialty. After that, NBC dropped *Martin Kane, Private Eye*, only to start a series called *The New Adventures of Martin Kane*, which starred Mark Stevens. Stevens, considerably younger than the three earlier actors, was expected to bring new life into the character.

Gargan soon learned that, even in those primitive days when comparatively few Americans owned televisions, the identification of the performer with one particular role was a powerful thing. After he left the Kane character behind, he was offered an almost identical part. The show was called, not too originally, *Barry Craig, Private Detective*, and its star had much more say in the way things were done. But as so often happens, the public did not share the performer's fondness for a project. The new series never enjoyed the popularity of its predecessor, with the radio version produced by Himan Brown much better.

For all intents and purposes, Gargan was in a state of semi-retirement. His two boys had been put through school and he had no other major goals left. He certainly did not have any driving ambitions that would have caused him to wage any more Hollywood battles. Relying on an occasional TV role just to keep his hand in, Gargan was learning for the first time in his life to lead a life of leisure. A few years hence, he would have reason to regret these "wasted years."

In the mid-'50s, Gargan returned to active filmmaking. He made his last two feature films in 1954 and 1955; both were directed by Rudolph Maté, whose prior work as cinematographer of such films as William Wyler's *Dodsworth* and Alfred Hitchcock's *Foreign Correspondent* makes him far better known in that capacity. Nevertheless, in their own ways, both are good films of their type. They were released within a few months of each other in early 1956. The first, Warners' *Miracle in the Rain*, gave him a good role as a musician who long ago had deserted his wife and daughter. When grown daughter Jane Wyman's romance with soldier Van Johnson leads to tragedy, it reunites the parents. Since by this time Johnson and Wyman were too mature for the type of roles they had played in the

'40s, acting honors went to the supporting players. Gargan and Josephine Hutchinson, as his estranged wife, were given some attention by publicists who noted the return to Warner Bros. of two former contractees.

At Universal, Tony Curtis was the star of *The Rawhide Years*, a rarity for Gargan, who had never had the opportunity to appear in a western. He played a U.S. marshall hunting Curtis, who had been framed for the murder of a wealthy man. It is basically an inconsequential film, but director Maté gives it good pace and there are fine performances by the always excellent Arthur Kennedy as Curtis' buddy and William Demarest in an offbeat villainous role. For fifth-billed Gargan, there was little critical mention. He knew he could have continued in such character roles, continually diminishing in size, but filmmaking had lost all of its excitement for him. While in Hollywood, he also acted in "Man on the Ledge" on the CBS-TV show *The Twentieth Century–Fox Hour*. This was a mini-version of the film *Fourteen Hours* (1951), aired in December 1955. Gargan had the role so well played by Paul Douglas in the film—the very humane officer Dunnegan, trying to save a would-be suicide. It was an excellent showcase for Gargan's warm manner and his performance was complemented by those of Cameron Mitchell, as the man who is trying to kill himself, Sylvia Sidney and James Bell, as the parents who have unwittingly driven him to do this, and Vera Miles, as the girl who cares about him. This was the kind of role an actor of Gargan's caliber should have played more often in this new medium. But the actor had given up his agency representation, indicating that he was no longer interested in playing roles that would keep him in Hollywood any longer than he had to be.

Though Gargan considered himself a middle-aged actor who had retired, others did not think of him that way. When a West Coast production of *The Desperate Hours* (a Tony-winner on Broadway and a good film as well) was in the planning stages, Gargan was asked to play Dan Hilliard, the middle-class businessman whose home is taken over by three killers. It was too good to pass up. Karl Malden had created the role of Hilliard on the New York stage and Fredric March played it in the 1955 William Wyler film for Paramount. Because Humphrey Bogart was cast as the chief criminal in the film, that version was the one that prompted many to notice the plot similarities between this play by Joseph Hayes and Robert E. Sherwood's *The Petrified Forest*. Gargan was praised for his performance as Hilliard. Personally, he was pleased with the way *The*

Desperate Hours turned out; having not played such a lengthy role in his younger Broadway days, it was a new experience. He was pleased enough to leave the door open for other limited, close-to-home stage productions.

The Gargans had plenty of time to travel, in a typically casual manner. His visit to New York usually meant renewing acquaintances among Saratoga racetrack pari-mutuel clerks, reliving his childhood memories every August. He did travel further afield for work when asked to appear in some filmed TV episodes as Martin Kane, doing his detecting in several European locales. Apparently kinescopes of the old shows had found their way abroad and become hits. Here was a chance to make up for all his years of studio-confined shooting and Gargan eagerly accepted. American audiences did not get to see the fruits of his labors: It appears that none of these programs has ever been telecast in the United States.

One of the best political plays ever written was Gore Vidal's *The Best Man*, a cynical dissection of convention politics. Some of the characters were sharply drawn from several well-known public figures. The play opened on Broadway with Melvyn Douglas and Frank Lovejoy as two leading presidential candidates of the same party and Lee Tracy as an ex-president whose endorsement both are seeking. For Tracy, the role of President Hockstader revitalized a too-long-dormant career. (Gargan had crossed Tracy's path when Tracy became TV's third Martin Kane.) So great was Tracy in the role that he recreated it in the 1964 film, winning an Oscar nomination to boot. It was a gratifying comeback.

While Tracy was still playing the role in New York, Gargan was asked to play Hockstader in the West Coast production, appearing with Leon Ames and old pal Gene Raymond. Gargan was taken aback at the casting; he may have once "met" a president on screen, but that had been Lewis Stone, who looked the part. He couldn't imagine himself being the chief executive and also had some doubts that he was old enough to be a former one. But second company casting usually had a lot to do with the role's originator and, since Tracy had always been known for his glib, street-wise characterizations, the producers had looked for an actor in the same vein. Had a more dignified type been cast in the original company, Gargan probably wouldn't have been considered.

It was no coincidence that *The Best Man* was scheduled to play at the Huntington Hartford Theater in Los Angeles that summer of 1960, just when the Democratic convention would be held in that very same city. It was the perfect device to boost the sale of tickets, since plays about politics were not always the best box office. At least one member of the cast got to meet the "superstar" of that convention. Although a man of conservative politics, Gargan admits to being impressed with Senator John F. Kennedy when they were introduced that summer. After all, they had two things in common: Both were Irish Catholics and both were preparing to be presidents of the United States.

Gargan found his role to be one of the richest and most rewarding of his long career. He did not even worry about how stocky he had become since his last public appearance, or for that matter how white his hair now was. Many of his old fans were most likely to think he had been "aged" for the part anyway. He also found that something else about his physical condition—something he had not previously been aware of—blended in well with his character. In the play, former President Hockstader is dying of cancer, expiring before the play ends. As Gargan settled into the role, some observers noticed that aside from the vigor and feisty qualities he brought to the characterization, an added touch of reality was the hoarseness of voice that had not been there when he first started playing the part. But this was something that had not been intentionally planned by him. He also noticed that this was no temporary thing, that his voice was not returning to its old style.

Not wanting to continue croaking on stage, he consulted his doctor. He was sent to a specialist, Dr. Alden Miller. It was his tests that produced the alarming news that Gargan had a growth on his larynx and it was cancerous. The situation was spelled out to the family. The cancer had already spread so that the larynx had to be removed or the patient would die. There was no way for the doctor to soften this tragic news; time was of the essence and a decision had to be made. Yet it was no easy decision for anyone, let alone a man who had acted for most of his life. It had occurred just at a time when he was rediscovering the pleasure of performing in front of a live audience. But this did not make him lose faith. After all, he had experienced a full career and even a comeback of sorts; he knew of many actors who were denied that much. Maybe it was a blessing it had come at this age. He knew what was in store for him, having been told that he would have to learn how to talk a whole new way, through a hole in his trachea. He had a pretty good idea what he would sound like. But William Gargan wanted to live. He, his wife and their two sons came to a swift decision and gave Dr. Miller the go-ahead to perform the operation.

Surgery was performed on November 10, 1960, the Thursday following the election of John Kennedy as thirty-fifth president of the United States. As soon as he completed the operation, Dr. Miller came out to see Mary Gargan and son Leslie. He showed them something—the larynx he just had removed, with the potentially deadly lump in evidence. It was a kind of affirmation that they had done the right thing, the only thing possible.

The way he adapted to this unfortunate situation earned Gargan some of the most heartfelt praise he ever received. Some performers had undergone similar operations and had gone into secluded retirement, never revealing their experiences. Others had put off what was necessary and it had killed them. That was why the Gargan situation drew so much publicity: For a celebrity of any kind to admit he had cancer and had an operation to have it removed was almost unheard of in the early '60s. Before Gargan, only Arthur Godfrey had talked to the press about his cancer operation in 1959. (As serious as his surgery was, it saved Godfrey's life without rendering him incapable to perform before a radio microphone or TV camera.)

First there was the period of healing, after which came what was possibly the most difficult experience of all. Gargan had to be fitted with and taught how to use an apparatus that would allow him to speak through a hole in his windpipe. No one deluded Gargan into believing that his "new voice" would be anything like the old one. He had been warned about everything. Some friends advised him that he would be eligible to receive government disability benefits. Soon after leaving the hospital, he did begin collecting unemployment insurance. He was the kind that did not like to take money for nothing, but realized he had to be realistic. At this point, every little bit of money coming in was a help to him.

The first year was the toughest because he could only communicate with pad and pencil. What was maddening was that he still had a strong, healthy body and was not making use of it simply because he had lost his voice. Later in 1961, the American Cancer Society called to ask him to be a spokesman, which would mean he would have to talk in public with his new voice. He still was not used to the hollow sounds that came from this throat; would others accept it? Amazingly, he also received the offer of an acting job—one where he did not have to speak at all. In what would be his last performance as an actor, Gargan played a mute circus performer who uses his agility to perform some daring thefts. This was on the half-hour syndicated adventure show *King of Diamonds* which starred Broderick Crawford (who also seemed to have a say in the casting). Crawford had had an enormously successful earlier series, *Highway Patrol*, the first syndicated series to enjoy a lengthy afterlife through reruns. Crawford and company followed the same policy in *King of Diamonds*: inexpensive casts and backgrounds. Fortunately, the shooting schedule was not physically taxing on an occasional guest star like Gargan. What saddened him was the knowledge that few such "tailor-made" roles would come his way.

Work for the Cancer Society proved anything but sparse as Gargan was turned into a kind of roving ambassador, travelling the country and making speeches. While educating others about the disease, he did himself some good as well. He quite naturally felt at first that others might regard him as a kind of freak, but the receptions he was given told him otherwise. He also seemed to be making up for all the lack of publicity he had garnered during his moviemaking days. An article about Gargan appeared in the September 1963 issue of *Reader's Digest*. His courage was heralded in a *Life* magazine story of December 3, 1965, in honor of his receiving the prestigious Criss Award in a ceremony televised by NBC the previous month. On November 12, 1967, William Gargan was named Man of the Year by the Screen Actors Guild.

The '60s were not without their touches of sadness. He shared the sorrow of the nation over JFK's assassination in November 1963; it was particularly poignant for him because of his contact with Kennedy just three years earlier. He saw the swearing-in of a new president who had not been the first choice of a running mate, for Kennedy's aide Dave Powers had confided to Gargan at convention time that Senator Symington rather than Senator Johnson had been Kennedy's choice for veep. Gargan mourned for the president he had felt such an empathy for. Three months later, he experienced a more personal tragedy. His beloved brother Ed died on February 19, 1964. He had been retired from films since the early '50s and seemed to enjoy doing nothing. Until his own final illness, Ed had always seemed to have the ability to cheer his younger brother in moments of crisis. Only recently had Bill Gargan realized that he was imbued with his own inner strength.

In 1966, the Gargans moved further away from the Hollywood scene, getting a desert home near Carlsbad. But he did not cut down on his travel on behalf of the American Cancer Society, while finding that it was not so hard making those speeches. He also found time to start working on his autobiography, which would be titled *Why Me?* That was a rather misleading title, because it brings to mind self-pity and bitterness and the author had little of that. The question he poses was rather something he already knew the answer to: It was him because he had the God-given strength to meet the challenge and go on and help others. However, the book, when published in 1969, was no serious bit of preachment. It was framed at beginning and end by events leading up to his operation and its aftermath, but Gargan candidly and wittily took on his career as an actor, displaying a heretofore unexplored gift for writing.

Approximately five years after his laryngectomy, Gargan suddenly became the *second* most famous actor known to have had that operation. He was never as big a name as England's Jack Hawkins, who had leads in three Academy Award–winning films (*The Bridge on the River Kwai*, *Ben-Hur* and *Lawrence of Arabia*). Like Gargan, Hawkins was in his mid-fifties when surgery for throat cancer proved necessary. The British actor was still very much in demand afterwards and he did continue, in markedly inferior roles, usually with a dubbed-in voice but sometimes in awkwardly silent characterizations. Hawkins never could consider his new "voice box" a viable substitute. He clung to the hope that further surgery would restore his unique sound. But further surgery only led to complications and, after hemorrhaging, he died in 1973. He had lived with the apparatus for less than eight years.

In his last years, Gargan curtailed his activities slightly, but continued to talk about how he had overcome his affliction. He was, as always, eager to get on with whatever life had in store for him. Perhaps he felt somewhat indestructible, having survived the major illness of his life. But on February 16, 1979, while on a New York–bound plane, Gargan suffered a heart attack. By the time the plane landed, the 73-year-old actor was dead.

For the last 18 years of his life, Gargan became well-known to many people who may not even have been aware of his extensive film career. Those who did remember him thought of him primarily as the cocky Irish man with the wide grin. Unlike most of the other actors mentioned in this book, he did not get a chance to play vicious killers, nor was he fondly remembered for occasionally playing rugged heroes. Is it any wonder that he was thought of more as a personality than actor? When the time came for him to tell his own story, he did not try for very long to convince the readers of *Why Me?* that he was a serious thespian. As he derided the majority of his films, he offered little indication that he could do better. He even took a swipe at his inability to carry a tune: On the set of *The Bells of St. Mary's,* Bing Crosby gathered together members of cast and crew for a little harmony. When Gargan raised his voice in song, Crosby, in that mock-serious manner he had perfected, asked the actor if he were feeling ill. Gargan wrote that this incident helped persuade him not to consider any sort of public "warbling."

But that story had a meaning far beyond an easy joke at his own expense. The actor had never needed the ability to sing to celebrate life; when he lost his voice completely, he still held onto his optimistic outlook. That was why he harked back to the Crosby incident at the end of the book. His point was that he never lost his zest for living, no matter what his affliction. He said it all in three words: "Inside I'm singing."

That alone qualifies William Gargan for the title of bravest, and nicest, tough guy.

The Films of William Gargan

WG began appearing in silent films back as far as 1917. Below are his talking film appearances.

1. ***Lucky Boy.*** Tiffany 1929. Norman Taurog. George Jessel, Rosa Rosanova, Glenda Farrell, William Strauss, Margaret Quimby. Playing himself, Jessel has a shot at his own "The Jazz Singer."

2. ***Follow the Leader.*** Par 1930. Norman Taurog. Ed Wynn, Ginger Rogers, Lou Holtz, Ethel Merman, Stanley Smith, Preston Foster, Lida Kane.

3. ***His Woman.*** Par 1931. Edward Sloman. Gary Cooper, Claudette Colbert, Richard Spiro, Douglass Dumbrille, Harry Davenport, Preston Foster, Joseph Spurin-Calleia, Barton MacLane (uncredited bit). WG is a crew member on Cooper's ocean liner.

4. ***Misleading Lady.*** Par 1932. Stuart Walker. Claudette Colbert, Edmund Lowe, Stuart Erwin, George Meeker, Selena Royle, Harry Ellerbe, Curtis Cooksey. WG is a Broadway character.

5. ***Rain.*** UA 1932. Lewis Milestone. Joan Crawford, Walter Huston, Matt Moore, Guy Kibbee, Beulah Bondi, Walter Catlett, Fredric Howard, Ben Hendricks, Kendall Lee. WG has his first major film role, as the marine sergeant.

6. ***The Sport Parade.*** RKO 1932. Dudley Murphy. Joel McCrea, Marian Marsh, Skeets Gallagher, Walter Catlett, Robert Benchley, Clarence Wilson, Ivan Linow. WG is a friend and manager of promising athlete McCrea.

7. ***The Animal Kingdom.*** RKO 1932. Edward H. Griffith. Ann

Harding, Leslie Howard, Myrna Loy, Neil Hamilton, Henry Stephenson, Ilka Chase, Donald Dillaway, Leni Stengel. WG repeats his stage role as Howard's offbeat servant Red Regan.

8. **Lucky Devils.** RKO 1933. Ralph Ince. William Boyd, Dorothy Wilson, Bruce Cabot, Julie Haydon, Rosco Ates, William Bakewell, Creighton (Lon) Chaney, Betty Furness. WG is one of a group of fliers who become movie stuntmen and have typical fallings-out.

9. **Sweepings.** RKO 1933. John Cromwell. Lionel Barrymore, Eric Linden, Alan Dinehart, Gloria Stuart, Gregory Ratoff, George Meeker, Lucien Littlefield, Helen Mack, Ivan Lebedeff, Nan Sunderland, Esther Muir. WG is one of the heirs to a department store dynasty started by patriarch Barrymore.

10. **Emergency Call.** RKO 1933. Edward L. Cahn. William Boyd, Wynne Gibson, Betty Furness, Reginald Mason, George E. Stone, Merna Kennedy, Edwin Maxwell, Ruth Fallows, Jane Darwell. Ambulance driver WG and medic Boyd become romantic rivals for Gibson.

11. **Headline Shooters.** RKO 1933. Otto Brower. Ralph Bellamy, Frances Dee, Wallace Ford, Dorothy Burgess, Gregory Ratoff, Robert Benchley, Jack LaRue, Hobart Cavanaugh, Franklin Pangborn. WG and Bellamy are a pair of fast-moving newsreel reporters.

12. **Aggie Appleby, Maker of Men.** RKO 1933. Mark Sandrich. Charles Farrell, Wynne Gibson, Zasu Pitts, Betty Furness, Blanche Frederici, Jane Darwell. Streetwise WG loses the title character to a doltish rival.

13. **The Story of Temple Drake.** Par 1933. Stephen Roberts. Miriam Hopkins, Jack LaRue, Sir Guy Standing, Florence Eldredge, Elizabeth Patterson, Irving Pichel, William Collier, Jr., Grady Sutton, Hattie McDaniel, Kent Taylor. Risque William Faulkner story has WG as the attorney trying to help Hopkins, who plays the title role.

14. **Night Flight.** MGM 1933. Clarence Brown. John Barrymore, Lionel Barrymore, Clark Gable, Helen Hayes, Myrna Loy, Robert Montgomery, Frank Conroy, Leslie Fenton, C. Henry Gordon, Ralf Harolde. This is WG's most inaccessible film due to neverending literary rights problems with the survivors of author Antoine de Saint-Exupéry. He plays one of the mail-transporting pilots.

15. **Four Frightened People.** Par 1934. Cecil B. DeMille. Claudette Colbert, Herbert Marshall, Mary Boland, Leo Carrillo, Chris-Pin Martin, Ethel Griffies, Tetsu Komai, Nella Walker. WG is the "expert" among the foursome lost in the jungle.

16. **The Lineup.** Col 1934. Howard Higgin. Marian Nixon, John Miljan, Paul Hurst, Noel Francis, Harold Huber, Joseph Crehan. WG is a policeman who develops an interest in a female witness (Nixon).

17. **Strictly Dynamite.** RKO 1934. Elliott Nugent. Jimmy Durante, Lupe Velez, Norman Foster, Eugene Pallette, Marian Nixon, Minna Gombell, Franklin Pangborn, The Mills Brothers, Sterling Holloway. WG is a show business know-it-all.

18. *British Agent.* WB 1934. Michael Curtiz. Leslie Howard, Kay Francis, Phillip Reed, Walter Byron, Irving Pichel, Cesar Romero, Halliwell Hobbes, Ivan Simpson, Alphonse Ethier, J. Carrol Naish. WG is one of a group of foreigners stuck in pre–Revolution Russia.

19. *Black Fury.* WB 1935. Michael Curtiz. Paul Muni, Karen Morley, Barton MacLane, Vince Barnett, Joseph Crehan, Sara Haden, Mae Marsh, Tully Marshall, J. Carrol Naish, Henry O'Neil, John Qualen, Willard Robertson, Akim Tamiroff, Ward Bond. WG is a decent company cop involved with Morley, the girl of coal miner Muni (who goes on a wild rampage).

20. *Night at the Ritz.* WB 1935. William McGann. Patricia Ellis, Allen Jenkins, Erik Rhodes, Dorothy Tree, Berton Churchill, Gordon Westcott, Bodil Rosing. WG manages the career of a (so-called) world-famous chef (Rhodes).

21. *Traveling Saleslady.* WB 1935. Ray Enright. Joan Blondell, Glenda Farrell, Hugh Herbert, Grant Mitchell, Ruth Donnelly, Al Shean, Bert Roach, Johnny Arthur, Joseph Crehan. WG offers romantic stability to Blondell, in the title role.

22. *Broadway Gondolier.* WB 1935. Lloyd Bacon. Dick Powell, Joan Blondell, Adolphe Menjou, Louise Fazenda, George Barbier, Grant Mitchell, Hobart Cavanaugh, The Mills Brothers, The Canova Family, Joseph Sawyer, James Burke. WG is a public relations specialist pushing crooner Powell.

23. *Bright Lights.* WB 1935. Busby Berkeley. Joe E. Brown, Ann Dvorak, Patricia Ellis, Joseph Cawthorn, Henry O'Neill, Gordon Westcott, Arthur Treacher, William Demarest, Joseph Crehan. WG courts Dvorak, the estranged wife of entertainer Brown.

24. *Don't Bet on Blondes.* WB 1935. Robert Florey. Warren William, Claire Dodd, Guy Kibbee, Vince Barnett, Errol Flynn, Walter Byron, Clay Clement, Mary Treen, Maude Eburne, Spencer Charters, Herman Bing. WG is a shady associate of gambler William.

25. *Man Hunt.* WB 1936. William Clemens. Ricardo Cortez, Marguerite Churchill, Charles "Chic" Sale, Dick Purcell, Olin Howlin, George E. Stone, Addison Richards, Russell Simpson, Anita Kerry, Kenneth Harlan. Law officer WG nabs gangster Cortez, who was hiding in a rural town.

26. *The Milky Way.* Par 1936. Leo McCarey. Harold Lloyd, Adolphe Menjou, Verre Teasdale, Helen Mack, George Barbier, Marjorie Gateson, Lionel Stander, Dorothy Wilson, Charles Lane. Milkman Lloyd is turned into a prizefighter after accidentally knocking out middleweight champion WG (in the role played on Broadway by Brian Donlevy).

27. *Sky Parade.* Par 1936. Otto Lovering. Kent Taylor, Jimmie Allen, Katherine DeMille, Grant Withers, Bennie Bartlett, Sid Saylor, Richard Fiske, Edgar Dearing. WB is one of a group of pilots who take care of a dead buddy's little boy.

28. *Navy Born.* Rep 1936. Nate Watt. Claire Dodd, Douglas Fowley, George Irving, William Newell, Addison Randall, Claudia Coleman, Paul

Fix, Douglas Wood, Hooper Atchley. Navy man WG once again assumes responsibility for a dead buddy's son.

29. **Alibi for Murder.** Col 1936. D. Ross Lederman. Marguerite Churchill, Gene Morgan, Dwight Frye, John Gallaudet. WG is a private detective.

30. **Blackmailer.** Col 1936. Gordon Wiles. Florence Rice, H. B. Warner, Paul Hurst, Nana Bryant, George McKay, Kenneth Thomson. WG is an amateur sleuth.

31. **Flying Hostess.** Univ 1936. Murray Roth. William Hall, Judith Barrett, Andy Devine, Ella Logan, Astrid Allwyn, Addison Randall. WG conducts a training program for stewardesses.

32. **Breezing Home.** Univ 1936. Milton Carruth. Wendy Barrie, Binnie Barnes, Raymond Walburn, Alan Baxter, Alma Kruger, William (Willie) Best, Elisha Cook, Jr. WG is a horse trainer.

33. **You Only Live Once.** UA 1937. Fritz Lang. Sylvia Sidney, Henry Fonda, Barton MacLane, Jean Dixon, Jerome Cowan, Margaret Hamilton, Warren Hymer, Guinn Williams, Ward Bond, Wade Boteler. WG is a prison chaplain who loses his life trying to help convict Fonda.

34. **Fury and the Woman.** Rialto 1937. Lewis Collins. Molly Lamont, James McGrath, J. P. McGowan, Libby Taylor, David Clyde, Reginald Hincks, Harry Hastings. WG is a new addition to a logging camp who must prove himself to the other men. The film's highlights are the actual Canadian locales.

35. **Wings Over Honolulu.** Univ 1937. H. C. Potter, Wendy Barrie, Ray Milland, Kent Taylor, Polly Rowles, Samuel S. Hinds, Louise Beavers, Joyce Compton, Clara Blandick. WG is a flying buddy of newlyweds trying to adjust to married life.

36. **Reported Missing.** Univ 1937. Milton Carruth. Jean Rogers, Dick Purcell, Hobart Cavanaugh, Joe Sawyer, Michael Fitzmaurice, Jack Carson. WG is a pilot who invents a new flying device.

37. **She Asked for It.** Par 1937. Erle C. Kenton. Vivienne Osborne, Orien Heyward, Roland Drew, Tully Marshall, Harry Beresford, Joyce Compton, Miki Morita, Carol Tevis, Alan Birmingham, Nora Cecil, Edward Earle. WG is an amateur sleuth.

38. **Some Blondes Are Dangerous.** Univ 1937. Noah Beery, Jr., Dorothea Kent, Nan Grey, Polly Rowles, Roland Drew, John Butler, Lew Kelly. WG is a fight manager who doesn't like his young boxer's tramp wife.

39. **You're a Sweetheart.** Univ 1937. David Butler. Alice Faye, George Murphy, Charles Winninger, Andy Devine, Ken Murray, Donald Meek, Bobby Watson, Four Playboys, Norelle Brothers. WG is a promoter of musical shows.

40. **The Crime of Dr. Hallett.** Univ 1938. S. Sylvan Simon. Ralph Bellamy, Josephine Hutchinson, John King, Barbara Read, Constance Moore, Charles Stevens, Nella Walker, Honorable Wu. WG is one of a group of medical researchers in a jungle laboratory.

41. ***The Devil's Party.*** Univ 1938. Ray McCarey. Victor McLaglen, Paul Kelly, Beatrice Roberts, Frank Jenks, Samuel S. Hinds, Gordon (Bill) Elliott, John Gallaudet. WG is one of four old pals from New York's Hell's Kitchen who has become a cop.

42. ***The Crowd Roars.*** MGM 1938. Richard Thorpe. Robert Taylor, Edward Arnold, Frank Morgan, Maureen O'Sullivan, Jane Wyman, Nat Pendleton, Lionel Stander, Gene Reynolds, Charles D. Brown, Isabel Jewell, Don Douglas, Donald Barry. Rising boxer Taylor inadvertently causes the death of his childhood idol WG, a washed-up ex-champ.

43. ***Behind the Mike.*** Univ 1938. Sidney Salkow. Judith Barrett, Don Wilson, Sterling Holloway, Grady Sutton, Gerald Oliver Smith, William Davidson. WG is a radio station manager.

44. ***Personal Secretary.*** Univ 1938. Otis Garrett. Joy Hodges, Andy Devine, Ruth Donnelly, Florence Roberts, Kay Linaker, Samuel S. Hinds. WG is a columnist.

45. ***The House of Fear.*** Univ 1939. Joe May. Irene Hervey, Dorothy Arnold, Alan Dinehart, Harvey Stephens, Robert Coote, Walter Woolf King, El Brendel. WG buys a theater and begins producing a play, with the intention of solving an old murder.

46. ***Broadway Serenade.*** MGM 1939. Robert Z. Leonard. Jeanette MacDonald, Lew Ayres, Frank Morgan, Ian Hunter, Rita Johnson, Virginia Grey, Wally Vernon, Katharine Alexander, Paul Hurst, Frank Orth, Franklin Pangborn, Al Shean, Esther Dale, Mary Beth Hughes. WG is one of Broadway producer Morgan's associates.

47. ***Woman in the Wind.*** WB 1939. John Farrow. Kay Francis, Victor Jory, Eve Arden, Eddie Foy, Jr., Sheila Bromley, Maxie Rosenbloom, Rosella Towne, John Dilson, Frankie Burke. WG is the romantic interest for aviatrix Francis.

48. ***Adventures of Jane Arden.*** WB 1939. Gerry Morse. Rosella Towne, Benny Rubin, Peggy Shannon, Dennie Moore, Pierre Watkin, Maris Wrixon, Frankie Burke. WG is a tough-on-the-exterior newspaper editor.

49. ***Three Sons.*** RKO 1939. Jack Hively. Edward Ellis, Kent Taylor, J. Edward Bromberg, Katharine Alexander, Virginia Vale, Robert Stanton, Kirby Grant. Remake of *Sweepings* (1933) with WB as a scion of a well-to-do family.

50. ***Within the Law.*** MGM 1939. Gustav Machaty. Ruth Hussey, Paul Kelly, Rita Johnson, Tom Neal, Lynne Carver, Sidney Blackmer, Paul Cavanagh, Samuel S. Hinds. Cop WG is suspicious of parolee Hussey.

51. ***Joe and Ethel Turp Call on the President.*** MGM 1939. Robert Sinclair. Ann Sothern, Lewis Stone, Walter Brennan, Marsha Hunt, Tom Neal, Don Costello, Muriel Hutchinson, Mary Gordon, Louis Jean Heydt, James Bush, Jack Mulhall, Lon McCallister. WG and wife Sothern champion the cause of their neighborhood mailman Brennan, telling president Stone about the man's life.

52. ***The Housekeeper's Daughter.*** UA 1939. Hal Roach. Joan Bennett,

Adolphe Menjou, John Hubbard, Peggy Wood, Donald Meek, George E. Stone, Victor Mature, Marc Lawrence. Arguing newspapermen Menjou and WG compete for a story.

53. *Double Alibi.* Univ 1940. Phil Rosen. Wayne Morris, Margaret Lindsay, Roscoe Karns, Cliff Clark, Robert Emmett Keane, James Burke. Newspaper editor WG concentrates on the case of Morris, suspected of killing his wife.

54. *Isle of Destiny.* RKO 1940. Elmer Clifton. Wallace Ford, June Lang, Gilbert Roland, Katherine DeMille, Etienne Girardot, Harry Woods. WG is an adventurer.

55. *Star Dust.* 20th 1940. Walter Lang. Linda Darnell, John Payne, Roland Young, Charlotte Greenwood, Mary Beth Hughes, Jessie Ralph, Donald Meek, Mary Healy, George Montgomery, Robert Lowery, Joan Brodel (Leslie), Mantan Moreland. WG is a Zanuck-like film executive on a talent hunt.

56. *Turnabout.* UA 1940. Hal Roach. Carole Landis, Adolphe Menjou, John Hubbard, Mary Astor, Verree Teasdale, Donald Meek, Joyce Compton, Marjorie Main, Franklin Pangborn, Inez Courtney, Berton Churchill. WG is a business associate of a couple (Landis and Hubbard) who inadvertently switch sexes.

57. *Sporting Blood.* MGM 1940. S. Sylvan Simon. Robert Young, Maureen O'Sullivan, Lewis Stone, Lynne Carver, Clarence Muse, Lloyd Corrigan, Tom Kennedy, Russell Hicks. WG is a horse trainer preparing for a big race.

58. *They Knew What They Wanted.* RKO 1940. Garson Kanin. Carole Lombard, Charles Laughton, Harry Carey, Frank Fay, Tom Ewell, Karl Malden, Victor Kilian, Joseph Bernard, Janet Fox. The third (and last to date) film version of Sidney Howard's play. WG nabbed his only Oscar nomination as the ranch foreman who unwittingly cuckolds his boss, immigrant winegrower Laughton.

59. *Sealed Lips.* Univ 1941. George Waggner. June Clyde, John Litel, Anne Nagel, Mary Gordon, Ralf Harolde, Joseph Crehan. WG is the sleuth trying to nail a criminal with a dual identity.

60. *Cheers for Miss Bishop.* UA 1941. Tay Garnett. Martha Scott, Edmund Gwenn, Marsha Hunt, Sidney Blackmer, Sterling Holloway, Dorothy Peterson, Mary Anderson, Rosemary DeCamp, Don Douglas, William Farnum, William Bakewell. WG is a longtime friend and admirer who grows old with dedicated teacher Scott.

61. *I Wake Up Screaming.* 20th 1941. H. Bruce Humberstone. Betty Grable, Victor Mature, Carole Landis, Laird Cregar, Alan Mowbray, Allyn Joslyn, Elisha Cook, Jr., Chick Chandler, Morris Ankrum, Frank Orth, May Beatty, Charles Lane. New York police detective (WG) and his neurotic colleague (Cregar) investigate a girl's murder.

62. *Keep 'Em Flying.* Univ 1941. Arthur Lubin. Bud Abbott, Lou Costello, Martha Raye, Dick Foran, Carol Bruce, Loring Smith, Truman Bradley, William Davidson, James Seay. WG is an Air Corps flying instructor at odds with pilot Foran.

63. *Flying Cadets.* Univ 1941. Erle C. Kenton. Edmund Lowe, Peggy Moran, Frankie Thomas, Frank Albertson, Roy Harris. WG is one of the men operating a school for flyers.

64. *Close Call for Ellery Queen.* Col 1942. James Hogan. Margaret Lindsay, Charley Grapewin, Ralph Morgan, Edward Norris, Kay Linaker, Addison Richards, Charles Judels. With this film, WG replaced Ralph Bellamy in the series title role.

65. *The Mayor of 44th Street.* RKO 1942. Alfred E. Green. George Murphy, Anne Shirley, Richard Barthelmess, Joan Merrill, Rex Downing, Millard Mitchell, Mary Wickes, Freddy Martin and His Orchestra, Esther Muir. WG is a cop friend of Murphy.

66. *Bombay Clipper.* Univ 1942. John Rawlins. Irene Hervey, Maria Montez, Lloyd Corrigan, Mary Gordon, Phillip Trent, Turhan Bey, Charles Lang, Truman Bradley. WG is a news correspondent.

67. *Miss Annie Rooney.* UA 1942. Edwin L. Marin. Shirley Temple, Guy Kibbee, Dickie Moore, Gloria Holden, Peggy Ryan, June Lockhart, Selmer Jackson, Virginia Sale, Ronald Dupree, Jonathan Hale, Mary Field, George Lloyd. WG is Temple's widowed father.

68. *Destination Unknown.* Univ 1942. Ray Taylor. Irene Hervey, Sam Levene, Keye Luke, Turhan Bey, Willie Fung, Felix Basch. WG is a pilot in the Orient.

69. *Enemy Agents Meet Ellery Queen.* Col 1942. James Hogan. Margaret Lindsay, Gale Sondergaard, Charley Grapewin, Gilbert Roland, Sig Ruman, Minor Watson, Felix Basch, Ludwig Donath, Ernest Dorian. WG is Ellery Queen.

70. *Who Done It?* Univ 1942. Erle C. Kenton. Bud Abbott, Lou Costello, Patric Knowles, Louise Allbritton, William Bendix, Don Porter, Thomas Gomez, Jerome Cowan, Mary Wickes, Ludwig Stossel. Police detective WG investigates a murder at a radio station.

71. *A Desperate Chance for Ellery Queen.* Col 1942. James Hogan. Margaret Lindsay, John Litel, Charley Grapewin, Lillian Bond, James Burke, Jack LaRue. WG's last appearance as the title sleuth.

72. *Harrigan's Kid.* MGM 1943. Charles Reisner. Bobby Readick, Frank Craven, J. Carrol Naish, Douglas Croft, Bill Cartledge, Selmer Jackson, Irving Leo. WG is a former jockey trying to groom Readick in the same line of work.

73. *No Place for a Lady.* Col 1943. James Hogan. Margaret Lindsay, John Litel, Phyllis Brooks, Dick Purcell, Jerome Cowan, Edward Norris, James Burke. WG plays a detective.

74. *Swing Fever.* MGM 1943. Tim Whelan. Kay Kyser, Marilyn Maxwell, Nat Pendleton, Curt Bois, Maxie Rosenbloom, Mike Mazurki, Lena Horne, Morris Ankrum, Andrew Tombes, Pamela Blake, Harry Babbitt. WG is a shady promoter who takes advantage of naive Kyser.

75. *The Canterville Ghost.* MGM 1944. Jules Dassin. Charles Laughton, Robert Young, Margaret O'Brien, Rags Ragland, Reginald

Owen, Una O'Connor, Frank Faylen, Jack Lambert, Peter Lawford, Mike Mazurki, Elisabeth Risdon. WG is a sergeant among a group of American soldiers billeted at a British castle during World War II.

76. *She Gets Her Man.* Univ 1945. Erle C. Kenton. Joan Davis, Leon Errol, Donald MacBride, Vivian Austin, Milburn Stone, Russell Hicks, Cy Kendall, Eddie Acuff, Paul Stanton. Davis is the offspring of a famous law officer and WG is her loyal protector.

77. *Song of the Sarong.* Univ 1945. Harold Young. Nancy Kelly, Eddie Quillan, George Cleveland, George Dolenz, Fuzzy Knight, Mariska Aldrich, Larry Keating, Clarence Lung, Jay Silverheels, Jack Slattery. WG is a promoter in this sendup of "island" pictures.

78. *Midnight Manhunt.* Par 1945. William Thomas. Ann Savage, Leo Gorcey, George Zucco, Don Beddoe, Paul Hurst, Charles Halton. WG is a reporter.

79. *Follow That Woman.* Par 1945. Lew Landers. Nancy Kelly, Regis Toomey, Ed Gargan, Byron Barr, Pierre Watkin, Audrey Young. WG is a detective with an interfering wife (Kelly).

80. *The Bells of St. Mary's.* RKO 1945. Leo McCarey. Bing Crosby, Ingrid Bergman, Henry Travers, Ruth Donnelly, Joan Carroll, Martha Sleeper, Rhys Williams, Una O'Connor, Dickie Tyler, Bobby Frasco. WG is an unreliable father. Priest Crosby reunites him with his wife and daughter.

81. *One Exciting Night.* Par 1945. William Thomas. Ann Savage, George Zucco, Paul Hurst, Don Beddoe, George E. Stone, Raymond Hatton. WG is a reporter.

82. *Behind Green Lights.* 20th 1946. Otto Brower. Carole Landis, Richard Crane, Mary Anderson, John Ireland, Mabel Paige, Charles Russell, Roy Roberts, Don Beddoe, Bernard Nedell, Charles Tannen. WG is a police detective investigating a murder.

83. *Murder in the Music Hall.* Rep 1946. John English. Vera Hruba Ralston, William Marshall, Nancy Kelly, Ann Rutherford, Helen Walker, Julie Bishop, Jerome Cowan, Paul Hurst, Jack LaRue, Anne Nagel, Edward Norris, Frank Orth. WG is again a homicide detective, this time looking into the death of a producer.

84. *Strange Impersonation.* Rep 1946. John English, Anthony Mann. Brenda Marshall, Hillary Brooke, H. B. Warner, Ruth Ford, Lyle Talbot, George Chandler, Mary Treen, Dick Scott. After WB breaks up with fellow scientist Marshall, she assumes another identity to rectify her personal and professional lives.

85. *Night Editor.* Col 1946. Henry Levin. Janis Carter, Jeff Donnell, Coulter Irwin, Charles D. Brown, Harry Shannon, Paul Burns, Frank Wilcox, Roy Gordon. Married cop WG witnesses a crime during an illicit meeting with his beautiful paramour Carter.

86. *Rendezvous 24.* 20th 1946. James Tinling. Pat O'Moore, Maria Palmer, David Leonard, Kurt Katch, John Bleifer, Henry Rowland. WG is

an American undercover man in France during the last days of the Nazi regime.

87. *Till the End of Time.* RKO 1946. Edward Dmytryk. Dorothy McGuire, Guy Madison, Robert Mitchum, Bill Williams, Tom Tully, Jean Porter, Ruth Melson, Johnny Sands, Loren Tindall, Selena Royle, Harry Von Zell, Richard Benedict, Blake Edwards, Paul Birch. Story of three returning World War II soldiers was overshadowed by the same year's award-winning *The Best Years of Our Lives.* WG is seen briefly as their ex-sergeant, who helps vets adjust to civilian life.

88. *Hot Cargo.* Par 1946. Lew Landers. Jean Rogers, Philip Reed, David Holt, Virginia Brissac, Will Wright, Harry Cording, Dick Elliott, Larry Young. WG is the boss of a work crew.

89. *Swell Guy.* Univ 1946. Frank Tuttle. Sonny Tufts, Ann Blyth, Ruth Warrick, Thomas Gomez, John Litel, Mary Nash, Millard Mitchell, John Craven, Howard Freeman, Vince Barnett, Charles Lane, Frank Ferguson, Patrick McVey, Garry Owen. WG is the big brother trying to put Tufts on the straight and narrow. Behind-the-scenes personnel include producer Mark Hellinger and screenwriter Richard Brooks, who adapted a play written years earlier by actor Gilbert Emery.

90. *The Argyle Secrets.* Eronel 1947. Cy Enfield. Marjorie Lord, Ralph Byrd, Barbara Billingsley, John Banner, Jack Reitzen, Peter Brocco. Reporter WG uncovers a neo–Nazi plot.

91. *Waterfront at Midnight.* Par 1948. William Berke. Mary Beth Hughes, Richard Travis, Richard Crane, Keye Luke, Cheryl Walker, Douglas Fowley, Horace MacMahon, Paul Harvey. WG is an agent trying to put waterfront racketeers out of business.

92. *Dynamite.* Pr. 1948. William Pine. Virginia Welles, Richard Crane, Irving Bacon, Edward Gargan, Frank Ferguson, Mary Newton. Construction workers WG and Crane see their friendship go up in smoke over the same woman (Welles).

93. *Miracle in the Rain.* WB 1956. Rudolph Maté. Jane Wyman, Van Johnson, Peggie Castle, Fred Clark, Eileen Heckart, Halliwell Hobbes, Josephine Hutchinson, Arte Johnson, Alan King, Barbara Nichols, Paul Picerni, Marcel Dalio, George Givot, Irene Seidner. WG is a musician who returns to long deserted wife (Hutchinson) when tragedy strikes their daughter Wyman.

94. *The Rawhide Years.* Univ 1956. Rudolph Maté. Tony Curtis, Arthur Kennedy, Colleen Miller, William Demarest, Peter Van Eyck, Minor Watson, Leigh Snowden, Trevor Bardette, Donald Randolph, Don Beddoe. U.S. marshal WG pursues gambler Curtis, who has been framed for a wealthy man's murder.

Barton MacLane

The fans of the great old gangster films remember Barton MacLane as an important member of the Warner Bros. stock company. His supreme villainy was so closely associated with that studio and that era that people forget that this period comprised less than one-quarter of his total film career. The most familiar image of MacLane in his heyday can be described thusly: "a weapon in his hand; a leer on his face." He seemed to never have been young, though he became prominent while in his early thirties. (The record books indicate he was only 32 when he played the cold-blooded gangster in *G-Men*.) When he dished out orders to Humphrey Bogart in *Bullets or Ballots*, the only film in which MacLane received higher billing, no one could have guessed that this authority figure was three years younger than the punk gangster who was waiting for his chance to dethrone his boss. You could almost plot his cinematic downfall in the films he made with Bogart over the years.

By virtue of the roles he played, MacLane was one of the most inhuman of all the tough guys. That inhumanity gave him an ageless quality that made him a survivor. When the Warner gangster royalty was shifted over to the ranks of the heroes to please the censors, MacLane became the studio's chief evildoer. He made these monsters he portrayed believable without any psychological motivation to fall back on; this indicates just how talented he really was. He once said he hated playing such roles, yet he mastered them.

He was born in Columbia, South Carolina, on December 2, 1902. This man who would someday personify evil so well had a strict puritanical upbringing. One thing that did not please his father was young Barton's love for the nickelodeons. He had taken to the early films and he eventually brought his father over to his way of thinking. He did this by taking the elder MacLane to see D. W.

A typical leering pose for Barton MacLane in the '30s.

Griffith's *The Birth of a Nation*. The film impressed his father, who would never again refer to the motion picture as the instrument of evil he had originally thought it to be.

His Methodist upbringing was the reason he was sent north to Wesleyan University. There he excelled in basketball and particularly football. He set a record as a running back of 105 yards, against Massachusetts State, a figure that was only beaten by football great Johnny Mack Brown, who also had some later success in motion pictures. As was the case with other college football stars, MacLane made his screen debut in the background of a film dealing with the sport, *The Quarterback* with Richard Dix. When this film was made in 1924, he was in his senior year of college and could have actively pursued a career in films. Unlike Brown, Ward Bond and a few others, MacLane did not use his gridiron success to launch him into the movies. By the time he decided he was ready to act on screen, talking pictures had arrived.

The reason MacLane put off making movies was because he was serious enough about it to try and learn the craft first. He enrolled in the prestigious American Academy of Dramatic Arts and from there he went out and picked up his first professional credits (stock in Brooklyn). He first appeared on Broadway in a walk-on in *The Trial of Mary Dugan*. During this period, he married Martha Stewart. This union produced two children, William and Martha, but was not a happy one. Mrs. MacLane was a Southern girl who preferred to live in that part of the country. When they split up, she took the children with her and he was unable to see them for a dozen years.

His first notable Broadway role was in Maxwell Anderson's play *Gods of Lightning*, in which two of the leads were taken by Charles Bickford and Sylvia Sidney, future Hollywood co-stars of his. This was one of several '20s plays that was designed to reflect the times, but the subject matter, the Sacco and Vanzetti case, contributed to its short run. Today, the play is just a critically acclaimed memory. This became a standard problem that had a lingering effect on MacLane's theatrical career: He was in some good plays but never got the part that would have made the big difference. Instead, he became an able supporting actor, just as he would be throughout his long film career.

In between plays, he did just what every other stage actor of the day seemed to be doing: picking up some bit work at Paramount's Astoria studio. He could be seen in the background, for those who were not confused by the hectic events in the foreground, in the Marx Brothers debut film *The Cocoanuts* (1929).* This was hardly in keeping with the serious stage work MacLane usually was considered for. Whether in the melodramatic *Subway Express* or the highly acclaimed *Yellow Jack*, in which he had a rare opportunity to play a medical man, he was always considered for dramatic parts. He was hoping that one of these parts would catapult him to the higher echelon, but no such luck.

He tried to rectify the situation by writing a play for himself. It was a risky proposition, especially during the early part of the Depression. But actors were suffering loss of work just like everyone else. MacLane relied upon those occasional trips to the Astoria Studios to pay some bills. He and William Gargan got a few days work in a Paramount film called *His Woman* (1931), but it was only important because it had Gary Cooper and Claudette Colbert as stars. His stage roles may have been bigger, but during that period, they were also a means to an end to support him until his play was ready. They also set the pattern for his later screen work. *Steel*, which ran on Broadway for 14 performances in November 1931, involved labor unrest and *The Tree*, which ran only half as long five months later, found him cast in his first racist role, as the lyncher of a young black boy. His own play was not without social significance: *Rendezvous* was about a World War I veteran embittered to the point of turning racketeer. One of the day's leading producers, Arthur Hopkins, not only brought the play to Broadway, but saw that the author himself was a natural for the lead. *Rendezvous* opened to respectful reviews in October 1932, but only managed to stay alive a scant 21 performances. A lot of flop plays were purchased by the movies and his fell into the plus column when MGM purchased the rights, but a film version was never made.

There was a 1935 MGM movie called *Rendezvous* (1935), notable as the first lead role for Rosalind Russell, whose best friend Charlotte Wynters was the future Mrs. Barton MacLane. Wynters had a substantial motion picture credit before either MacLane or Russell; a prominent role in D. W. Griffith's final film *The Struggle*. Other parts followed. Though her career in films would span a quarter of a century, many of her later roles would be obtained through her friend Russell (*Woman of Distinction*) or her husband (numer-

---

*A precursor of things to come: Paramount more than any other studio saw him as a straight man for comics including Burns and Allen in an early short film.

ous films). It was Wynters who supplied temporary West Coast lodgings for Russell, who went through an abortive period under contract to Universal before being signed by MGM. The relationship between Wynters and MacLane began in earnest when he came west in 1933, for the show that succeeded *Rendezvous* had ten less performances. He saw no reason not to accept a contract offered by Paramount Pictures.

In rapid succession, he made eleven films which did absolutely no harm, or good. They weren't an undistinguished lot; half of them were Henry Hathaway–directed versions of Zane Grey westerns and the others had stars like Claudette Colbert and W. C. Fields. The trouble was that MacLane was not given the type of role suitable for him. No one there seemed to see him as the personification of evil he would soon play; then cast him as mild secondary villains or just colorless minor roles. They offered no special bits of business usually associated with the more successful character performers of the era. It was not surprising that Paramount did not pick up his option.

"I've never liked playing heavies," MacLane would say some three decades later. "In fact, I hated 'em." This incredible admission would be made to *TV Guide* after he had finally made it as a western "hero" in a continuing series. But it was the title of the article, "What Happens to Old Heavies," that told the story. The label really first applied after Paramount, for in early 1934, he was signed to a players contract at Warner Bros. Unlike his previous place of employment, that studio had a first-rate publicity department that worked almost as hard for supporting actors as they did for the stars. An item appeared in the December 5, 1934, edition of the *Los Angeles Times* about new Warners contractee Barton MacLane. Ironically, the blurb involved the studio's acquisition of a possible rival to Charles Bickford,[*] who was hardly among the motion picture elite at the time. But at least, this showed that they had an idea of what they planned to do with him. In fact, by this time, he had already completed several Warners films.

It may not have been noticeable with the first films, but things were beginning to pick up. There were signs of the type of characterizations that he would become identified with in his first three films at Warners, but it was the fourth one, *G-Men* (1935), that really

---

[*]*In the then-recent* White Woman (1933), *Bickford played the screen version role MacLane had played on stage earlier that year, in* Hangman's Whip.

established him. In that film, MacLane created a chilling portrait of vicious criminal Brad Collins. He is a man so single-mindedly evil that he does not hesitate in firing a bullet into the heart of his mistress Ann Dvorak when he discovers her in a phone booth calling the Feds about him. He would have never gotten the chance to commit this brutal act if not for the state of Hollywood censorship at the time.

Many of the objections the reformers of movie violence had in those days were directed at the gangster films of the early talkie period, in which the protagonists like Rico Bandello in *Little Caesar* and Tom Powers in *Public Enemy* were unrepentant killers. Although they were punished in the end, those who worried about the nation's morality felt that a main character such as that, played by popular actors, would have the wrong effect on the impressionable. The studio tried to comply by giving Cagney and Robinson comic gangster or con men roles, but the Legion of Decency screamed about the lack of morality these men displayed, proving that the violence was not the main objection to begin with. No, these big stars had to be heroes, upholders of law and order. Cagney was none too happy about this and only consented to doing one "law and order" film before returning to the more typical "bad boy turned good" roles he was getting in the mid-'30s. *G-Men* was it, with the star playing a young lawyer who joins the FBI to avenge a friend's death. Even here, Cagney had to be cocky until he learned the ropes from his superiors, Robert Armstrong and Lloyd Nolan. Director William Keighley and writer Seton I. Miller were responsible for setting the pattern for MacLane as the screen's most menacing underworld czar; in both this film and their *Bullets or Ballots* the following year, the actor is at his best. In those days, it was surprisingly difficult to cast the role of a gang lord using members of Warner's rogue's gallery. Actors like Joseph Downing, Jack LaRue, Marc Lawrence, Dick Purcell, Joe Sawyer and Ben Welden, as talented as they were, were simply not authoritative enough to play the big boss; they were definitely "henchmen" type. Though these actors were MacLane's contemporaries, there was something about his stocky build and wide face that made him seem much older, and much more important. And the audiences began to notice him.

Two other films released early in 1935 showed how the newly created MacLane image could be used to represent a variety of things. One should remember that Warner Bros. in the '30s was the most socially conscious of studios. And when director Frank Borzage

Russell Hopton, James Cagney, William Pawley and Barton MacLane in *G-Men* (1935).

wanted to show a labor union making trouble on George Brent's construction crew in *Stranded*, he cast MacLane as the man behind the strike. On the other hand, Michael Curtiz wanted to show in his film *Black Fury* how management cruelly dealt with union members so he secured the same actor's services as a brutal company cop who thinks nothing of cracking the skull of poor John Qualen. Here is another typical MacLane persona, the brute who commits the unpremeditated murder and shows no signs of remorse. His action serves to rouse star Paul Muni out of his apathy. Muni, like Cagney and Robinson, had starred in one gangster classic, *Scarface*, but since he had become the studio's number one prestige actor, he was even less likely to be cast as a denizen of the underworld. So MacLane was pressed into duty again in Muni's next film *Dr. Socrates* (1935), as a gangster who forces a country doctor to treat him. Naturally, Muni played the title role.

MacLane's enormous 1935 workload also included inconsequential roles in the films *Go Into Your Dance*, *Page Miss Glory* and *I Found Stella Parish*, all with important stars. He also did two more with Cagney that weren't gangster films (*Frisco Kid* and *Ceiling Zero*) and played the cop in a pair of Perry Mason films starring Warren William. And, like almost every other featured player on the Warners lot, he was given a lead in a small film. The title could have applied to many an average studio contractee of the day: *Man of Iron*. MacLane played a tough "hard hat" softened by his involvement with a lovely and refined woman, played by Mary Astor. Though the picture was a quickie, it had an importance to MacLane, being his first starring role. He felt he had every reason to expect even better starring roles.

But Warner Bros. was still only a motion picture factory, turning out a quantity of product with only an occasional hint of quality. In 1936 came such high quality films as *The Story of Louis Pasteur*, *The Petrified Forest*, *Anthony Adverse* and *Green Pastures*, but they made more than 50 other films—some so inconsequential that top stars like James Cagney and Bette Davis went out on costly suspensions rather than act in them. Secondary performers like William Gargan also walked out on their contracts. So MacLane was one who persevered, realizing that his employers represented security. They also continued to get his name in the papers on occasion.

He was not such a "work horse" in his second year with Warners, having only seven films released in 1936 compared to the previous year's dozen. Leading roles in B-films came his way, often using him as a backstop for more conventional but callow juvenile stars like Warren Hull or Craig Reynolds. In Michael Curtiz's *The Walking Dead*, MacLane and Ricardo Cortez framed Boris Karloff for the murder of a judge, only to get their just desserts when the electrocuted Karloff is brought back to life. He got into more lightweight fare in *Times Square Playboy*, one of the studio's versions of a George M. Cohan property (*The Hometowners*) they often revised. Warren

William had the title role and MacLane was his buddy, but the film was easily stolen by Gene Lockhart as William's old friend from his small town days. The policy of the Warners second unit, usually presided over by producer Bryan Foy, was to use their contractees as an unofficial repertory company. What made Warners players more recognizable to the public was the studio policy of showing the performer in a shot from the picture as his or her name flashed on the screen. This was done on big-budget films for a short period in the early '30s, but continued on B products made as late as 1940, thereby giving character people and screen newcomers the public exposure that few of their contemporaries received. This helped MacLane's name become almost as familiar as his face.

After having his name appear below a new discovery named June Travis in two films, MacLane had his name appear over hers in his top-billed film of 1936, *Bengal Tiger*. This fast-paced film about a big game hunter whose young wife falls for his best friend was a studio perennial. The plot had been used many times, with only the new adaptor given screen credit so that its origins were well-camouflaged. All the adaptor did was to change the profession of the protagonists. So Edward G. Robinson's accented fisherman in Howard Hawks' *Tiger Shark* (1932) became MacLane's all-American hunter here. Director Louis King did not demand anything like the realism that had almost cost Charles Bickford his life the year before in Universal's; the tiger used was edited in from another film and MacLane grappled with a man in a tiger's skin. He might have gotten along with a big cat; he certainly did with small ones: One of the publicity items that made the papers said that MacLane became the "trusty" for a stray cat that had been adopted by the studio personnel. Evidently, they were trying a new publicity angle; this hardly sounded like Bickford's tough rival. In fact, rumor had it that he was actually a big softie at heart.

His best picture of 1936 had one of MacLane's best performances ever, as mob leader Al Kruger in *Bullets or Ballots*. Not required to display the ruthlessness shown in some other films, he could have easily held his own against Edward G. Robinson's hero had it not been for the presence in the cast of Humphrey Bogart. Too soon after his triumph in *The Petrified Forest* to be given higher than fourth billing (after Robinson, Joan Blondell and MacLane), the film gave him a break nonetheless. As Kruger's vicious henchman, Bogart played one of his first cold-blooded roles, showing disapproval of his boss' reticence about rubbing out troublesome reformers. Kruger, caught between the secret group of businessmen who give him orders and trigger-happy underlings, begins to trust ex-cop Robinson, who has infiltrated his gang to get him. Midway through the film, the emphasis shifted from MacLane to Bogart. Up until then, MacLane had been giving one of his best performances. Then Bogie, who may just have been as jealous of his position at the studio as his character Bugs Fenner was jealous of Kruger, comes into his boss' office and shoots him dead. This was well before the picture's end, so it was a tremendous boost to the standing of the new contractee. It was also a sign that MacLane's recently acquired success was already starting to peak. In all the two actors' subsequent films together, he would receive lower billing, usually playing a cruel nemesis. This would not be the last bullet MacLane would take from Bogart's gun.

Though he hadn't lived in California for too many years, by 1936, MacLane and much of his family were firmly ensconced on the West Coast. He had moved his parents and his two sisters to his five-acre ranch in Encino, where he did much of the construction work. Besides the enjoyment he got from the work, it added a new dimension to the relationship between the actor and his father. It actually seemed a stronger bond than between the two when MacLane was a child. The only blot on his personal life was his inability to see his two children by his first marriage. His steady income helped him acquire good legal advice, but even the best lawyers could not battle the tough custody laws of Tennessee. The children resided with their mother in Memphis and even an affluent father like MacLane could not obtain visitation rights. To his children William and Martha, Barton MacLane was a stranger.

Series films, those with continuing characters, were popular in the '30s, but for some reason Warners had little luck with their entries. MacLane got his shot at one about a fast-talking lady reporter named Torchy Blane. Glenda Farrell, who was the prototype for such roles, played the lead and he played McBride, her police detective boyfriend, usually one step behind her. The two had worked together previously in an Al Jolson vehicle and both were often wasted in films. The Torchy Blane features were inexpensively made, but when a series caught on with the public, it could make the fortunes of those in it. However, Warners was a studio with a short attention span. While MGM made ten years worth of Dr. Kildare or Dr. Gillespie films and Columbia ground out Blondie movies for an incredible 12 years, Warners series rarely last beyond five films, not even retaining the same actors for the duration. Perhaps this was because they based their series on characters who were already popular in books; Perry Mason, Philo Vance and Nancy Drew all had strong literary images to live up to. By comparison, the lesser-known Torchy Blane ran for an unprecedented three years and nine films, and Farrell and MacLane were starred in all but two of them.*

MacLane's future wife Charlotte Wynters had a featured role in the first of the Torchy mysteries, *Smart Blonde* (1936), a possible good luck charm as she almost never worked at MacLane's studio. Among her films of that period were Columbia's *The Calling of Dan Matthews* (1936) and Universal's *Girl Overboard* (1937), programmers at best. Her specialty was the wise secondary woman who had been around. A freelance actress, Wynters never garnered a following as one of the important character performers of Hollywood's "golden era." She would continue in films, usually on the fringe of Hollywood's Poverty Row, into the 1950s.

Series work did not immediately cut down on the busy MacLane schedule. He continued to be cast in rugged roles: a villainous timberman in *God's Country and the Woman* (1936), his first Technicolor film, and a coal miner in *Draegerman Courage* (1937). In 1937, he was loaned out twice, the first time since he'd gone to work for Warners. Fritz Lang's *You Only Live Once* for United Artists release offered a change of pace: It was a film about criminals in which he was on the right side of the law. He was the decent businessman who loved Sylvia Sidney but understood her feeling for Henry Fonda, a man propelled by circumstance into a life of crime. Frequently shown on television in the early days, this film later achieved near-cult status as the best of the '30s films to be loosely based upon the story of Bonnie and Clyde. MacLane was back in a more familiar role as a racketeer preying on taxi companies in Fox's *Born Reckless*, which teamed him with his counterpart at that studio, Brian Donlevy. Since the latter was a member of the "home team," he was the good guy, though at the time, they were of equal importance to their respective employers.

MacLane's own studio made good use of that mean countenance and it was not at all surprising that his best films of 1937 were the ones in which he was the most hateful. He used his villainy in an earlier period of history in an adaptation of Mark Twain's *The Prince*

One of the teams considered as replacements, but ultimately too popular for the roles, were Ann Sheridan and Humphrey Bogart.

and the Pauper, his fourth film with the director who had given him his best gangster roles, William Keighley. Playing the cruel John Canty, father of the pauper Tom (Billy Mauch),* he again personifies evil so well that he could not have been more frightening to children of the time had he been created by Charles Dickens. MacLane may have been surprised to find himself among a primarily British cast, but he blended in just fine.

In *San Quentin*, he was on more familiar ground. As Lt. Druggin, a brutal old-school prison guard who resents Pat O'Brien's rehabilitation program for convicts, he was excellent in a role that required a bit more shading (his motivation for the evil he performs is more understandable here). His vicious treatment of the inmates is "rewarded" when escaping con Joe Sawyer "takes him for a ride." (Surprisingly, when lamenting the passing of the old gangster films in his book *The Bad Guys*, William K. Everson singles out in an amusing manner the days when MacLane and Sawyer would go "storming into the First National Bank with tommy guns." While Sawyer might have participated in such a scene, MacLane would surely never have done such a thing when he could assign others to that task.) Humphrey Bogart, going through a brief period of playing criminals who only needed a chance to reform, was incongruously cast here as the weak kid brother of heroine Ann Sheridan; his redemption was stymied by MacLane. *Wine, Women and Horses*, which was filmed at about the same time, was a low-budget remake of an Edward G. Robinson film, *Dark Hazard* (1934); MacLane played a horseplayer who tries to reform for the sake of his decent wife Peggy Bates, before deciding he is better off with Sheridan, a woman with the same interests. This, one of his better B pictures, put him in the unusual position of being involved with two women. Another pleasurable extra was that director Louis King strove for authenticity by leaving the studio confines and taking cast and crew out to the Santa Anita racetrack. King allowed his performers and extras to watch the actual running of a race, to work up the proper excitement. But it worked too well: MacLane not only bet on the races that day, he became so hoarse screaming for the nags he bet on that he was unable to finish the day's shooting. The star went home and the director contented himself with shooting enough racetrack color for his backgrounds.

MacLane had two more *Torchy Blane* films released in 1937 and

---

*Billy's twin brother Bobby played Prince, later King, Edward.

two the following year. But between the 1938 pair, another film about the same characters was released. Tom Kennedy still appeared as McBride's dumb assistant, but the rest of the cast was different; Paul Kelly as McBride and Lola Lane as the reporter were the stars of *Torchy Blane in Panama* (1938). Farrell, who had been with the studio a lot longer than MacLane, had not signed a new contract with Warners and Lola Lane was under contract. So the studio, in their usual "wisdom," decided to change leading players and pick up extra bucks by loaning MacLane out. Around the time *Panama* was being made, Farrell and MacLane were at Universal, working in a film called *Prison Break*, in which the latter was a non-criminal railroaded into jail. After its completion, the stars returned to Warners for *Torchy Gets Her Man* (1938).

MacLane was experiencing the same situation his contemporaries at Fox and Paramount were. The major studios were cutting back on their second feature departments at the end of the 1930s, causing Brian Donlevy and Lloyd Nolan to seek work elsewhere. While they found new employment even more lucrative than their previous jobs, MacLane was unable to find another studio that would sustain him as a top character actor. He soon found himself drifting from one lot to another, with the willing approval of the Warner people.

With the phasing-out of their low-budget films, the size of MacLane's role in their A products also began to diminish. After two more *Torchy* films, MacLane did not work at Warners for almost two years. (The studio did make one more *Torchy*; Jane Wyman was the last Torchy and Allen Jenkins was McBride.)

MacLane didn't lack for work during this period away from the studio. Fritz Lang called him over to his first Hollywood home, Paramount, for *You and Me* (1938) with Sylvia Sidney and George Raft, but gave him the one-dimensional role of a criminal recruiting a group of ex-convicts for a big heist. The film had much too light a touch to compare with Lang's earlier classics or to establish MacLane as a formidable menace. In 1939, he had two title roles. In Universal's *Big Town Czar*, he was more corrupt than brutal and any evil deeds he did were explained away by the usual excuse, a hard childhood. Despite its title, *I Was a Convict* was a comedy-drama in which he is given a job in big business by financier Clarence Kolb, who did a stretch in prison with him. The story had possibilities, but the film was a product of Republic studios, an outfit whose style of making movies had defeated many a good idea over the years. Both these films gave him just about his last chance to play romantic scenes, for his days as a leading man in even the cheapies were numbered. It was fitting that these roles came in 1939, a particularly "romantic" year for him, as it was the year he and Miss Wynters married. Their union was worth the wait; it lasted the rest of his life.

At three different studios, MacLane squared off against Charles Bickford: in Universal's *The Storm* (1938), MGM's *Stand Up and Fight* (1939) and Monogram's *Mutiny in the Big House* (1939). In the latter film, Bickford had to save an impressionable young convict from MacLane's hardened con boss. He played the same exact character in his very next film, Columbia's *Men Without Souls* (1940). This time the chaplain was John Litel and the boy he influenced was played by a young Glenn Ford, but as far as MacLane was concerned, it was the same picture.

Although he had enjoyed displaying his brand of villainy in expensive Warners products, the early '40s proved a disquieting experience for him. He found himself being taken for granted in quickies in which he had no time to make anything of the evil men he had to play. Since Warners was not calling upon him quite so often, he labored in imitations of that studio's product by Columbia, Republic and Universal. In Republic's *Gangs of Chicago* (1940), he played a Humphrey Bogart–like character to Lloyd Nolan's James Cagney type in a bargain basement *The Roaring Twenties*; the two fine actors managed to give their film the shine of one made by the majors. Nolan was still rising in the film world, but his co-star was no longer upwardly mobile.

In 1941, the quality of the films he appeared in improved, but the size of his roles was noticeably lessened. In many ways, this would be his last "important" year in a career that had close to three decades to run. In addition to a return to Warners, he made three films for MGM and two for Fox. At Metro, an actor had the habit of getting lost amid all the expense. In *Come Live with Me*, he appeared in his smallest role in years, an immigration investigator who admires Hedy Lamarr's spunk so much, he advises her to marry an American so she can stay in the U.S. He then disappears from the film, giving the illegal alien the rest of the running time to find a husband (James Stewart). But while one can carp about the size of this part, one is less inclined to complain about his part in another MGM feature, Victor Fleming's *Dr. Jekyll and Mr. Hyde* with Spencer Tracy and Ingrid Bergman. Although not as well received as the earlier versions of the Robert Louis Stevenson story, its psychological approach and the excellent performances made the film worthwhile. MacLane's minute bit was also the most unusual part he ever had in films. Almost unrecognizable behind a large walrus mustache, he was the maddened Cockney husband of Sara Allgood. In the very beginning of the film, he causes a disturbance in church which is one of the underlying factors in leading Tracy-Jekyll to explore "man's darker side." Tracy did a more subtle job than the other great actors (John Barrymore and Fredric March) who had previously tackled the role and the change of character was accomplished primarily through the way the film was lighted rather than by any hideous makeup. As good as the star was, he was still Spencer Tracy, with no trace of a required British accent, while MacLane completely subordinated his well-known image for just a short amount of screen time. This says a lot about character actors and what they are allowed (or forced) to do, depending on the circumstances. MGM would not have taken a chance on having a well-known star in total disguise, even a prestige performer like Tracy. As fine as MacLane was, his characterization went unnoticed by critics, dooming the chances of his branching out into another direction, away from tough guy roles. Around the same time, he had another small part as a government man in Metro's *Barnacle Bill* starring Wallace Beery.

At Fox, he made his third appearance in a Fritz Lang picture, *Western Union*. As the brutal Old West outlaw Jack Slade, MacLane found one of the most heinous villains of the genre and etched one of his most memorable characterizations of a human monster. Through much of the film, he and his gang are disguised as Indians as they stage raids on the workmen putting up the first telegraph lines in the Old West. Randolph Scott plays an old cohort of his who has reformed and is working for Western Union. At the film's end, Scott goes to face his former comrade, who is having a shave in the barber shop. MacLane's Slade shoots his old buddy from under the barber's sheet. Scott is only wounded and manages to finish off all the other baddies before MacLane fires a fatal volley of shots into him (naturally not facing him at the time). It is then left to the last-minute act of heroism by dude Robert Young (who, after all, was top-billed) to finally dispatch MacLane. This description does not do justice to the scene, which is superbly staged by Lang, complete with MacLane having his last gunfight with shaving cream on his face, making him the epitome of a "mad dog" that must be put to death.

He also appeared in three 1941 films for Warners, two of which were the classics that firmly established Humphrey Bogart as a star. In Raoul Walsh's *High Sierra*, MacLane played Kramner, an ex-cop turned gangster underling who tries to gun Bogie down after a jewel robbery goes awry. Naturally, Bogie, who didn't like the guy anyway, kills him. (Mrs. MacLane had a bit part in that film.) The relationship between MacLane and Bogart was little better in John Huston's *The Maltese Falcon*, in which the former played Police Lt. Dundy and clashes with Bogart's Sam Spade over a string of murders linked to the quest for the elusive and priceless Maltese Falcon. MacLane's old status at Warners, rather than the size of the part, was possibly the reason he was billed above Sydney Greenstreet, who was making a belated screen debut in the memorable role of Kasper Gutman.

George Raft, who turned down both of the forementioned Bogart roles, was one of the stars of *Manpower*, also directed by Raoul Walsh. MacLane had little to do as a nasty nightclub owner who employs Marlene Dietrich. His only leading role during that entire year was in Universal's *Hit the Road*, in which he played a reformed racketeer who makes a home for some transplanted Dead End Kids (now known as "The Little Tough Guys").

MacLane made an appearance in John Huston's second directorial effort, *In This Our Life* (1942), in which virtually the whole cast of *The Maltese Falcon* had unbilled parts. He completed his obligation to Warners with *All Through the Night* (1942). This was yet another Bogart starrer, the best of a group of gangsters-vs.-Nazis films made or at least in the planning stages before the U.S. officially entered the war. Vincent Sherman did an expert job of pacing the action and the comedy and Bogart emerged a true hero when up against the really vile Germany spy Conrad Veidt. MacLane plummeted to eleventh place in the cast listing, as an underworld figure who thinks Bogie is doing in his men (they are actually being killed by the Nazis). His part is superfluous, a sad ending to his regular collaboration with a studio to which he would only infrequently return. In fact, though he would continue to film for another quarter of a century, he would rarely work for any of the majors—and only two of Hollywood's really important directors would make use of his services in all that time.

MacLane was only guilty of becoming too familiar to the public and he found himself in a rut, limited by the type of roles he played. As his agent got him parts at various studios, he gradually began to realize it. He would continue to play ruffians of a more colorless variety than those of the old Warner days. His good guy roles were limited, usually playing a hard-boiled police detective in cheap horror films. He would try to break out with various projects, but it proved next to impossible.

RKO was the only major studio to continuously employ MacLane through the '40s, mostly in undistinguished films. Yet it was for them that he played his last really formidable modern-day underworld czar (in 1942's *The Big Street*). Thereafter, his villainy would be practiced either in some primitive jungle or in the Old West. His role in *The Big Street* was not a conventional villain part because its creator, Damon Runyon, did not put such types in his offbeat stories. The part he played, nightclub owner Case Ables, was a second cousin to Charles Bickford's "Big Steve" without a "Little Miss Marker" to redeem him, though his story was just as sentimental. Both had an insanely jealous streak concerning their women, in both cases a singer in their clubs; Lucille Ball played the part here. One of *The Big Street*'s chief assets is Ball's dramatic performance. As the callous nightclub thrush, she thinks nothing of cheating on lover MacLane whenever some eligible and handsome playboy looks her way. During an argument in his club, he hits her (what else would anyone expect of him?) and her fall down a flight of stairs causes paralysis. Nevertheless, she remains just as egotistical in her wheelchair and uses the only man who still cares about her, an adoring busboy played by Henry Fonda. Doomed to die, she has him wheel her to Florida where she foolishly believes she will "conquer society." This incongruous plot has caused some people to suggest that these two characters were the heterosexual inspiration for the characters of Ratzo Rizzo and Joe Buck in *Midnight Cowboy*. But everything in the later film was completely plausible and not the kind of fable one gets here. The film is routinely directed by Irving Reis, and Fonda was by then too mature to be playing a naive boy. But Ball shines in her role and MacLane holds his own in a supporting cast that includes Mercury Theater dropouts Agnes Moorehead and Ray Collins, fresh from giving great performances in Orson Welles' *The Magnificent Ambersons*.

MacLane had pretty much had it with leading roles after he starred in *Man of Courage* (1942) for Producers Releasing Corporation and *A Gentle Gangster* (1943) for Republic. Fittingly, both films cast him as a man who had already seen his best days. The former was mainly notable because Mrs. MacLane had a large role in it and her husband was also given screenwriting credit. Aside from some of their horror films, the films of PRC aren't seen much today; their low production values and their Poverty Row casts have doomed them. MacLane's two subsequent films for PRC, *Underdog* (1943) and *Nabonga* (1944), only utilized him as an actor.

The war years sparked another kind of ambition in MacLane. He had been a little too young to serve in the first World War and now he was too old by draft board standards. Feeling he was still in good physical shape, he offered his services to the United States Navy as an athletic instructor.* The service MacLane gave his country went largely unnoticed.

The world situation did have an effect on his screen image. In many World War II–era films, the villains were Germans and Japanese; compared to them, the American tough guy seemed heroic. As a tough non-commissioned officer, MacLane found a niche in RKO's *Bombardier* (1943) and *Marine Raiders* (1944), both starring another ex–Warners regular, Pat O'Brien. In secondary crime or horror films, MacLane was usually cast as a police detective who usually was too busy suspecting the film's hero that he never catches the real baddie or ghoul until he's led right to him. But audiences, who were still meant to dislike him, reacted differently to him now. His older-than-his-years appearance now worked in his favor; you expected a man his age to be upholding the law.

On the western scene, MacLane tried to get his hands on Roy Rogers' ranch in Republic's *Song of Texas* (1943) and was a bad sheriff stalking Marjorie Main and her outlaw sons in MGM's *Gentle Annie* (1944). RKO used him as a sneaky pirate in *The Spanish Main* (1945) and as the everpresent trouble-making jungle poacher in two Tarzan films. At the end of the war, he was allowed to be meaner than he had been in years, playing a ruthless convict in RKO's *San Quentin* (1946) and doing his best to wreck fellow convict Lawrence Tierney's plans for rehabilitation. This was a throwback to the old MacLane: the vicious killer with no regard for his fellow man. The post war era saw a reemergence of prison pictures, and MacLane was the first of the '30s gangsters to resume wearing stripes; later on, James Cagney (in *White Heat* and *Kiss Tomorrow Goodbye*) and Edward G. Robinson (in *Black Tuesday*) once again planned prison breakouts.

The MacLanes led a moderate social life and never presumed

He had considerable experience as a pilot, flying with a corps of actors on weekends since 1940, but that meant little to the Navy.

on friendship to obtain parts. They saw Rosalind Russell and her husband Frederick Brisson; they had married a couple of years after Wynters and MacLane. Another old chum of the girls was Nedda Harrigan, who was now primarily based in New York as Mrs. Joshua Logan. Harrigan, like Wynters, had had a fairly undistinguished career in minor league crime films as had her brother William, who had acted with MacLane in *G-Men*. While on vacation in New York, the MacLanes were the Logans' guests at what was then the hottest show in town, Irving Berlin's *Annie Get Your Gun* with Ethel Merman. Joshua Logan remembered MacLane's great enthusiasm for the show in one of the vignettes he used in his book *Movie Stars, Reel People and Me*. So thrilled was MacLane by the performance that at intermission time, he said to Logan in that big booming voice that it was the "greatest fucking thing" he'd ever seen. Logan decided that this was the true mark of a show's success and thereafter, when a show looked like a hit, producers and directors would be seen in the theater yelling to one another that the show was a "Barton MacLane." Only the "in" people knew what that meant. And that was how MacLane's name became part of theatrical folklore.

Much of MacLane's enthusiasm was for the live performance itself, a branch of show business in which he knew he would never again participate. He had never been too pleased with his own stage work and refused to chance a return to live performing. The few film actors who found new success after years of Hollywood (people like Paul Kelly and Lloyd Nolan) were in the minority. As dismal as some of his screen roles were, he at least felt he had an affinity for film acting.

After a five-year absence, MacLane was called back to Warner Bros., primarily because two of his former directors wanted him. When Raoul Walsh cast him in small roles as a lawman in *Cheyenne* (1947) and a roughneck in *Silver River* (1948), MacLane worked with many co-stars from the old days. John Huston took him to Mexico to play the role of McCormick in the classic *The Treasure of the Sierra Madre* (1948). As the conniving hiring boss who cheats the men who work for him, he had one last opportunity to antagonize Humphrey Bogart. He knew that Huston could have taken a cheaper actor for the part, since only the gold prospectors and a few Mexicans were considered principal characters, and it was Huston's kindness that made MacLane a part of one of the great films of all time.

One of his bigger roles of the period was as a surly ship's captain in an atrocious film called *Unknown Island* (1948), made by a studio called Film Classics (they never made any). His last scene is memorable, as he tries to have his way with heroine Virginia Grey, he is thwarted by the arrival of one of the badly constructed prehistoric monsters that are on the island. Happily, his meanness doesn't desert him; he does scream like most non-heroic types do in such pictures but stays to fight the monster as if it were just another human opponent, a tough guy to the last. This became one of his most televised films, having been sold to TV almost immediately after being made.

MacLane also started working in television in its prehistoric days, in filmed anthology series like Frank Wisbar's *Fireside Theater*. He also continued to answer calls to appear in major productions for the big studios, though the director he worked for had no feel for the kind of thing he did best. He was still engaged in vile acts, like framing Robert Young in Columbia's *Relentless* (1948) and playing a small town bum who attacks innocent girls in Fox's *The Walls of Jericho* (1948), but these characters had none of the color of his old villains and had little screen time to make an impression. He was equally lost in good guy parts in United Artists' *Red Light* (1949) and Paramount's *Let's Dance* (1950), in which he was the club owner who employed Fred Astaire. Even if there had been some acting opportunity in such pictures, MacLane did not have directors of Huston's caliber to allow him even a distinguished cameo. The industry was already in a hurry to keep up with television and craftsmen with more liberal shooting schedules and bigger budgets were becoming as insensitive to an actor's needs as the makers of quickies had always been. The bulk of his '50s work was for Republic and Allied Artists, the two last remnants of Poverty Row, which were themselves dying.

Thanks to another old co-star, James Cagney, MacLane made two films that were released by Warners in the early '50s. Cagney, in partnership with his brother William, produced both films and Cagney starred in the first, *Kiss Tomorrow Goodbye* (1950). Gordon Douglas directed this tough crime thriller that benefited from its strong cast, not the least of the players being MacLane and Ward Bond as dishonest cops whom hoodlum Cagney uses for his own ends.*

---

*Bond and MacLane had a long professional relationship. Bond was a bit player in G-Men *and* Black Fury, *was on an almost equal footing with MacLane in* Prison Break, The Maltese Falcon *and* Manpower *and had higher billing in* Kiss Tomorrow Goodbye *and Republic's* Thunderbirds *(1952). A decade later, when Bond died, MacLane's was one of the names thrown around as a replacement for Bond as* Wagon Train's *beloved Major Adams. It would have been interesting to see how well one ex–tough guy could do in a part created by another ex–tough guy.*

Warners prevailed upon the Cagney brothers to produce westerns; while Cagney the actor did not take part in them, Bond and MacLane did one apiece. MacLane once again wore sergeant's stripes for a routine cavalry picture called *Bugles in the Afternoon* (1952). In the '50s, MacLane was in 20 westerns, a surprising turn of events. Underworld pictures were still being made, but there were many new actors to play the psychopathic killers. The tough mugs had been replaced by the baby faces. When MacLane appeared in a modern-day crime story, it was generally in the role of law enforcer, not lawbreaker.

MacLane's career was perhaps at its lowest ebb in the mid-'50s. His featured roles in pictures like Republic's *Sea of Lost Ships* (1953) and *Jubilee Trail* (1954) were so unimportant to the plot that they could easily have been excised and no damage would have been done; in the former, he's killed off right after the picture's first scene. Around the same time, he received his first star billing in ten years (it also turned out to be his last). It was the title role of *Captain Scarface* (1953) a miserable cheapie released by Astor, a low-budget company even by Poverty Row standards. As in *Unknown Island*, he played a ship's captain and the leading lady was again Virginia Grey; this time the villains were human and there were no dinosaurs in sight. (Except maybe for the movie, a dinosaur of another kind.)

There were a few pictures that deserve some note. Allied Artists' *Jack Slade* (1953) was an uncompromisingly bleak western; Mark Stevens played Slade and MacLane played his tormentor. *The Glenn Miller Story* (1954) was perhaps his biggest film of the decade; the first of several small parts he played at Universal, it was a rare opportunity to play a real-life character, Gen. "Hap" Arnold, who arranges for the Miller band's USO tour. Another Universal film, *Foxfire* (1955) had him playing a mining company boss, with his wife Charlotte making what was by then a rare screen appearance, playing his wife. These were at least respectable films, but there were many more pictures like *Jail Busters* (1955) with the remnants of the Dead End Kids (now called the Bowery Boys) and *Jaguar* (1956), in which he tried to menace Sabu. And in 1958, he had an experience that too many good actors have had to endure, playing straight man in a Jerry Lewis film (in this case *Geisha Boy*). Strangely enough, these surroundings made MacLane, as another officer, look positively dignified in comparison. He was used to such things, having started at the same studio (Paramount) in films starring the Marx Brothers and W. C. Fields.

Though few of his films had any merit, MacLane (now past 50) still was convincing as the tough guy. When he allowed himself to be drawn into fistfights with much younger men such as Howard Duff and Charlton Heston, he looked as though he really believed he could beat them. But the type of characters he had excelled in were becoming a thing of the past. The new villains were a more subtle, less flamboyant type that he had never had an opportunity to play because no one thought it within his range. He was exposed to real-life tough guys while working on location in Florida on the film *Naked in the Sun* (1957), about conflicts between ruthless slave traders and the Seminole Indians led by courageous Chief Osceola. MacLane and James Craig, the star of the picture, went to get a bite to eat and found themselves surrounded by a lot of menacing young hot rodders in an open parking area of Daytona Beach. The worst that happened was that they were a bit shook up, but the papers made more of it than that. It was certainly more publicity than the usual cheapjack Lippert production received.

The late '50s saw an increase in television work for MacLane, who appeared on programs like *The Kaiser Aluminum Hour* and *Laramie*. He returned to his alma mater for a guest spot on *Warner Bros. Presents*, a short-lived anthology series, then played another police detective in what would have been his last feature film for Warners. But the studio decided that the film, *Girl on the Run* (1958), would made a good pilot for a TV series focusing on private detective Stuart Bailey (Efrem Zimbalist, Jr.). So *Girl on the Run* became the opening segment of the successful *77 Sunset Strip* series and did not go the usual B picture route. Billed directly above MacLane as a punk killer was Edward "Kookie" Byrnes, who then proceeded to become one of the show's biggest draws in its five-year history. MacLane also made several guest appearances as a suspect on another long-running show of that era, the very durable *Perry Mason* series. The show's executive producer Gail Patrick Jackson, who co-starred with MacLane in Paramount's *To the Last Man* (1933), may have had a hand in his casting. In one, he played a senator; the next time around, he was cast as a small-town sheriff (at least he was an honest one).

The good lawman image resulted in a 1960–62 TV series for MacLane. *The Outlaws* was originally conceived as a sort of Western *Untouchables*, the then-popular series set in the Prohibition era. The concept was to focus each week on a real-life notorious outlaw with a cast of regular lawmen connecting the episodes. The regulars, who were expected to be even less colorful than Robert Stack's Elliot Ness, were Don Collier and Jock Gaynor as young deputy marshals and MacLane as their chief, Frank Caine. Collier had the billing and more footage, but MacLane amply supplied the TV father figure required by any series that had younger leads with little experience. *The Outlaws* aired on NBC on Thursdays. The network wanted the series to make it and tried to help it along with publicity about its regulars. For MacLane, that meant the usual items about a former movie bad guy becoming a TV good guy in columns and a *TV Guide* profile (April 1961). By that time, however, there was disenchantment with the series, although the ratings were good enough to ensure renewal. The writers were running out of outlaws that they could work into that historical period, so the scripts were basically fiction. They also decided that the public needed more identification with the series' regulars and, more importantly perhaps, the locale. Western series of the day generally had a place viewers could become familiar and comfortable with (the towns of *Gunsmoke* and *The Rifleman*, the relay station of *Laramie*, etc.). To keep the heroes in one place, the show was revamped for 1961-62 and the cast was changed with the exception of Collier, who was now confined to being a small town marshal. The new regulars were Bruce Yarnell, Slim Pickens and Loretta Young's daughter Judy Lewis, all of whom seemed to have been instructed to emulate the regulars on *Gunsmoke*. The tampering did not pay off and *The Outlaws* barely made it through a second season. MacLane may have been missed more than anyone realized. As he told *TV Guide*, his season of *The Outlaws* at least gave him standing with the kids in the neighborhood.

Immediately after completing his stint on *The Outlaws*, MacLane went to work in Frank Capra's *Pocketful of Miracles* (1961), a lavish remake of Capra's own *Lady for a Day* (1933). MacLane had never worked for Capra, but found many familiar faces among the cast of mostly veteran performers. The film's producer-star Glenn Ford may have had more to do with the casting than Capra; he reportedly picked Bette Davis for the role of "Apple Annie" because she had picked him as her leading man in a film 15 years earlier.* Having been cast amid other "senior actors" may have made MacLane feel his age, but at least the film was the biggest pic-

---

*Davis replaced the original choice, Helen Hayes, but any feelings of gratitude toward Ford vanished in a dispute over dressing rooms.

ture he had been in for years, directed by one of the top men in the business.

As MacLane inched towards his sixtieth birthday, he drifted into a semi-retirement, save for an occasional TV role. For the first time in 30-odd years, he went through two calendar years, 1962 and 1963, with no film release to his credit. And he only returned because producer A. C. Lyles contracted with Paramount to do a series of low-budget westerns. Other reunions of veteran screen actors pale in comparison to Lyles'; on the first film, *Law of the Lawless* (1964), he found himself completely surrounded by other weather-beaten old Hollywood faces: William Bendix, Bruce Cabot and Lon Chaney, Jr., as well as one-time leading men John Agar, Richard Arlen and Kent Taylor. He had a role that was already a cliché: the most powerful man in a western town, whose son is on trial for murder. The presiding judge (Dale Robertson) happens to be an old friend of both father and son, the latter played by Agar. The conflicts were mostly verbal ones, although there were some clumsily staged barroom fights (with younger men obviously doubling for the aging actors). The acting is much better than that seen in the later films, particularly a scene near the end between MacLane and Cabot, his hired gunman.

As part of this atypical repertory company, MacLane worked in three other westerns without playing one of his dyed-in-the-wool villains. In *Town Tamer* (1965) and *Buckskin* (1968), he played respectable citizens who back up the heroes (Dana Andrews and Barry Sullivan, respectively). In *Arizona Bushwackers* (1968), he was a crooked lawman, but he redeems himself by turning on chief villain Scott Brady before the final fadeout; in his final death scene, he is shot off the top of the building.

The balance of MacLane's work during his last years was in television, primarily in the role of Air Force Gen. Peterson in the comedy success *I Dream of Jeannie*. He was brought in after the series had already begun; he played the super-straight authority figure befuddled by whatever troubles genie Barbara Eden's antics had caused. The show's premise was painfully similar to that of *Bewitched*, also packaged by Columbia–Screen Gems. The fact that both shows were successful proves that fantasy-comedies were extremely popular during the '60s. *I Dream of Jeannie* was developed by veteran screenwriter-director Sidney Sheldon, who later gave it all up to become a successful novelist. The professionalism that went into the series, from those behind and in front of the camera, were the things that gave it its long run and the show is still popular in many markets around the country. Almost everyone on the show got a chance to be funny except MacLane, who remained stuck in the role of dignified patsy. The opportunity never seemed to arise for him to say or do anything funny.

The series was still running when MacLane left his role (he was replaced by another general, just as stodgy). And it was still on the air when, in the early hours of New Year's Day, 1969, Barton MacLane died. He had had a short bout with double pneumonia and his death was quite unexpected. At 66, the tough guy who had been cut down by most of the immortals of the screen, died peacefully.

MacLane has a definite place in the history of film if only because of his association with Warner Bros. He provided a badly needed presence in their films and when they no longer needed him, he was good enough to continue making a living as an actor until the day he died. His parts got progressively smaller, yet he did not end his days in unbilled walk-ons. Few movie tough guys could top MacLane's larger-than-life portraits of men of pure evil. For those, he will be remembered.

The Films of Barton MacLane

MacLane began in films as a bit player in the silent film *The Quarterback* (1924) and continued in such films as *The Cocoanuts* (1929) and *His Woman* (1931) among other non-speaking bits he did at Paramount's Astoria Studios while appearing on the Broadway stage.

1. **To the Last Man.** Par 1933. Henry Hathaway. Randolph Scott, Esther Ralston, Noah Beery, Sr., Larry "Buster" Crabbe, Gail Patrick, Jack LaRue, Muriel Kirkland, Fuzzy Knight, Eugenie Besserer, Shirley Temple. BM is a rancher with a family.

2. **Man of the Forest.** Par 1933. Henry Hathaway. Randolph Scott, Verna Hillie, Harry Carey, Buster Crabbe, Noah Beery, Sr., Blanche Frederici, Guinn "Big Boy" Williams, Vince Barnett, Tom Kennedy. BM participates in the kidnapping of a rancher's daughter.

3. **Big Executive.** Par 1933. Erle C. Kenton. Ricardo Cortez, Richard Bennett, Elizabeth Young, Sharon Lynne, Dorothy Peterson, Charles Middleton, Charles Grapewin.

4. **Sunset Pass.** Par 1933. Henry Hathaway. Randolph Scott, Tom Keene, Harry Carey, Kathleen Burke, Noah Beery, Sr., Kent Taylor, Fred Kohler, Leila Bennett, Fuzzy Knight, George Barbier, Vince Barnett, Charles Middleton, Patricia Farley.

5. ***Tillie and Gus.*** Par 1933. Francis Martin. W. C. Fields, Alison Skipworth, Jacqueline Wells (Julie Bishop), Clifford Jones, Baby Leroy, Edgar Kennedy, Clarence Wilson. BM is the commissioner judging a boat race crucial to a young couple's well-being.

6. ***Torch Singer.*** Par 1933. Alexander Hall. Claudette Colbert, Ricardo Cortez, David Manners, Baby Leroy, Lyda Roberti, Cora Sue Collins, Kathleen Burke, Helen Jerome Eddy, Charles Grapewin, Ethel Griffies, Florence Roberts.

7. ***Hell and High Water.*** Par 1933. Grover Jones and William Slavins McNutt. Richard Arlen, Judith Allen, Sir Guy Standing, William Frawley, Charles Grapewin, Robert Knettes, Gertrude Hoffman. BM works on a boat hauling garbage.

8. ***Thundering Herd.*** Par 1933. Henry Hathaway. Randolph Scott, Judith Allen, Noah Beery, Sr., Harry Carey, Raymond Hatton, Blanche Frederici, Monte Blue, Al Bridge, Dick Rush, Frank Rice. BM is the bad guy's hireling.

9. ***All of Me.*** Par 1934. James Flood. Fredric March, Miriam Hopkins, George Raft, Helen Mack, Nella Walker, William Collier, Jr., Gilbert Emery, Blanche Frederici, Kitty Kelly, Edgar Kennedy. BM has a bit part as a policeman.

10. ***The Last Roundup.*** Par 1934. Henry Hathaway. Randolph Scott, Barbara Fritchie, Monte Blue, Fred Kohler, Richard Carle, Fuzzy Knight, Charles Middleton, Frank Rice, Dick Rush, Jim Corbett. BM is a cattle thief.

11. ***Lone Cowboy.*** Par 1934. Paul Sloane. Jackie Cooper, Lila Lee, J. M. Kerrigan, Gavin Gordon, Addison Richards, Charles Middleton, John Wray, Irving Bacon, Herbert Corthell, Lillian Harmon, Dell Henderson. BM stands in the way of young Cooper's hopes of finding surrogate parents.

12. ***Go Into Your Dance.*** WB 1935. Archie Mayo. Al Jolson, Ruby Keeler, Glenda Farrell, Patsy Kelly, Helen Morgan, Benny Rubin, Gordon Westcott, Joseph Cawthorne, Phil Regan, Akim Tamiroff, Sharon Lynne, William Davidson. BM starts his Warners tenure as a hoodlum muscling in on show business.

13. ***Stranded.*** WB 1935. Frank Borzage. Kay Francis, George Brent, Patricia Ellis, Donald Woods, Robert Barrat, William Harrigan, Joseph Crehan, Henry O'Neill, Gavin Gordon, John Wray, June Travis, Mae Busch. BM leads a bunch of strikers delaying a bridge construction project.

14. ***The Case of the Curious Bride.*** WB 1935. Michael Curtiz. Warren William, Margaret Lindsay, Donald Woods, Claire Dodd, Allen Jenkins, Winifred Shaw, Philip Reed, Warren Hymer, Mayo Methot, Errol Flynn. Perry Mason mystery with BM as a police detective.

15. ***G-Men.*** WB 1935. William Keighley. James Cagney, Ann Dvorak, Margaret Lindsay, Robert Armstrong, Lloyd Nolan, William Harrigan, Russell Hopton, Noel Madison, Regis Toomey, Edward Pawley, Monte Blue,

Addison Richards, Harold Huber. BM is murderous public enemy Brad Collins.

16. *Black Fury.* WB 1935. Michael Curtiz. Paul Muni, Karen Morley, William Gargan, John Qualen, J. Carrol Naish, Vince Barnett, Tully Marshall, Henry O'Neill, Mae Marsh, Willard Robertson, Ward Bond, Akim Tamiroff, Joseph Crehan. BM is a brutal enforcer for a mining company.

17. *Page Miss Glory.* WB 1935. Mervyn Leroy. Marion Davies, Pat O'Brien, Dick Powell, Mary Astor, Patsy Kelly, Frank McHugh, Allen Jenkins, Lyle Talbot, Joseph Cawthorne, Hobart Cavanaugh, Al Shean, Berton Churchill, Lionel Stander, Gavin Gordon, Helen Lowell. Crooks BM and Jenkins get involved in a deception to pass chambermaid Davies off as a dream girl.

18. *Dr. Socrates.* WB 1935. William Dieterle. Paul Muni, Ann Dvorak, Robert Barrat, John Eldredge, Hobart Cavanaugh, Helen Lowell, Mayo Methot, Henry O'Neill, June Travis, Samuel S. Hinds. When small town doctor Muni saves his life, gangster BM forces him to go to work for him.

19. *The Case of the Lucky Legs.* WB 1935. Archie Mayo. Warren William, Genevieve Tobin, Patricia Ellis, Lyle Talbot, Allen Jenkins, Peggy Shannon, Porter Hall, Craig Reynolds, Henry O'Neill. BM again as a detective in his second and last appearance in a Perry Mason drama until the TV series 24 years later.

20. *Frisco Kid.* WB 1935. Lloyd Bacon. James Cagney, Ricardo Cortez, Margaret Lindsay, Lili Damita, Donald Woods, George E. Stone, Joseph King, Addison Richards, Robert McWade, Joseph Crehan, Joseph Sawyer. BM is a Barbary Coast ruffian who stymies civic attempts to clean up the area.

21. *I Found Stella Parish.* WB 1935. Mervyn Leroy. Kay Francis, Ian Hunter, Paul Lukas, Sybil Jason, Jessie Ralph, Eddie Acuff, Walter Kingsford, Joseph Sawyer, Harry Beresford. BM is a man who knows a secret in the past of stage star Francis.

22. *Man of Iron.* WB 1935. William McGann. Mary Astor, John Eldredge, Dorothy Peterson, Joseph Crehan, Craig Reynolds, Joseph King, John Qualen, Joseph Sawyer, Gordon (William) Elliott. In his first leading role, MacLane plays a construction worker who rises to executive. He was compared to George Bancroft by the reviewer for *Variety*.

23. *Ceiling Zero.* WB 1936. Howard Hawks. James Cagney, Pat O'Brien, June Travis, Stuart Erwin, Isabel Jewell, Dick Purcell, Craig Reynolds, Addison Richards, Martha Tibbetts, Henry Wadsworth, Edward Gargan. BM is a flight dispatcher.

24. *The Walking Dead.* WB 1936. Michael Curtiz. Boris Karloff, Ricardo Cortez, Edmund Gwenn, Marguerite Churchill, Warren Hull, Henry O'Neill, Joseph King, Paul Harvey, Addison Richards. Gangsters BM and Cortez frame ex-con Karloff, who comes back from the dead to get his revenge.

25. *Times Square Playboy.* WB 1936. William McGann. Warren William, Gene Lockhart, June Travis, Kathleen Lockhart, Dick Purcell,

Craig Reynolds, Granville Bates. BM is a combination friend, personal trainer and sometime butler to man-about-town William.

26. *Jailbreak.* WB 1936. Nick Grinde. June Travis, Craig Reynolds, Dick Purcell, George E. Stone, Eddie Acuff, Addison Richards, Joseph King, Joseph Crehan, Charles Middleton, Mary Treen. BM is a dangerous criminal attempting a breakout.

27. *Bullets or Ballots.* WB 1936. William Keighley. Edward G. Robinson, Joan Blondell, Humphrey Bogart, Frank McHugh, Joseph King, Dick Purcell, George E. Stone, Henry O'Neill, Henry Kolker, Gilbert Emery, Louise Beavers, Joseph Crehan, Herbert Rawlinson. BM is mob boss Al Kruger, in the only film where he's billed above Bogart.

28. *Bengal Tiger.* WB 1936. Louis King. June Travis, Warren Hull, Paul Graetz, Joseph King, Gordon Hart, Don Barclay, Carlyle Moore, Jr. Wild animal trainer BM comes to believe that his wife and best friend are cuckolding him.

29. *God's Country and the Woman.* WB 1936. William Keighley. George Brent, Beverly Roberts, Robert Barrat, Alan Hale, Joseph King, El Brendel, Joseph Crehan, Addison Richards, Roscoe Ates, Mary Treen. BM gives trouble to a logging company.

30. *Smart Blonde.* WB 1936. Frank McDonald. Glenda Farrell, Winifred Shaw, Craig Reynolds, Addison Richards, Charlotte Wynters, David Carlyle, Joseph Crehan, Tom Kennedy, Jane Wyman. First in the series of eight Torchy Blane mysteries with BM as Steve, the police lieutenant who cares about her.

31. *You Only Live Once.* UA 1937. Fritz Lang. Sylvia Sidney, Henry Fonda, Jean Dixon, William Gargan, Margaret Hamilton, Warren Hymer, Charles "Chic" Sale, John Wray, Jerome Cowan, Ward Bond. In his first non–Warners film in over two years, BM is Sidney's attorney-employer who loves her.

32. *Draegerman Courage.* WB 1937. Louis King. Jean Muir, Robert Barrat, Henry O'Neill, Addison Richards, Helen MacKellar, Gordon Oliver, Joseph Crehan, Priscilla Lyon, Walter Miller. BM is a miner involved in a rescue operation after a cave-in.

33. *The Prince and the Pauper.* WB 1937. William Keighley. Errol Flynn, Claude Rains, Billy Mauch, Bobby Mauch, Henry Stephenson, Alan Hale, Eric Portman, Lionel Pape, Montagu Love, Halliwell Hobbes, Murray Kinnell, Phyllis Barry, Ivan Simpson, Mary Field, Fritz Leiber. BM is the pauper's abusive father, Cockney accent and all, in this adaptation of Mark Twain's classic.

34. *Fly Away, Baby.* WB 1937. Frank McDonald. Glenda Farrell, Gordon Oliver, Hugh O'Connell, Marcia Ralston, Tom Kennedy, Joseph King, Raymond Hatton, Gordon Hart, Harry Davenport. The second *Torchy Blane*, with BM again the police lieutenant foil.

35. *Ever Since Eve.* WB 1937. Lloyd Bacon. Marion Davies, Robert Montgomery, Frank McHugh, Patsy Kelly, Allen Jenkins, Louise Fazenda, Marcia Ralston, Frederic Clark, Arthur Hoyt, Mary Treen, Harry Hayden.

BM is seen briefly as Jenkins' low-class buddy, who is set up as Davies' blind date.

36. **San Quentin.** WB 1937. Lloyd Bacon. Pat O'Brien, Humphrey Bogart, Ann Sheridan, Joseph Sawyer, Veda Ann Borg, Joseph King, James Robbins, Gordon Oliver, Garry Owen, Marc Lawrence, Emmett Vogan. BM is the hateful prison guard Druggin, passed over for promotion in favor of O'Brien.

37. **Wine, Women and Horses.** WB 1937. Louis King. Ann Sheridan, Dick Purcell, Peggy Bates, Walter Cassel, Lottie Williams, Kenneth Harlan, Charley Foy, James Robbins. BM is an incurable horseplayer whose habit wrecks his marriage.

38. **Born Reckless.** 20th 1937. Mal St. Clair. Brian Donlevy, Rochelle Hudson, Robert Kent, Harry Carey, Chick Chandler, Pauline Moore, William Pawley, Frances MacDonald, Joseph Crehan, Lon Chaney, Jr. BM runs a racket that preys on small taxi cab companies.

39. **Adventurous Blonde.** WB 1937. Frank McDonald. Glenda Farrell, Anne Nagel, Tom Kennedy, George E. Stone, William Hopper, Natalie Moorhead, Anderson Lawler, Charley Foy, Bobby Watson, Charles Wilson, Virginia Brissac. BM is Police Lt. Steve to Farrell's Torchy Blane.

40. **Blondes at Work.** WB 1938. Frank McDonald. Glenda Farrell, Tom Kennedy, Rosella Towne, Donald Briggs, John Ridgely, Betty Compson, Thomas Jackson, Frank Shannon, Carole Landis. Fourth in the *Blane* series.

41. **The Kid Comes Back.** WB 1938. B. Reeves Eason. Wayne Morris, June Travis, Maxie Rosenbloom, James Robbins, Joseph Crehan, Dickie Davis, David Carlyle, Herbert Rawlinson. BM again follows in Edward G. Robinson's footsteps in a lower-level follow-up to *Kid Galahad*: He plays an aging fighter still hungering for the championship whose kid sister finds love with young contender Morris. (In a rare tribute, the *New York Times* reviewer praised his performance as the fighter-turned-manager, saying he held the film together.)

42. **Gold Is Where You Find It.** WB 1938. Michael Curtiz. George Brent, Olivia de Havilland, Claude Rains, Margaret Lindsay, John Litel, Marcia Ralston, Tim Holt, Henry O'Neill, Sidney Toler, Willie Best, Robert McWade, George "Gabby" Hayes, Harry Davenport, Clarence Kolb. Battle between landowners and miners finds BM on the wrong side of the issue.

43. **You and Me.** Par 1938. Fritz Lang. George Raft, Sylvia Sidney, Harry Carey, Robert Cummings, Roscoe Karns, George E. Stone, Cecil Cunningham, Guinn Williams, Bernadene Hayes. BM is the leader of a gang planning a department store robbery.

44. **Prison Break.** Univ 1938. Arthur Lubin. Glenda Farrell, Ward Bond, Constance Moore, William Pawley, Paul Hurst, Edmund MacDonald, Victor Kilian. For once, BM plays a man wrongfully sent to prison and Bond is a bad con who influences him.

45. **Torchy Gets Her Man.** WB 1938. William Beaudine. Glenda Far-

rell, Tom Kennedy, Willard Robertson, George Guhl, John Ridgely, Thomas Jackson, Frank Reicher, Edward Raquello. BM is back as Police Lt. McBride.

46. *The Storm.* Univ 1938. Harold Young. Charles Bickford, Preston Foster, Tom Brown, Nan Grey, Andy Devine, Samuel S. Hinds, Frank Jenks, Florence Roberts, Jack Mulhall, Dorothy Arnold. In the first of three almost consecutive films together, Bickford and BM play a pair of battling brothers.

47. *Stand Up and Fight.* MGM 1939. W. S. Van Dyke. Wallace Beery, Robert Taylor, Helen Broderick, Florence Rice, Charles Bickford, Charley Grapewin, John Waulen, Selmer Jackson, Jonathan Hale. BM is a mercenary involved in a war between Taylor's railroad and Beery's stagecoach line.

48. *Torchy Blane in Chinatown.* WB 1939. William Beaudine. Glenda Farrell, Patric Knowles, Henry O'Neill, James Stephenson, Tom Kennedy, Janet Shaw, Frank Shannon, George Guhl. BM returns as Lt. McBride after being replaced by Paul Kelly in *Torchy Blane in Panama*, reunited with Farrell after their sojourn at Universal.

49. *Big Town Czar.* Univ 1939. Arthur Lubin. Tom Brown, Eve Arden, Jack LaRue, Walter Woolf King, Frank Jenks, Esther Dale, Ed Sullivan. Famed columnist and future TV star Sullivan is credited with writing this familiar tale of a mobster (BM) who changes his ways when the kid brother he tried to keep out of the mob (Brown) is killed.

50. *Mutiny in the Big House.* Monogram 1939. William Nigh. Charles Bickford, Dennis Moore, Pat Moriarity, George Cleveland, Nigel DeBrulier, Charley Foy, Russell Hopton, William Royal, Jack Daley, Wheeler Oakman, Charles King. Priest Bickford and con BM wage war for the soul of young prisoner Moore.

51. *Torchy Runs For Mayor.* WB 1939. Ray McCarey. Glenda Farrell, Tom Kennedy, John Miljan, Frank Shannon, Joe Cunningham, Joseph Downing, George Guhl, Irving Bacon. BM's last outing as Steve McBride. (There would be one other entry in the series, with Allen Jenkins broadening the comic aspects of the character.)

52. *I Was a Convict.* Rep 1939. Aubrey Scotto. Beverly Roberts, Clarence Kolb, Janet Beecher, Leon Ames, Horace MacMahon, Ben Welden, Clara Blandick, Russell Hicks, John Harmon. Parolee BM goes to work for his former cellmate, a millionaire, and finds his baser instincts changed by the experience.

53. *Men Without Souls.* Col 1940. Nick Grinde. John Litel, Rochelle Hudson, Glenn Ford, Don Beddoe, Cy Kendall, Richard Fiske, Eddie Laughton, Dick Curtis. BM is again a hardened con waging battle with the prison chaplain (Litel) over convict Ford.

54. *The Secret Seven.* Col 1940. James Moore. Florence Rice, Bruce Bennett, Joseph Crehan, Edward Van Sloan, Joseph Downing, Don Beddoe, Howard Hickman. A group of responsible citizens target mob boss BM in their campaign to clean up their city.

55. *Gangs of Chicago.* Rep 1940. Arthur Lubin. Lloyd Nolan, Lola

Lane, Ray Middleton, Astrid Allwyn, Horace MacMahon, Leona Roberts, Charles Halton, Addison Richards, Dwight Frye, Alan Ladd. BM is another mob kingpin.

56. *Melody Ranch.* Rep 1940. Joseph Santley. Gene Autry, Jimmy Durante, Ann Miller, George "Gabby" Hayes, Barbara Jo Allen (Vera Vague), Joseph Sawyer, Horace MacMahon, Mary Lee, Jerome Cowan, Veda Ann Borg, Clarence Wilson, William Benedict, Ruth Gifford, George Chandler. BM is the leader of the gang that runs the hometown of cowboy star Autry.

57. *Come Live with Me.* MGM 1941. Clarence Brown. James Stewart, Hedy Lamarr, Ian Hunter, Verree Teasdale, Donald Meek, Edward Ashley, Fritz Feld, Adeline deWalt Reynolds, Ann Codee, King Baggott. Kindly immigration officer BM gives foreign-born Lamarr an idea on how she could become an American citizen before the time she must leave the country.

58. *High Sierra.* WB 1941. Raoul Walsh. Ida Lupino, Humphrey Bogart, Alan Curtis, Arthur Kennedy, Joan Leslie, Henry Hull, Henry Travers, Jerome Cowan, Minna Gombell, Isabel Jewell, Donald MacBride, Elisabeth Risdon, Cornel Wilde, Paul Harvey. BM is an ex-cop employed by a dying crime boss, putting him at odds once again with Bogart.

59. *Hit the Road.* Univ 1941. Joe May. Gladys George, Billy Halop, Huntz Hall, Evelyn Ankers, Gabriel Dell, Bernard Punsley, Bobs Watson, Charles Lang, Walter Kingsford, Shemp Howard. Reformed racketeer BM tries to help his dead cohorts' sons, many of them remnants of Warners' Dead End Kids.

60. *Western Union.* 20th 1941. Fritz Lang. Randolph Scott, Robert Young, Dean Jagger, Virginia Gilmore, Slim Summerville, John Carradine, Chill Wills, Minor Watson, Russell Hicks, Victor Kilian, Chief Big Tree, Chief Thundercloud, George Chandler, Dick Rich. Villainous Jack Slade (BM) makes trouble for the people putting up the Western Union lines.

61. *Barnacle Bill.* MGM 1941. Richard Thorpe. Wallace Beery, Marjorie Main, Leo Carrillo, Virginia Weidler, Donald Meek, Connie Gilchrist, Sara Haden, Don Terry. BM is a ruthless fishing contractor.

62. *Dr. Jekyll and Mr. Hyde.* MGM 1941. Victor Fleming. Spencer Tracy, Ingrid Bergman, Lana Turner, Ian Hunter, Donald Crisp, C. Aubrey Smith, Sara Allgood, Peter Godfrey, Frederick Worlock, Frances Robinson, William Tannen, Billy Bevan. BM, the Cockney husband of Allgood, has a fit of insanity while at church services and is calmed by Dr. Jekyll (Tracy).

63. *Wild Geese Calling.* 20th 1941. John Brahm. Henry Fonda, Joan Bennett, Warren William, Ona Munson, Iris Adrian, Russell Simpson, Mary Field, James Morton. After losing his hotel to Fonda in a card game, BM seeks revenge.

64. *Manpower.* WB 1941. Raoul Walsh. Edward G. Robinson, Marlene Dietrich, George Raft, Alan Hale, Frank McHugh, Ward Bond, Eve Arden, Egon Brecher, Walter Catlett, Joyce Compton, Lucia Carroll, Joseph Crehan, Cliff Clark. BM runs the nightclub where Dietrich works.

65. *The Maltese Falcon.* WB 1941. John Huston. Humphrey Bogart,

Mary Astor, Gladys George, Peter Lorre, Sydney Greenstreet, Lee Patrick, Ward Bond, Jerome Dowan, Elisha Cook Jr., James Burke, Walter Huston (unbilled). BM is the police lieutenant who hasn't much use for private eye Sam Spade (Bogart).

66. *All Through the Night.* WB 1942. Vincent Sherman. Humphrey Bogart, Conrad Veidt, Judith Anderson, Jane Darwell, William Demarest, Jackie Gleason, Peter Lorre, Frank McHugh, Phil Silvers, Kaaren Verne, Edward Brophy, Wallace Ford, Hans Schumm, Ludwig Stossel. BM drops to his lowest ever billing at Warners, eleventh in the cast listing, as another shady rival of gangster Gloves Donahue (Bogart), who eventually becomes his ally when he realizes they have a common enemy, the Nazis.

67. *Highways by Night.* RKO 1942. Peter Godfrey. Richard Carlson, Jane Randolph, Jane Darwell, Ray Collins, George Cleveland, Gordon Jones, Marten Lamont, Paul Fix. Carlson, an heir to a fortune, goes on the road to learn the ways of life and runs afoul of racketeer BM.

68. *The Big Street.* RKO 1942. Irving Reis. Henry Fonda, Lucille Ball, Eugene Pallette, Ray Collins, Agnes Moorehead, Sam Levene, Louise Beavers, William T. Orr, Marian Martin, Hans Conreid, Millard Mitchell, Ozzie Nelson and His Orchestra. BM is the gambler who causes girlfriend Ball to become paralyzed after knocking her down.

69. *Man of Courage.* Producers Releasing Corporation 1942. Alexis ThurnTaxis. Charlotte Wynters, Lyle Talbot, Dorothy Burgess, Forrest Taylor. BM co-wrote the script and plays an honest district attorney involved with a nightclub singer (played by his real-life wife Wynters).

70. *A Gentle Gangster.* Rep 1943. Phil Rosen. Molly Lamont, Jack LaRue, Dick Wessel, Joyce Compton, Cy Kendall, Rosella Towne, Ray Teal, Elliott Sullivan, Anthony Warde. Reformed racketeer BM and some associates find their peaceful small-town existence threatened by an old crony.

71. *Song of Texas.* Rep 1943. Joseph Kane. Roy Rogers, Sheila Ryan, Arline Judge, Harry Shannon, Pat Brady, William Haade, Eve March, Hal Taliaferro, Yakima Canutt, Maxine Doyle, Bob Nolan, The Sons of the Pioneers. Scheming BM tries to get control of a ranch by underhanded methods.

72. *Bombardier.* RKO 1943. Richard Wallace. Pat O'Brien, Randolph Scott, Anne Shirley, Eddie Albert, Walter Reed, Robert Ryan, Bernard Nedell, Russell Wade, Richard Martin, John Miljan, Charles Russell. BM is a veteran Air Force man training new recruits (something he would have liked doing in real life).

73. *Crime Doctor's Strangest Case.* Col 1943. Eugene J. Forde. Warner Baxter, Lynn Merrick, Reginald Denny, Gloria Dickson, Jerome Cowan, Rose Hobart, Constance Worth, Lloyd Bridges, Virginia Brissac. BM is a cop.

74. *Underdog.* PRC 1943. William Nigh. Billy Larson, Charlotte Wynters, Jan Wiley, Conrad Binyon, Elizabeth Valentine, Kenneth Harlan. BM is an impoverished farmer whose life is saved by a boy and his dog.

75. *Nabonga.* PRC 1944. Sam Newfield. Buster Crabbe, Julie London,

Fifi D'Orsay, Bryant Washburn, Herbert Rawlinson. In another role that would recur for BM, he plays a mercenary hunter searching for a lost white girl in the jungle.

76. *Secret Command.* Col 1944. Edward Sutherland. Pat O'Brien, Chester Morris, Carole Landis, Ruth Warrick, Tom Tully, Wallace Ford, Frank Sully, Matt McHugh. O'Brien is an undercover man trying to find the source of sabotage at a wartime defense plant. BM is one of his suspects.

77. *Cry of the Werewolf.* Col 1944. Henry Levin. Nina Foch, Osa Massen, Stephen Crane, Blanche Yurka, John Abbott, Fritz Leiber, Ivan Triesault. BM is a police detective hunting for a seemingly werewolf-inspired murderer.

78. *Marine Raiders.* RKO 1944. Harold Schuster. Pat O'Brien, Robert Ryan, Ruth Hussey, Frank McHugh, Richard Martin, Russell Wade, Michael St. Angel, Martha MacVicar (Martha Vickers), Sammy Stein, Blake Edwards, William Forrest. BM is another courageous non-com.

79. *The Mummy's Ghost.* Univ 1944. Reginald LeBorg. Lon Chaney, Jr., John Carradine, Robert Lowery, Ramsay Ames, George Zucco, Frank Reicher, Harry Shannon, Emmett Vogan, Claire Whitney, Oscar O'Shea, Lester Sharpe, Martha MacVicar (Martha Vickers). BM is another perplexed policeman dealing with murders committed by a monster.

80. *Gentle Annie.* MGM 1944. Andrew Marton. Marjorie Main, James Craig, Donna Reed, Henry (Harry) Morgan, Paul Langton, Noah Beery, Sr., Morris Ankrum, Tom London. BM is a dishonest sheriff stalking Main and her outlaw sons.

81. *Tarzan and the Amazons.* RKO 1945. Kurt Neumann. Johnny Weissmuller, Brenda Joyce, Johnny Sheffield, Henry Stephenson, Maria Ouspenskaya, Don Douglas, J. M. Kerrigan. BM is a corrupt man tempted by the riches of a tribe of natives.

82. *The Spanish Main.* RKO 1945. Frank Borzage. Paul Henreid, Maureen O'Hara, Walter Slezak, Binnie Barnes, John Emery, Jack LaRue, J. M. Kerrigan, Curt Bois, Nancy Gates, Mike Mazurki, Antonio Moreno, Ian Keith, Fritz Leiber. BM is a surly pirate who shows his usual ingratitude by trying to kill pirate Henreid, who has spared his life.

83. *Scared Stiff.* Par 1945. Frank McDonald. Jack Haley, Ann Savage, Veda Ann Borg, George E. Stone, Lucien Littlefield, Paul Hurst, Arthur Aylesworth. BM is a gangster who has a special interest in a haunted house. There is little similarity to the 1953 Martin & Lewis film of the same name.

84. *Mysterious Intruder.* Col 1946. William Castle. Richard Dix, Nina Vale, Pamela Blake, Regis Toomey, Mike Mazurki, Charles Lane, Helen Mowery. In this entry in the *Whistler* series, Dix is a private eye who needs an antagonist—and who better than BM as another police detective.

85. *Santa Fe Uprising.* Rep 1946. R. G. Springsteen. Allan (Rocky) Lane, Bobby Blake, Jack LaRue, Martha Wentworth, Tom London, Dick Curtis, Forrest Taylor, Emmett Lynn, Pat Michaels, Hank Patterson. Western from the *Red Ryder* series with BM another scheming bad guy.

86. *San Quentin.* RKO 1946. Gordon Douglas. Lawrence Tierney, Marian Carr, Harry Shannon, Carol Forman, Richard Powers (Tom Keene), Joe Devlin, Raymond Burr, Tony Barrett. BM's prison escape jeopardizes the future of a reform program started by his fellow ex-con Tierney.

87. *Tarzan and the Huntress.* RKO 1947. Kurt Neumann. Johnny Weissmuller, Brenda Joyce, Johnny Sheffield, Patricia Morison, John Warburton, Charles Trowbridge, Ted Hecht. BM, again a jungle mercenary, hires out to villainess Morison.

88. *Jungle Flight.* Par 1947. Peter Stewart. Robert Lowery, Ann Savage, Douglas Fowley, Douglas Blackley, Duncan Renaldo, Curt Bois. BM is a mine owner in Latin America.

89. *Cheyenne.* WB 1947. Raoul Walsh. Dennis Morgan, Jane Wyman, Janis Paige, Bruce Bennett, Alan Hale, Arthur Kennedy, John Ridgely, Tom Tyler, Bob Steele, John Compton, John Alvin, Anne O'Neal, Monte Blue. BM returns to his former Hollywood home Warner Bros. in the small role of a government man who gives agent Morgan his assignment.

90. *The Treasure of the Sierra Madre.* WB 1948. John Huston. Humphrey Bogart, Walter Huston, Tim Holt, Bruce Bennett, Alfonso Bedoya, Manuel Donde, Jose Torvay, Jacqueline Dalya, Bobby Blake, John Huston (unbilled), Ann Sheridan (unbilled). BM is the dishonest hiring boss whose treatment of Bogart and Holt early in the film leads them to go into gold prospecting.

91. *Relentless.* Col 1948. George Sherman. Robert Young, Marguerite Chapman, Akim Tamiroff, Willard Parker, Mike Mazurki, Robert Barrat, Clem Bevans, Frank Fenton, Paul Burns, Hank Patterson. BM frames Young for a murder that he committed, precipitating a chase that lasts the length of the movie.

92. *The Dude Goes West.* Allied Artists 1948. Kurt Neumann. Eddie Albert, Gale Storm, James Gleason, Gilbert Roland, Binnie Barnes, Douglas Fowley, Tom Tyler, Harry Hayden, Sarah Padden, Chief Yowlachie, Edward Gargan. Outlaw BM is one of the menaces faced by Albert, a gunsmith from New York.

93. *Silver River.* WB 1948. Raoul Walsh. Errol Flynn, Ann Sheridan, Thomas Mitchell, Bruce Bennett, Tom D'Andrea, Art Baker, Monte Blue, Alan Bridge, Joseph Crehan, Jonathan Hale, Arthur Space. BM is a ruffian who incites others to cause trouble for Western entrepreneur Flynn following the Civil War.

94. *The Walls of Jericho.* 20th 1948. John M. Stahl. Cornel Wilde, Anne Baxter, Linda Darnell, Kirk Douglas, Ann Dvorak, Marjorie Rambeau, Henry Hull, Colleen Townsend, William Tracy, Griff Barnett, Art Baker, Frank Ferguson, Hope Landin, Ann Morrison, J. Farrell MacDonald, Gene Nelson, Will Wright. Small town lowlife BM's attack upon a young girl results in a court case that affects most of the citizenry.

95. *Angel in Exile.* Rep 1948. Allan Dwan. John Carroll, Adele Mara, Thomas Gomez, Alfonso Bedoya, Grant Withers, Paul Fix, Art Smith, Tom Powers, Howland Chamberlin, Ian Wolfe, Mary Currier. Reformed thief

Carroll changes his mind about reclaiming his stolen loot, which automatically puts him in conflict with ex-partner BM.

96. *Unknown Island.* Film Classics 1948. Jack Bernhard. Virginia Grey, Richard Denning, Phillip Reed, Dick Wessel, Daniel White, Phillip Nazir. BM, a charter boat captain with more courage than brains, meets his match in a confrontation with a prehistoric gorilla.

97. *Red Light.* UA 1949. Roy Del Ruth. George Raft, Virginia Mayo, Gene Lockhart, Arthur Franz, Raymond Burr, Henry (Harry) Morgan, Arthur Shields, William "Bill" Phillips, Movita Castenada, Phillip Pine, Paul Frees. BM is a cop who can't get the goods on killer Burr, inciting his victim's brother Raft to seek revenge in his own way.

98. *The Bandit Queen.* Lippert 1949. William Berke. Barbara Britton, Willard Parker, Phillip Reed, Margia Dean, Victor Kilian, Thurston Hall, Jack Perrin, Martin Garralaga, Pepe Hern. BM is another crook, in league with Parker.

99. *Let's Dance.* Par 1950. Norman Z. McLeod. Fred Astaire, Betty Hutton, Roland Young, Ruth Warrick, Lucile Watson, Shepperd Strudwick, Melville Cooper, Gregory Moffett, George Zucco, Ida Moore, Bess Flowers. BM is a nightclub owner who employs Astaire.

100. *Kiss Tomorrow Goodbye.* WB 1950. Gordon Douglas. James Cagney, Barbara Payton, Helena Carter, Luther Adler, Ward Bond, Neville Brand, Steve Brodie, William Frawley, Herbert Heyes, Robert Karnes, John Litel, Dan Riss, Rhys Williams. BM and Bond are a pair of crooked cops ensnared in ex-con Cagney's plans.

101. *Rookie Fireman.* Col 1950. Seymour Friedman. Bill Williams, Marjorie Reynolds, Gloria Henry, Richard Quine, John Ridgely, Cliff Clark, Frank Sully. BM is a fire chief who comes down hard at first on moonlighting newcomer Williams.

102. *Best of the Badmen.* RKO 1951. William D. Russell. Robert Ryan, Claire Trevor, Robert Preston, Walter Brennan, Jack Buetel, Bruce Cabot, Lawrence Tierney, John Archer, Carleton Young, Carlos Sepulveda. Ryan is assigned the task of setting a trap for a gang that includes some of the most notorious outlaws of the post–Civil War era. BM is a henchman of Preston.

103. *Drums in the Deep South.* RKO 1951. William Cameron Menzies. James Craig, Guy Madison, Barbara Payton, Craig Stevens, Taylor Holmes, Louis Jean Heydt, Tom Fadden, Robert Osterloh, Robert Easton, Lewis Martin. BM is a sergeant in the Confederate Army.

104. *Bugles in the Afternoon.* WB 1952. Roy Rowland. Ray Milland, Helena Carter, Hugh Marlowe, Forrest Tucker, George Reeves, James Millican, Gertrude Michael, Stuart Randall, William "Bill" Phillips, Sheb Wooley, John Pickard. BM is a cavalry non-com immediately following the Civil War.

105. *The Half-Breed.* RKO 1952. Stuart Gilmore. Robert Young, Janis Carter, Jack Buetel, Reed Hadley, Porter Hall, Connie Gilchrist, Sammy White, Damian O'Flynn, Tom Monroe, Chief Thundercloud, Stuart Randall, Al Hill. BM is an upholder of the law.

106. ***Thunderbirds.*** Rep 1952. John H. Auer. John Derek, John Barrymore, Jr., Mona Freeman, Gene Evans, Ward Bond, Eileen Christy, Ben Cooper, Wally Cassell, Mae Clarke, Slim Pickens, Benny Baker, Allene Roberts. BM is once again a tough training officer.

107. ***Cow Country.*** AA 1953. Lesley Selander. Edmond O'Brien, Helen Westcott, Peggie Castle, Robert Barrat, Raymond Hatton, Robert Lowery, Marshall Reed. BM is a banker allied with the bad guys in a range war.

108. ***Kansas Pacific.*** AA 1953. Ray Nazarro. Sterling Hayden, Eve Miller, Reed Hadley, Irving Bacon, Douglas Fowley, James Griffith, Myron Healey, Clayton Moore, Tom Fadden, Lane Chandler, I. Stanford Jolley. BM is the foreman of a railroad construction crew whose daughter falls for his superior Hayden.

109. ***Captain Scarface.*** Astor 1953. Paul Guilfoyle. Virginia Grey, Leif Erickson, Peter Coe, Rudolph Anders, Howard Wendell, Don Dillaway, Isabel Randolph, Paul Brinegar, Martin Garralaga, John Mylong. BM's charter boat is used by agents who want to destroy the Panama Canal with an atom bomb.

110. ***Jack Slade.*** AA 1953. Harold Schuster. Mark Stevens, Dorothy Malone, Paul Langton, John Litel, Jim Bannon, John Harmon, Sammy Ogg, Ron Hargrave, Nelson Leigh, Harry Shannon, Lee Van Cleef. Stevens plays a more sympathetic version of the outlaw in *Western Union* and BM, his portrayer a dozen years earlier, plays one of his antagonists.

111. ***Sea of Lost Ships.*** Rep 1953. Joseph Kane. John Derek, Wanda Hendrix, Walter Brennan, Tom Tully, Richard Jaeckel, Ben Cooper, Erin O'Brien Moore, Darryl Hickman, Roy Roberts, Tom Powers, Steve Brodie, James Brown, Douglas Kennedy. When veteran Coast Guardsman BM dies, loyal friend Brennan takes on the rearing of his son (who grows up to be trouble-prone Derek).

112. ***Jubilee Trail.*** Rep 1954. Joseph Kane. Vera Ralston, Joan Leslie, Forrest Tucker, John Russell, Pat O'Brien, Ray Middleton, Jim Davis, Buddy Baer, Richard Webb, Grant Withers, James Millican, Nina Varela, Jack Elam. Pioneers Leslie and Russell meet several troublesome characters, BM included, on their trip west.

113. ***The Glenn Miller Story.*** Univ 1954. Anthony Mann. James Stewart, June Allyson, Henry Morgan, Charles Drake, George Tobias, Sig Ruman, Irving Bacon, James Bell, Kathleen Lockhart, Louis Armstrong, Gene Krupa, Frances Langford, The Modernaires, Ben Pollack, Carleton Young. BM plays Gen. Hap Arnold, a rare real-life characterization.

114. ***Rails into Laramie.*** Univ 1954. Jesse Hibbs. John Payne, Dan Duryea, Mari Blanchard, Joyce Mackenzie, Harry Shannon, Lee Van Cleef, James Griffith, Ralph Dumke, Myron Healey, Douglas Kennedy, Charles Horvath. BM is involved in another war with the laying of railway tracks.

115. ***Hell's Outpost.*** Rep 1954. Joseph Kane. Rod Cameron, Joan Leslie, Chill Wills, John Russell, Jim Davis, Ben Cooper, Kristine Miller, Taylor Holmes, Ruth Lee, Oliver Blake. BM is a sheriff in the modern West.

116. ***Treasure of Ruby Hills.*** AA 1955. Frank McDonald. Zachary Scott, Carole Mathews, Dick Foran, Lola Albright, Raymond Hatton, Rick Vallin, Steve Darrell, Stanley Andrews. BM is involved in another land-grabbing scheme.

117. ***The Silver Star.*** Lippert 1955. Richard Bartlett. Edgar Buchanan, Marie Windsor, Lon Chaney, Jr., Richard Bartlett, Earle Lyon, Morris Ankrum, Steve Rowland, Michael Whalen, Edith Evanson. BM is a Western blacksmith who doesn't want to help a new lawman (Lyon) battle town boss Chaney.

118. ***Foxfire.*** Univ 1955. Joseph Pevney. Jane Russell, Jeff Chandler, Dan Duryea, Mara Corday, Frieda Inescort, Robert Simon, Charlotte Wynters, Celia Lovsky, Eddy C. Waller, Phil Chambers. BM is an oil company executive.

119. ***Jail Busters.*** AA 1955. William Beaudine. Leo Gorcey, Huntz Hall, Bernard Gorcey, Anthony Caruso, Percy Helton, David Gorcey, Lyle Talbot, Bennie Bartlett, Murray Alper, Fritz Feld, Henry Kulky. BM is a prison guard captain.

120. ***Jaguar.*** Rep 1956. George Blair. Sabu, Chiquita, Touch (Mike) Connors, Jonathan Hale, Jay Novello, Fortunio Bonanova, Nacho Galindo. BM arranges a frame-up of Sabu for murder in a story involving crooked oil dealings in Africa.

121. ***Wetbacks.*** Bob Banner Associates 1956. Hank McCune. Lloyd Bridges, Nancy Gates, John Hoyt, Harold Peary, Jose Gonzalez-Gonzalez, Robert Keyes, Wally Cassell, Nacho Galindo, Louis Jean Heydt. BM is a government man posing as a trafficker smuggling Mexicans into the U.S.

122. ***Backlash.*** Univ 1956. John Sturges. Richard Widmark, Donna Reed, William Campbell, John McIntire, Henry (Harry) Morgan, Robert J. Wilke, Edward Platt, Jack Lambert, Frank Chase. Cavalry sergeant BM survives a massacre only to be killed later while trying to help Widmark get information about it.

123. ***Last of the Desperados.*** Lippert 1956. Sam Newfield. James Craig, Jim Davis, Margia Dean, Myrna Dell, Stanley Clements, Donna Martell, Bob Steele. BM is one of the bad guys being stalked by lawman Pat Garrett (Craig).

124. ***The Naked Gun.*** Associated 1956. Jack Lewis. Willard Parker, Mara Corday, Veda Ann Borg, Tom Brown, Billy House, Chick Chandler, Morris Ankrum, William "Bill" Phillips, Rick Vallin, Timothy Carey, X. Brands, Jody McCrea. BM is yet another thorn in the side of a Western hero, this time Parker.

125. ***The Man Is Armed.*** Rep 1956. Franklin Adreon. Dane Clark, William Talman, May Wynn, Robert Horton, Richard Benedict, Fredd Wayne, Richard Reeves, Harry Lewis, Darlene Fields, Larry Blake. BM is a police detective.

126. ***Three Violent People.*** Par 1956. Rudolph Maté. Charlton Heston, Anne Baxter, Gilbert Roland, Tom Tryon, Forrest Tucker, Bruce Ben-

nett, Elaine Stritch, Robert Blake, Peter Hanson, John Harmon, Robert Arthur, Ross Bagdasarian, Jameel Farrah (Jamie Farr). Carpetbagger BM gets into a brawl over Baxter with returning Confederate officer Heston.

127. *Sierra Stranger.* Col 1957. Lee Sholem. Howard Duff, Gloria McGhee, Dick Foran, John Hoyt, Edward Kemmer, George E. Stone, Eve McVeagh, Robert Foulk, Henry Kulky. Outsider Duff earns the enmity of townsmen like BM when he takes the part of a man who is a town pariah.

128. *Hell's Crossroads.* Rep 1957. Franklin Adreon. Stephen McNally, Peggie Castle, Robert Vaughn, Harry Shannon, Douglas Kennedy, Henry Brandon, Grant Withers, Myron Healey, Frank Wilcox. BM is a lawman charged with bringing in members of the James gang.

129. *Naked in the Sun.* Lippert 1957. R. John Hugh. James Craig, Lita Milan, Tony Hunter, Dennis Cross, Jim Boles, Bill Armstrong, Peter Dearing, Tony Morris, Mike Recco. BM is a slave trader who foments trouble between whites and Seminole chief Osceola (Craig) in the Florida of the 1830s.

130. *Girl on the Run.* WB 1958. Richard L. Bare, Efrem Zimbalist, Jr., Erin O'Brien, Shepperd Strudwick, Edward Byrnes, Charles Cane. Pilot for the hit TV series *77 Sunset Strip* was originally planned as a feature. BM is a police detective acquainted with private eye Stuart Bailey (Zimbalist).

131. *Girl in the Woods.* Rep 1958. Tom Gries. Forrest Tucker, Margaret Hayes, Murvyn Vye, Diana Francis, Paul Langton, Kim Charney, Joyce Compton, Bartlett Robinson, Mickey Finn, George Lynn. BM is a logging boss involved in a competition with a rival company.

132. *Geisha Boy.* Par 1958. Frank Tashlin. Jerry Lewis, Nobu McCarthy, Marie McDonald, Sessue Hayakawa, Suzanne Pleshette, Robert Kazuyoshi, Alex Gerry, Douglas Fowley, The L.A. Dodgers. BM is an army major leading a USO tour (which includes bumbling magician Lewis) in Japan.

133. *Frontier Gun.* 20th 1958. Paul Landres. John Agar, Robert Strauss, Joyce Meadows, Leslie Bradley, Morris Ankrum, Lyn Thomas, Sammy Ogg, Doodles Weaver, Holly Bane. Disabled lawman Agar goes up against the villain (Strauss) who killed his father BM.

134. *Noose for a Gunman.* UA 1959. Edward L. Cahn. Jim Davis, Lyn Thomas, Ted De Corsia, Walter Sande, Harry Carey, Jr., Leo Gordon, John Hart, Lane Chandler, William Tannen. Hero Davis cleans up a community despite the usual opposition from BM and others.

135. *Gunfighters of Abilene.* UA 1960. Edward L. Cahn. Buster Crabbe, Judith Ames, Eugenia Paul, Kenneth MacDonald, Richard Cutting, Richard Devon. Crabbe seeks revenge against villainous rancher BM, the father of the girl Crabbe loves.

136. *Pocketful of Miracles.* UA 1961. Frank Capra. Bette Davis, Glenn Ford, Hope Lange, David Brian, Peter Falk, Edward Everett Horton, Sheldon Leonard, Thomas Mitchell, Arthur O'Connell, Mickey Shaughnessy, Ann-Margret, Jerome Cowan, Fritz Feld, Frank Ferguson, John Litel, Peter

Mann. In Capra's remake of his own *Lady for a Day*, BM plays the New York police commissioner.

137. ***Law of the Lawless.*** Par 1964. William Claxton. Dale Robertson, Yvonne De Carlo, John Agar, Richard Arlen, Donald Barry, William Bendix, Bruce Cabot, Lon Chaney, Jr., Rod Lauren, Kent Taylor, Bill Williams, Roy Jenson. BM is a powerful man putting pressure on judge Robertson to get his murderous son Agar off. The first and best of BM's four A. C. Lyles productions.

138. ***The Rounders.*** MGM 1965. Burt Kennedy. Glenn Ford, Henry Fonda, Chill Wills, Sue Ane Langdon, Hope Holliday, Edgar Buchanan, Joan Freeman, Kathleen Freeman, Denver Pyle, Doodles Weaver, Casey Tibbs, Allegra Varron. Saddle buddies Ford and Fonda try to make a business deal with well-to-do BM.

139. ***Town Tamer.*** Par 1965. Lesley Selander. Dana Andrews, Terry Moore, Richard Arlen, Lyle Bettger, Bruce Cabot, Jeanne Cagney, Phillip Carey, Lon Chaney, Jr., Coleen Gray, Richard Jaeckel, DeForest Kelley, Sonny Tufts, Donald Barry, Pat O'Brien. Prominent businessman BM's uncharacteristic honesty does him no good when he is shot by a drunken jealous husband.

140. ***Arizona Bushwackers.*** Par 1967. Lesley Selander. Howard Keel, Yvonne De Carlo, John Ireland, Brian Donlevy, Marilyn Maxwell, Scott Brady, James Craig, Roy Rogers, Jr., Reg Parton; narrated by James Cagney. BM is a crooked sheriff in a town torn apart by the Civil War.

141. ***Buckskin.*** Par 1968. Michael Moore. Barry Sullivan, Joan Caulfield, Wendell Corey, Barbara Hale, Lon Chaney, Jr., John Russell, Bill Williams, Leo Gordon, Richard Arlen, Gerald Michenaud, George Chandler, Aki Aleong, Michael Larrain. Small town doctor BM is one of Sullivan's allies in his effort to clean up a Western town dominated by Corey. The last film for both Corey and BM, who died within five months of the film's release in August 1968.

Lloyd Nolan

Of all the actors chronicled in this text, the one who probably garnered the most respect among his peers would have to be Lloyd Nolan. Although his talent has a great deal to do with it, another major factor was that he was a survivor. After a half-century of performing, the sight of his name in the cast listing of any film or TV show assured the viewer of at least one quality performance. Coming from the same beginnings as many of his contemporaries, Nolan enjoyed a distinguished career as a character man apart from his successful career as both tough hero and heavy. Aside from that, he had a great stage role which he brought to television with unqualified success. The other actors discussed enjoyed some of these types of career triumphs, but he was the only one who had it all.

His durability was due in part to how well the reliable Nolan countenance fit into so many genres. His outstanding roles included law enforcers and lawbreakers, lowly soldiers and generals, baseball managers and players, small town general practitioners and big city psychiatrists, spy chiefs, customs officials—you name it and Nolan has probably played it. Some of the films are now considered classics, but the majority of them aren't. Typically, his best stage roles went to top film stars when they received the Hollywood treatment, but critics remembered Nolan. His friends Brian Donlevy and Alan Ladd achieved stardom at Paramount where he had been taken for granted. Yet while he was being used badly, the great director John Ford was being advised to select him for the plum role of the Ringo Kid in *Stagecoach* (1939). Nolan didn't get the role; in true John Alden fashion, the person who said he was the best man for the part was chosen by Ford ... John Wayne.

Lloyd Benedict Nolan was born August 11, 1903, in San Francisco, California. His father James, a shoe manufacturer, had emigrated

Lloyd Nolan as Captain Queeg in the 1954 Broadway play *The Caine Mutiny Court-Martial*.

from County Cork, Ireland. The Nolans lived well thanks to the father's business. Young Lloyd spent his formative years in the City by the Bay. As a student at Santa Clara Prep, studying acting never crossed his mind.

When Nolan went to Stanford University, he had every intention of becoming a newspaperman. But after his first year, he realized that Santa Clara really hadn't prepared him sufficiently for college and he flunked out. He jokingly said that most journalists had flunked college, but seriously began to rethink his values. To a certain extent, he had been spoiled by his family and he decided a little rebelliousness was called for. For young men of his generation, a little too young for the Great War, that meant a tour of duty at sea. By not seeking to continue a "formal education," Nolan knew he was giving up his dreams of being a reporter, but he never lost his liking for the profession. When he became famous, he would never think of refusing an interview request by a member of the press.

When he resumed his education, it was at the Pasadena Playhouse, from whose ranks many screen favorites leaped into film. But it proved to be no immediate springboard for Nolan. So beginning in 1927, he became what was known as a "touring actor." That touring eventually got him to Broadway: His New York debut was in a minor revue-type show called *Cape Cod Follies*. Once in the big city, he had no intention of going back out on the road. He joined the ranks of the groups of young actors hunting for jobs shortly before the Depression began.

Nolan developed a style that was to stand him in good stead through his career. He quickly proved to be as adept in musicals and witty farces as he was in straight plays, which enabled him to find a job soon after his previous show flopped. One 1930 play probably qualified in the flop category. It was called *Sweet Stranger*, but it was a memorable experience for him. It was in that show that he first worked with a young actress named Mel Efird. They began to see each other regularly. He received far more attention for his out-of-town work as Kruger, one of the reporters, in the Hecht-MacArthur classic *The Front Page*. His first good New York reviews came for a mild little musical called *High Hat* in 1931. The notices were good enough to win him a character part with Alfred Lunt and Lynn Fontanne in *Reunion in Vienna*. The Lunts, already acknowledged as giants of the stage, had just returned from their unpleasant experience filming *The Guardsman* for MGM. *Reunion in Vienna* by Robert E. Sherwood was (like *The Guardsman*) made to order for them, but when MGM bought it, the couple didn't even consider making the film. The Lunt company was always a happy one, with good reason; they usually enjoyed long runs. This one opened in November of 1931 and played a total of 264 performances.

Nolan now had the security he had hoped for. However, he put off his plans to marry Mel; his practical nature made him wonder if he could support a wife. What gave him confidence was the starring role of Biff Grimes in *One Sunday Afternoon*, which opened on Broadway on February 15, 1933. The play, a seemingly lightweight nostalgia piece by James Hogan, did not attract any of the leading male performers of the day, which was just as well. A big star could have destroyed this fragile story of a dentist who has lost the girl of his dreams to a "friend" and also has taken a criminal rap for that same man and spent time in jail. Plotting revenge when he sees the man again after many years, Grimes finds out that no revenge is necessary because he has found a better life with the right girl. Such material could have easily been labelled corn in those hard-bitten Depression days, but something about it struck a chord with audiences. And no small credit was given Nolan by the critics. John Chapman of the *Daily News* wrote that Nolan deserved "the honors for his human and holding portrayal." Word of mouth made the play a runaway hit that played an incredible 322 performances on Broadway,* outdoing Nolan's run with the Lunts. This success in a year like 1933 was enough security for any actor. During the run of the play, Mel Efird became Mrs. Lloyd Nolan, one of the most durable of show business marriages.

Nolan had started on the road, not far from the bright lights of Broadway, playing the Shubert Theater in Newark, New Jersey. It was there that *One Sunday Afternoon* opened in November; *Newark Star* critic Richard Murray wrote, "If you saw Gary Cooper in the movie version, you may have some idea of what a really fine actor Mr. Nolan is." No critic who saw Nolan in that play failed to be impressed by the naturalness he projected; this seemed the perfect wedding of actor and role. After a year together, Nolan and Biff Grimes parted company, never to be reunited. Other actors would reprise their great stage roles in later years, but this actor never returned to what was clearly "the role of his youth."

Hollywood had taken notice of Nolan's success, but although offers had started to come in, he bided his time. Instead, he went from his hit to a less commercial enterprise: appearing in *Gentle-*

---

*As soon as One Sunday Afternoon *clicked, Paramount bought the rights for Gary Cooper. Warner Bros. later purchased the property and it was filmed twice for them by director Raoul Walsh, once as* The Strawberry Blonde *(with James Cagney as Biff to give it all the pace the Cooper picture lacked) and the second time under its original title, with Dennis Morgan in the lead and songs to fill in the gaps. A Lux TV version in the '50s with Gordon MacRae had only brevity on its side.*

James Cagney is trained by Lloyd Nolan (second from right) and Robert Armstrong (extreme right) in *G-Men* (1935).

woman, the latest production of the Group Theater. Nolan worked with such famed Group members as Stella Adler, Roman Bohnen, Morris Carnovsky and Russell Collins. The author of the play was John Howard Lawson, who would become one of the infamous Hollywood Ten. The play, about American politics, did not succeed.

Harry Cohn's Columbia Pictures was the company that first acquired Nolan's services, needing a sturdy leading man for their B pictures. But in true Hollywood fashion, his new employers loaned him out at first. For Paramount, he was paired with George Raft in a musical-drama, *Stolen Harmony* (1935), and at Warners, he played an FBI official who gets killed in the same year's *G-Men* with James Cagney. Sharing the screen with two top tough guys would seem to indicate the direction his career was going to go, but Columbia didn't follow this pattern. They would use him in some character roles, but they also wanted to make him familiar to audiences as the star of their second feature.

His first Columbia film, *Atlantic Adventure* (1935), was promising. As a fast-talking reporter solving a shipboard mystery, Nolan was given the talented but faded star Nancy Carroll as a leading lady. One of the most luminous personalities of early talkies, Carroll was finishing up her contract after a series of programmers in which she co-starred with George Murphy. From the way she looked and acted, no one would have suspected that her film career was practically over, even though she was not yet 30. Also in the cast was the great silent screen comic Harry Langdon, cast as Nolan's sidekick.

His second leading role, also released in 1935, was *One Way Ticket*, a comedy-drama in which he plays a man who robs a bank in order to recover money the bank cheated him out of. He's caught and sent to jail, where he becomes involved with the warden's daughter. It was inconsequential fun as was his subsequent lead, in *You May Be Next* (1936). One of several '30s films on radio broadcasting, it had Nolan as a station employee who helps Ann Sothern succeed in the medium. Interspersed with these films were his secondary roles in more expensive features. Because he was a utility man for a relatively small studio without a large stockpile of contract players, he worked in more genres than he would later on. That would have been all right but the smallish parts he was given did not add much gloss to his career. An actor who had recently been a tremendous hit on Broadway appeared to be wasting his golden opportunities. He was making pictures in which no one even noticed him.

He was in the semi-screwball comedy *She Couldn't Take It* (1935), again with George Raft, on loan to Nolan's studio this time. He was a third male lead in *Lady of Secrets* (1936), Harry Cohn's attempt to make a Ruth Chatterton tearjerker after Warners had bled the lady (and the genre) dry. This would be the last time Chatterton would sacrifice herself for her child on screen. He was put in a plane along with Richard Dix in the aviation drama, *Devil's Squadron* (1936). As it turned out, his most interesting role for Columbia was his last: *Counterfeit* (1936) was fairly typical crime stuff, with agent Chester Morris infiltrating a ring of counterfeiters. But Nolan, as the gang's leader, had his first chance to prove he could snarl with the best of them. If any part that he'd played in his first year in films set the model for the parts he would play at his new home, this was the one.

Nolan accepted an offer from Paramount and began working there. One of the prime incentives in working with one of the major studios was the quality of the directors. For his first two Paramount outings in 1936, Nolan drew Raoul Walsh and King Vidor, two of the best. In Walsh's *Big Brown Eyes*, he was cast as a villain heinous enough to make Barton MacLane jealous. Early in the film, Nolan tries to perform a gangland killing in a park and accidentally fires into a baby carriage. He later shows no remorse, even though the film is a comedy-drama. He supported Joan Bennett (a frequent star of Nolan films), Cary Grant and Walter Pidgeon in that one. More memorable was Vidor's *The Texas Rangers*, in which he played an outlaw whose partners (Fred MacMurray and Jack Oakie) reform, joining the title organization. Nolan guns down Oakie in a classic card game scene, so MacMurray has to go after his old sidekick. By adding that wry humorous manner that was becoming his trademark, Nolan made his character far more interesting that it normally would have been, certainly more than Macdonald Carey did in the uninspired remake *Streets of Laredo* (1949). Not only did Nolan get himself a good role from *The Texas Rangers*, but also a longtime friendship with Fred MacMurray.

While the Paramount people tried to decide what heinous acts he would next perform, he was loaned to the newly formed 20th Century–Fox for a programmer called *15 Maiden Lane* (1936). He was to play a cop investigating a jewel heist. It seemed odd to bring him over from another studio when they had recently signed Brian Donlevy to play such parts. Dwan, the most prolific director in Sol Wurtzel's second feature unit, cast outsider Nolan in the good guy role because the leading male character was actually a villain, a suave jewel thief played by Cesar Romero. The next time Nolan would visit the Fox studio, it would be under better circumstances.

Nolan played well with Claire Trevor, and one picture later she became his leading lady at his home studio. Unfortunately, *King of Gamblers* (1937) was his least important one of the year and represented the beginning of a trend at Paramount that ultimately did his career little good. The most colorful character in the film was the title one, played by Akim Tamiroff, and the simple plot involved Nolan getting the goods on him. It was his only heroic role in a year of more interesting character work.

In his other 1937 films, he was cast as four very different types of villains—all of them interesting to a point. He played a racketeer who takes over a newspaper and turns it into a scandal sheet in *Exclusive*, another Fred MacMurray starrer in which the tragic Frances Farmer had the female lead. Reporter MacMurray shows Farmer the error of her ways after she willfully goes to work for

Nolan.* Farmer was also leading lady in the offbeat *Ebb Tide*, a strange film which benefited from its performers and Technicolor photography. Although Paramount did a lot of South Seas Island stories, this one was slightly different. It starred the famed Austrian actor Oscar Homolka (who was introduced with much fanfare but not signed because the studio's Akim Tamiroff worked cheaper) and also gave a strong, scenery-chewing role to another recent émigré, Ireland's Barry Fitzgerald. Ray Milland and Farmer had the romantic leads, but the big surprise was Nolan. As the sinister ruler of the island visited by the other four leads, he looked suavely handsome, sporting a Melvyn Douglas–type mustache. But no one was quite sure what the allegorical script really meant. After that, the studios South Seas films would all be the innocuous kind that usually starred Dorothy Lamour.

On horseback again, Nolan battled stalwart Joel McCrea who was trying to set up the first *Wells Fargo* line in the picture of the same name. It was directed by Frank Lloyd, whose career as a maker of epics was somewhat overshadowed by Cecil B. DeMille, whose style was similar. Almost two hours in length, the film allowed Nolan much time to be a thorn in McCrea's side. Earlier that year, Nolan had appeared with McCrea (in his only appearance as Dr. Kildare) and Barbara Stanwyck in the trivial *Interns Can't Take Money*, but had played a "nice gangster" rather than the villain of the piece. In another change of pace, he whitened his temples to play "Honest John," a grafting politician, in Mae West's Gay Nineties comedy *Every Day's a Holiday*. He emerged as one of the few actors who did not serve merely as straight man for West, whose contractual ties with Paramount ended with this film. This may have been the reason that Nolan and leading man Edmund Lowe were given funny lines all for themselves. In office scenes with his stooges present and no Mae West in sight, Nolan has a field day displaying his gift for comedy. But comedy roles were to become as rare for the actor as would parts in high budget films for the next few years.

As Nolan's face became familiar to the moviegoing public, the studio's publicity machine began to grind out copy on him. He still had a warm spot in his heart for the press, and in 1937 he was given the opportunity to write a piece which would be syndicated throughout the country. The piece was filled with many laudatory words

---

*Nolan also met a longtime friend, Lucille Ball, through this film; she was dating its director, Alexander Hall.

about journalists. Strangely, one unnamed paper mistakenly substituted a photograph of actor Paul Fix for Nolan's.

The success of *King of Gamblers* revitalized Paramount's inexpensive B-picture unit, which had previously turned out films of uneven value. They realized they had actors under contract who could duplicate the performers at a studio like Warner Bros. (They now had directors Robert Florey and Louis King who had turned out programmers for Warners.) At the same time, the studio acquired some J. Edgar Hoover stories about how the FBI brought several criminals to justice. Most of the films were fictional and inexpensive, although the quality of the casts make them look better than they really were, even today. Florey's *Daughter of Shanghai* (1937) with Anna May Wong and Charles Bickford set the pace, compressing a great deal of action into a little more than an hour's running time. Florey's next, *Dangerous to Know* (1938), although based on an Edgar Wallace play, was simply a rehash of *King of Gamblers*. Akim Tamiroff, the Russian character actor who had started out as a studio bit player less than five years earlier, was the pivotal character, a big-time underworld figure. Wong played his mistress and Nolan was the sardonic cop who waits for the opportunity to nail him. All in all, it was an entertaining time-filler.

The pattern was set. When the chief villainous role called for a foreign type, particularly Italian or Chinese, Tamiroff would play the part. If the villain was subordinate to the hero, the studio's utility man J. Carrol Naish would be the bad guy while Nolan usually played the breezy undercover man, cop or occasionally an innocent bystander thrown into the thick of things. If the leading role called for a Caucasian gangster, Nolan put on his best snarl and played that role. The casts were often more interesting than the stories. Mary Carlisle was usually the innocent heroine while Gail Patrick played the more worldly types. Former Paramount star Evelyn Brent was given the shady older women parts, while the gangster's top underlings were usually played by two handsome young actors famous for other accomplishments, Larry "Buster" Crabbe and Anthony Quinn. The typecasting worked well and such films were made into the early '40s. While entertaining, they ground many fine actors' careers to a standstill.

The two bad guy roles Nolan essayed in 1938 were interesting, mainly due to the way he played them. In *Hunted Men*, he appeared as a gangster who needs a hiding place after gunning down Crabbe. Only his confederates Naish and Quinn know that he has taken refuge in the middle-class home of Lynne Overman, whose daughter Carlisle eventually brings out the good in this ruthless thug. It took an actor of Nolan's stature to make this change convincing in the film's relatively brief running time. He had no opportunity for reformation in *Prison Farm*, even though he was temporarily loved by the heroine (Shirley Ross, on temporary leave from the studio's musical wing). His characterization can be considered that of an unrepentant heel. The crime he commits causes unsuspecting Ross to be imprisoned along with him in the same prison complex. There was little chance for his rehabilitation with corrupt prison official Naish on hand, but audiences knew Ross would make it once she met handsome prison doctor John Howard. When Nolan played a baddie, he seemed to be Paramount's answer to Humphrey Bogart.

Nolan was cast as guys who were not necessarily in the business of being courageous in both *King of Alcatraz* (1938) and *Ambush* (1939). The former, which had no prison scenes, had Nolan as an officer of a ship taken over by escaped killer J. Carrol Naish and his henchmen, who are outwitted by Nolan once he becomes angry enough. This film is chiefly remembered because it contained one of the best casts any second feature ever had, including (in his screen debut) Robert Preston as Nolan's buddy. *Ambush* once again gave Nolan a musical leading lady; opera star Gladys Swarthout needed one more picture to round out her contract and this was it. Here he's a trucker unwittingly involved with a gang of thieves which includes Broderick Crawford. Crawford was also in *Undercover Doctor* (1939), in which Nolan was once more an upholder of the law on the trail of J. Carrol Naish, a doctor with underworld connections. But even a change of pace away from criminals, as a riverboat captain who shields runaway movie star Dorothy Lamour in *St. Louis Blues* (1939), was no help.* It was a nothing leading man's role.

Nolan chose not to sign a new contract with Paramount. His last film for them, *The Magnificent Fraud* (1939) was another Akim Tamiroff tour de force in which Nolan once again played straight man. It seemed to indicate that he'd made the right decision by leaving, although he did not reap any immediate benefits. He was seen in leading roles in ten movies released in 1940, his most prolific year. Of course, some of these films had even lower production values

---

Forty-five years later, Lamour and Nolan (playing themselves on TV's Remington Steele*) recalled this and another co-starring vehicle,* Johnny Apollo.

than his Paramount quickies, for he had to freelance until his contract with Fox was negotiated. One of his better pictures that year had him reunited with George Raft and Joan Bennett in her then-fiancée Walter Wanger's independent production *The House Across the Bay*. As gangster Raft's scheming lawyer, he has designs on his client's wife Bennett when Raft goes to prison. But Bennett falls for dependable Walter Pidgeon, so Nolan stirs up Raft, with typical results. Nolan's role was well-written and he easily took acting honors, which helped his standing during this transitional period.

Nolan soon found that freelancing was good only when one was a star like Ronald Colman or Fredric March. For second-string tough guys like Bickford, MacLane and now Nolan, their independence quickly led them along Poverty Row to little Republic Studios. At least he got away with doing only two quickies on Herbert J. Yates' lot, playing a gangster in one and a conniving reporter in the other. These were just two of Republic's attempts to expand beyond their two best genres, the serial and the western, and were made with just enough know-how to make them interesting.

Fox's B pictures of the early '40s were mostly remakes, quickies designed as companion pieces to Darryl Zanuck's increasingly lavish main features. Nolan's first, almost an elongated screen test, was *The Man Who Wouldn't Talk* (1940), a remake of 1929's *The Valiant* (the film debut of the electrifying Paul Muni). The '29 version, like most stagebound early talkies, was heavy with dialogue although its leading character prefers to go to his death silently rather than bring shame upon his mother and sister, on whose account he has committed murder. The 1940 remake featured flashbacks and more-modern techniques, and Nolan's playing was low-keyed, wisely not imitating Muni's bravura Oscar-nominated performance. Nolan's first film with Fox's B queen Lynn Bari was a remake of *Me and My Gal* (1932). In this new film, *Pier 13*, Nolan played Spencer Tracy's old part (a waterfront cop) and Bari recreated Joan Bennett's role of his waitress girlfriend.

Nolan did yet another picture with Bennett that year. Fox's *The Man I Married* was one of a horde of 1940 films which took a decided anti–Nazi stance. Bennett played an American woman who marries German Frances Lederer and goes to live in his country, only to find that he is a Nazi. Nolan is her American friend who comes to her rescue. As usual in a "shaky A," his part was comparatively small. He then did another with Bari, *Charter Pilot*, which proved that the best way to be top-billed in a film was to play the title role. That was certainly the case with his next Fox film which closed out 1940 very well indeed and told the powers-that-be that he did have audience appeal. The film that did it was *Michael Shayne, Private Detective.*

During the '30s, many film series were inspired by the so-called "gentlemen detectives" personified by Philo Vance and Nick Charles, who solved crimes with deductive reasoning rather than their fists. And who was more of a gentleman than Fox's own Charlie Chan? Fox had been looking for another successful sleuth for a series of low-budgeters, especially since anti–Japanese feeling had led to the end of the Mr. Moto series. When Basil Rathbone scored in their *The Hound of the Baskervilles* (1939), they considered a Sherlock Holmes series, but dropped the idea after one additional film. The following year, Fox chose Brett Halliday's somewhat unorthodox but American sleuth Michael Shayne and emphasized his Irish ancestry by casting Nolan. They weren't sure that a smart-aleck private eye who used his fists would sit well with the public. It immediately caught on. It preceded by several months not only Humphrey Bogart's Sam Spade (in *The Maltese Falcon*) but also the beginning of Chester Morris' Boston Blackie series. Nolan's Shayne can rightfully be classified as the first successful, slightly uncouth screen detective. Gentlemen private eyes were on their way out.

The first entry did not seem much different than the average detective films made up to that time; it had the prerequisites of rich family, countless suspects and interesting background (in this instance, a racetrack). Besides Shayne's own wisecracking manner,* there was usually a feisty leading lady who would trade quips with the detective while helping him out; Mary Beth Hughes, Marjorie Weaver and Lynn Bari filled this slot. The other players also had quality, but if the series was to succeed, it had to have an attractive star. And Nolan soon found that this character was garnering him a substantial number of female admirers. It may have been their interest more than anything else that turned the supposed one-shot into a seven-picture series. It certainly made a difference in the way Nolan's new bosses looked at him. When Nolan first came to Fox, he was cast as ruthless gangster Mickey Dwyer in *Johnny Apollo* (1940), playing against hero Tyrone Power just the way Brian Donlevy had done when he was under contract. This, like most of Power's

---

*Thomas Pryor in The New York Times *wrote,* "Mr. Nolan does this sort of thing to perfection," *an apt summary of the entire series.*

films, was personally produced by the boss, Darryl F. Zanuck, who wasn't likely to be adverse to continual typecasting. But Shayne came along a few months later and Nolan never again played the villain in any of the countless Fox movies he made in the '40s. If he wasn't the hero of a second feature, he would be playing a prominent "nice guy" role in some big-budgeter. Most of the meanness was taken out of this effective tough guy.

The Shayne pictures stand up well despite the passage of time, thanks to several gimmicks employed. Mysteries always worked well on trains, so there was *Sleepers West* (1941). The threat of marriage loomed over the detective in *Dressed to Kill* (1941) and industrial spies were brought into the same year's *Blue, White and Perfect*. *The Man Who Wouldn't Die* (1942) rounded up all the suspects in a typically creepy house, while *Just Off Broadway* (1942) had Shayne serving on a jury; additional comedy relief was supplied by Phil Silvers. But the ideas ran out and in the last of the series' 1942 *Time to Kill*, Fox did just as RKO did with the same year's *The Falcon Takes Over*: utilize a Raymond Chandler story and a "disguised" Phillip Marlowe. In the two-year Shayne series, advertising stressed the actor's name equally with the part he played—proof that audiences were not just interested in a Michael Shayne mystery. Nolan had developed some box office clout.

As he became more important to Fox as younger leading men were going into service, the actor found his contract was to be renegotiated so he would work exclusively at Fox. His first two years there had made him appear to be a freelance actor. He had made two films apiece for Warners and MGM and had even returned to the Paramount lot for a Runyonesque comedy, *Buy Me That Town* (1941). The knowledge that his old studio thought its own contractees too important to play the lead in this film did not phase Nolan; he was in the midst of the most tranquil time in his life. And this was reflected in his private life. These were the years that the Nolans got down to the serious business of raising a family. First came a daughter (Melinda, like her mother). But modesty prevailed two years later when a son was born to the Nolans and the boy was named Jay rather than Lloyd, Jr., as is more customary in Irish families. The great affection felt for the child was so evident that magazine pieces often swerved away from the performer and concentrated on the doting father. The image still counted to the Hollywood press and any publicity item about him in those days would have been incomplete without a photo of father frolicking with son Jay and the expected caption, "Not So Tough." The Nolan home in Brentwood was also a major project and he used much of his spare time finding ways of redecorating to suit their needs.

One of his Warner Bros. films was Anatole Litvak's offbeat *Blues in the Night* (1941). Nolan, a gangster, gives a job to a group of young musicians whom he eventually turns against. (This plot was superficially similar to his first film *Stolen Harmony*, in which he was a gangster who kidnapped Ben Bernie's band.) Two of the musicians are better known for their directorial work in film, Richard Whorf and Elia Kazan, the latter previously with the Group Theater. The picture has over the years developed a cult following among critics. Some talk about Litvak's direction or the inventive montages of Don Siegel, some about the screenplay of yet another future director Robert Rossen, while others admired the now-clichéd femme fatale of Betty Field or her male doormat, Howard Da Silva. Those who admire the *film noir* techniques popular in the '40s consider this film one of that form's originators. Knowledgeable film historian William K. Everson recognized all these things. In a March 1980 *Films in Review*, he wrote that *Blues in the Night* "offers an excellent example of studio ensemble-acting although as is often the case, it is the confident, subtle and unmannered playing of Lloyd Nolan that is the best single performance in the film." But even Everson suggested that had Warners considered this project more commercial, it would have been their own Humphrey Bogart who would have played it. It is interesting to note that this was Nolan's last serious gangster role on film.

Thanks to the Shayne pictures, Nolan got to use his wry sense of humor in other roles, including several films about baseball. In Universal's *Mr. Dynamite* (1941), he played a star pitcher for a St. Louis team, who gets involved with secret agent Irene Hervey and saboteurs while in Coney Island. He remained in Brooklyn, this time as team manager, in Fox's *It Happened in Flatbush* (1942). He and Carole Landis played so well together that they were reteamed later that year for the more serious *Manila Calling*. With the end of the Shayne series, he was thrown into another topical war film, *Guadalcanal Diary* (1943). In this movie, the primary relief from the pressures of war came in the form of a crucial ballgame between the New York Yankees and the St. Louis Cardinals, heard by the men on the radio with William Bendix and Nolan taking opposing sides.

MGM's *Bataan* (1943), directed by Tay Garnett, proved to be one of the best combat films made during World War II, almost totally devoid of the patriotic fervor that destroyed the realism of many other wartime films. Some considered the script a steal from Dudley Nichols' *The Lost Patrol* (1934), but one could say that about countless films in which a group of men were wiped out by an enemy one by one. The characterizations were altogether different here and the script (credited to Robert D. Andrews) did not appear to be the allegorical type as in the earlier film. Within the excellent cast, three characters were particularly well-etched. Robert Taylor's Sgt. Bill Dane takes command when his superior officers are killed; he gives one of his best performances as the battle-hardened non-com. Nolan was the shadowy Corp. Barney Todd, a good soldier with a blot on his record. And newcomer Robert Walker, as young sailor Leonard Purckett, thrown in with a group of tough G.I.s, easily won audience sympathy with his sensitive portrayal. Nolan felt that his death scene would be anti-climactic, coming immediately after Purckett's death. He conspired, with the help of director Garnett and Taylor, to make *his* death every bit as moving. Taylor's grief over Nolan's death after audiences thought they did not like each other gave the film's star the best dramatic scene he would ever have. *Bataan* is an indictment of war rather than just a blind story of sacrifice, making it stand tall in its genre.

Despite that film's success, Nolan balked at doing another war film thereafter and did not do *Wing and a Prayer* for which he had been announced. He also vetoed another 1944 film, *Roger Touhy, Gangster*, which would have put him back where he was five years earlier at Paramount; it even had Robert Florey as the director. Fox was perturbed by this sudden change in the usually cooperative actor. And Nolan, with no more loan-outs to fall back on, knew he faced suspension. But the extra time to spend with his family and work on his house looked pretty good to him. In 1944, his only acting was done for the radio microphone, in the series *Results, Inc*. Nolan made up for this by appearing in four 1945 releases of his home studio.

The first and last of the four films are the most important, even though his roles offered the actor little in the way of challenge. That he accepted these roles after a period of selectivity proves a desire to contribute at least in part to a worthy film rather than a desperate need to work. The first was the adaptation of Betty Smith's novel *A Tree Grows in Brooklyn* and directing it was Nolan's *Blues in the Night* co-star Elia Kazan. It is an auspicious debut; Kazan keeps the nostalgia and the sentiment in check and gets wonderful performances out of Dorothy McGuire, Joan Blondell, James Dunn, James Gleason and the two children, Peggy Ann Garner and Ted Donaldson, who are really the film's stars. The film was a particular triumph for Dunn, a leading Fox player of the early '30s who had fallen on hard times. As the lovable failure of a father, he was memorable enough to be remembered nearly a year later when the Best Supporting Actor Academy Award for 1945 was given him. Nolan has the somewhat thankless role of McShane, the local patrolman who seeks to fill the void in the life of McGuire and the children left by the death of Dunn. Thanks to the way Kazan had handled that important character's passing, the audience unconsciously resented McShane, even though the character was a most decent man who would be an ideal stepfather for the children.

His other important film that year was Henry Hathaway's *The House on 92nd Street*, which also took an Oscar (Best Original Story). The total content of the film was again more important than Nolan's role, that of FBI Inspector Briggs. The film was the first of a group produced by Louis de Rochemont that pioneered an area which today is called docudrama. De Rochemont made several of these for Fox in the mid- to late '40s, many of them directed by Henry Hathaway and the best one *Boomerang* (1947), directed by Elia Kazan. *The House on 92nd Street* became extremely popular, with its factual locales and a supporting cast of New York actors adding a more naturalistic quality than audiences of the day were used to. Nolan had been involved with the FBI before, at both Warners and Paramount, but those films were almost irreverent in comparison to the sanctification the Bureau underwent here. The fact that the script won an award only reflects the mood of the period; this sort of film remained popular well into the '50s. (Nolan continued to turn up in films and television series in the employ of the government and would go full circle in the late '70s, appearing in the less-than-flattering biography of J. Edgar Hoover, played by Broderick Crawford.)

His other 1945 films elicited nothing more than yawns. *Circumstantial Evidence* was an unpretentious B in which Nolan and a group of kids try to clear their friend Michael O'Shea of a murder charge. However, *Captain Eddie* had practically no saving graces. It was a big budgeter starring Nolan's pal Fred MacMurray as World War I ace flyer Eddie Rickenbacker. Nolan's former leading lady Lynn Bari was given a rare shot at the big time as Mrs. Rickenbacker, but it was a dubious honor at best. Badly needed was more aerial footage, even if it had to be culled from a prior World War I film, but the script opted for all the biographical clichés which minimized its subject's accomplishments. It also brought in the present war: The story was told in flashbacks, remembered by Rickenbacker on a lifeboat after a ship was torpedoed. As one of the men on the lifeboat, Nolan has virtually nothing to do and may have just taken the part to work with such friendly co-stars as MacMurray and Richard Conte. All in all, whether the films were good or bad, the parts he was receiving at Fox offered him little to no challenge.

Once again, Fox began loaning him to other studios. MGM's first (*Two Smart People* 1946) had Lucille Ball and John Hodiak as confidence people being tracked by amiable cop Nolan and it was minor league all the way. The second for Metro was a version of Raymond Chandler's *Lady in the Lake* (1946), directed by and starring Robert Montgomery as detective Phillip Marlowe. The film was unusual because all the action was viewed through his eyes; audiences heard his voice (and occasionally saw his reflection) as the other actors stared at him. (This must have made the job of acting and directing a lot easier.) The former Michael Shayne was this time a dishonest police detective, involved in the crime being investigated by Marlowe. Paramount's *Wild Harvest* (1947) had some more old friends—director Tay Garnett, Dorothy Lamour and Robert Preston, as well as a new friend in star Alan Ladd. The popular Ladd, in reality a very insecure man, seemed to gravitate towards older actors and he formed a lasting friendship with the Nolans during the making of the film. This was during a period when Ladd and his friend William Bendix were not speaking to one another and Nolan filled some kind of void in the life of Ladd, who had lost his father at an early age. Nolan found him to be a good friend and didn't mind occasionally playing the "father figure."

Meanwhile, the Nolans' little boy Jay was showing a noticeable inability to learn. At times, he was very hyperactive and other times he became withdrawn. It was determined that Jay was autistic because, unlike the retarded child, he perceived the world around him. He had a functioning brain; it was only his outward behavior that was erratic. Once it was diagnosed, the Nolans realized their son would find it difficult to adapt to the world of the average school child. A special school was recommended and Jay was enrolled.

This personal sadness seemed to reflect itself in Nolan's screen work, as producers suddenly began casting him in parts calling for a sympathetic nature. In a relatively short period of time, he was involved in several films in which either kids or animals (or both) figured prominently in the plot. Previously associated with urban settings, Nolan was now turning up almost as frequently in rural areas. The two films in which he ended his long association with Fox point up this diversity. He recreated his *House on 92nd Street* role of FBI Inspector Briggs in *The Street with No Name* (1948), once again sending a young agent out on an undercover assignment. Because the film was directed by William Keighley, the director of *G-Men* and many other Warners crime dramas, it seemed faster paced than the other Fox docudramas. It also provided Richard Widmark with a snarling villain to follow up his successful Tommy Udo in *Kiss of Death*. Nolan's other 1948 film, *Green Grass of Wyoming* found him in a completely different setting. Because the contracts of Preston Foster and Roddy McDowall had not been renewed by Fox, Nolan and Robert Arthur assumed their roles of father and son in this third entry in the *My Friend Flicka* series. The Technicolor picture was lovely to look at, but this story about turning Flicka into a successful trotting horse didn't do as well as its predecessors.

Nolan went over to MGM, where he was involved with another soon-to-fade animal series: He was paired with Lassie and Jeanette MacDonald in her last film, *The Sun Comes Up* (1949). Nolan wins her by helping her recover from her grief over the tragic death of her son. He then had another Good Samaritan role, running a ranch for wayward kids in Allied Artists' *Bad Boy* (1949), taking special pains to rehabilitate Audie Murphy (who had his first lead in the title role). Nolan's image had been so changed that when he next got to play a gangster, it was in a comedy, the Bob Hope version of Damon Runyon's *The Lemon Drop Kid* (1951).

Nolan made his television debut in January 1950, in CBS' production of "The Barker" on their *Theater Hour* program. In 1951, he was asked to replace William Gargan in the *Martin Kane, Private Eye* series. His portrayal had much of the wry sense of humor of Michael Shayne.

Nolan made only two features in the next five years, a big comedown after 15 years of heavy activity. He got to play with John Wayne, the man who had recommended him for his role in *Stagecoach*, in a William Wellman film for Warners, *Island in the Sky* (1953). The plot involved rescue operations in Greenland, where Wayne and his crew have crashlanded in their plane. In Republic's *Crazylegs* (1953), he did the same service for football star Elroy Hirsh as Charles Bickford had done for Jim Thorpe and Ward Bond was about to do for Olympic star Bob Mathias; and just as in the latter case, the subject played himself.

Nolan was wise enough to know that the golden days of Hollywood were over and that an actor had to diversify. He bought an interest in a frozen food plant at a time when it was becoming popular with the public. With Fred MacMurray, he shared ownership of an apartment house (it has long been rumored that MacMurray became one of the wealthiest actors in California). No such fate awaited Nolan, though this enabled him to take a career risk: He returned to Broadway on January 10, 1954. His commitment to *Martin Kane* was over; now he fulfilled a commitment to Lloyd Nolan.

His role was that of Capt. Queeg in Herman Wouk's adaptation of a segment of his novel *The Caine Mutiny*; the play was called *The Caine Mutiny Court-Martial*. The main thrust of the play was the plight of Lt. Maryk (John Hodiak), who took command of the navy minesweeper *Caine* away from Queeg when he came to believe that Queeg was unfit for duty. There was no factual basis for this, for the U.S. Navy had no recorded instances of mutiny during World War II or at any time. But the book had made excellent reading, and (later that same year) would make an extremely entertaining film. It was exciting theater. Although mutineer Maryk is a sympathetic character, a dupe for a more devious brother officer, the scene in the play with the strongest impact is the one in which Lt. Greenwald (Henry Fonda), Maryk's counsel, cross-examines Queeg, the supposedly perfect officer. Those who saw those two actors performing this unforgettable piece of theater considered it to be a supreme lesson in the art of acting. Bit player James Garner, who had only to sit on the stage and wordlessly listen to testimony, has said as much. After two decades, this was a stage comeback worth the wait. When Humphrey Bogart appeared as Queeg in the Columbia film released that summer, he was praised on one hand and compared unfavorably to Nolan on the other. The play was successful enough to remain on Broadway for 415 performances, all through the popular film's initial run. Nolan remained with the play after Fonda left for the filming of *Mister Roberts* and Barry Sullivan assumed the role of Greenwald. The quality of the cast had a great deal to do with the play's continuing success. For his performance, Nolan received the coveted Donaldson Award and, a year later, he was awarded an Emmy when he repeated the role of Queeg on CBS TV. (Barry Sullivan, again his co-star, claimed to have voted for Nolan to win the Emmy even though he too was nominated in the same category.) Around the same time, he played another man who loved the sea, writer Jack London, on the CBS series *Climax*.

When the producers of *The Caine Mutiny Court-Martial*, Paul Gregory and Charles Laughton, put together a touring company, they had to do without the original stars. Both Fonda and Sullivan had film commitments and Hodiak, an underrated actor who had worked with Nolan in Hollywood, died suddenly in October 1955, at the age of 41. Nolan had found the experience artistically gratifying but not financially remunerative, especially in comparison to the higher quality film and TV roles now being offered. A major consideration was his son Jay. In Philadelphia, the Nolans found a school better equipped to deal with the autistic child. The school (The Institute for Achievement of the Human Potential) was obviously the best thing for Jay, but it was no easy decision; the Nolans agonized over the thought of having their son so far away from them. At the time they made the decision to keep him there, Nolan hoped he would be doing more stage work in the East. Outside of an appearance as Queeg in the London production the following year, however, he would only get one further theatrical role: In 1960, he picked a play called *One More River*, but it died upon its Broadway arrival.

Nolan returned to a somewhat different Hollywood, in which many of the big actors were now their own producers. It certainly benefited him as a character actor, since he was on good terms with practically all the top names. This may have been the real reason his next few years were so fruitful; the movie capital was not always impressed by the theatrical accolades given by the Eastern establishment.

The first star he worked with upon his return to movies in 1955 was Robert Taylor, who (unlike most of his contemporaries) was still toiling as an employee of a studio. The film was Richard Brooks' *The Last Hunt* and, just as in their previous MGM film together (*Bataan*), Taylor and Nolan were doomed men. The latter got to do a lot of uncharacteristic scenery-chewing as a one-legged old buffalo hunter. Taylor continuously sought villainous roles in the postwar era, playing against his image more than other stars of his ilk; here he played a cold-hearted character who killed man and buffalo alike with no qualms. He left the heroics this time to Stewart Granger and dies a particularly unpleasant death: With rifle in hand, he is frozen solid during a very cold night while Granger is saved by the warmth of a cave and Indian maiden Debra Paget. What made this film better than average was the parallel made between a dying breed of men and the dying species they were hunting.

Nolan next had two meaty roles in 1956 Warner Bros. releases. That studio leaned heavily on independent producers. One was Nolan's old friend Alan Ladd, whose Jaguar Productions were distributed by Warners. Ladd usually exercised his clout by filling his films with old Paramount buddies like Bendix, Donlevy, William Demarest and Frank Faylen. Nolan was handed a good old-fashioned villain's role in the adventure *Santiago*. There was nothing original about the script, set in that Cuban seaport; Italian actress Rosanna Podesta was leading a rebellion against Spain with the help of good soldier of fortune Ladd and his not-so-good counterpart Nolan. The latter had not played a colorful heavy in ages and he obviously relished the chance. He easily stole the film, though in truth there was little worth stealing. As producer, Ladd could probably have edited Nolan's part (other stars in the same position would have). But the two actors were very close friends and Ladd was just glad to have him around. Eighteen years after Ladd's untimely death in 1964, Nolan contributed a warmly moving introduction for the book *The Films of Alan Ladd*.

The next actor-producer Nolan worked with was William Holden. *Toward the Unknown* was released three months after *Santiago*, but was far superior. Old pro Mervyn LeRoy produced and directed from a good script about an Air Force officer (Holden) who was brainwashed as a POW in Korea and is now trying to rebuild his flying career. He comes into frequent conflict with his commanding general, another superb Nolan portrayal. Their clashes are realistic and dramatic, making this one of the better films about peacetime service. It may have been surprising to some that Nolan's part was almost as large as Holden's; actually, the general's scenes had had to be written down. The film had originally been conceived to star a dream team that would never be: Clark Gable and Gregory Peck. Though it was not publicized at the time, Nolan had replaced "The King" of Hollywood.

Another superstar, Tyrone Power, Nolan's *Johnny Apollo* co-star, had also formed a production company, so Nolan was next off to England for his first overseas filming, in Columbia's *Abandon Ship!* (1957). His was a small role and he and Power were the only Americans cast. It was about a luxury liner that hits a leftover World War II mine and the survivors' struggle for survival on one overcrowded life raft in the mid–Atlantic. This modern-day fact-based story takes place totally within the confines of the lifeboats. Nolan portrays a seaman dying of injuries sustained in the explosion. But Nolan's primary reason for being in England was to again portray that survivor of a different type of sea disaster, Capt. Queeg, for a short period on the London stage, which was easy to do as his footage in *Abandon Ship!* was minimal. Queeg was a role that had never failed to win him acclaim and this brief run was no exception.

Nolan's first two film roles upon return to the U.S. represent some of his best screen work. These important properties, one based on a successful play and the other on the biggest best-selling book of the day, were Twentieth Century–Fox productions. But it was a Fox that Nolan barely recognized. Darryl Zanuck had relinquished his head of production job in favor of independent movie making in Europe. He had never worked with the two directors involved and the casts of both films were made up of many new young actors he barely knew—quite a change from his recent superstar co-stars. None of this really mattered once he realized that his parts were the best any character actor could want.

Producer Buddy Adler's personal production of *A Hatful of Rain* was excellently directed by Fred Zinneman, based on the Michael Gazzo play. As a film, it was the first truly realistic study of drug addiction, concerning an average user and suppliers who are rightfully shown as common street punks. The film is about ordinary families; the addict here is Johnny Pope (Don Murray), who is protected by his brother Polo (Anthony Franciosa), who covers up for Johnny in front of the latter's pregnant wife (Eva Marie Saint) and John Pope, Sr. (Nolan). John, Jr., is the preferred son and Polo loves his father and brother enough to practice his deceit until the shattering denouement exposes all secrets. As the self-sacrificing Polo, Franciosa deservedly takes top honors; he is the only one of the four leads to have played his part on Broadway and his familiarity with the character shows. Murray's boyish quality works well as the junkie and Henry Silva is frightening as his main supplier. Saint is the only casting weakness, being too matter-of-fact about her husband's addiction and her brother-in-law's consuming passion for her.

Nolan performed with a depth of characterization never required in his previous films. He plays an intolerant man who has found minor flaws in the better of his two sons; his discovery of a major weakness possessing his favored child causes Nolan to instinctively turn on *him*, too. However, beneath the man's domineering manner, Nolan uses small gestures to reveal a caring person unable to verbalize his feelings. Other versions of the play have found Pope, Sr., portrayed as an overbearing stereotype, making the near-end confrontations not nearly as moving. Arthur Miller's plays, so often dealing with sibling rivalry for a father's affections, are generally tougher because the Miller elders are usually unworthy of any devotion. Thanks to Nolan, the audience sees something worth loving in the man. If part of his identification with a man unable to deal with a son who is ill came from his own personal tragedy, he can't be faulted for that. Isn't the utilization of some internal thing to convey feelings what acting is all about?

The veteran actor found a few more familiar faces on the set of his next film, *Peyton Place* (1957). Former co-stars Betty Field (*Blues in the Night*), Russ Tamblyn (*The Last Hunt*) and his longtime friend Leon Ames (*Lady in the Lake*) were part of the enormous cast. Yet when Grace Metalious, the authoress of the original novel, appraised the players, it was only Nolan's performance she called great. The book's success warranted the film's production, but while a box office success was expected, the surprise was that the film was the recipient of many Oscar nominations, Best Picture included. This is not a definite sign of artistic achievement, but director Mark Robson and screenwriter John Michael Hayes had worked something of a miracle. Most of the book's steamier passages were either deleted or toned down, the morals of several characters were vastly improved and the emphasis was shifted. Hayes and Robson imbued the film with a kind of wistfulness reminiscent of earlier small town stories like *The Human Comedy*, William Saroyan's lovely tale of the World War II homefront. They did this without seriously changing the face of the novel they were adapting. So even though Rodney and Betty were still making out in the back seat of his car and Selena's stepfather Lucas still rapes her, there is also innocent young Norman who goes off to war and the dying but dignified schoolteacher Miss Thornton. One might argue that it is easy to revamp such a novel into a film that the Production Code would never object to, but it doesn't seem to have been done since.

The film received several nominations for its acting, including a Best Actress nod to Lana Turner, who was playing a middle-aged mother for the first time. In the supporting category were the new young actresses Hope Lange and Diane Varsi, and Arthur Kennedy and Russ Tamblyn were in the male division. All were admittedly fine, but Nolan was even better as the kindly Doc Swain, who knew all the town's secrets but cared enough about the people to be discreet.* He gives a strong, caring performance unlike any he had given up to that time.

The character of Matthew Swain was not needed in the sequel *Return to Peyton Place* (1961), which was just as well; it was far less successful. In fact, for the next few years, Nolan's film work was limited to the small screen. It was a wise move; the film scripts that started to come in paled in comparison to his last two feature roles. Instead he worked in all of the better TV series, including *Playhouse 90* and *Wagon Train*. For the prestigious *Hallmark Hall of Fame*, he played editor Nat Miller opposite Helen Hayes in Eugene O'Neill's *Ah, Wilderness!* He also took on another TV series: In June 1959, he debuted as the star of an inexpensive syndicated show called *Special Agent*. The title tells it all; it played out its initial run on mostly local stations around the country, making its star little profit.

After completing work on the series, he made a series of features which were of the potboiler variety. In Universal's *Portrait in Black* (1960), another lavish Lana Turner vehicle, he was billed as a special guest star as Turner's dying tycoon husband whose mysterious death causes all kinds of suspicions. It was a relatively brief role that required him to be merely unpleasant, but there was one interesting fringe benefit to the film. He was reunited with two former compatriots from his Paramount quickie days: Anthony Quinn played his doctor (who was, unfortunately for Nolan, also Miss Turner's lover) and Anna May Wong played Nolan's housekeeper. This was one of those films where the cast was much better than the material.

Nolan then did another pair for Warner Bros. *Girl of the Night* (1960), filmed in New York, was basically a case history of a call girl (Anne Francis) who seeks psychiatric help from kindly New York analyst Nolan. This was one of the first films about the basically decent hooker trying to get out of her seedy profession and it wasn't that bad, but suffered a quick death mainly due to competition from MGM's flashier Elizabeth Taylor vehicle *Butterfield 8*. *Susan Slade* (1961) offered Nolan another reunion: His wife was played by Dorothy McGuire, whom he courted 16 years earlier in *A Tree Grows in Brooklyn*. Sadly, this fine actress was in the same position as Nolan, having to prop up films that starred currently popular but inexperienced young stars, in this case Connie Stevens

---

*Nolan's last role ever was that of a TV soap opera actor, a Doc Swain type in an episode of *Murder, She Wrote*.

and Troy Donahue. The incredible plot would have audiences believe that because Nolan had an engineering job in a remote part of Latin America for many years, his daughter Stevens would have grown up completely unaware of sex, which is strange since McGuire and Nolan do not act in the film like repressive parents. Stevens naturally gets pregnant by the first man she meets, who almost immediately gets killed off. When the folks find out, Nolan (who had evidently wanted to give up travelling to remote parts of the world) takes another such job. The sacrifice allows him to get out of the film when he suffers a fatal heart attack. He doesn't have to be around when McGuire tries to pass off her illegitimate grandchild as her own change-of-life baby; even a pro like him might have difficulty keeping a straight face amid such happenings.

His television work in the early '60s was reminiscent of some of his older parts. He proved he could still do the snarling gangster bit though pushing 60 in an episode of *The Untouchables*. On the western front, he played the comically troublesome father of one of the regulars on the series *The Outlaws* and reprised his Pope, Sr., in a western setting as a father who shows preference for one son over the other on *The Virginian*. He took part in an all-star episode of *The Dick Powell Theater*, as a dying millionaire who hires detective Powell to investigate potential heirs to his fortune. (Nolan had had Powell as director for the pre–Broadway tryouts for *The Caine Mutiny Court-Martial*.) Nolan got to like working in all-star episodes of series like *77 Sunset Strip* and *The Great Adventure* because they invariably provided well-written cameo roles.

He also found time for a bit of European-based filmmaking. In England, he was used to help give an American flavor to a Kenneth More comedy called *We Joined the Navy* (1962), an attempt to duplicate the success of the service comedies of the late '50s. Then he was recruited by American director Roy Rowland, who had the unenviable task of doing a Mike Hammer detective picture (1963's *The Girl Hunters*) in England with that character's creator Mickey Spillane playing the role. Nolan played a stereotyped role with little interest.

Nolan made a trip to Spain to take part in the international production *Circus World* (1964), featuring John Wayne and Rita Hayworth. Even this large-scale Paramount picture was a disappointment; production was slowed down after the original director, Frank Capra, split with producer Samuel Bronston, who replaced him with Henry Hathaway. (Hathaway had directed Nolan in *Johnny Apollo* and *The House on 92nd Street*.) But producer Bronston fancied himself a new Cecil B. DeMille, turning out a string of super-spectaculars that were not making back their massive costs. By plunging into *Circus World* before his previous epic *The Fall of the Roman Empire* was ready for release, he left himself open for failure on two fronts. Delays caused Bronston to go broke before the film was completed and the distributors salvaged what was left, for some less-than-spectacular showings. Ironically, one of the other titles the film had been known by was *The Magnificent Showman*. That title could never be applied to the film's producer, who was unable to raise money for any of his lofty projects thereafter. Nolan's role, as Wayne's longtime friend and confidante, was another one of those parts he could have played in his sleep, which was also the preferable way to view the film.

After being bogged down in Spain, Nolan returned to the U.S. in mid–1963, almost glad for a return to the relatively uncomplicated world of television. Many veteran performers now preferred appearing in an episode of a weekly series to an inflationary motion picture; the former more closely resembled the old days of filmmaking.

When Nolan wasn't in an officer's uniform, he was at the very least an employee of the government. A good example of his TV work of the period was an episode of the short-lived science fiction series *The Outer Limits*. In the episode "Soldier," he played Tom Kagan, a sympathetic government man who tries to get through to a soldier from another planet (Michael Ansara) who had been unintentionally propelled through time and landed on present-day Earth. Kagan takes the alien to live among his family to try and eliminate much of his warlike training. It seems to be working, but before there are any positive results, an enemy from the alien's world comes after him and they destroy each other. This leaves Kagan to wonder if the alien had not changed or if he had sacrificed himself to save the Kagan family. It was a thoughtful, well-made show and once again Nolan etched a believable portrait of an authority figure, never performing as though he was acting in a fantasy. This made the story seem a lot more probable than it normally would.

With the arrival of the television movie era, the banality of the theatrical variety seemed to be increasing. Nolan's next three appearances on the big screen, all distributed by Warners, were all mediocre versions of material that had originally seemed promising. It might have been a lot better if the Norman Lear production *Never Too Late* (1965) had had Nolan playing the middle-aged father-to-be instead of the nothing part of the town mayor. The lead in both the stage and screen versions of this mildly humorous story was unfortunately in the incompetent hands of Paul Ford. Nolan then went into *An American Dream* (1966), which was no credit to the acclaimed Norman Mailer novel from which it was adapted. He had a few good scenes as the tough old political boss with a bitch of a daughter (Eleanor Parker) who is killed in a fight with her radio commentator husband (Stuart Whitman). The book's controversial elements were watered down by a weak script. *The Double Man* (1967) was an attempt to cash in on the spy movie craze and had a quality director, Franklin Schaffner. But the plot was based on the old chestnut of having the same actor play both hero and villain. Since no two men could accidentally look like Yul Brynner, who was the star, the modern approach was that the bad guy had had plastic surgery to make him resemble the master spy who was the hero. Nolan was kept on the sidelines as a CIA chief confined to a wheelchair. As in other '60s pictures like *Portrait in Black* and *Never Too Late*, he was afforded special guest billing, usually indicating that he had a role very unworthy of his talents. The same held true for MGM's confused Cold War epic *Ice Station Zebra* (1968), in which he had another prop role; the officer (this time an admiral) who sends the hero (this time Rock Hudson) on a mission that will constitute the film's running time.

All during this period, it was television which gave him the real creative sustenance. The pilot script for the series that ultimately became *Julia* offered him the chance to appear in a new and different type of TV series. When he said yes, he had no way of knowing that more people would come to know him as Dr. Morton Chegley than had known him throughout his long career. Considering the original conception of the role, this was quite amazing.

The first series to spotlight the modern black woman, *Julia* was either lauded or criticized. The heroine, a middle-class war widow, seemed to have a much-too-lavish wardrobe considering her modest earnings as a nurse; this was the cause of some of the complaints. Many thought that the star Diahann Carroll was too beautiful to be representative of the average black woman, but nobody had really planned that she be just that. The show was just meant to be a pleasant comedy-drama about a young mother raising a small boy by herself while holding down a job, and her relationships with the people she lived and worked with. Most people accepted it as just that, which was what helped the show last three seasons.

Julia, produced at Nolan's old stomping grounds of Twentieth Century–Fox, was the brainchild of veteran comedy writer Hal Kanter. Nolan signed on the dotted line simply because Dr. Chegley was not one of the usual TV stick figures. As the head of a busy medical unit in an aerospace industry, he played a man of both intelligence and wit, not a springboard for the jibes of other characters. The script of the pilot established this immediately. In applying for the job of nurse over the phone, Julia expects to be treated with the usual stereotyping and accidentally uses the word "colored" to describe herself. Dr. Chegley asks what color she was and, upon being told, asks her if she always was a Negro or had just become one because it was fashionable. With a few brief lines of dialogue, it is established that Chegley is no bigot. The only trouble Julia will have with him is those anyone would have with a boss who was something of a curmudgeon.

Nolan's billing on the show was unusual: He had adverbs like "frequently" or "occasionally" tacked onto the word "starring." Since much of the show was to be about the home life of Julia and her son, no one expected Dr. Chegley to be in every episode, least of all the actor who played him. But this portrayal was so deft that fans of the show also became fans of the doctor. They enjoyed his run-ins with veteran nurse Yarby, played by Lurene Tuttle.* More and more, Dr. Chegley began meddling in Julia's private life, but Nolan always made viewers feel comfortable with his character. By the third season, the padding of his part would become obvious, when his previously unseen wife suddenly surfaced in the form of Mary Wickes. Even when the character fell into typical TV situation comedy traps (such as having Nolan play his own sprightly father), he handled this episode so well that one's credibility was not greatly strained. The show's hit status dictated that *TV Guide* do an article on him; it appeared in the Christmas 1969 issue. He was referred to in it as "the unforgettable man from many forgettable movies."

The article was a fine tribute to Nolan. Diahann Carroll probably summed up what many of his co-stars felt throughout the years when she told the interviewer, "Aside from the fact that Lloyd is a nice human being to spend time with on a film set, I love the sense of professionalism he contributes to the atmosphere. All of us consider ourselves lucky to have him around." And around he was, even though his original contract had required him to only work 44 days

---

Ironically, Nolan and Tuttle made their last appearance in the same show, a 1985 episode of Murder, She Wrote.

a year. As soon as his first hiatus from the series came along in early 1969, he went into Ross Hunter's expensive Universal production *Airport* (1970) and wound up in the biggest box office hit of his career. As a veteran customs official who is equally adept at ferreting out old lady stowaways and mad bombers, he still stands out in the star-laden cast. Its release at the beginning of a new decade gave him the rare honor of being in at least one top-grosser in every decade from the '30s into the '70s.

The *Julia* years were not totally happy ones in Nolan's life. In the early part of 1969, 25-year-old Jay Nolan choked to death on a piece of food. Besides the grief, there was some guilt—the feeling that they had not done enough. Nolan had avoided mentioning Jay's affliction over the years to interviewers. In the *TV Guide* article, published months after Jay's death, it was only mentioned that his son, aged 25, had died.

The Nolans were no different from most parents with afflicted children: They felt that other people would not understand, so they kept quiet. After his son's death, Nolan realized that as long as the general public was allowed to remain ignorant about autism, it would be more difficult finding ways of treating it. Since there were some methods of treatment possible, funds had to be raised. So when the newly formed National Society for Autistic Children began making headway in the early '70s, the ideal honorary chairman was Nolan, a parent who had suffered a great loss and now was willing to discuss it in public.

The last *Julia* episode aired in May 1971 and Nolan then began giving much of his time to his new post. Through the first half of this decade, he shunned most of the TV and movie roles offered him, feeling that his energies should be used towards a worthier cause. In the days when his career was being handled by the mammoth agency MCA, he was constantly forced to take jobs he didn't really want, such as his two series prior to *Julia*. His agent since 1959, Bill Robinson, understood his client's need and got Nolan less taxing roles, when he wanted any. Ten years after their relationship began, no contract had yet been signed. Robinson himself said, "That's unheard of." But when Nolan began approaching 70, there seemed little need for him to have an agent at all.

TV commercials are for the most part tiresome; that includes the so-called "public service" announcements, usually brief pitches for various charities. But in the late '60s, this changed, due to three moving and courageous spot announcements. The first featured actor William Talman, former movie heavy and courtroom adversary to

TV's *Perry Mason* obviously ravaged from his bout with lung cancer, doing an anti-smoking ad surrounded by the family he said he was about to lose. This commercial aired before and after Talman's death in 1968. Dana Andrews was not dying, but his spot concerning drunken driving was equally courageous. Here was a one-time star who was still a working actor, admitting to the world that he was an alcoholic, just for the purpose of telling his fellow man not to drive while intoxicated.

Nolan's announcement consisted of a brief discussion of Jay's affliction. Even if the listener had been unaware that the actor was talking about his own son, there was something in his tone of voice that said this was more than just another performance, that his words had great meaning for him.

The message was slowly getting to the public and Nolan sought to speed up the processing by going on television talk shows. But the bigger ones were not interested, preferring their actor guests to discuss their latest film or golf tournament and leaving diseases to an occasional doctor squeezed into the show's last few minutes. In 1974, Irv Kupcinet, the Chicago newspaper columnist, allowed Nolan ample time to discuss autism on his syndicated talk show. But he did not get a prime time network audience until October of 1978. On the NBC series *Quincy*, Nolan guested as a psychiatrist trying to educate parents about the differences between retardation and autism, assisted by the star of the show, Jack Klugman as a coroner always involving himself in noble causes outside his own field. But this episode ("A Test for Living") did not become as farfetched as the usual series entries, and the performances of Nolan and a fine young actor named David Hollander, as an autistic seven-year-old, made their points. Thereafter, autism was "in" on the networks, with several TV movies which concentrated on the problem through the eyes of the parents. The floodgates had been opened.

Nolan's *Peyton Place* director Mark Robson offered him the small role of a doctor in the disaster film *Earthquake* (1974). His old friend from the *Caine Mutiny* days, Barry Sullivan, was also in the cast, and both gave performances far superior to some of the higher billed cast members. He also worked in such Universal-produced teleseries as *McCloud* and *McMillan and Wife*.

Well into his seventies, Nolan picked up a working pace that belied his years. In 1972, he played an aging small town deputy who becomes the victim of a bizarre ritual-like murder in *Isn't It Shocking?*; young police chief Alan Alda has a moving moment when he learns of Nolan's death. Two years later, he was on the wrong side of the law for the first time in years, abducting a fellow gangster's daughter because she is said to have the power to make miracles in *They Kidnapped Anne Benedict*. His work in *Airport* and *Earthquake* may have led to his being cast in two small-screen disaster films in the 1976-77 season, *Fire* and *Flight to Holocaust*. Nolan looked forward to working with pal Fred MacMurray in *Fire*, but MacMurray had to bow out due to ill health and was replaced by Ernest Borgnine. Nolan teamed with Pat O'Brien, plus some other veterans, in a Disney two-parter about two old men who used to be barnstorming pilots. In the ABC 1979 telefilm *Valentine*, Nolan has only one scene but he effortlessly snatches the story and the film away from the stars, Mary Martin and Jack Albertson. As Albertson's spiteful brother, he is more interested in dredging up past animosities than listening to the news that his brother has found romance late in life with Martin.

Nolan took time out from acting to appear at a testimonial dinner for Rita Hayworth in 1977. Around that time he was seen on the movie screen in two feature films. Sharing no scenes with star Broderick Crawford, Nolan played the U.S. Attorney General who appoints young J. Edgar Hoover (James Wainwright) in an unsubtle film aptly titled *The Private Files of J. Edgar Hoover*. Ida Lupino and Ralph Meeker starred in *My Boys Are Good Boys* (1977), in which Nolan was once more the responsible law enforcement officer who finds that Lupino engineered the robbery of husband Meeker's armored car.

Early in 1978, Nolan appeared in an NBC comedy special, working with the likes of Milton Berle and Martha Raye in some funny sketches. He seized the role of an archaeologist in an episode of Universal's *Hardy Boys* series, primarily because he and Mrs. Nolan had become interested in that science on their frequent trips to the Middle East. He portrayed a mine owner on *The Waltons* and this may have been due to the fact that Ellen Corby, the actress who suffered a stroke while playing Granny, was an old friend of the Nolans. And as the decade changed, he followed in the path of Henry Fonda, Laurence Olivier and other estimable performers who had succumbed to the lure of advertisers' dollars; Nolan hawked denture cream. He did the spot superbly, never giving the impression that what he was doing was demeaning.

He began an unprecedented seventh decade as an actor with an appearance in a two-part episode of *Archie Bunker's Place*, looking about the same as he had for the past 25 years. In January 1981, the series that had evolved from the immensely popular *All in the Family* was in its second season—a season that had begun on an unpleasant note (the off-camera death of Edith Bunker, one of TV's most beloved and decent people). That left Archie (Carroll O'Connor) alone with his wife's young niece Stephanie (Danielle Brisebois). The girl's wealthy grandmother (Celeste Holm) turned up and, in just two half-hour episodes, the writers had to convince Judge McGuire (Nolan) and the audience that Archie was a more fit guardian for the child than her maternal grandparent.

The outcome might have shattered the series' justly deserved reputation for credibility had not the acting been so professional. The participants made you believe. From the first moment Nolan enters the courtroom, the role seemed no less important to him than any roles dating back over half a century of performing. His attitude towards Archie is predictable for any longtime viewers and it is only in the second part of the episode that we see the judge's compassionate side.

In January 1981, Mel Efird Nolan passed away rather suddenly. Nolan didn't work for a year after this tragedy* and next appeared as a cantankerous oldster in the pilot for *Adam's House*, a projected Karen Valentine series about a social worker. Besides being funny, he is also touching as he opposes the demolition of his apartment building, describing his apartment's meaning to him and his late wife. Those who saw Nolan break into tears knew this was more than just acting. Once again, the actor was identifying with his role.

Having proved his durability, Nolan began to ease off after his eightieth birthday. He played himself in an amusingly nostalgic episode of NBC's *Remington Steele*; he then played a Catholic priest who was the childhood mentor of Mickey Rooney in a syndicated Christmas special. These were to be his last roles. He died of lung cancer on September 27, 1985, still residing to the end in the Brentwood house.

His obituaries called him a tough guy, but in his 50 years on film he rarely used a weapon to project that quality. Playing the elderly lawbreakers bucking an unfair bureaucracy were really logical extensions of earlier roles. Young or old, always present was the Lloyd Nolan style, marked by an ability to make audiences believe all that he said.

He even managed to prove himself after death. While some obits

---

Around the same time his career resumed, he married Virginia Florey, the widow of his one-time director Robert Florey, who died in 1979.

were calling *Earthquake* his last film, a new Nolan film appeared: Woody Allen's *Hannah and Her Sisters* (1985), in which he and Maureen O'Sullivan played the show business parents of the title characters. There were glowing posthumous reviews. Vincent Canby in *The New York Times* Sunday Section said that Nolan and O'Sullivan "bring to it the kind of emotional reserves that are acquired only after years of experience." For one last time, Nolan stood out among a fine ensemble.

The Films of Lloyd Nolan

1. *Stolen Harmony.* Par 1935. Alfred Werker. George Raft, Ben Bernie, Grace Bradley, Goodee Montgomery, Leslie Fenton, William Cagney, Iris Adrian, Ralf Harolde, Charles Arnt, Jane Wyman (unbilled). A travelling orchestra runs afoul of gangster LN.

2. *G-Men.* WB 1935. William Keighley. James Cagney, Ann Dvorak, Margaret Lindsay, Robert Armstrong, Barton MacLane, William Harrigan, Harold Huber, Regis Toomey, Noel Madison, Ed Pawley, Russell Hopton, Addison Richards. LN is one of fledgling FBI agent Cagney's superiors.

3. *Atlantic Adventure.* Col 1935. D. Ross Lederman. Nancy Carroll, Harry Langdon, Arthur Hohl, E. E. Clive, John Wray, Dwight Frye, Robert Middlemass. LN investigates a murder on an ocean liner and passes with flying colors in this, his first leading role.

4. *She Couldn't Take It.* Col 1935. Tay Garnett, George Raft, Joan Bennett, Walter Connolly, Billie Burke, Alan Mowbray, Wallace Ford, Donald Meek, Franklin Pangborn, James Blakely, William Tannen, Bess Flowers. LN interferes with Raft's attempts to honor the wishes of a millionaire and aid his helpless family by taking heiress Bennett's kidnapping hoax seriously.

5. *One Way Ticket.* Col 1935. Herbert Biberman. Peggy Conklin, Walter Connolly, Edith Fellows, Nana Bryant, Thurston Hall. Convict LN reforms enough to win the warden's daughter in this comedy.

6. *Lady of Secrets.* Col 1936. Marion Gering. Ruth Chatterton, Lionel Atwill, Otto Kruger, Marian Marsh, Robert Allen, Elisabeth Risdom. Domineering Atwill splits up daughter Chatterton and doomed doughboy LN, the father of her unborn child.

7. *You May Be Next.* Col 1936. Albert Rogell. Ann Sothern, Douglass Dumbrille, John Arledge, Thurston Hall, Nana Bryant, Berton Churchill, Robert Middlemass, Gene Morgan, George McKay. LN gets involved with Sothern and some zany happenings at a radio station.

8. *Devil's Squadron.* Col 1936. Erle C. Kenton. Richard Dix, Karen Morley, Shirley Ross, Henry Mollison, Gene Morgan, Gordon Jones. Dix and LN are a pair of daredevil test pilots.

9. *Counterfeit.* Col 1936. Erle C. Kenton. Chester Morris, Margot Grahame, Marian Marsh, Claude Gillingwater, Pierre Watkin, Marc Lawrence. Undercover agent Morris infiltrates LN's gang.

10. *Big Brown Eyes.* Par 1936. Raoul Walsh. Joan Bennett, Cary Grant, Walter Pidgeon, Alan Baxter, Isabel Jewell, Marjorie Gateson, Douglas Fowley, Henry Brandon. Public enemy LN spoils the film's lighthearted mood by inadvertently firing bullets into an occupied baby carriage.

11. *The Texas Rangers.* Par 1936. King Vidor. Fred MacMurray, Jack Oakie, Jean Parker, Edward Ellis, Bennie Bartlett, Jed Prouty, George "Gabby" Hayes, Elena Martinez, Frank Shannon. By accident, badmen MacMurray and Oakie become rangers, leaving behind partner LN to continue alone in a life of crime.

12. *15 Maiden Lane.* 20th 1936. Allan Dwan. Claire Trevor, Cesar Romero, Lester Matthews, Douglas Fowley, Ralf Harolde, Robert McWade, Russell Hicks. LN is on the right side of the law, as a police detective on the trail of jewel thieves.

13. *Interns Can't Take Money.* Par 1937. Alfred Santell. Barbara Stanwyck, Joel McCrea, Stanley Ridges, Lee Bowman, Barry Macollum, Irving Bacon, Pierre Watkin, Fay Holden, Gaylord (Steve) Pendleton, Charles Lane, Terry Ray (Ellen Drew). McCrea as the first Dr. Kildare is repaid for a favor by mobster LN.

14. *King of Gamblers.* Par 1937. Robert Florey. Claire Trevor, Akim Tamiroff, Larry "Buster" Crabbe, Helen Burgess, Porter Hall, Evelyn Brent, Harvey Stephens, Colin Tapley, Purnell Pratt, Cecil Cunningham, Nick Lukats, Fay Holden, Paul Fix. Reporter LN sets a trap for Tamiroff, playing title character.

15. *Exclusive.* Par 1937. Alexander Hall. Fred MacMurray, Frances Farmer, Charles Ruggles, Ralph Morgan, Bennie Bartlett, Edward H. Robins, Fay Holden, Horace MacMahon, Harlan Briggs, Willard Robertson, Gaylord (Steve) Pendleton. LN takes over a respectable newspaper and turns it into a scandal sheet.

16. *Ebb Tide.* Par 1937. James Hogan. Oscar Homolka, Frances Farmer, Ray Milland, Barry Fitzgerald, Lina Basquette, David Torrance, Charles Judels. A suave but fanatical LN rules an island hideaway as his personal kingdom.

17. *Wells Fargo.* Par 1937. Frank Lloyd. Joel McCrea, Frances Dee, Bob Burns, Ralph Morgan, Henry O'Neill, Mary Nash, John Mack Brown, Porter Hall, Clarence Kolb, Robert Cummings, Stanley Fields, Granville Bates, Frank Conroy, Harry Davenport, Peggy Stewart. Badman LN is a longtime thorn in the side of pioneering Wells Fargo man McCrea.

18. *Every Day's a Holiday.* Par 1937. Edward Sutherland. Mae West, Edmund Lowe, Charles Butterworth, Charles Winninger, Louis Armstrong, Walter Catlett, Herman Bing, Chester Conklin, Roger Imhof. Con woman West easily brings down LN (playing a grafting New York politician of the 1890s).

19. *Dangerous to Know.* Par 1938. Robert Florey. Anna May Wong, Akim Tamiroff, Gail Patrick, Harvey Stephens, Anthony Quinn, Roscoe Karns, Porter Hall, Hedda Hopper, Hugh Sothern, Pierre Watkin, Barlowe Borland. LN waits to get the goods on racket boss Tamiroff.

20. *Tip-off Girls.* Par 1938. Louis King. Mary Carlisle, J. Carrol Naish,

Larry "Buster" Crabbe, Anthony Quinn, Roscoe Karns, Harvey Stephens, Benny Baker, Evelyn Brent, Irving Bacon, Gertrude Short, Archie Twitchell, Pierre Watkin, Barlowe Borland. LN is again on the right side of the law.

21. **Hunted Men.** Par 1938. Louis King. Mary Carlisle, Lynne Overman, J. Carrol Naish, Anthony Quinn, Larry "Buster" Crabbe, Dorothy Peterson, Regis Toomey, Johnny Downs. Killer LN finds refuge in a suburban home in this precursor of *The Desperate Hours*.

22. **Prison Farm.** Par 1938. Louis King. Shirley Ross, John Howard, J. Carrol Naish, Porter Hall, Esther Dale, Marjorie Main, Anna Q. Nilsson, Mae Busch, May Boley, John Hart, Diane Wood, William Holden (unbilled). LN causes innocent girlfriend Ross to be sent to a woman's prison adjoining the facility he's been confined to.

23. **King of Alcatraz.** Par 1938. Robert Florey. Gail Patrick, J. Carrol Naish, Robert Preston, Harry Carey, Anthony Quinn, Porter Hall, Dorothy Howe, Richard Denning, Gustav von Seyffertitz, Tom Tyler, Konstantin Shayne, Emory Parnell, Stanley Morner (Dennis Morgan). Ship's officer LN thwarts the plans of gangster-passenger Naish.

24. **St. Louis Blues.** Par 1939. Raoul Walsh. Dorothy Lamour, Tito Guizar, Jessie Ralph, William Frawley, Jerome Cowan, Mary Parker, Cliff Nazarro, Joseph Crehan, Florence Dudley, Virginia Howell. Riverboat captain LN offers runaway entertainer Lamour refuge from the celebrity spotlight.

25. **Ambush.** Par 1939. Kurt Neumann. Gladys Swarthout, William Henry, Ernest Truex, Broderick Crawford, William Frawley, Antonio Moreno, Richard Denning, Polly Moran, Wade Boteler, Raymond Hatton, Ethel Clayton. Trucker LN innocently becomes involved with a gang of hijackers.

26. **Undercover Doctor.** Par 1939. Louis King. J. Carrol Naish, Heather Angel, Broderick Crawford, Janice Logan, Robert Wilcox, Richard Carle. Agent LN tries to get the goods on a physician (Naish) linked with the mob.

27. **The Magnificent Fraud.** Par 1939. Robert Florey. Akim Tamiroff, Mary Boland, Patricia Morison, George Zucco, Steffi Duna, Ralph Forbes, Frank Reicher, Ernest Cossart, Abner Biberman, Robert Warwick, Barbara Pepper, Robert Middlemass. LN is an American adventurer trapped in a Latin American country where actor Tamiroff is impersonating the country's dictator.

28. **The Man Who Wouldn't Talk.** 20th 1940. David Burton. Jean Rogers, Onslow Stevens, Robert Kellard, Eric Blore, Mae Marsh, Joan Valerie, Paul Stanton, Mantan Moreland, Harlan Briggs, Douglas Wood. LN is a murder suspect who refuses to defend himself.

29. **The House Across the Bay.** UA 1940. Archie Mayo. George Raft, Joan Bennett, Walter Pidgeon, Gladys George, June Knight, Joseph Sawyer, Peggy Shannon, Cy Kendall, Mack Grey, Etta McDaniel, James Craig. LN betrays his racket boss Raft out of love for Bennett, who later rejects both underworld types for true love with Pidgeon.

30. **Johnny Apollo.** 20th 1940. Henry Hathaway. Tyrone Power, Dorothy Lamour, Edward Arnold, Charley Grapewin, Lionel Atwill, Marc Lawrence, Fuzzy Knight, Jonathan Hale, Russell Hicks, Charles Trowbridge, Charles Lane. LN is gangster Mickey Dwyer.

31. **Gangs of Chicago.** Republic 1940. Arthur Lubin. Barton MacLane, Lola Lane, Ray Middleton, Astrid Allwyn, Horace MacMahon, Leona Roberts, Charles Halton, Addison Richards, Dwight Frye, Alan Ladd. Low-budget variation on *The Roaring Twenties* with LN as a mouthpiece working for racketeer MacLane.

32. **The Man I Married.** 20th 1940. Irving Pichel. Joan Bennett, Francis Lederer, Anna Sten, Otto Kruger, Maria Ouspenskaya, Johnny Russell, Ludwig Stossel, Lionel Royce, Frederick Vogeding. LN aids American friend Bennett and her young son escape from German husband Lederer, who has been influenced by the Nazis.

33. **Pier 13.** 20th 1940. Eugene Forde. Lynn Bari, Joan Valerie, Douglas Fowley, Chick Chandler, Oscar O'Shea, Louis Jean Heydt. Waterfront cop LN solves a case with the help of waitress girlfriend Bari.

34. **The Golden Fleecing.** MGM 1940. Leslie Fenton. Lew Ayres, Rita Johnson, Leon Errol, Virginia Grey, Nat Pendleton, William Demarest, Marc Lawrence, Thurston Hall. LN is a gangster who buys an insurance policy and then menaces Ayres, who sold it to him.

35. **Behind the News.** Rep 1940. Joseph Santley. Doris Davenport, Frank Albertson, Robert Armstrong, Paul Harvey, Charles Halton, Veda Ann Borg, Eddie Conrad, Dick Elliott. Over-the-hill newspaperman LN gets a new lease on life as mentor to a cub reporter.

36. **Charter Pilot.** 20th 1940. Eugene Forde. Lynn Bari, Arleen Whelan, George Montgomery, Hobart Cavanaugh, Henry Victor, Etta McDaniel. Marriage does not keep pilot LN away from dangerous jobs.

37. **Michael Shayne, Private Detective.** 20th 1940. Eugene Forde. Marjorie Weaver, Walter Abel, Joan Valerie, Douglass Dumbrille, Elizabeth Patterson, Donald MacBride, Clarence Kolb. The first in a series of features with LN as the wisecracking private detective.

38. **Sleepers West.** 20th 1941. Eugene Forde. Lynn Bari, Mary Beth Hughes, Edward Brophy, Don Douglas, Louis Jean Heydt, Ben Carter, Oscar O'Shea, George Chandler, Ferike Boros. Michael Shayne (LN) must see to it that a female witness makes it to court, and takes her on an arduous train trip.

39. **Mr. Dynamite.** Univ 1941. John Rawlins. Irene Hervey, J. Carrol Naish, Robert Armstrong, Ann Gillis, Elisabeth Risdon, Shemp Howard, Cliff Nazarro. A baseball pitcher (LN) becomes involved with a gang of spies while visiting New York.

40. **Dressed to Kill.** 20th 1941. Eugene Forde, Mary Beth Hughes, Sheila Ryan, Henry Daniell, William Demarest, Ben Carter, Virginia Brissac, Emmet Vogan, Minerva Urecal, William Benedict, Milton Parsons. LN gets precariously close to marriage while solving a murder in this Michael Shayne entry.

41. **Buy Me That Town.** Par 1941. Eugene Forde. Albert Dekker, Constance Moore, Sheldon Leonard, Vera Vague, Warren Hymer, Edward Brophy, Horace MacMahon, Russell Hicks, Rod Cameron. LN is a gangster who acquires a small town as a hideout for his underworld cohorts.

42. **Blues in the Night.** WB 1941. Anatole Litvak. Priscilla Lane, Richard Whorf, Betty Field, Jack Carson, Billy Halop, Elia Kazan, Wallace

Ford, Peter Whitney, George Lloyd, Joyce Compton, Matt McHugh, Charles Wilson. Gangster LN takes a fancy to a group of struggling musicians. The plot is similar to that of his first film, although with more pretension.

43. *Steel Against the Sky.* WB 1941. A. Edward Sutherland. Alexis Smith, Craig Stevens, Gene Lockhart, Edward Ellis, Walter Catlett, Julie Bishop, Edward Brophy, Howard Da Silva. Steel worker LN vies with his younger brother for the same woman.

44. *Blue, White and Perfect.* 20th 1941. Herbert Leeds. Mary Beth Hughes, Helene Reynolds, George Reeves, Curt Bois, Steven Geray, Mae Marsh, Ann Doran. LN's Shayne clears up a mystery involving industrial diamonds.

45. *It Happened in Flatbush.* 20th 1942. Ray McCarey. Carole Landis, Sara Allgood, Jane Darwell, Robert Armstrong, William Frawley, George Holmes, Joseph Allen, Jr., Scotty Beckett, Roger Imhof, Matt McHugh, James Burke, Leroy Mason. Former ballplayer LN is recruited as the manager of the slumping Brooklyn Dodgers.

46. *The Man Who Wouldn't Die.* 20th 1942. Herbert I. Leeds. Marjorie Weaver, Henry Wilcoxon, Richard Derr, Helene Reynolds, Paul Harvey, Olin Howlin, Billy Bevan, Jeff Corey. LN investigates a murder in a well-to-do family's house.

47. *Apache Trail.* MGM 1942. Richard Thorpe. Donna Reed, William Lundigan, Ann Ayars, Gloria Holden, Chill Wills, Connie Gilchrist, Grant Withers, Miles Mander, Ray Teal. Western bandit LN waylays assorted stagecoach passengers and is opposed by his decent brother Lundigan.

48. *Just Off Broadway.* 20th 1942. Herbert I. Leeds. Marjorie Weaver, Phil Silvers, Janis Carter, Richard Derr, Joan Valerie, Don Costello, Chester Clute. Detective Shayne (LN) solves a crime while serving on a jury.

49. *Manila Calling.* 20th 1942. Herbert I. Leeds. Carole Landis, Cornel Wilde, James Gleason, Ralph Byrd, Elisha Cook, Jr., Louis Jean Heydt, Martin Kosleck, Ted North, Charles Tannen. One of the fastest of the post–Pearl Harbor productions (and therefore the seams show). LN is a heroic team leader in the path of invading Japanese.

50. *Time to Kill.* 20th 1942. Herbert I. Leeds. Heather Angel, Richard Lane, Doris Merrick, Ralph Byrd, Ethel Griffies, Sheila Bromley, Morris Ankrum, James Seay, William Pawley. Final Shayne film is like the same year's *The Falcon Takes Over*, a disguised version of a Raymond Chandler-Phillip Marlowe mystery novel.

51. *Guadalcanal Diary.* 20th 1943. Lewis Seiler. Preston Foster, William Bendix, Anthony Quinn, Richard Conte, Richard Jaeckel, Roy Roberts, Lionel Stander, John Archer, Reed Hadley, Eddie Acuff, Miles Mander. LN is Gunner in the second of an unofficial LN trilogy of Pacific heroism films, this one enhanced by its faithfulness to Richard Tregaskis' book.

52. *Bataan.* MGM 1943. Tay Garnett. Robert Taylor, Thomas Mitchell, George Murphy, Robert Walker, Desi Arnaz, Lee Bowman, Tom Dugan, Roque Espiritu, Barry Nelson, Kenneth Spencer, Phillip Terry. The best of its kind of film. LN is at the top of his game, as the shadowy Corp. Barney Todd.

53. ***A Tree Grows in Brooklyn.*** 20th 1945. Elia Kazan. Dorothy McGuire, Joan Blondell, James Dunn, Peggy Ann Garner, Ted Donaldson, James Gleason, Ruth Nelson, John Alexander, B. S. Pully, Ferike Boros, Charles Halton. LN is the kindly police office McShane.

54. ***Circumstantial Evidence.*** 20th 1945. John Larkin. Michael O'Shea, Trudy Marshall, Billy Cummings, Ruth Ford, Scotty Beckett, Reed Hadley, Roy Roberts. LN leads a group of kids in a race against time to prove his friend, sentenced to die in the electric chair, is not guilty of murder.

55. ***Captain Eddie.*** 20th 1945. Lloyd Bacon. Fred MacMurray, Lynn Bari, Charles Bickford, Richard Conte, Thomas Mitchell, Spring Byington, James Gleason, Darryl Hickman, Mary Phillips, Stanley Ridges, John Dehner. LN shares a lifeboat with Eddie Rickenbacker (MacMurray) during World War II and has to listen to a boring account of the latter's life, which constitutes the bulk of the film.

56. ***The House on 92nd Street.*** 20th 1945. Henry Hathaway. William Eythe, Signe Hasso, Gene Lockhart, Leo G. Carroll, Lydia St. Clair, Harry Bellaver, William Post, Jr., Bruno Wick, Charles Wagenheim, Reed Hadley (narrator). The first of the popular Louis de Rochemont docudramas and the first of LN's two appearances as FBI Inspector Briggs, a more believable Fed than the kind he played a few years earlier at Paramount.

57. ***Somewhere in the Night.*** 20th 1946. Joseph Mankiewicz. John Hodiak, Nancy Guild, Richard Conte, Josephine Hutchinson, Fritz Kortner, Sheldon Leonard, Lou Nova, Jeff Corey, Margo Wood, John Russell, Charles Arnt, Whit Bissell. Amnesiac hero Hodiak is helped by cop LN in this noirish thriller.

58. ***Two Smart People.*** MGM 1946. Jules Dassin. Lucille Ball, John Hodiak, Hugo Haas, Leonore Ulric, Elisha Cook, Jr., Lloyd Corrigan, Clarence Muse, Bess Flowers. LN is a cop tracking Hodiak, a swindler pulling an art fraud, who goes on the lam south of the border.

59. ***Lady in the Lake.*** MGM 1946. Robert Montgomery. Montgomery, Audrey Totter, Tom Tully, Leon Ames, Jayne Meadows, Morris Ankrum, Lila Leeds, Richard Simmons, Kathleen Lockhart. Montgomery is detective Phillip Marlowe, whose attempt to become an author involves him with characters like shady cop LN.

60. ***Wild Harvest.*** Par 1947. Tay Garnett. Alan Ladd, Dorothy Lamour, Robert Preston, Allen Jenkins, Richard Erdman, Anthony Caruso, Will Wright, Griff Barnett. LN is part of a group of traveling crop dusters.

61. ***Green Grass of Wyoming.*** 20th 1948. Louis King. Charles Coburn, Peggy Cummins, Robert Arthur, Burl Ives, Geraldine Wall, Will Wright, Herbert Heywood, Richard Garrick. LN inherits the role of Rob McLaughlin from Preston Foster, who was in the two earlier *My Friend Flicka* flicks. He is an understanding father whose family horse is turned into a trotter.

62. ***The Street with No Name.*** 20th 1948. William Keighley. Mark Stevens, Richard Widmark, Barbara Lawrence, Ed Begley, Donald Buka, John McIntire, Robert Karnes, Joseph Pevney, Howard Smith, Walter Greaza, Randy Stuart. LN is again Inspector Briggs, the character he played

in *The House on 92nd Street* for the director who first put him in the FBI (in 1935's *G-Men*).

63. *The Sun Comes Up.* MGM 1948. Richard Thorpe. Jeanette MacDonald, Claude Jarman, Jr., Lassie, Lewis Stone, Percy Kilbride, Margaret Hamilton, Nicholas Joy, Dwayne Hickman, Ida Moore, Hope Landin, Esther Somers. LN wins over grieving MacDonald, a singer who lost her son, with the help of a boy and Lassie.

64. *Bad Boy.* Allied Artists 1949. Kurt Neumann. Audie Murphy, Jane Wyatt, James Gleason, Martha Vickers, Stanley Clements, James Lydon, Selena Royle, Rhys Williams, Tommy Cook, Dickie Moore, William Lester, Walter Sande. LN is a rancher trying to redeem troubled boys.

65. *Easy Living.* RKO 1949. Jacques Tourneur. Victor Mature, Lucille Ball, Lizabeth Scott, Sonny Tufts, Paul Stewart, Jeff Donnell, Jack Paar, Richard Erdman, Art Baker, Jim Backus, Don Beddoe. LN is a sympathetic football coach who doesn't know that star player Mature has a bad heart.

66. *The Lemon Drop Kid.* Par 1951. Sidney Lanfield. Bob Hope, Marilyn Maxwell, Jane Darwell, Fred Clark, Andrea King, Jay C. Flippen, William Frawley, Harry Bellaver, Sid Melton, Ida Moore, Ben Welden, Harry Shannon, Francis Pierlot. Hope owes money to underworld type LN in this Damon Runyon comedy.

67. *Island in the Sky.* WB 1953. William Wellman. John Wayne, Walter Abel, James Arness, Harry Carey, Jr., Andy Devine, Paul Fix, Darryl Hickman, Allyn Joslyn, Sean McClory, Bob Steele, Carl "Alfalfa" Switzer, Regis Toomey, Touch (Michael) Connors, Wally Cassell. LN spearheads a rescue operation in Greenland to save Wayne's downed crew during World War II.

68. *Crazylegs.* Rep 1953. Francis Lyon. Elroy Hirsh, Joan Vohs, James Millican, James Brown, Louise Lorimer, Bob Waterfield, Bob Kelley, John Brown, Joseph Crehan. LN does double duty as narrator and coach-mentor to football player Hirsch, who began his brief movie career playing himself here.

69. *The Last Hunt.* MGM 1955. Richard Brooks. Robert Taylor, Stewart Granger, Debra Paget, Russ Tamblyn, Constance Ford, Ainslie Pryor, Joe DeSantis, Ralph Moody, Fred Graham. LN is a grizzled old hunter on an ill-fated quest for buffalo.

70. *Santiago.* WB 1956. Gordon Douglas. Alan Ladd, Rosanna Podesta, Chill Wills, Paul Fix, L. Q. Jones, Frank DeKova, George J. Lewis, Royal Dano, Clegg Hoyt, Ernest Sarracino. Old associates Ladd and LN are competing gunrunners in Cuba.

71. *Toward the Unknown.* WB 1956. Mervyn Leroy. William Holden, Virginia Leith, Charles McGraw, Paul Fix, Karen Steele, James Garner, Murray Hamilton, L. Q. Jones, Ralph Moody, Maura Murphy. Former POW Holden returns to active duty in the Air Force, where he has frequent clashes with commanding officer LN.

72. *Abandon Ship!* Col 1957. Richard Sale. Tyrone Power, Mai Zetterling, Stephen Boyd, Moira Lister, James Hayter, Gordon Jackson, Marie Lohr, Moultrie Kelsall, Noel Willman, Laurence Naismith, Clive Morton, Victor Maddern, David Langton. LN appears briefly as a dying seaman on

a lifeboat who tells surviving ranking officer Power what to do to save as many shipwreck victims as possible.

73. *A Hatful of Rain.* 20th 1957. Fred Zinneman. Anthony Franciosa, Don Murray, Eva Marie Saint, Henry Silva, Gerald O'Laughlin, William Hickey, Art Fleming. LN is at the peak of his talents as narrow-minded John Pope, Sr., father of two grown sons.

74. *Peyton Place.* 20th 1957. Mark Robson. Lana Turner, Arthur Kennedy, Hope Lange, Terry Moore, Lee Phillips, Russ Tamblyn, Diane Varsi, Leon Ames, Barry Coe, Mildred Dunnock, Betty Field, Lorne Greene, David Nelson, Erin O'Brien Moore, Tami Conner, Robert H. Harris. LN manages to match the standard of his preceding role with his exceptionally sensitive portrayal of small town doctor Matthew Swain in this classic.

75. *Portrait in Black.* Univ 1960. Michael Gordon. Lana Turner, Anthony Quinn, Richard Basehart, Sandra Dee, John Saxon, Ray Walston, Virginia Grey, Anna May Wong, Dennis Kohler, Paul Birch, John Wengraf, Robert P. Lieb, Richard Morris. Shipping tycoon LN is done in by his younger wife Turner and his doctor Quinn.

76. *Girl of the Night.* WB 1960. Joseph Cates. Anne Francis, John Kerr, Kay Medford, James Broderick, Arthur Storch, Eileen Fulton, Julius Monk, Lauren Gilbert. LN is a New York psychiatrist who tries to help call girl Francis.

77. *Susan Slade.* WB 1961. Delmer Daves. Connie Stevens, Troy Donahue, Dorothy McGuire, Brian Aherne, Grant Williams, Natalie Schafer, Kent Smith, Bert Convy, Guy Wilkerson. LN is a father whose career choices have a definite effect on his withdrawn daughter Stevens ... and vice versa.

78. *We Joined the Navy.* Dial 1962. Wendy Toye. Kenneth More, Joan O'Brien, Mischa Auer, Jeremy Lloyd, Dinsdale Landen, Derek Fowlds, Dirk Bogarde. Typical lend-lease comedy has British hero More a lot looser than American naval officer LN.

79. *The Girl Hunters.* Colorama 1963. Roy Rowland. Mickey Spillane, Shirley Eaton, Hy Gardner, Scott Peters, Charles Farrell, Bill Nagy, James Dyrenforth, Guy Kingsley Poynter. Putrid Mike Hammer film with LN as an American federal agent.

80. *Circus World.* Par 1964. Henry Hathaway. John Wayne, Rita Hayworth, Claudia Cardinale, Richard Conte, John Smith, Katherine Kath, Kay Walsh, Miles Malleson, Henry Dantes. LN is the business associate and friend of circus owner Wayne.

81. *Never Too Late.* WB 1965. Bud Yorkin. Paul Ford, Maureen O'Sullivan, Connie Stevens, Jim Hutton, Jane Wyatt, Henry Jones, Timothy Hutton. Small town mayor LN is amused that a contemporary of his, local businessman Ford, is about to become a father.

82. *An American Dream.* WB 1966. Robert Gist. Stuart Whitman, Eleanor Parker, Janet Leigh, Barry Sullivan, Murray Hamilton, J. D. Cannon, Susan Denberg, Les Crane, Warren Stevens, Joe De Santis, Stacy Harris, Harold Gould, Paul Mantee. Second-rate Norman Mailer, with LN as an old-fashioned political boss and father of Parker.

83. ***The Double Man.*** WB 1967. Franklin Schaffner. Yul Brynner, Britt Ekland, Clive Revill, Anton Diffring, Moira Lister, Julia Arnall, George Mikell, Ronald Radd, David Bauer, Kenneth J. Warren. LN is a crippled CIA chief.

84. ***Ice Station Zebra.*** MGM 1968. John Sturges. Rock Hudson, Ernest Borgnine, Jim Brown, Patrick McGoohan, Tony Bill, Gerald O'Loughlin, Murray Rose, Ted Hartley, Ron Masak. Admiral LN gives submarine commander Hudson his assignment in this Cold War drama.

85. ***Airport.*** Univ 1970. George Seaton. Burt Lancaster, Dean Martin, Jacqueline Bisset, Helen Hayes, Van Heflin, George Kennedy, Barry Nelson, Jean Seberg, Maureen Stapleton, Dana Wynter, Gary Collins, John Findlater, Larry Gates, Barbara Hale, Jessie Royce Landis, Peter Turgeon, Merry Anders, Whit Bissell, Virginia Grey. LN is a sharp-eyed airport customs official whose suspicions are aroused by mad bomber Heflin.

86. ***Earthquake.*** Univ 1974. Mark Robson. Charlton Heston, Ava Gardner, Genevieve Bujold, Marjoe Gortner, Lorne Greene, George Kennedy, Victoria Principal, Richard Roundtree, Barry Sullivan, Lloyd Gough, Scott Hylands, Monica Lewis, Kip Niven, John Randolph, Walter Matthau (unbilled). Doctor LN tends to the victims of an L.A. earthquake.

87. ***The Private Files of J. Edgar Hoover.*** AIP 1976. Larry Cohen. Broderick Crawford, James Wainwright, Ronee Blakely, Dan Dailey, Howard Da Silva, Andrew Duggan, Jose Ferrer, June Havoc, Celeste Holm, William Jordan, John Marley, Michael Parks, Raymond St. Jacques, Rip Torn. LN is the U.S. Attorney General who first establishes the FBI with a young Hoover in charge.

88. ***My Boys Are Good Boys.*** Media Arts 1977. Bethel Buckalew. Ida Lupino, Ralph Meeker, David Doyle, Sean Thomas Roche, Ron Lake. LN is a law officer who nabs the kids who hijacked Meeker's armored car.

89. ***Prince Jack.*** New World 1984. Bert Lovitt. Dana Andrews, Jim Backus, Theodore Bikel, Robert Guillaume, Robert Hogan, James F. Kelly, Kenneth Mars, Cameron Mitchell, William Windom. Somewhat tasteless spoof of the Kennedy family with LN standing in for the family patriarch.

90. ***Hannah and Her Sisters.*** Orion 1985. Woody Allen. Allen, Michael Caine, Mia Farrow, Barbara Hershey, Maureen O'Sullivan, Tony Roberts, Daniel Stern, Max Von Sydow, Dianne Wiest, Carrie Fisher, Julie Kavner, Bobby Short, Sam Waterston. In his final film role, LN is the cantankerous show business father of Farrow, Hershey and Wiest and husband of O'Sullivan.

LN's extensive TV work also produced a number of full-length films which adds to his above total. The 1968 theatrical release *Sergeant Ryker* was a compilation of two hour-long segments of *Kraft Mystery Theatre.* Features made exclusively for TV were *Wings of Fire* (1967), *Isn't It Shocking?* (1973), *The Abduction of Saint Anne* (1975), *Fire* (1977), *Flight to Holocaust* (1977) and *It Came Upon a Midnight Clear* (1984).

Bibliography

Anger, Kenneth. *Hollywood Babylon II*. New York: E. P. Dutton, 1984.
Bickford, Charles. *Bulls, Balls, Bicycles and Actors*. New York: Paul S. Eriksson, 1965.
Bosworth, Patricia. *Montgomery Clift*. New York & London: Harcourt, Brace and Jovanovich, 1978.
Bronner, Edwin J. *Encyclopedia of American Theatre*. New York: A. S. Barnes, 1980.
Catalog of Copyright Entries, cumulative series. *Motion Pictures*, 1912–1939, 1940–1949, 1950–1959, 1960–1969 volumes. Washington, D.C.: Copyright Office, Library of Congress, 1951, 1953, 1963, 1973.
Everson, William K. *The Bad Guys*. New York: Cadillac Publishing, 1964.
Films in Review. New York: National Board of Review. Monthly.
Gargan, William. *Why Me?* Garden City, New York: Doubleday, 1969.
Garnett, Tay, and Fredda Dudley Balling. *Light Up Your Torches and Pull Up Your Tights*. New Rochelle, New York: Arlington House, 1973.
Halliwell, Leslie. *Film Guide*. New York: Scribners and Son, 1977.
_____. *The Filmgoers Companion*. New York: Hill and Wang, Scribner and Son, 1965, 1967, 1970, 1974, 1976, 1977, 1980.
Henry, Marilyn, and Ron De Sourdis. *The Films of Alan Ladd*. Secaucus, New Jersey: Citadel Press, 1981.
Houseman, John. *Front and Center*. New York: Simon and Schuster, 1979.
Kobal, John. *Rita Hayworth: The Time, The Place, The Woman*. New York: W. W. Norton, 1978.
Linet, Beverly. *Ladd: The Life, the Legend, the Legacy of Alan Ladd*. New York: Arbor House, 1979.
Logan, Joshua. *Movie Stars, Reel People and Me*. New York: Delacorte Press, 1978.
McBride, Joseph, and Michael Wilmington. *John Ford*. New York: D. A. Capo Press, 1975.
Michael, Paul. *The American Movies Reference Book: The Sound Era*. Englewood Cliffs, New Jersey: Prentice Hall, 1969.
Milland, Ray. *Wide-Eyed in Babylon*. New York: William Morrow, 1974.
Parish, James Robert, and William T. Leonard. *Hollywood Players—The Thirties*. New Rochelle, New York: Arlington House, 1976.

Parish, James Robert, and Michael Pitts. *The Great Gangster Pictures.* Metuchen, New Jersey: Scarecrow Press, 1976.
Russell, Rosalind, and Chris Chase. *Life Is a Banquet.* New York: Random House, 1977.
St. John, Adela Rogers. *The Honeycomb.* Garden City, New York: Doubleday, 1969.
Sennett, Ted. *Warner Brothers Presents.* Secaucus, New Jersey: Castle Books, 1971.
Shipman, David. *The Great Movie Stars: The International Years.* London: Angus and Robertson, 1972.
Spoto, Donald. *Stanley Kramer—Filmmaker.* New York: G. P. Putnam's, 1978.
Terrace, Vincent. *Complete Encyclopedia of Television Programs.* South Brunswick & New York: A. S. Barnes, 1976.
Thomas, Bob. *Golden Boy: The Untold Story of William Holden.* New York: St. Martin's Press, 1983.
_____. *King Cohn.* New York: G. P. Putnam's, 1967.
TV Guide. Radnor, Pennsylvania: Triangle Publications. Weekly.
Weales, Gerald. *Canned Goods as Caviar.* Chicago: University of Chicago Press, 1985.
Weiss, Ken, & Ed Goodgold. *To Be Continued...* New York: Crown, 1972.
Willis, John, ed. *Screen World.* New York: Crown. Annual.
Zinman, David. *Fifty from the Fifties.* New Rochelle: Arlington House, 1979.
Zolotow, Maurice. *Shooting Star.* New York: Simon and Schuster, 1974.

Index

Abandon Ship! 315, 316, 333
Abbott, Bud 233
Abbott, George 34
Abroad with Two Yanks 26
Accusing Finger 75
Adams, Julie 211
Adams, Neile 209
Adam's House (TV pilot) 326
Adler, Stella 299
The Admirable Crichton (play) 225
Adventures of Jane Arden 251
Adventurous Blonde 284
Against the Law 74
Agar, John 83, 279
Aggie Appelby, Maker of Men 248
Ah, Wilderness! 318
Air Mail 73, 107
Airport 323, 325, 335
Akins, Claude 150
Albertson, Frank 45
Albertson, Jack 325
Alda, Alan 324
Alexander, John 196
Alias Jesse James 100
Alibi for Murder 250
All About Eve 204
All of Me 281
All the King's Men 131–133, 154
All Through the Night 271–272, 287
Allen, Fred 202
Allen, Gracie 189, 192
Allen, Woody 327
Allyson, June 204
Aloma of the South Seas (play) 219, 233
Amazing Dr. Clitterhouse 112
Ambush 143, 304, 329
American Dream 321, 334

An American Romance 171, 184
Ames, Leon 242, 317
Anderson, Dame Judith 102
Anderson, Maxwell 34
Andersson, Bibi 145
Andrews, Dana 47, 324
Andrews, Robert D. 309
Angel in Exile 289
Angels in the Outfield 201, 214
Animal Kingdom 221–224, 247
Anna Christie 36–37, 130, 202
Anna Lucasta 131, 154
Annie Get Your Gun (play) 274
Another Face 163, 181
Ansara, Michael 320
Anthony Adverse 263
Apache Trail 331
The Apartment 213
Arden, Eve 202–203
Argyle Secrets 255
Arizona Bushwackers 179, 188, 279, 294
Arlen, Richard 22, 101
Armstrong, Robert 223, 299
Arnold, Edward 49, 230
Arthur, Jean 193, 208
Astaire, Adele 123
Astaire, Fred 123, 275
Astor, Mary 78, 263
Atlantic Adventure 300, 327
The Awful Truth 233
Aykroyd, Dan 149
Ayres, Lew 49

The Babe Ruth Story 13, 27, 49, 65
Backlash 292
Bacon, Lloyd 124, 128, 198
Bad Boy 312, 333

Bad Men of Tombstone 154
Badlands of Dakota 127, 153
Baker, Carroll 54
Baker, Diane 56
Ball, Lucille 11, 125, 301, 311
Balsam, Martin 19
The Bandit Queen 290
Bankhead, Tallulah 39
Barbary Coast 163, 181
Bari, Lynn 305, 310
Barnacle Bill 270, 286
Barnett, Mike 239
Barry, Phillip 221–222
Barrymore, Ethel 35, 48
Barrymore, John 34, 43
Barrymore, Lionel 37, 47, 80
Basehart, Richard 139, 200
Bataan 309, 331
Bates, Peggy 267
Battle of Broadway 164, 182
Battle Stations 18, 29
Beau Geste 35, 126, 152, 165–166, 182
Beau James 209, 216
Because of Him 129
Beery, Noah 165
Beery, Noah, Jr. 102, 230
Beery, Wallace 5, 14, 23, 37–38, 73
Behind Green Lights 254
Behind Prison Gates 165, 182
Behind the Mike 251
Behind the News 330
Bel Geddes, Barbara 200
Bell, James 241
A Bell for Adano 11, 27
Bellamy, Ralph 74, 230, 233–234, 239
The Bells of St. Mary's 238, 247, 254
Ben-Hur 246
Bendix, Lorraine 7, 16
Bendix, Stephanie 9, 21
Bendix, Theresa (Stefanotti) 6, 21
Bendix, William 5–30, 49, 93, 101, 206, 233, 308 311, 315
Bengal Tiger 264, 283
Bennett, Constance 129
Bennett, Joan 48, 201, 301, 305
Benny, Jack 189, 192
Berkeley Square 226
Berle, Milton 325
Bernie, Ben 307
The Best Man (play) 242–243
Between Heaven and Hell 142, 156
Bewitched (TV series) 279

Biberman, Herbert 230
Bickford, Beatrice (Loring) 33
Bickford, Charles 13, 33–69, 74, 90, 130, 136, 138, 260, 264, 269, 303
Bickford, Doris 33
Bickford, Mary Ellen 33
Bickford, Rex 33
Il Bidone 139–140; see also *The Swindle*
Big Brown Eyes 301, 328
Big Cage 41
The Big Combo 176, 187
The Big Country 54, 66
Big Executive 280
A Big Hand for a Little Lady 58, 67
Big House 38
Big House, U.S.A. 138, 156
The Big Steal 28
The Big Street 272–273, 287
Big Town Czar 268, 285
The Big Trail 72, 106
Birch, Paul 103
Bishop, Joey 23
Black Angel 129, 154
The Black Cat 127, 153
Black Fury 108, 227, 249, 262, 282
Black Tuesday 273
Blackbeard the Pirate 15, 28
Blackboard Jungle 141, 142
Blackmailer 250
Blaze of Noon 12, 27
Blondell, Gloria 16
Blondell, Joan 209, 228, 264, 310
Blondes at Work 284
Blowing Wild 89, 119
Blue Dahlia 11, 27
Blue, White and Perfect 307, 331
Blues in the Night 308, 330
Blyth, Ann 173
The Bob Mathias Story 90, 119
Bogart, Humphrey 75, 77, 78, 134, 197, 206, 207, 227, 228, 264, 265, 271, 272, 306, 308, 313
Bohnen, Roman 44, 299
Bombardier 273, 287
Bombay Clipper 253
Bonanza 102
Bond, Doris (Sellers Childs) 74, 82
Bond, John 71
Bond, Mabel 71
Bond, Mary Lou (May) 88
Bond, Ward 18, 49, 69–120, 121, 276
Boomerang 310
Borgnine, Ernest 101, 134, 146, 325

Born Reckless (1930) 72
Born Reckless (1937) 182, 284
Born to Be Wild 111
Born Yesterday 133–134, 155, 193–197, 204, 208
Borzage, Frank 261
Boteler, Wade 74
Bouchey, Willis 103
Bowman, Lee 235
Boyd, William 223
Brady, Alice 34
Brady, Scott 279
Brand, Neville 86
Branded 50–51, 66
Brando, Marlon 91
The Brat 72, 106
Breezing Home 250
Brennan, Walter 82, 100, 146, 231, 233
Brent, Evelyn 101, 303
Brent, George 124, 129, 262
The Bride Walks Out 109
The Bridge on the River Kwai 246
Bright Lights 228, 249
Bringing Up Baby 112
Brisebois, Danielle 326
Brisson, Frederick 274
British Agent 226, 249
Broadway 129, 153
Broadway Bill 50, 74, 82–83, 108
Broadway Gondolier 249
Broadway Serenade 231, 251
Broderick, Bill 144
Broderick, Helen 123, 124, 125, 128, 129, 144, 145
Brodie, Steve 86
Bronson, Charles 68, 134
Bronston, Samuel 319, 320
Brooks, Stephen 147
Brophy, Edward 128
Brown, Clarence 201, 202
Brown, Joe E. 228
Brown, Johnny Mack 258
Brute Force 48, 65
Buchinsky, Charles *see* Bronson, Charles
Buckskin (TV series) 102
Buckskin 279, 294
Bugles in the Afternoon 276, 290
Bullets or Ballots 261, 264, 283
Burke, Paul 56
Burma Convoy 45, 63
Burns, George 189, 192, 207
Butch Minds the Baby 128, 153

Butterfield 8 318
Buy Me That Town 307, 330

Cabot, Bruce 75, 143, 279
Caged 196
Cagney, James 13, 34, 85, 86, 130, 150, 261, 263, 299
Cagney, Jeanne 13
Cagney, William 78, 86, 276
The Caine Mutiny Court-Martial (play) 206, 211, 313, 319
Calcutta 12, 27
Calhern, Louis 203, 204
Calhoun, Rory 23
The Calling of Dan Matthews 266
Cannon, Dyan 144
The Canterville Ghost 235–236, 253
Cantor, Eddie 163, 219
Canyon Passage 84, 117, 173, 185
Cape Cod Follies (play) 297
Capra, Frank 50, 74, 75, 82, 278, 319
Captain Eddie 47, 64, 310, 332
Captain Scarface 276, 291
Carey, Harry 84
Carey, Harry, Jr. 84, 91
Carey, Macdonald 170, 301
Carey, Philip 91
Cargo to Capetown 133, 155
Carnovsky, Morris 299
Carradine, John 105
Carrillo, Leo 83
Carroll, Diahann 321, 322
Carroll, Nancy 23, 300
Carson, Jack 128, 212, 223
Carter, Janis 237
Casablanca 207
Case Against Mrs. Ames 109
Case of the Curious Bride 281
Case of the Lucky Legs 282
Casey Jones (play) 43
The Castilian 144, 156
The Cat and the Canary 127
Cattle Thief 110
Ceiling Zero 263, 282
Chained 74
Chandler, Raymond 11, 78
Chaney, Lon, Jr. 125, 138
Chapman, Marguerite 74
Charlie Chan 305
Charter Pilot 305, 330
Chatterton, Ruth 300
Cheers for Miss Bishop 233, 252
Chevalier, Maurice 121
Cheyenne 274, 289

Chicago (play) 35
China 9, 25
China Doll 100, 120
Christie, Agatha 211–212
Churchill, Marguerite 228
Cimarron 37
Cimarron City (TV series) 102
Circumstantial Evidence 310, 332
Circus World 320, 334
The Cisco Kid and the Lady 114
Clark, Fred 54
Clash by Night 202, 215
Clift, Montgomery 198
Clipper Ship 54, 68
Clork, Harry 229
Close Call for Ellery Queen 235, 253
Cobb, Lee J. 21, 57
The Cocoanuts 259, 280
Cohn, Harry 39, 42, 73, 90, 234, 299
Colbert, Claudette 220, 225, 260
College Coach 79, 107
Collier, Don 278
Collins, Ray 11, 272
Collins, Russell 299
"The Colter Craven Story" (TV play) 103
Comden, Betty 194
Come Live with Me 269, 286
Command Decision 49, 64, 174, 185
Confessions of a Nazi Spy 113
Conflict 110
Connecticut Yankee in King Arthur's Court 13, 27
Connolly, Walter 132
Conreid, Hans 19
Conte, Richard 51, 137, 176, 311
Convicted 133, 155
Convicts Four 143, 156
Cook, Donald 73, 235
Cooper, Gary 42, 53, 77, 298
Corbett, James J. 34, 78
Corby, Ellen 325
Corcoran, Donna 89
Corey, Wendell 206
Cortesa, Valentina 145
Cortez, Ricardo 228
Cotten, Joseph 48, 96
Counterfeit 300, 327
The Country Girl (play) 177
The Court-Martial of Billy Mitchell 53–54
Cover-Up 28
Cow Country 291
Coward, Noel 124

Cowboy 177, 187
Crabbe, Buster 303
Crack-Up 181
Cradle Song (TV play) 53
Crash Donovan 110
Crashout 18, 29
Crawford, Broderick 45, 52, 53, 121–158, 197, 208, 310, 325
Crawford, Joan 174, 221, 222
Crawford, Joan (Tabor) 144–147
Crawford, Kay (Griffith) 127, 140
Crawford, Kelly 147
Crawford, Kim 147
Crawford, Lester 122–124, 162
Crawford, Mary Alice (Mitchell) 148
Crazylegs 312, 333
Creeping Unknown (*The Quatermass Xperiment*) 176, 187
The Crime Doctor's Strangest Case 287
Crime of Dr. Hallett 230, 250
The Criminal Code 133
Crisp, Donald 89, 90, 212
Crosby, Bing 5, 13, 50, 238, 247
The Crowd Roars 230, 251
Crowther, Bosley 189, 198
A Cry in the Night 177, 187
Cry of the Werewolf 288
Crystal Ball 9, 25
Cummings, Robert 178, 203
Curse of the Fly 178, 188
Curtis, Tony 241
Curtiz, Michael 226–227, 263
Cyclone Lover (play) 35

Dailey, Dan 149
Dakota 81, 116
Dakota Incident 96, 119
D'Andrea, Tom 15, 16
Danger Island (*Mr. Moto in Danger Island*) 112
Dangerous Assigment (TV series) 171, 175
Dangerous Mission 16, 29
Dangerous to Know 303, 328
Dark Corner 11, 26
Dark Hazard 267
Darnell, Linda 47, 101
Da Silva, Howard 11, 175, 200, 308
Dassin, Jules 48, 235
Daughter of Shanghai 62
Davis, Bette 102, 279
Day, Doris 135
The Days of Wine and Roses 55, 67

Dead End 75, 111
Death of a Salesman (TV play) 57
Death on the Diamond 108
DeCamp, Rosemary 14, 18
The Decks Ran Red 142, 156
Dee, Frances 72, 89
Deep Six 18, 29
The Defense Rests 108
de Havilland, Olivia 53
Della (TV pilot aka Royal Bay) 57
del Rio, Dolores 83
Demarest, William 177, 241, 314
DeMille, Cecil B. 35, 38–40, 42, 53, 320
DeMille, William 38
Denning, Richard 238
Derek, John 136, 208
deRochemont, Louis 310
Desperate Chance for Ellery Queen 235, 253
Desperate Hours (play) 241
Destination Unknown 253
Destry Rides Again 166, 183
Detective Story 15, 28
Devil Dogs of the Air 108
The Devil's Party 230, 251
The Devil's Playground 110
The Devil's Squadron 300, 327
Devine, Andy 127, 128
The Dick Powell Theater (TV series) 55–56, 319
Dickens, Charles 267
Dickenson, Angie 100
Dinner at Eight 134, 197, 199
Dix, Richard 235, 300
Dr. Jekyll and Mr. Hyde 269, 286
Dr. Socrates 263, 282
Doctors Don't Tell 115
Dodge City 75, 112
Don Juan Quilligan 11, 26
Donahue, Troy 319
Donaldson, Ted 310
Donlevy, Brian 8, 49, 126, 127, 128, 159–188, 295, 301, 306, 314
Donlevy, Judith 171, 174
Donlevy, Lillian (Arch Lugosi) 176, 179, 180
Donlevy, Marjorie (Lane) 163
Donlevy, Yvonne (Grey) 162, 163
Donnell, Jeff 237
Don't Bet on Blondes 228,
Double Alibi 252
Double Dummy (play) 192
Double Indemnity 171

The Double Man 321, 335
Douglas, Adam 206
Douglas, Elizabeth (Farnsworth) 191
Douglas, Geraldine (Higgins) 192
Douglas, Gordon 86
Douglas, Jan (Sterling) 195–196, 199–213
Douglas, Kirk 23, 200
Douglas, Margaret 193
Douglas, Melvyn 302
Douglas, Paul 21, 189–216, 241
Douglas, Sussie (Welles) 191
Douglas, Virginia (Field) 192, 195
Down Three Dark Streets 137, 155
Downing, Joseph 261
Draegerman Courage 266, 283
Dressler, Marie 23, 37
Drums Along the Mohawk 76, 113
Drums in the Deep South 290
Drury, James 57
The Dude Goes West 289
Duel in the Sun 47–48, 54, 64
Duff, Howard 277
Duffy's Tavern 30, 188
The Dungeon (TV play) 211
Dunn, James 310
Dunne, Irene 39, 43
Durbin, Deanna 11, 128, 129
Dust Be My Destiny 75, 113
Dvorak, Ann 228, 261
Dynamite (1929) 35, 59
Dynamite (1948) 237, 255

Earthquake 325, 327, 335
East of Borneo 39, 41, 60
East of Java 41–42, 45, 61
Easy Living 333
Ebb Tide 302, 328
Eddy, Nelson 224, 231
Eden, Barbara 279
Ellery Queen 231
Ellis, Patricia 227
Elopement 51, 65
Embassy 148, 157
Emergency Call 223, 248
Enemy Agents Meet Ellery Queen 235, 253
Enemy from Space (Quatermass II) 176, 187
Errand Boy 178, 187
Erwin, Stuart 14, 167
Escape by Night 111
Escape from Red Rock 187
Eternally Yours 126, 152

Ever Since Eve 283
Everson, William K. 267, 308
Every Day's a Holiday 302, 328
Everybody Does It 190, 198, 214
Ewell, Tom 203
Exclusive 301, 328
Executive Suite 204, 212, 215
Eythe, William 238

The Falcon Takes Over 78, 115, 307
Fallen Angel 47, 64
A Family Affair (TV series) 179
Farmer, Frances 301
Farmer Takes a Wife 41, 61
The Farmer's Daughter 48, 64
Farrell, Charles 223
Farrell, Glenda 228, 265
Farrow, Mia 145
Fastest Gun Alive 141, 156
The Fat Spy 178, 188
Faylen, Frank 177, 314
Fellini, Federico 139–140, 211
Ferrer, Jose 85, 149
Ferrer, Mel 85
Field, Betty 45, 308, 317
Fields, W.C. 260, 276
15 Maiden Lane 301, 328
Fifty Million Frenchmen 124
Fighting Coast Guard 186
Fighting Shadows 109
Fire (TV movie) 335
Fitzgerald, Barry 77, 87, 302
Five Golden Dragons 178, 188
Fix, Paul 79, 303
The Flame 129, 154
Fleming, Victor 75, 79, 88
Flesh 73, 107
Flight to Holocaust (TV movie) 325, 335
Florey, Robert 309, 325
Fly Away, Baby 283
Flying Cadets 253
Flying Hostess 250
Flynn, Errol 76, 78, 228
Foch, Nina 204
Follow That Woman 237, 254
Follow the Leader 220, 247
Fonda, Henry 20, 41, 58, 76, 82–83, 91–92, 266, 272, 313, 314
Fontanne, Lynn 35, 123, 297
For Love or Money 23, 29
Foran, Dick 59
Ford, Glenn 133, 136, 141, 177, 269, 279
Ford, John 69, 70, 71–73, 75–78, 82–84, 86–87, 90–92, 94–97, 103–105, 295
Ford, Paul 58, 321
Ford, Wallace 124
Forest, Mark 143
Forever Female 204, 215
Fort Apache 83, 117
Fortunella 211, 216
Foster, Preston 225, 312
Four Faces West 49, 64
Four Frightened People 225, 248
Fourteen Hours 200, 214, 241
Foxfire 276, 292
Franciosa, Anthony 316
Francis, Anne 318
Francis, Kay 231
Frederick, Hal 147
Frisco Kid 263, 282
The Front Page 231, 297
Frontier Gun 293
Frontier Marshal (1934) 107
Frontier Marshal (1939) 82, 113
Fugitive 83, 117
Fury and the Woman 230, 250
Fury 74

Gable, Clark 49, 74, 75, 174, 196, 223–224, 315
Gabor, Zsa Zsa 202
Gambling House 28
Gamera, the Invincible 175, 188
The Gamma People 207, 216
Gangs of Chicago 269, 285, 330
Gangs of New York 43, 62
Garbo, Greta 36, 37
Garfield, John 75
Gargan, Ed 219, 225, 237, 245
Gargan, Leslie 229, 244
Gargan, Mary (Kenny) 219, 244
Gargan, William 144, 163, 200, 217–255, 312
Gargan, William, Jr. 229
Garner, James 313
Garner, Peggy Ann 310
Garnett, Tay 126, 308, 311
Gaynor, Jock 278
Geisha Boy 178, 276, 293
General Seeger (play) 22
Gentle Annie 273, 288
A Gentle Gangster 272, 287
Gentleman Jim 78, 115
Gentlewomen (play) 298, 299
Giftos, Elaine 147
Girl from God's Country 63

Girl from Mexico 113
The Girl Hunters 319, 334
A Girl in Every Port 15, 28
Girl in Room 13 178, 187
Girl in the Woods 293
Girl of the Night 318, 334
Girl on the Run 277, 293
Girl Overboard 266
The Glass Key 8, 25, 170, 184
Gleason, Jackie 21, 128
Gleason, James 7, 14, 310
The Glenn Miller Story 276, 291–292
G-Men 260, 262, 281, 299, 327
Go Into Your Dance 263, 281
Goddard, Paulette 131, 236
Godfrey, Arthur 210
God's Country and the Woman 266, 283
Gods of Lightning (play) 35, 258
The Go-Getter 110
Going Places 112
Gold Diggers of 1937 124
Gold Is Where You Find It 284
Goldbeck, Willis 14
The Golden Fleecing 330
Goldwyn, Samuel 50, 163
Goliath and the Dragon 143, 156
Gomez, Thomas 211
Gone with the Wind 75, 113
Goodwin, Bill 192
Gordon, Michael 23
Gordon, Ruth 193
The Gorgeous Hussey 74, 106
Gorshin, Frank 141
Goulding, Edmund 198
Grable, Betty 198
Grand Old Girl 108
Grant, Cary 46, 145, 300
The Grapes of Wrath 76, 113
The Great Adventure (TV series) 319
The Great Man's Lady 168, 183
The Great McGinty 168, 180, 183
The Great Missouri Raid 118
Green, Adolph 194
Green Fire 204, 215
Green Grass of Wyoming 312, 332
Greene, Clarence 137, 141, 146
Gregory, Paul 206, 314
Grey, Virginia 275, 276
Guadalcanal Diary 9, 25, 308, 331
Guard That Girl 109
The Guardsman 297
Guest, Val 176
Guilty as Hell 43

Guilty of Treason 50, 65
Gulager, Clu 57
Gunfighters of Abilene 293
A Guy Named Joe 79–80, 116
Guy Who Came Back 201, 214
Gypsy Colt 89, 119

The Hairy Ape 10, 25
The Half Breed 290
Hall, Alexander 198, 301
Hall, Jon 237
Hall, Porter 43
Halliday, Brett 306
The Halliday Brand 96, 120
Hallmark Hall of Fame (TV series) 53, 318
Hamilton, Ray 144
Hamlet 121
Hannah and Her Sisters 327, 335
Harding, Ann 22, 222
Harlequin 158
Harrigan's Kid 235, 253
Harris, Phil 198
A Hatful of Rain 316–317, 334
Hathaway, Henry 166, 260, 310, 319
Havoc, June 149
Hawaii Calls 111
Hawks, Howard 100
Hayden, Sterling 90
Hayes, Helen 318
Hayes, John Michael 317
Hayes, Joseph 224
Hayward, Susan 10–11, 165, 173
Hayworth, Rita 133, 136, 319, 325
The Heart's a Lonely Hotel (TV play) 209
Heaven Only Knows (aka *Montana Mike*) 174, 185
Heaven with a Barbed Wire Fence 114
Hecht, Ben 231, 297, 321
The Heffernan Family (TV play) 208
Hell and High Water 281
Hellgate 87, 118
Hello Frisco, Hello 79, 116
Hello, Trouble 106
Hell's Bloody Devils (aka *The Fakers*) 157
Hell's Crossroads 293
Hell's Outpost 291
Hepburn, Katharine 8, 221
Here Comes the Groom 108
Herlie, Eileen 11
Heroes for Sale 73, 107
Hervey, Irene 308
Heston, Charlton 205, 277

Heyes, Herbert 86
High and Dry (aka *The Maggie*) 203, 215
The High and the Mighty 205
High Hat (play) 297
High Noon 100
High Sierra 271, 286
High Speed 106
Highway Patrol (TV series) 140–141, 144
Highways by Night 287
His Woman 220, 247, 280
Hit the Road 271, 286
Hitchcock, Alfred 10
Hitler—Dead or Alive 79, 116
Hobart, Rose 39
Hodiak, John 11, 311, 313, 314
Holden, William 133, 134, 150, 168, 169, 170, 197, 204, 315
A Hole in the Head 209
Hollander, David 324
Holliday, Judy 133–134, 194–197, 207–208
Holloway, Sterling 16
Holm, Celeste 196, 198, 325
Holt, Jack 73
Home in Indiana 116
Hometowners (play) 263
Homolka, Oscar 302
Hondo 89, 119
Hoover, J. Edgar 149, 310
Hope, Bob 9, 100, 208, 312
Hopper, DeWolf 144
Horton, Robert 20, 98, 105
Hostile Guns 179, 188
Hot Cargo 255
The Hound of the Baskervilles 306
A House Is Not a Home 145, 157
House of Fear 251
House on 92nd Street 310, 312, 320, 333
The Housekeeper's Daughter 231–233, 251
Houseman, John 93
How Did a Nice Girl Like You Get Into This Business? 157
How to Stuff a Wild Bikini 178, 188
Howard, Leslie 221–222, 226–229
Hubbard, John 231–232
Hudson, Rock 321
Hughes, Mary Beth 306
The Human Comedy 317
The Hunchback of Notre Dame 227
Hunted Men 303, 329

Hunter, Jeffrey 94, 200
Hunter, Ross 323
Husing, Ted 189
Huston, Walter 133, 172
Hutchinson, Josephine 241
Hutton, Betty 205
Hymer, Warren 79, 88

I Can't Give You Anything but Love, Baby 152
I Found Stella Parish 263, 282
I Love Lucy (TV show) 211
I Wake Up Screaming 233, 252
I Wanted Wings 168, 183
I Was a Convict 268, 285
Ice Station Zebra 321, 335
Idol on Parade 20, 29
I'll Be Yours 11, 27
Impact 174, 186
In Old Chicago 164, 182
In This Our Life 77, 106, 271
The Informer 87
Interns Can't Take Money 302, 328
Ireland, John 131, 132, 133
Island in the Sky 312, 333
Island of Lost Men 152
Isle of Destiny 252
Isn't It Shocking? (TV movie) 324, 335
It Came Upon a Midnight Clear (TV movie) 335
It Happened One Night 74, 107
It Happens Every Spring 198, 214
It's a Wonderful Life 82, 117
Ives, Burl 54

Jacobi, Lou 11
Jaffee, Sam 57
Jagger, Dean 57, 168
Jaguar 276, 292
Jail Busters 276, 292
Jailbreak 283
Jesse James 164, 182
Jewell, Isabel 230
Jim Thorpe—All American 51, 66
Joan of Arc 84, 117
Joe MacBeth 207, 215
John Loves Mary 195
Johnny Apollo 306, 319, 329
Johnny Belinda 49, 65
Johnny Dollar (radio series) 238
Johnny Guitar 89–90, 118
Johnny Holliday 14, 28
Johnny Nobody 22, 29

Johnson, Ben 86
Johnson, Lyndon B. 245
Johnson, Rita 125
Johnson, Van 202, 240
The Jolson Story 132
Jones, Jennifer 46–48
Juke Box Rhythm 178, 187
Julia (TV series) 321–323
Julie 143
Jungle Flight 289
Just Off Broadway 307, 331
Justice of the Range 108

Kanin, Garson 193, 232
Kansas Pacific 291
Kansas Raiders 175, 186
Kanter, Hal 322
Karloff, Boris 263
Karns, Roscoe 240
Kaufman, George S. 124, 125
Kazan, Elia 308, 310
Keith, Robert 200
Kelly, Gene 7
Kelly, Grace 205
Kelly, Paul 5, 177, 218, 222, 230, 268, 274
Kennedy, Arthur 241, 318
Kennedy, John F. 104, 243, 245
The Kid Comes Back 284
The Kid from Brooklyn 163
The Kid from Kokomo 112
Kid Rodelo 157
Kiley, Richard 134
Kill the Umpire 14, 28
Killer McCoy 173, 185
King of Alcatraz 304, 329
King of Gamblers 301, 303, 328
A Kiss in the Dark 131, 154
Kiss of Death 174, 185, 312
Kiss Tomorrow Goodbye 85–86, 118, 275, 290
Kit Carson 114
Kitt, Eartha 131
Krasna, Norman 202
Kulky, Henry 16
Kupcinet, Irv 324
Kyria Katina (TV play) 18

La Strada 139, 211
Ladd, Alan 8, 9, 18, 50–51, 170, 172, 177, 295, 311, 315
Ladd, Sue Carol 18
Lady for a Day 278
Lady in the Lake 311, 332

Lady of Secrets 300, 327
Lake, Veronica 8, 170
Lamour, Dorothy 304, 311
Landis, Carole 308
Lane, Sara 58
Langdon, Harry 300
Lange, Hope 317
Larceny, Inc. 128, 153
The Last Hunt 314, 333
The Last Man 60
The Last of the Commanches 134, 155
Last of the Desperados 292
The Last Posse 52, 66, 136, 155
The Last Roundup 281
Laughton, Charles 40, 171, 232–233, 236, 314
Laurie, Piper 53, 55
Law of the Lawless 23, 29, 279, 294
Law West of Tombstone 111
Leather Saint 207, 216
Lederer, Francis 305
Lee, Belinda 143
Legion of Terror 110
Lemmon, Jack 55, 91, 177, 213
The Lemon Drop Kid 312, 333
A Letter to Three Wives 196–197, 198, 202, 214
Levin, Ira 22
Lewis, Jerry 178, 276
Liar's Moon 158
Life of Riley 11–12, 14, 16–19, 27
Lifeboat 10, 11, 26
Lindfors, Viveca 18, 130
Lindsay, Howard 134
The Lineup 248
Little Big Shot 109
Little Caeser 261
Little Miss Marker 40, 61, 272
Little Old New York 114
A Little Romance 122, 129, 158
Littlest Rebel 41, 42, 67
Litvak, Anatole 308
Lloyd, Frank 301
Lloyd, Harold 75, 229
Lombard, Carole 40, 232
Lone Cowboy 281
Lone Star 134, 155
The Long Gray Line 90–91, 119
The Long Voyage Home 77, 114
The Lost Patrol 309
Love That Brute 199, 214
Lovejoy, Frank 212
Lowe, Edmund 40, 132, 164

348 Index

Lowery, Robert 206
Loy, Myrna 223–224
Lucky Boy 219, 220, 247
The Lucky Stiff 174, 186
Lugosi, Bela 127, 176
Lugosi, Bela, Jr. 176
Lunt, Alfred 297
Lupino, Ida 325
Lyles, A.C. 22–24, 179, 279
Lynn, Diana 173

MacLaine, Shirley 213
MacLane, Barton 22, 44, 71, 74, 78, 85–86, 104, 179, 227, 229, 256–294, 301
MacLane, Charlotte (Wynters) 259, 266, 269, 276
MacLane, Martha (Stewart) 258, 265
MacLane, Martha (daughter) 258, 265
MacLane, William 258, 265
MacMurray, Fred 47, 89, 160, 170, 213, 301, 311, 313, 325
Made for Each Other 112
The Magnificent Ambersons 272
The Magnificent Fraud 304, 329
Mailer, Norman 321
Main, Marjorie 101, 273
Malden, Karl 241
The Maltese Falcon 77, 85, 115, 271, 276, 286, 306
A Man Alone 96, 109
A Man Betrayed (aka *Wheel of Fortune*) 77, 115
Man Hunt 228, 249
The Man I Married 305, 330
Man of Courage 272, 287
Man of Iron 262–263, 282
Man of the Forest 280
The Man Who Lived Twice 74, 110
The Man Who Wouldn't Die 307, 331
The Man Who Wouldn't Talk 305, 329
Manilla Calling 308, 331
Manpower 115, 272, 276, 286
A Man's Game 108
March, Fredric 178, 204, 241
Marry the Girl 111
Marshall, E.G. 19
Martin, Mary 208, 325
Martin Kane, Private Eye 238–240, 242, 313
Marvin, Lee 53, 138
Marx, Groucho 16
Marx, Harpo 21

The Marx Brothers 258, 276
Masina, Giuletta 139, 211
Massey, Raymond 50
Mature, Victor 13, 16, 233
The Mayor of 44th Street 253
McCambridge, Mercedes 90, 132
McCoy, Tim 73
McCrea, Joel 49, 65, 165, 169, 302
McGrath, Frank 87, 98–99
McGuire, Dorothy 310, 318, 319
McIntire, John 58, 105
McLaglen, Victor 40, 43, 83, 87, 133, 164, 230
McMahon, Ed 189
McNally, Stephen 49
McNamee, Graham 189
Meeker, Ralph 325
Melody Ranch 286
Men in Her Life 60
Men of Texas 153
Men of the Night 108
Men Without Souls 269, 285
Menjou, Adolphe 40, 52, 229, 231
Meredith, Burgess 44, 58
Merman, Ethel 220
Michael Shayne, Private Detective 306, 329
Midnight Manhunt 254
Miles, Vera 94, 241
Milestone, Lewis 125
The Milky Way 162, 163, 229, 231, 249
Milland, Ray 126, 130, 148, 151, 165–166, 168, 172, 302
Miller, Dr. Alden 243–244
Miracle in the Rain 240, 255
Miracle of Morgan's Creek 171, 184
Miss Annie Rooney 233, 253
Mister Cory 54, 67
Mr. Dynamite 308, 330
Mr. Lucky 46, 64
Mr. Moto on Danger Island 112
Mr. Moto's Gamble 75, 111
Mister Roberts 91–92, 120
Mitchell, Cameron 143, 241
Mitchell, Thomas 33, 77
Mitchum, Robert 13, 15, 53, 138
The Mob 134, 155
Monroe, Marilyn 202
Monsieur Beaucaire 162, 181
Montez, Maria 128, 169
Montgomery, Robert 82, 311
The Moonlighter 89, 119
Moorehead, Agnes 49, 200 272

Index

Morgan, Dennis 298
Morris, Chester 38, 45, 300, 306
Morris, Wayne 168
The Mortal Storm 76, 114
The Most Precious Thing in Life 108
Mostel, Zero 199
Mother's Boy 162, 181
Muni, Paul 226, 263, 305
Murder in the Fleet 109
Murder in the Music Hall 254
Murphy, Audie 174, 342
Murphy, George 300
Murray, Don 316
Muss 'Em Up 109
Mutiny at Fort Sharp 157
Mutiny in the Big House 44, 63, 269, 285
My Boys Are Good Boys 325, 335
My Darling Clementine 82, 117
Mysterious Intruder 288

Nabonga 273, 287
Nader, George 235
Nagel, Conrad 36
Naish, J. Carroll 165, 227, 303, 304
The Naked Gun 292
Naked in the Sun 277, 293
National Society for Autistic Children 323
Natwick, Mildred 77
Navy Born 249
Negulesco, Jean 49
Never So Few 177, 187
Never Too Late 321, 334
Never Wave at a WAC 203, 215
New York Confidential 137, 141, 156
Newlen, Anthony 20
Newton, Robert 16
Nicol, Alex 51
Night Club Scandal 43, 62
Night Editor 237–238, 254
Night Flight 233–224, 248
Night Key 110
Night People 136–137, 155
Night Unto Night 132, 154
Nightmare 170–171, 184
Niven, David 126, 131, 146
Nixon, Richard 149
No Other Woman 39, 60
No Place for a Lady 235, 253
Nolan, Jay 307, 311, 314, 323, 324
Nolan, Lloyd 148, 177, 240, 261, 269, 295–335
Nolan, Mel (Efird) 297, 298, 307, 322, 326

Nolan, Melinda (daughter) 307
Noose for a Gunman 293
North to the Klondike 153
Not as a Stranger 53, 66, 138, 155
A Notorious Gentleman 41, 60

Oakie, Jack 301
O'Brien, Edmond 177, 209
O'Brien, George 71, 83
O'Brien, Pat 124, 129, 169, 230, 267, 273, 325
O'Connor, Carroll 326
Of Human Bondage 226
Of Human Hearts 111
Of Mice and Men 41, 63, 124, 125
O'Keefe, Dennis 171, 232
Olivier, Laurence 121
On Dangerous Ground 93, 118
One Hour to Live 63
One More Tomorrow 223
O'Neill, Eugene 16, 21, 36, 77, 318
Only the Valiant 86, 118
Operation Pacific 86, 118
The Oscar 146, 157
O'Sullivan, Maureen 327
Our Hearts Were Growing Up 173, 184
Our Hearts Were Young and Gay 173
Our Leading Citizen 63
The Outlaws (TV series) 277, 319
Outside Looking In (play) 35
Over the Wall 111
Overland Trail (TV series) 20–21
Overman, Lynne 303

Pagan Lady 60
Page, Geraldine 93
Page Miss Glory 263, 282
Paget, Debra 314
Palmer, Betsy 91
Panama Flo 39, 60
Panic in the Streets 199–200, 214
The Paramount Pretties (book) 230
Pardon Our Nerve 112
Paris Bound (play) 221–222
Parish, James Robert 79, 230
Park Avenue Logger 110
Parker, Eleanor 321
Passion Flower 38, 60
Patrick Jackson, Gail 278
Payne, John 97
Payton, Barbara 85, 86
Peck, Gregory 48, 54, 85, 137
Penitentiary 75, 111

Perry Mason (TV series) 277, 324
Personal Secretary 251
Peters, Jean 198, 199
The Petrified Forest 226–227, 241, 264
Peyton Place 317, 324, 334
The Phony American 22, 29
Pickens, Slim 278
Pidgeon, Walter 21, 49, 174, 204, 300, 305
Pier 13, 330
Pillars of the Sky 96, 120
Pit Stop 180, 188
The Plainsman 42–43, 62
Pocketful of Miracles 278, 293
Podesta, Rossana 315
Point of No Return (play) 91
Police Car 17, 107
Poor Rich 107
Portrait in Black 318, 321, 334
Portrait of a Sinner (aka *The Rough and the Smooth*) 20, 29
Powell, Dick 55–56, 319
Powell, William 91–92, 224
Power, Tyrone 90, 163, 164, 168, 196, 306, 315
Presley, Elvis 20
Preston, Robert 8, 165, 166, 170, 304, 311
Price, Vincent 16
Pride of the Marines 42, 61, 74, 110
The Prince and the Pauper 266, 267, 283
Prince Jack 335
The Prince of Players 52, 66
Prison Break 276, 284
Prison Farm 304, 329
The Private Files of J. Edgar Hoover 149, 158, 325, 335
Professor Beware 112
Public Enemy 261
Purcell, Dick 261

Qualen, John 77, 105, 262
Queen of the Yukon 64
The Quiet Man 87–88, 119
Quine, Don 58
Quinn, Anthony 89, 139, 196, 303, 318

Race Street 13, 27
Rackety Rax 73, 107
Raft, George 13, 159, 170, 178, 268, 271, 299, 300, 305
Raging Tide 66

Rails Into Laramie 291
Rain 222–223
Rally 'Round the Flag Boys 212
Ralston, Vera 129
Ransom Money 158
The Rawhide Years 241, 255
Raye, Martha 23, 325
Reagan, Ronald 124, 131
The Real Glory 126, 152
Reap the Wild Wind 45, 64
Red Harvest (novel) 159
Red Light 275, 289
Red Tomahawk 156
Red Wagon 40, 61
Reformatory 111
Relentless 275, 289
The Remarkable Andrew 169, 184
Remick, Lee 55
Rendezvous (play) (1935) 259
Rendezvous (1935) 259, 260
Rendezvous 24 (1946) 254
Reported Missing 250
Requiem for a Nun 225
Return to Peyton Place 318
Reunion in Vienna (play)
Ride the Man Down 186
Riders of Death Valley 45, 67–68
Riding High 50, 65
Rio Bravo 101
Ritter, Thelma 23
The River's End 38, 60
Roar, China! 220
The Roaring Twenties 132
Robards, Jason, Jr. 58
Robertson, Cliff 55
Robertson, Dale 279
Robinson, Bill 323
Robinson, Edward G. 1, 78, 128, 130, 163, 172, 264
Rogue's Gallery 179, 188
Roman, Ruth 89, 207
Romance of the Redwoods 63
Romero, Cesar 144, 199, 301
Rookie Fireman 290
Rooney, Mickey 173, 326
Rose of the Ranchero 42, 61
Roseanna McCoy 50, 65
Ross, Shirley 304
The Rounders 294
Rowland, Roy 319
Royal Ban (TV pilot) 56–57
Ruggles, Charles 14
The Runaround 129, 153–154
Russell, Jane 15, 179

Russell, Rosalind 203, 259, 260, 274
Ryans, Robert 49, 53, 85, 202

Sadie Thompson 222
Sailor's Lady 76, 114
St. John, Howard 134
Salute 72, 106
San Quentin (1937) 267, 284
San Quentin (1946) 273, 289
Sanctuary 224
Sanders, Lugene 16
Santa Fe Trail 76, 114
Santa Fe Uprising 288
Santiago 315
Sawyer, Joseph 7, 261
Scandal for Sale 39
Scandal Sheet 134, 155
Scared Stiff 288
Scott, Randolph 165, 167, 270–271
The Sea Bat 37, 59
Sea of Lost Ships 276, 291
Sealed Lips 252
Sealed Verdict 130, 154
The Searchers 94–96, 120
Secret Command 288
The Secret Seven 285
Sentimental Journey 11, 26
Sergeant York 77, 115
Serling, Rod 19, 213
Seven Sinners 126, 152
The Seven Year Itch 209
Shakedown 174, 186
She Asked for It 250
She Couldn't Take It 300, 327
She Gets Her Man 237, 254
Sheffield, Johnny 46
The Shepherd of the Hills 115
Sheridan, Ann 267
Shields, Arthur 87
The Shootist 43
Sidney, Sylvia 35, 229, 258, 266, 268
Sierra Stranger 293
Silva, Henry 316
Silver River 274, 289
The Silver Star 292
Silvers, Phil 307
Simmons, Jean 54, 209
Simon, Neal 21
Sin Town 115, 121, 129, 153
Sinatra, Frank 53, 138
The Singing Guns 118
Skelton, Red 173
Sky Parade 229, 249
Slaughter Trail 175, 186

Slave Girl 129, 154
Sleepers West 307, 330
Slight Case of Murder 135
Slightly Dangerous 79, 116
Smith, Sandra 147
Some Blondes Are Dangerous 79, 116
Song of Texas 287
Song of the Eagle 39, 60
Song of the Sarong 237, 254
Song of Scheherezade 173, 185
Sorrowful Jones 40
Sothern, Ann 197, 231, 299
South Sea Rose 36, 59
South to Karanga 63
A Southern Yankee 173, 185
The Spanish Main 288
Special Agent (TV series) 318
Spillane, Mickey 319
Sport Parade 247
Sporting Blood 252
Stack, Robert 127, 146
Stagecoach 77
Stallings, Lawrence 85
Stanke, Don E. 79
Stanwyck, Barbara 56, 89, 101
Star Dust 232, 252
A Star Is Born 52, 66
Star Spangled Rhythm 9, 30
Stars Over Hollywood (radio series) 238
Stevens, Connie 318, 319
Stockwell, Dean 55
Stolen Harmony 299, 308, 327
Stone, Christopher 147
Stop, You're Killing Me 135, 155
The Storm 44, 62
The Story of Louis Pasteur 263
The Story of Temple Drake 225, 248
Straightaway 107
Stranded 262, 281
Strange Impersonation 254
Street of Missing Men 63
Street with No Name 312, 332
Streets of Laredo 14, 28
Strictly Dynamite 225, 248
Strike Me Pink 163, 181
Submarine Command 15, 28
Submarine D-1 124, 151
Submarine Patrol 75, 112
Sudden Money 126, 151
Sullivan, Barry 49, 313, 314, 324
The Sullivans 81, 116
The Sun Comes Up 312, 333
Sundown Rider 106

352 Index

Susan Slade 318
Swamp Water 115
Swarthout, Gladys 304
Sweepings 231, 248
Swell Guy 255
Swing Fever 235, 253

Tall in the Saddle 81, 116
Tallman, William 323, 324
Tamiroff, Akim 168, 171, 301, 303, 304
Tap Roots 84–85, 117
Tarzan and the Amazons 288
Tarzan and the Huntress 289
Tarzan's New York Adventure 45–46, 64
Taxi, Mister 8, 25
Taylor, Robert 40, 44, 163, 168, 171, 230, 309, 314
Teenage Tragedies 142
Ten Gentlemen from West Point 79, 115
The Texas Rangers 14, 301, 328
The Texas Rangers Ride Again 153
The Texican 157
There Goes the Bride 158
They Came to Blow Up America 79, 116
They Gave Him a Gun 111
They Knew What They Wanted 202, 232–233, 252
They Made Me a Criminal 75, 112
They Met in a Taxi 110
They Were Expendable 82, 116
13 Hours by Air 163, 181
36 Hours to Kill 181
This Could Be the Night 209, 216
This Day and Age 39, 61
This Is My Affair 163–164, 181
This Man Is Armed 293
Thou Shalt Not Kill 63
Three Godfathers 84, 117
Three Sons 231, 251
Three Violent People 292
Three-Cornered Moon (play) 162
Thunder Below 39, 60
Thunder Trail 43, 62
Thunderbirds 87, 118
Thundering Herd 281
Tight Shoes 128, 153
Till the End of Time 238, 255
Tillie and Gus 281
Time Element (TV play) 19
The Time of Your Life 7, 13, 27, 85, 117, 130, 154

Time to Kill 307, 331
Times Square Playboy 282
To the Last Man 277, 280
Topper 19, 110, 231
Torch Singer 281
Torchy Blane in Chinatown 285
Torchy Blane in Panama 268
Torchy Gets Her Man 268, 284
Torchy Runs for Mayor 285
Toward the Unknown 315, 333
Tracy, Lee 240, 242
Trail of the Vigilantes 127, 152
Treasure of Ruby Hills 292
Treasure of the Sierra Madre 274, 289
A Tree Grows in Brooklyn 309, 318, 332
Trial of Vivienne Ware 73, 106
Trouble in Sundown 113
The Trouble with Women 172, 185
Turnabout 231, 252
Tuttle, Frank 177
Tuttle, Lurene 322
23½ Hours Leave 110
Two Mugs from Brooklyn (aka *McGuerins of Brooklyn*) 25
Two Smart People 311, 332
Two Yanks in Trinidad 169, 184
Two Years Before the Mast 11, 26, 172, 185

Unconquered 84, 117
Under Pressure 40–41, 61
Underdog 273, 287
Union Pacific 165, 182
Unknown Island 274, 290
Untouchables (TV series) 20, 277, 319
Up from the Beach 155
Upper Crust 158

Valentine, Karen 326
Valentine (TV movie) 325
The Valiant 305
Valley of the Giants 44, 62
Vanity Street 60
Variety Girl 12, 30
Virginia City 76, 114
The Virginian 57–59, 172, 184, 319
Virtue 73, 106
Voice in the Night 108

Wagner, Walter 84, 229, 304
Wagon Train (TV series) 98–105, 177, 318

Index

Wagonmaster 86
Wake Island 8, 25
Wald, Jerry 202
The Walking Dead 282
Walls of Jericho 275, 289
Walsh, Raoul 15, 78, 271, 274, 301
Waterfront 113
Waterfront Lady 109
Wayne, John 69, 71–74, 75, 77–79, 81–87, 89, 94–97, 100, 103, 165, 295, 312, 319
Wead, Frank 82, 96–97
Weaver, Marjorie 306
Webb, Clifton 11, 51, 196
Wee Willie Winkie 164
Wells Fargo 302, 328
We're Not Married 202, 215
West, Mae 302
Western Courage 109
Western Union 270, 286
Wetbacks 292
What Price Glory? (play) 85, 164
When in Rome 201, 214
When Strangers Marry 107
When the Daltons Rode 127, 152, 166–167, 183
Where There's Life 12, 27
Whirlpool (1934) 108
Whirlpool (1949) 50, 65
White Eagle 107
White Tie and Tails 11, 27
White Woman 40, 61
Whitman, Stuart 142–143, 321
Who Done It? 25, 233, 253
Whorf, Richard 308
Wicked Woman 40, 61
Wickes, Mary 322
Widmark, Richard 121, 174, 199, 312
Wild Bill Hickock Rides 115
Wild Boys of the Road 73, 107
Wild Geese Calling 286
Wild Harvest 311, 332
The Wildcatter 111
William, Warren 228, 263, 264
Wilmington, Michael 76
Wilson, Julie 303

Wilson, Marie 15
Wilson, Terry 87–88, 98–99, 102
Wine, Women and Horses 267–268, 284
Wing and a Prayer 47, 64, 309
Winged Victory 194
The Wings of Eagles 96–97, 120
Wings Over Honolulu 230, 250
Winters, Shelley 204
Winterset (TV play) 53
Withers, Grant 83
Within the Law 251
Without Orders 110
The Wizard of Oz 162
Wolheim, Louis 10, 162
Woman Chases Man 124, 151
Woman in the Wind 231, 251
Woman of the Year 8
Woman on the Beach 49, 64
The Woman They Almost Lynched 174, 186
Won Ton Ton, the Dog That Saved Hollywood 148, 158
Wong, Anna May 303, 318
Wood, Natalie 177
The Wreckers 108
Wyman, Jane 49, 154, 240
Wynn, Keenan 201, 236

Yarnell, Bruce 278
Yin and the Yang of Mr. Go 157
You and Me 268, 284
You Can't Run Away from It 54, 67
You Can't Take It with You 75, 112
You May Be Next 300
You Only Live Once 229
Young, Loretta 126
Young, Robert 236, 270, 275
Young and the Brave 23, 29
Young Fury 24, 30
Young Mr. Lincoln 76, 113
You're a Sweetheart 230, 250

Zander the Great (play) 34
Zanuck, Darryl F. 232

www.ingramcontent.com/pod-product-compliance
Ingram Content Group UK Ltd.
Pitfield, Milton Keynes, MK11 3LW, UK
UKHW041922140426
5217IPUK00014B/270